HANDBOOK
FOR
BASIC
COMPOSITION

HANDBOOK
FOR
BASIC
COMPOSITION

ALBERT R. KITZHABER

English Department
Dartmouth College

DONALD W. LEE

English Department
University of Houston

PRENTICE-HALL, INC.

Englewood Cliffs, N.J.   1961

LIBRARY OF CONGRESS
CATALOG CARD NUMBER: 61-11814

PRINTED IN THE UNITED STATES OF AMERICA
37249-C

PREFACE

This book is intended for the student who has considerable trouble with his writing—trouble in getting started, trouble in organizing his ideas, trouble in expressing them clearly, correctly, and effectively. Because we believe that a student so afflicted must concentrate his efforts on basic problems and principles, we have tried in this book to be selective rather than comprehensive. Instead of describing half a dozen or more patterns of organization for student writing, we have emphasized the two that are likely to be most generally useful. Instead of listing all the possible refinements of the use of the comma, we have centered attention on those with which, in our experience, students most frequently need help. Some matters often found in freshman English handbooks, such as semantics or propaganda analysis or forms of business correspondence, do not appear here. We do not mean to imply that these matters are therefore without value, but we think it more profitable, for the student we have in mind, to concentrate on what we think is most likely to bring about prompt and noticeable improvement in writing.

The book falls into two divisions: the first eleven chapters (done mainly by A.R.K.), which deal for the most part with rhetorical problems, and the remaining six (done mainly by D.W.L.), which concern grammar and usage. To encourage the student to view writing as a process consisting of fairly distinct steps, we have arranged the rhetorical chapters, from Chapter 3 on, in the order in which these steps normally occur. The order of the last six chapters is more arbitrary, although the arrangement of material in each is intended to help student and teacher to locate specific information.

We must add that the position taken on language matters in these chapters will not satisfy people of extreme views. This is an uncomfortable time for grammarians, with the discipline of grammar cut loose from the old moorings and not yet firmly anchored at new ones. We have tried to show that we are aware of this state of affairs, and our treatment of language

v

is therefore frankly transitional, although not, we trust, any the less useful to the student.

We have consistently assumed that the student, although he may be laboring under a variety of language disabilities, is a rational being and will respond appropriately if he is treated as one. We have not deluded him with easy formulas or recipes where none exist, and we have tried to avoid presenting the problems of writing to him as though there were a single right way of doing everything. Instead we have endeavored to show him that "good" writing is governed by many variables, and we have encouraged him to extend to the problems of writing the same processes of judgment that he applies to other aspects of his behavior. In this way, we hope, the student will be helped more rapidly on his way toward self-sufficiency as a writer and will not have to lean on rules and injunctions learned by rote and imperfectly understood.

In keeping with our desire to inform the student rather than indoctrinate him, we have given rather full explanations of rhetorical and grammatical matters. We have included illustrative examples, both of student and of professional writing. And whenever possible we have tried to deduce principles from these examples, believing that the student will more readily see the cogency of the principles than if they are merely enunciated and exemplified. Exercises, which we have tried always to make realistic, are copious and varied. Far more are offered than any teacher would want or need to assign; our intention has been to present a wide selection from which the teacher may choose those that best fit his purposes.

We gratefully acknowledge the assistance of our students and our colleagues—the former for the use of papers and parts of papers, both good and less than good; the latter for advice and perspective. We are especially indebted to Mr. James Daricek and Professor Leonard Dean of the University of Connecticut; to Professor J. Gordon Eaker of the University of Houston; to Professor Edgar Wolfe of the University of Kansas; and to Mr. Paul E. O'Connell, Editor, and Miss Mary F. Sherwood, Production Editor, of Prentice-Hall, Inc. We have also benefited from the criticisms of the following, who have read parts of the manuscript: Professor Harrison Hayford, Northwestern University, and Professor R. L. Montgomery, Jr., University of Texas.

ALBERT R. KITZHABER
DONALD W. LEE

ACKNOWLEDGMENTS

We are especially grateful to the firms and individuals named below for permission to reprint passages from the works indicated:

STEWART ALSOP: the selection from "The Strange Death of Louis Slotin," by Stewart Alsop and Ralph E. Lapp, in *The Saturday Evening Post* (March 6, 1954), used by special permission of Mr. Alsop.

THE AMERICAN MERCURY: the selection from Helena Kuo's "American Women Are Different" (June 1942), used by special permission of *The American Mercury*.

AMERICAN SCIENTIST: the selection from J. R. Dunning's "Nuclear Power in the Future" (January 1950), used by special permission of *American Scientist* and J. R. Dunning.

THE ATLANTIC MONTHLY: the selection from Alfred Fabre-Luce's "Chinese Journey" (December 1959); the selection from Donald H. Menzel's "The Astronomer's Stake in Outer Space" (November 1958); the selection from Frank W. Notestein's "Poverty and Population" (November 1959); the selection from Raoul de Roussy de Sales' "Love in America" (May 1938); the selection from C. W. Ceram's "The Man Who Found Troy" (November 1951); the selection from Allen Jackson's "Too Much Football" (November 1952); the selection from Grant Cannon's "Refilling Our Wells" (August 1954); the selection from Hanson W. Baldwin's "Limited War" (May 1959); the selection from George F. Kennan's "Foreign Policy and Christian Conscience" (May 1959), all used by special permission of *The Atlantic Monthly*.

BALLANTINE BOOKS, INC.: the selection from *Flood*, copyright 1956 by David Dempsey, reprinted by permission of the Publisher, Ballantine Books, Inc.

BLACK & VEATCH, CONSULTING ENGINEERS: the passage from *Consolidated Report on Water Works Improvements, San Antonio, Texas, 1956*, used by special permission of Black & Veatch.

BRANDT & BRANDT: the selection "All Around the Town" from *The Selected Works of Stephen Vincent Benét*, copyright 1942 by Farrar and Rinehart, now Holt, Rinehart and Winston, Inc., used by special permission of Brandt & Brandt, agents for the Estate of Stephen Vincent Benét.

BULOVA WATCH COMPANY, INC.: the Bulova watch advertisement from *The Saturday Evening Post* (June 6, 1959), used by special permission of the Bulova Watch Company.

CONSUMERS UNION: the selection from *Consumer Reports* (November 1957), used by special permission of Consumers Union.

DODD, MEAD & COMPANY, INC.: the selection from *My Remarkable Uncle* by Stephen Leacock, copyright 1942 by Dodd, Mead & Company, Inc., and the selections from *The Birth of Britain* and *The New World*, by Winston S. Churchill, copyright 1956 by Winston S. Churchill, reprinted by permission of Dodd, Mead & Company, Inc.

DOUBLEDAY & COMPANY, INC.: the selection from *To the Finland Station* by Edmund Wilson, copyright 1940 by Edmund Wilson, and the selections from *The Summing Up* by W. Somerset Maugham, copyright 1938 by W. Somerset Maugham, reprinted by permission of Doubleday & Company, Inc.

FORTUNE: the selection from "Soviet Society: From the Dacha Set Down" (February 1953), reprinted by courtesy of *Fortune* magazine.

THE GENERAL FIREPROOFING CO.: the selection from the advertisement of The General Fireproofing Co., appearing in *Time* (June 29, 1959), used by special permission of The General Fireproofing Co.

HARCOURT, BRACE & COMPANY, INC.: the selection from *Main Currents in American Thought* by Vernon L. Parrington, copyright 1927 by Harcourt, Brace & Company, Inc., and the selection from *Shooting an Elephant, and Other Essays* by George Orwell, copyright 1955 by Harcourt, Brace & Company, Inc., used by special permission of Harcourt, Brace & Company, Inc.

HARPER & BROTHERS: the passage from *Only Yesterday* by Frederick Lewis Allen, copyright 1939 by Harper & Brothers; the passage from *A History of American Civilization* by Merle Curti, Richard H. Shryock, Thomas C. Cochran, and Fred Harvey Harrington, copyright 1953 by Harper & Brothers; the selections from "Farewell My Lovely" and "Two Letters, Both Open" from *The Second Tree from the Corner* by E. B. White, copyright 1954 by Harper & Brothers; the selection from *You Can't Go Home Again* by Thomas Wolfe, copyright 1934, 1937, 1938, 1939, 1940 by Harper & Brothers; the selection from *The Coming Age of Rocket Power* by G. Edward Pendray, copyright 1945, 1947 by Harper & Brothers; the selection from *As France Goes* by David Schoenbrun, copyright 1957 by Harper & Brothers; and the selection fom *The Day Lincoln Was Shot* by Jim Bishop, copyright 1955 by Harper & Brothers, reprinted by special permission of Harper & Brothers.

HARPER'S MAGAZINE: the selection from John Bartlow Martin's "The Blast in Centralia No. 5" (March 1948), used by special permission of *Harper's Magazine*.

HOLT, RINEHART AND WINSTON, INC.: the selection from *Opus 21* by Philip Wylie, copyright 1949 by Philip Wylie, used by permission of Holt, Rinehart and Winston, Inc.

HOUGHTON MIFFLIN COMPANY: the selection from *Across the Wide Missouri* by Bernard De Voto, copyright 1947 by Houghton Mifflin Company, and the selection from *My Antonia* by Willa Cather, copyright 1918 by Houghton Mifflin Company, used by special permission of Houghton Mifflin Company.

ROBERT U. JAMESON: the selection from "How to Stay in College" in *The Saturday Evening Post* (October 6, 1954), used by special permission of the author.

THE JOURNAL OF THE AMERICAN MEDICAL ASSOCIATION: the selection from Jonas E. Salk's "Studies in Human Subjects on Active Immunization Against Poliomyelitis" (March 28, 1953), used by special permission of *The Journal of the American Medical Association* and Dr. Salk.

ALFRED A. KNOPF, INC.: the selection from *Report on the Atom* by Gordon Dean, copyright 1953 by Gordon Dean, and the selection from "His Majesty the King" in *Farewell to Sport* by Paul Gallico, copyright 1937, 1938 by Paul Gallico, reprinted by permission of Alfred A. Knopf, Inc.

WOLFGANG LANGEWIESCHE: the selection from *A Flier's World,* published by McGraw-Hill Book Company, Inc., copyright 1943, 1948, 1949, 1950, 1951 by Wolfgang Langewiesche, used by special permission of the author.

LIFE: the selection from Lincoln Barnett's "The World We Live In" (September 7, 1953), copyright 1953 by Time Inc., used by special permission of *Life* Magazine.

LITTLE, BROWN & COMPANY: the selections from *Point of No Return* by John P. Marquand, copyright 1949 by Little, Brown & Company; the selections from Walter Lippmann's *The Public Philosophy,* copyright 1955 by Little, Brown & Company, and from Walter Lippmann's *U.S. Foreign Policy: Shield of the Republic,* copyright 1943 by Little, Brown & Company, used by special permission of Little, Brown & Company.

MADEMOISELLE: the selection from Marybeth Little's "Are College Men Boys?" (September 1954), reprinted from *Mademoiselle,* copyright 1954 by Street and Smith Publications, Inc.

DAVID MCKAY CO., INC.: the selection from *The Hidden Persuaders* by Vance Packard, copyright 1957 by Vance Packard, used by special permission of the David McKay Co., Inc.

ALBERT R. MARCKWARDT: the selection from the essay "What Is Good English?" copyright 1937 by Albert R. Marckwardt, used by special permission of the author.

G. & C. MERRIAM CO.: the entry for *manage* in *Webster's New Collegiate Dictionary,* copyright 1960 by G. & C. Merriam Company, Publishers of the Merriam-Webster Dictionaries, used by permission of the G. & C. Merriam Co.

THE NEW LEADER: the selection from Bertrand Russell's "The Greatness of Albert Einstein" (May 30, 1955), used by special permission of *The New Leader.*

NEWSWEEK: the selection "6 Hours 12 Minutes" (October 13, 1958), used by special permission of *Newsweek.*

THE NEW YORKER: the selection from James Thurber's "The Dog that Bit People," reprinted by permission, copyright 1945 by James Thurber, and the selection from "Notes and Comment" (August 1, 1959), reprinted by permission, copyright 1959 by The New Yorker Magazine, Inc.

THE NORTHWESTERN MUTUAL LIFE INSURANCE COMPANY: the selection from the advertisement of The Northwestern Mutual Life Insurance Company, used by special permission of the company.

OXFORD UNIVERSITY PRESS, INC.: the selection from *The Sea Around Us* by Rachel Carson, copyright 1951 by Rachel Carson, used by special permission of the Oxford University Press, Inc.

PANTHEON BOOKS, INC.: the selection from *English Prose Style* by Herbert Read, copyright 1952 by Herbert Read, used by special permission of Pantheon Books, Inc.

PENGUIN BOOKS, INC.: the selection from *Henry Purcell* by A. K. Holland, copyright 1932; and the selections from *Tudor England* by S. T. Bindoff, copyright 1950, used by special permission of Penguin Books, Inc., Baltimore 11, Maryland.

POPULAR MECHANICS MAGAZINE: the selection from A. M. Wettzch's "How to Shape Trees" (September 1958), used by special permission of *Popular Mechanics Magazine*.

PRENTICE-HALL, INC.: the selections from *Physical Geology* by L. Don Leet and Sheldon Judson, copyright 1954 by Prentice-Hall, Inc., used by special permission of the publisher.

G. P. PUTNAM'S SONS: the selection from *Blood, Sweat, and Tears* by Winston Churchill, copyright 1941 by Winston Churchill, used by special permission of G. P. Putnam's Sons.

RANDOM HOUSE, INC.: the selection from *The Ox-Bow Incident* by Walter Van Tilburg Clark, copyright 1940 by Walter Van Tilburg Clark; the selections from *Rascals in Paradise* by James A. Michener and A. Grove Day, copyright 1957 by the authors; the selection from Robinson Jeffers' Foreword to *The Selected Poetry of Robinson Jeffers*, copyright 1937 by Random House, Inc.; the selection from *Intruder in the Dust* by William Faulkner, copyright 1948 by Random House, Inc.; the following selections from *The American College Dictionary*, copyright 1958 by Random House, Inc.: the entry for *metal*, and the synonymy under the entry for *brave*; and the selection from *The Young Lions* by Irwin Shaw, copyright 1948 by Irwin Shaw, all reprinted by permission of Random House, Inc.

THE REPORTER: the selection from John Steinbeck's "How to Tell the Good Guys from the Bad Guys" (March 10, 1955), used by special permission of *The Reporter* and of the author's agents, McIntosh and Otis, Inc.

THE SATURDAY REVIEW: the selection from Joseph Wood Krutch's "Is Our Common Man Too Common?" (January 10, 1953); the selection from Seymour St. John's "The Fifth Freedom" (October 10, 1953); the selection from Phyllis McGinley's "The Consolations of Illiteracy" (August 1, 1953); the selection from Richard Hanser's "A Plea for Literary Mayhem" (April 11, 1953); the selection from Alan Paton's "The White Man's Dilemma" (May 2, 1953); and the selection from Norman Cousins' "Don't Resign from the Human Race" (August 7, 1948), all used by special permission of *The Saturday Review*.

THE SCIENTIFIC AMERICAN: the selection from "The Army Ant" by S. C. Schneirle and Gerard Piel (June 1948); the selection from Christopher Howard Andrews' "The Common Cold" (February 1951); and the selection from Joseph Bernstein's "Tsunamis" (August 1954), all used by special permission of *The Scientific American*.

CHARLES SCRIBNER'S SONS: the selection reprinted from *A Farewell to Arms* by Ernest Hemingway, copyright 1929 by Charles Scribner's Sons, renewal copyright 1957 by Ernest Hemingway; the selection from "Alibi Ike" appearing in *How to Write Short Stories* by Ring Lardner, copyright 1915 by Curtis Publishing Company, renewal copyright 1943 by Ellis A. Lardner; the selection from *The Nature of Natural History* by Marston Bates, copyright 1950 by Marston Bates; and the selection from *So Red the Rose* by Stark Young, copyright 1934 by Charles Scribner's Sons, all used by permission of Charles Scribner's Sons.

SIMON & SCHUSTER, INC.: the selection from William H. Whyte, Jr.'s *The Organization Man*, copyright 1956 by William H. Whyte, Jr., used by special permission of Simon & Schuster, Inc.

ST. MARTIN'S PRESS, INC.: the selection from *Shakespearean Tragedy* by A. C. Bradley, copyright 1955 by Macmillan & Co., Ltd., used by permission of St. Martin's Press, Inc.

STANDARD OIL COMPANY: the selection from "Chemistry's Secret Agents," appearing in *The Lamp* (January 1948), used by permission of Standard Oil Company.

EDWIN WAY TEALE: the selections from "Those Phenomenal Insects" appearing in *PB, The Pocket Book Magazine* (No. 2, 1955), used by special permission of the author.

TIME: the selections from the issues of June 29, 1959, and December 7, 1959, reprinted by courtesy of *Time*, copyright Time Inc, 1959.

THE VIKING PRESS, INC.: the selections from *Exile's Return* by Malcolm Cowley, copyright 1951 by Malcolm Cowley, used by special permission of The Viking Press, Inc.

THE WORLD PUBLISHING COMPANY: the entry for *child* in the *Webster's New World Dictionary*, copyright 1960 by the World Publishing Company, used by special permission of The World Publishing Company.

CONTENTS

ADAPTING
WHAT YOU SAY

People speak and write for various reasons. Sometimes they do so with the deliberate and serious intention of influencing, often changing, the way others think or feel. Sometimes their purpose is to inform, sometimes merely to entertain. Sometimes they speak more to express sociability and friendliness to others than either to influence or to inform them. And sometimes people speak and write more to themselves than to others; they talk to themselves on occasion and they keep lecture notes and diaries written only for their own reading. The sort of writing and speaking which you need to study most is, of course, not this last kind; instead it is communication addressed to others. Quite probably the communication that you will need to be most concerned with is that in which you try to influence others to change their opinions or feelings, and that in which you try to inform others.

Adapting to Your Audience

In either case you will be writing or speaking to an audience—to one or more hearers or readers. To affect and communicate with this audience as you wish, you must *adapt* both what you say and how you say it. In the treatment of even the simplest things, both your content and your style—both what you say and how you say it—should be fitted to the intended hearers or readers. If you are trying to explain a baseball sacrifice play, you can readily realize that the things you say and the way you say them will differ with different audiences; you can't say the same things in the same way to a group of lettermen and to a group of girls. Comments you might be making as an adult on regulation of labor unions might vary considerably in tone and method of presentation depending on whether they were intended for union men or chamber of commerce members. This is by no means to suggest, if your audience were union members and you favored increased federal regulation of unions, that you should conceal your real views from this audience and create a false impression of what you believe. Your first duty should always be faithfulness to your own convictions. But, knowing that your views would conflict sharply with those of your audience, you would try to adapt the tone and presentation of your comments so as not to antagonize needlessly and hope to get a fair hearing for your argument.

Let's look at a rather obvious illustration of adapting, an advertisement aimed at the "often-a-bridesmaid-never-a-bride" girl:

> Nearly all the other girls that Janice had graduated with two years ago were already married . . . but she was still alone. She felt discouraged, for she was becoming convinced that she was doomed to be an old maid. It was all so puzzling, too. She knew she was not unattractive . . . men often sought her out and introduced themselves. But after one or two dates . . . they never came back. Why? Why? Poor girl, she couldn't guess . . . and of course no one would tell her.
>
> It's too bad that Janice hasn't discovered Beaujolais, the mouthwash that ends offensive breath instantly! Why be unpopular? Use Beaujolais before each date!

By way of contrast, look at the following advertisement, which is intended to appeal to industrial executives:

> GF partitions don't divide space . . . they multiply productivity. Irving Gilman, Vice President and Project Director of the Institute for Motivational Research, says: "When privacy is employed to eliminate work-robbing distractions, productivity shows marked improvement. This is especially true with workers whose jobs require intense concentration or those who receive business visitors. Privacy boosts morale, too—satisfies the employee's desire to work in quarters he regards as his own."
>
> You can create privacy for your workers—overnight—with GF partitions; and as space requirements change, you can rearrange your GF partitions, quickly and easily. To boost productivity in your offices as much as 25%, call on GF—America's largest maker of metal business furniture. Only GF offers complete planning, design and decorator

services that take into consideration, not just space utilization and work-flow, but the many *human* factors that make for efficiency.

An informative booklet, "PLAN TO PROFIT FROM YOUR OFFICE IN-VESTMENT," is yours for the asking. Just call your GF branch or dealer . . . (General Fireproofing Company).

Notice the difference between the wording of these advertisements. The language of the first is emotional, that of the second, factual. The vocabulary of the first is rather simple, that of the second, more difficult. Notice the familiar tone of the first advertisement, the more formal tone of the second.

Advertisements hardly deserve attention for their literary value; nevertheless, examining them may teach you a useful lesson: to be effective, any communication must show evidence that the speaker or writer has identified the audience, has analyzed it carefully, and has said what he had to say to appeal best to that particular audience. The devices he uses in his composition will vary accordingly.

Now let's turn to a pair of student themes written to persuade, or to try to persuade, and see how successfully they have been adapted to an audience.

The Independence of College

A frequent resentment of the average high school student is the fact that although in his own mind he is perfectly capable of looking out for himself, there are those in authority above him who continue to make sure that he follows along the right path. Whether it be the well-meaning high school principal who deems it necessary to hold a private consultation in his dreaded office for those who failed to be in attendance at assembly in order to bask in the more pleasant atmosphere of the soda fountain across the street, or the unworldly English teacher who does not comprehend that last night's basketball game was infinitely more important than today's assignment, the high school student feels that his ability to make his own decisions is unnecessarily inhibited and curbed by their actions.

After one semester of college classes and of university life in particular, I can recommend no better panacea for this situation than for a student to accept the responsibility of independence which college requires. Here one is provided with more than ample opportunity for testing his ability to utilize his own judgment.

Yet, no matter how long a student has desired this new feeling of independence, it still brings many adjustments which had not been previously anticipated. To be sure, there is no longer the ever-watch-ful high school teacher to see that each student comes to class or carefully prepares the following assignment, for upon accepting the right to act and think for himself the college student also accepts the consequences of his decisions. It is in this matter that trouble often befalls even those with the best of intentions.

Indeed, the high school student does find himself in a new and different situation when at long last he possesses the independence which for the four previous years was just beyond his reach. His reaction to it and his ability to control it successfully are measures of his maturity. One thing is certain, however; it is an experience which is necessary in the growing up of an individual. The falls are many, but the bumps soon heal.

After reading this paper, you will probably agree that the writer may have had in mind—although dimly—an audience of other college freshmen. But the language is stiff, unnatural, and pompous ("frequent resentment," "dreaded office," "utilize his own judgment"). The tone is stilted and formal, the structure of sentences sometimes unduly complicated (notice the second sentence of the paper, for example).

The following paper resulted from an assignment to select a specific audience and write a paper clearly directed at that audience. The author of this paper was able to imagine himself as an Air Force recruiting sergeant talking to high school boys:

Know Your Air Force

I want to thank your teachers for letting you out of class to hear what I have to say. Being new to this district I haven't had the opportunity to get to know many of you yet but I plan to visit most of you at home in the near future.

As seniors in high school you have probably been bothered by not being able to make any definite plans for your future without the threat of the draft catching up with you. This is my reason for being here. I don't have time to go into every detail concerning a career in the Air Force because I was informed that you boys want to be on time for that algebra test next period.

The first thing most fellows think of when I mention enlisting in the Air Force is the four year duration compared with a two year hitch in the Army. I usually retort, "Which would you rather do? Knock yourselves out digging ditches for two years or take it easier for four years and at the same time learn a valuable trade?" If you enlist in the Air Force now, during this enlistment drive, I can practically guarantee you the job of your choice, provided you have the ability, and assignment to a training school to help you learn this job. If you go into administrative or personnel work you will most likely be sent to a civilian college nearest your home of record. Munitions training is conducted in Utah, photography in Colorado. So you see you can have a variety of choices in schools and jobs.

I admit that the pay isn't the highest in the nation, but remember that all the branches of service are on the same pay scale. Air Force personnel, however, sometimes have a slight edge over men in the other branches of service in this regard, because many Air Force men draw extra pay for being on flying status. And don't forget about that new pay increase that the Armed Services Committee is asking of Congress. Twenty-five percent would be a big boost.

Don't let these Air Force recruits that are home on leave scare you. Sure, basic training is rough, but only as rough as you make it yourselves. I look back now and can honestly say that I really enjoyed my basic training. I think your experience would be the same as mine.

I see it's just about time for you boys to get back to class, so I'll have to cut this short. Tomorrow evening, here in the high school gym, I will be available to answer any questions you may have about the Air Force. These pamphlets I am about to pass out to you may be used for nothing more than book-marks but I urge you to at least glance through them. There are several personal experiences of Air Force men included in the booklet that you would like to read, I'm sure. Yes, the pay scale is listed on page five.

I'll see all of you tomorrow night, I hope. Bring your friends, too. I'll be glad to talk to them and answer their questions. So long, and take it easy!

Notice that this paper does try to appeal to twelfth-grade boys. The speaker emphasizes aspects of the Air Force that these boys would naturally be interested in—opportunities for career training, the higher pay for flight status. He tries to anticipate some of the objections that the boys would raise—the longer term of enlistment, the hardships of basic training—and to convince them that there are compensating advantages or that the disadvantages have been overrated. The tone of this composition is relaxed and conversational as it should be, considering the subject, the occasion, and the audience. The vocabulary is simple, sentences and paragraphs are short and uncomplicated, and the language includes numerous expressions ("sure," "take it easy," "cut this short") appropriate to the friendly and relaxed relationship that the speaker is trying to establish. (These expressions, by the way, would *not* be appropriate in compositions intended for most of the people you will be writing for in college.)

If your aim is to inform rather than persuade, you must also consider adapting to an audience that you have in mind. Note the following selection, written by a highly qualified scientist, addressed to an audience of general readers not well grounded in science:

The birth of a volcanic island is an event marked by prolonged and violent travail: the forces of the earth striving to create, and all the forces of the sea opposing. The sea floor, where an island begins, is probably nowhere more than about fifty miles thick—a thin covering over the vast bulk of the earth. In it are deep cracks and fissures, the results of unequal cooling and shrinkage in past ages. Along such lines of weakness the molten lava from the earth's interior presses up and finally bursts forth into the sea. But a submarine volcano is different from a terrestrial eruption, where the lava, molten rocks, gases, and other ejecta are hurled into the air through an open crater. Here on the bottom of the ocean the volcano has resisting it all the weight of the ocean water above it. Despite the immense pressure of, it may be, two or three miles of sea water, the new volcanic cone builds upward toward the surface, in flow after flow of lava. Once within reach of the waves, its soft ash and tuff are violently attacked, and for a long period the potential island may remain a shoal, unable to emerge. But, eventually, in new eruptions, the cone is pushed up into the air and a rampart against the waves is built of hardened lava (Rachel L. Carson, *The Sea Around Us*).

If Miss Carson had been writing on the same subject for an audience of other scientists who had studied the ocean or volcanic activity, she would have written very differently. Her language would almost certainly have been much more technical (there are really only two unfamiliar technical words in this passage: *ejecta* and *tuff*), for she could expect her readers to be familiar with the technical terms of the sciences dealing with her subject. She would have been able to go into much greater scientific detail than she does in the passage quoted above; in fact, experts in the subject would not be satisfied with the simplified treatment that we see in the quoted passage.

Now contrast the following paragraph from a report on the water distribution system of a large American city; the report was intended to be read mainly by engineers. Notice the technical terms unfamiliar to the average reader, the formal and impersonal style of writing, and the exactness with which the subject is discussed.

The system at present is composed of cast iron, transite, steel, copper, lead, and concrete pipe varying in diameter from ½ inch to 30 inches. Cast iron pipe, Class B or Class 150 pounds, is the predominating type. The interior of all pipe was found to be in excellent condition considering the age of the pipe. When pipe samples were removed from the system and examined, pipe 35 years old was found to have a very clean interior. Tests were also run on pipe in service to determine the coefficients of friction. Pipes 12 inches and 16 inches in diameter gave "C" values exceeding 140, indicating excellent internal condition (Black & Veatch, Consulting Engineers, *Consolidated Report on Water Works Improvements, San Antonio, Texas*).

Let us assume that your hobby is electronics and that you have considerable specialized knowledge of this subject. If you write a paper explaining the transistor, with the rest of your English class as the audience, you will certainly have to explain any technical terms you use, and you will have to bring in comparisons and examples to make yourself understood. After all, you may be the only person in class who knows anything about electronics. It might be a good idea, too, to make it clear to your audience why the transistor is important to *them*, to tell them how it has revolutionized the construction of radios, TV sets, and other familiar electronic devices that they use every day. In this way, you will interest them in what you are saying.

But if you become a major in electrical engineering and are writing a paper on transistor circuits, with one of your engineering professors as audience, you will want to use technical language so that you can express your meaning with precision, and you will necessarily go into far more detail than if you were writing a paper on the same subject for your classmates in freshman English.

Adapting to Your Purpose

Adapting what you speak or write to the purpose you are trying to accomplish is closely related to adapting what you say to a particular audience; in fact, the two processes are often the same. We can see adaptation to purpose in an obvious form in advertisements. But we can see the same adaptation to purpose in every careful use of language. A good letter of application has the single purpose of getting a certain job. A newspaper editorial on highway safety is written with the aim of reducing traffic accidents. A review of a play is written to guide the playgoer. A surgeon who publishes an article in a medical journal describing a new technique in brain surgery is sharing his discovery with other surgeons so that they may use it for the advantage of their patients. There is little writing in the adult world that is not adapted to purpose.

Awareness of purpose in your own writing and speaking is indispensable. It is like a rudder: it will keep you headed steadily in the direction you want to go, without aimless and time-consuming wanderings in other directions. Suppose your purpose in a theme is simply to tell about the time you got lost on a hunting trip in the mountains of central Idaho and to let your audience share your experience. You want to communicate to your readers the growing unease you felt as you first began to doubt that you knew where you were; the scared, hopeless feeling that suddenly welled up in you when you realized you were thoroughly lost; the desperation of your futile calls for help and your search for a familiar landmark; and finally the wonderful sense of relief and security when you unexpectedly came upon a logging road that you recognized as leading back to camp.

It would be a mistake, in telling of this experience, to go into a lot of detail about how you happened to be going on a hunting trip in central Idaho, or what you did that evening after you had returned safely. Both may be interesting, but they have nothing directly to do with your purpose, which is to tell as accurately as you can about being lost in a real wilderness and to describe what the experience feels like. Every decision to bring something into the theme or leave something out of it must be based on whether it will help to accomplish your purpose.

This is what is meant by adaptation to purpose. It will not only affect the material you include in the account but will also help to determine the sort of language you use and the general tone or style. You certainly would write this paper in the first person, for instance. You would strive for an informal, personal tone, because your purpose is to bring the experience as close as you can to your readers. A formal, impersonal style might put a barrier between you and the audience, and your paper would no longer seem like an account of a personal experience.

On the other hand, if you are writing a research paper on the growth of the closed shop in American industry, your purpose will be to present the facts as you have found them, as completely and faithfully as possible. The tone of the paper should be objective—that is, uncolored by any personal preferences or notions; you will guard yourself against being swayed by prejudice or drawing unwarranted conclusions. In this sort of paper, you will use the third person as a matter of course, because it is an indication to your readers that you have tried to eliminate your own personal attitudes and to present instead an unbiased picture of the subject.

This discussion of adaptation to purpose can be made more concrete if we look at two freshman themes. The author of the first paper has not done a very good job of adapting what he is saying, and how he is saying it, to the purpose he apparently has in mind. Part of this purpose is suggested by his title: he hopes to make clear to his readers what his views are on the limits of free speech. But, as you read through the paper, you see that he also is trying to persuade his readers to accept his opinions. Actually, he doesn't succeed very well on either score. His remarks are so vague and generalized, so lacking in supporting evidence, that we feel confused as to just what he does think about censorship and free speech. It is apparent that he has not thought through the subject carefully but instead has strung together a series of almost wholly unsupported opinions and tried to express them in a way that he hopes will seem profound. As a result, he clearly fails to achieve his purpose, for the paper strikes us as being neither informative nor persuasive: being unsure of his exact views, we are of course reluctant to give him our confidence and accept these hazy opinions.

How Far I Think Freedom of Speech Should Go

One of the qualifications of a democracy is that the people have freedom of speech; however, it is difficult, if not impossible, to set definite boundaries limiting freedom of speech which will be successful in this type of government. In a true democracy there would necessarily be complete freedom of speech—but are the people wise enough to exercise this complete freedom without hurting others and eventually destroying the democracy?

Apparently many people are not capable of judiciously exercising a complete freedom of speech because one does not exist today anywhere in the world. The censorship boards and committees now in existence often have sprung up from necessity. Freedom of speech was made possible for us when our democracy here in the United States was established; and if we had been worthy of that freedom, it would still be completely alive and functioning as it was intended to. Although censorship has no place in a true democracy, it had to be resorted to when officials realized that the people did not have good enough judgment to publicly express themselves without occasionally saying something offensive—or things infringing upon the rights of others. The problem became bigger and bigger with the innovations of new and more efficient communication media. The more money to be made, the more an off-color idea was exploited. Therefore, censorship became necessary.

On the other hand, if most people are not capable of deciding when their ideas should be expressed, why do other people have the right to censor what is said by the majority? The problem presented by this question is an obstacle, but I believe that censorship is necessary to a certain extent so as to balance or regulate our ideas. Freedom of speech could be a functioning reality only if people were always considerate of the feelings and rights of others.

In contrast to this theme, here are the first three paragraphs of a "library" paper. Notice that the writer's purpose clearly is to *inform* the reader about cholesterol and some of its effects on the human body. In keeping with this purpose, these paragraphs are not argumentative or emotional or otherwise personalized but instead are objective and factual. Since clear explanation of the subject is the main goal, definitions and factual details are used generously as the author adapts his material to his purpose.

The Relationship of Cholesterol to Disease
of the Heart and Arteries

Arteriosclerosis is the most common disease in the western world and, in certain areas of the world, is the greatest killer of mankind. For this reason, finding the cause and cure of this disease is vitally important to the improved health of the human race as a whole as well as to the relief of suffering of individual patients. Since cholesterol has recently been related to the cause of arteriosclerosis and coronary heart disease, its study is important not only for the scientist but for any person who is interested in good health. This paper will present a description of cholesterol, its effects upon the body, and the prevention and treatment of the diseases caused by its overabundance.

Cholesterol is a fat-like substance found in animal fats, bile, blood, the liver, and the kidneys. The chief food sources of this substance are animal fats, milk, eggs, butter, and cream, but it can also be synthesized in most of the tissues of the body, the liver being the principal organ for this synthesis. Altogether the average American diet furnishes about 400 or 500 milligrams of cholesterol a day, while the body normally synthesizes about twice this amount within its own tissues. Fats such as cholesterol are useful to the body because they give flavor to food and necessary because they provide fatty acids, calories for energy, and the fat-soluble vitamins A, D, E, and K.

Despite its uses in the body, cholesterol has been associated with a very harmful disease—atherosclerosis. This disease is one of the three forms of arteriosclerosis or hardening of the arteries and affects primarily the large elastic vessels: the aorta (the main trunk of the arterial system), and the large heart and brain vessels. Since there will not be room in this paper to discuss all three types of arteriosclerosis thoroughly, only the one associated with cholesterol will be explained. . . .

Adaptation to purpose requires first that you know clearly and in detail what you want to say and why you want to say it, then that you use this awareness as a guide in determining what to include and what to leave out in order to make the most appropriate kind of presentation.

Adaptation to audience requires first that you know the identity and main characteristics of your audience, then that you try to sense in advance the probable reactions of the audience to your material and purpose; you should next adjust your presentation to insure a favorable reception, but certainly not by concealing or falsifying your views and purposes.

These skills are special ones, no doubt, but they can be developed just as other skills can. It is chiefly a matter of practice, with someone to help you with criticism and advice when needed. You will get both the practice and the help in your freshman English course.

EXERCISES

1. In the periodicals section of the library examine three different magazines. What sort of readers is each apparently intended for? What evidence can you present to support your opinion?

2. Select an article in a magazine and analyze it as to audience and purpose. That is, what audience is being aimed at, what purpose is intended, what means have been used to adapt to audience and purpose, and how successful is the adaptation?

3. Are the advertisements in the same magazine apparently aimed at the same audience as the article you analyzed? What is your evidence for believing so?

4. Select five different advertisements from five different magazines (such as *Fortune, The New Yorker, The Saturday Evening Post, The Atlantic Monthly,* some of the detective, western, or confession magazines, a technical or scientific magazine such as *Popular Mechanics* or *Scientific American*). Write a thumbnail sketch of the sort of person who might be expected to be attracted by each advertisement.

5. Write three paragraphs of about one hundred words each, all on the same subject but each aimed at a different audience—such as an account of an incident from your first week or so of college for your parents, for a distant relative, and for a reporter for the campus newspaper. In what different ways do you try to adapt yourself to them?

6. Write an account of an imaginary automobile accident in which you try to communicate to your parents the shock and horror of the experience; then write about the same accident to tell your insurance company exactly what happened.

7. For what sort of audience is each of the following passages intended, what seems to be the ruling purpose, and what is your evidence for believing so?

(a) The urban middle-class family generally lives in a one- or two-room apartment with private kitchen and toilet facilities. Furniture tends to be Mid-Victorian in style. Many of the bourgeoisie have radio, mainly the special sets that are plugged into just a few channels. Television sets and private cars are uncommon. Lightweight company cars are at the disposal of the managers and high officials of middle-size enterprises and state farms. A car is often shared by the small-factory manager, his chief engineer, the secretary of the party organization, and their families. Almost every family owns a bicycle, but motorbikes are rare, as are spare parts for both ("Soviet Society: From the Dacha Set Down," *Fortune Magazine*, February, 1953).

(b) Whether you have a few fruit trees or a small orchard, it will pay to know the many corrective measures that can be employed to bring about and maintain yearly production of good quality fruit. To help you do this, growth correcting and grafting methods used by professional orchardists are explained in this article (A. M. Wettzch, "How to Shape Trees," *Popular Mechanics*, September, 1958).

(c) The Port of New York Authority last week took the cotton out of its ears—at long last—and decided that jet air transports are quiet enough to operate at the city's airports. Twelve hours later, the long-awaited era of commercial jet travel across the Atlantic was off to a screeching start (*Newsweek*, October 13, 1958).

(d) I am sore about your note, which didn't seem friendly. I am a friendly taxpayer and do not think the government should take a threatening tone, at least until we have exchanged a couple of letters kicking the thing around. Then it might be all right to talk about selling the place, if I proved stubborn. I showed the lawyer your notice about the warrant of seizure and sale, and do you know what he said? He said, "Oh, that doesn't mean anything, it's just a form" (E. B. White, "Two Letters, Both Open," from *The Second Tree from the Corner*).

(e) The portable typewriters rated . . . fell into two groups: the regular-size portables ranged in weight from 16 to 22 pounds, including carrying case. They were priced from about $80 to $142. The pint-sized portables, weighing from 8 to 11 pounds, were priced from about $60 to $93. Whether you should buy a very small portable depends on how much you value extreme compactness and portability, and how many other conveniences you are willing to sacrifice. Most of the very small portables did not offer the kind of "feel" typists expect—even in a portable. None of them rated better than Fair in overall quality (*Consumer Reports*, November, 1957, in *Buying Guide Issue*, 1958).

2

LEVELS AND VARIETIES
OF ENGLISH

Although probably you have been hearing the phrase "good English" ever since you were in grade school, you may not have formed a clear notion of exactly what it is that makes English good. Many students come to college with the idea that English is good if it breaks none of the rules of grammar, punctuation, spelling, or pronunciation. But English of this sort is only *correct* English; and correctness, though certainly important, is not enough by itself to make English *good*. The question of what makes good English is a little more complicated. This chapter will try to give you a basis for deciding what is and what is not good English.

Levels of English: Standard and Non-standard

Though we do not have a titled aristocracy in this country (as England, for example, has), it is true nevertheless that we do have what probably should be called class differences. We can look around us and see that some people have more education than others, some more money, more influence, more social prestige. These people are, in a sense, a privileged class; they are usually looked up to by most other members of the community. There is no hard-and-fast boundary between this group or class and others, nor is it impossible for someone who originally was not in this group to enter it.

The members of this group make up what usually is called *the edu-*

cated class, since a better-than-average education is the one thing that nearly all of them have in common. Most of the leadership of our country is drawn from this class: the people who have positions of authority and responsibility in business, in civic enterprises, in education, and in government. A large part of their prestige, in fact, is due to the influence they have on our affairs. Because less influential groups of people in our population look to them for leadership, many of the things they do are copied by others. Many of their habits are accepted as standards, chief among these being their habits in language. They have a particular way of speaking and writing, a sort of class dialect that is used by nearly all members of this group. Because most of the country's affairs are conducted in this dialect, it enjoys the same prestige as the people who habitually speak and write it. It is accepted, in other words, as the standard and is commonly regarded as the source material for standards of usage.

In some ways, this variety of language (called the level of *Standard English*) is not at all better *as language* than the sort used by uneducated people (usually called the level of *Non-standard English*). Your meaning is perfectly clear whether you say "I didn't think no more about him," or "I didn't think any more about him." Non-standard English is entirely adequate for many uses of language; it can communicate simple meanings clearly and often effectively. After all, it is not a totally different language from Standard English. Both are still English and have far more points of similarity than of difference.

There are, however, certain words, expressions, grammatical constructions, and sentence patterns found in one level that are not usually found in the other. Standard English, for instance, does not use the double negative ("she never meant no harm"), or "done" as the third person singular form of "do" in the past tense ("she done it herself"), or the very useful "ain't." There is no *logical* reason why these forms are avoided in Standard English, but the fact remains that they are not used.

Non-standard English is seldom used for writing, except when an author wants to reproduce in a book or story the conversation of someone who uses Non-standard English as his normal way of expressing himself. (This is what Mark Twain did in *Huckleberry Finn.*) There are two chief reasons why it is not often written. The people who use non-standard English write rarely, except for letters to friends and relatives, and publish even less often. Most of the writing in our society—business letters, scientific reports, news writing, magazine articles, advertising, books, stories, plays—is done by people who are members of the educated class. Because these people use Standard English, Non-standard does not often appear in print.

The second reason is based on a characteristic of Non-standard English itself. Because the people who use it are not, as a rule, highly educated, and because ordinarily they do not occupy positions where they have to express complicated ideas with precision, Non-standard English is usually considerably narrower in scope than Standard is. For example, its vocabulary is smaller, its range of language patterns or constructions is more limited, and the meanings it attaches to words are often less exact. It is not the most useful sort of language, therefore, in which to express the ideas and problems that must often be dealt with by educated people. An engineering report, or a magazine article on the possible relation between cigarettes and lung cancer, could not very well be written in Non-standard English; the ideas would usually be more complex than the language could manage to express.

Look, for example, at the following passage, in which a former chairman of the Atomic Energy Commission explains how atom-smashing machines, such as the cyclotron, operate:

> So important are these particle-accelerating machines in the atomic scheme of things that I believe it would be useful to take a moment to explain roughly how they work. Let us assume we wish to accelerate protons. You will recall that a single proton constitutes the nucleus of ordinary hydrogen gas. It is therefore fairly easy to obtain a plentiful supply of protons by simply buying some hydrogen gas from a chemical supply house. But in normal hydrogen gas the protons come as parts of atoms, complete with accompanying electrons. Our first job is to get rid of these electrons. We are helped in this by the fact that some metals, such as tungsten, release electrons when they are heated. Thus, if we pass our hydrogen gas into a chamber containing a heated tungsten wire, the electrons being released by the tungsten will knock the electrons out of the atoms of hydrogen gas, leaving only the proton nuclei. The gas is now said to be ionized, or electrically charged.
>
> Once ionized, the gas is allowed to diffuse upward into the particle accelerator. If the accelerator is a cyclotron, it is essentially a giant cake-shaped, hollow magnet, split vertically down the middle into two parts called "dees." Protons enter the machine in the space between the two dees. At the time of entry, one of the dees is positively charged and the other negatively charged. The positive dee repels the proton and the negative one attracts it. Thus begins the proton's acceleration. But hardly does it get under way before the charge in the dees is reversed. This starts the proton on a circular course inside the

cyclotron. In the 184-inch (the diameter of the 4,000-ton magnet) cyclotron at Berkeley the charge in the two dees is reversed at a rate of 20 million times a second, causing the particle to pick up speed swiftly as it travels in an ever-widening circle within the machine. Particles make 10,000 revolutions in a thousandth of a second and emerge at a speed which is nearly half that of light. When they leave the cyclotron they are pointed at a target material containing the atoms to be smashed. The fragments of the resulting collisions are then studied for clues as to the nature of the nucleus (Gordon Dean, *Report on the Atom*).

Mr. Dean's book is not aimed at an audience of atomic scientists but rather at educated people with no specialized knowledge of nuclear physics. (See pp. 20–21 for a discussion of nuclear physics that *is* intended for scientists.) He has taken pains, therefore, to write as simply and clearly as he can. Even so, the complexity of the ideas he is trying to communicate requires the use of Standard English. Besides a number of technical words from the specialized language of physics, there are other words in this passage that are part of the vocabulary of Standard English but that are unknown to Non-standard—"accelerate," "constitutes," "diffuse," "emerge," and so on. Still other words, though they may be found in Non-standard English, are used here with much more exact meanings: "scheme," "release," "pass," "attracts," "charge," "particle." The more limited resources of Non-standard would not have been equal to the job of explaining this subject.

As a college student you will be meeting a great variety of new ideas every day in your courses. The complexity and importance of these ideas require the full resources of Standard English for their proper discussion—in textbooks, in lectures and recitations, and in the papers and examinations you will be asked to write.

Varieties of English: Informal and Formal

Though you are mainly concerned with the level of language that we have called *Standard English,* remember that this term takes in a good deal of territory. We have limited it somewhat by calling it the language used by educated people. But of course people do not always write and speak in the same way; instead they vary their language, just as they do the rest of their behavior, according to the circumstances they are in and the purposes they are trying to accomplish. There is one way to act and talk when you are chatting with a group of close friends about the football schedule; there is a different way when you are explaining to the dean why you need to put off taking a required course in mathematics. A chief difference between these two situations is in the degree of formality or informality that is called for. With your friends you will be informal; with the dean, formal. Both your language and your general behavior will differ accordingly.

There are, in other words, formal and informal varieties of Standard English, each entirely respectable and appropriate for its own purposes, just as there are formal and informal kinds of conduct. It probably would be possible to give names to half a dozen or more of these varieties, ranging from the very familiar to the extremely formal, but for our purposes here such a list would not be especially useful. All you really need to know is that Standard English is sometimes more formal, sometimes less so; why it varies as it does; and how it varies.

The best way to study the problem is to look at several selections, all of them in Standard English but showing various degrees of formality. First, read this excerpt from a news story published in *Time* magazine:

> Everybody agreed that James Worley, head of the English department at big (1,160 students) Fox Lane High School near Mt. Kisco, N.Y., was just about the finest teacher they knew. And academic standards are high in the suburban Westchester County area, home of many a well-heeled Manhattan commuter with an eye on Harvard for his son. But last week able, balding Teacher Worley, 38, was fired. Reason: he refused to file lesson plans with the front office two weeks ahead of class.
>
> Worley blew his stack over an irritation familiar to many a classroom teacher—the seeming fondness of administrators for more and more paper work. Fox Lane teachers have always submitted outlines during the summer of what they plan to teach in the new year. Last year they also began filing achievement summaries at the end of each month, plus a plan for the next week. This year, when the teachers were ordered to tack on another week, Worley refused (*Time,* Dec. 7, 1959).

Several characteristics of this selection mark it as an example of informal English—considerably more informal, in fact, than you will want to use in your own writing in college. Notice first the several slang terms: "well-heeled," "fired," "blew his stack," "front office." Ordinarily, if other traits were in keeping with this use of slang, we would say that the passage was Non-standard English. But with one possible exception, the language structure of the selection conforms to the rules of usage that are typical of Standard English. The possible exception is "Everybody . . . they" in the first sentence, a construction about which there is a good deal of argument just now; but this use of debatable constructions is a frequent characteristic of informal English. Other traits of informality are seen here in the relaxed tone, the fairly short and uncomplicated sentences, and the relatively simple vocabulary.

This next selection, though still written in informal English, is less informal than the one just quoted:

> One morning when Muggs bit me slightly, more or less in passing, I reached down and grabbed his short stumpy tail and hoisted him into the air. It was a foolhardy thing to do and the last time I saw mother, about six months ago, she said she didn't know what possessed me. I don't either, except that I was pretty mad. As long as I held the dog off the floor by his tail he couldn't get at me, but he twisted and jerked so, snarling all the time, that I realized I couldn't hold him that way very long. I carried him to the kitchen and flung him onto the floor and shut the door on him just as he crashed against it. But I forgot about the backstairs. Muggs went up the backstairs and down the frontstairs and had me cornered in the living room. I managed to get up onto the mantelpiece above the fireplace, but it gave way and came down with a tremendous crash throwing a large marble clock, several vases, and myself heavily to the floor. Muggs was so alarmed by the racket that when I picked myself up he had disappeared. We couldn't find him anywhere, although we whistled and shouted, until Old Mrs. Detweiler called after dinner that night. Muggs had bitten her once, in the leg, and she came into the living room only after we assured her that Muggs had run away. She had just seated herself when, with a great growling and scratching of claws, Muggs emerged from under a davenport where he had been quietly hiding all the time, and bit her again. Mother examined the bite and put arnica on it and told Mrs. Detweiler that it was only a bruise. "He just bumped you," she said. But Mrs. Detweiler left the house in a nasty state of mind (James Thurber, "The Dog That Bit People," from *My Life and Hard Times*).

There are several contractions in this passage ("didn't," "don't," "couldn't") and a few rather slangy words ("mad," "racket") but nothing approaching the breeziness of "blew his stack" and "well-heeled" in the first selection. Yet these words help to create an easy informality of tone. Other words in this excerpt are rather infrequent in conversation, being more typical of written English: "foolhardy," "flung," "assured," "emerged." Sentences are generally longer and more complicated in structure than in the *Time* quotation, but these differences and those in vocabulary are not so great that the language becomes formal English instead of informal.

The next selection is a paragraph from *The Organization Man,* by William H. Whyte, Jr.:

> The descent, every spring, of the corporations' recruiters has now become a built-in feature of campus life. If the college is large and its placement director efficient, the processing operation is visibly impressive. I have never been able to erase from my mind the memory of an ordinary day at Purdue's placement center. It is probably the largest and most effective placement operation in the country, yet, much as in a well-run group clinic, there seemed hardly any activity. In the main room some students were quietly studying company literature arranged on the tables for them; others were checking the interview timetables to find what recruiter they would see and to which cubicle he was assigned; at the central filing desk college employees were sorting the hundreds of names of men who had registered for placement. Except for a murmur from the row of cubicles there was little to indicate that scores of young men were, every hour on the half hour, making the decisions that would determine their whole future life.

The style of this passage represents a sort of middle ground of Standard English, neither too familiar nor too stiff. The first person pronouns "I" and "my" are used to suggest a personal tone in the selection but this tone never becomes as directly personal as in the Thurber passage. The structure of the sentences in the paragraph varies as much as does their length. The vocabulary contains no slang, no contractions. The passage is typical of much expository writing today: informal but dignified.

Just as there is no sharp dividing line between Standard and Nonstandard English, there is no distinct boundary between formal and informal language. The two varieties have many things in common; they use many of the same words and forms of words, often the same word order, sometimes the same kinds of sentence structure. But there are differences. The three selections already quoted have all been written in informal English; the two that follow illustrate different uses of formal English. First is the concluding paragraph of the address that Winston Churchill delivered to the British House of Commons when he became Prime Minister during the early months of World War II.

> We have before us an ordeal of the most grievous kind. We have before us many, many long months of struggle and of suffering. You ask, What is our policy? I will say: "It is to wage war, by sea, land and air, with all our might and with all the strength that God can give us: to wage war against a monstrous tyranny, never surpassed in the dark, lamentable catalogue of human crime. That is our policy." You

ask, What is our aim? I can answer in one word: Victory—victory at all costs, victory in spite of all terror, victory however long and hard the road may be; for without victory there is no survival. Let that be realized; no survival for the British Empire; no survival for all that the British Empire has stood for; no survival for the urge and impulse of the ages, that mankind will move forward towards its goal. But I take up my task with buoyancy and hope. I feel sure that our cause will not be suffered to fail among men. At this time I feel entitled to claim the aid of all, and I say, "Come, then, let us go forward together with our united strength" (Speech delivered to the House of Commons, May 13, 1940, from *Blood, Sweat, and Tears*).

The tone of Churchill's speech reflects the seriousness and importance of the occasion. It is solemn, stately, formal. Many of the words are typical of learned English—"suffered" (in the sense of "allowed"), "grievous," "monstrous," "surpassed," "lamentable," "buoyancy." But more significant than the words are the ways in which they have been put together. Notice the repetition of words and phrases to drive home a point and to give a sweeping rhythm to sentences, a frequent characteristic of formal oratory: "We have before us an ordeal of the most grievous kind. We have before us many, many long months of struggle and of suffering." Or again, "Victory—victory at all costs, victory in spite of all terror, victory however long and hard the road may be. . . ." This sort of pattern, which is called *parallel structure,* runs all through the paragraph. The effect is one of dignity and solemnity, appropriate here to Churchill's official position, to his subject, and to the occasion on which he was speaking. Informal English uses this device, but seldom so many times in a short space as Churchill has used it here.

The second example of formal English shows how this variety of language is used in writing of the results of scientific and other investigation, where the aim is to present factual information as objectively as possible. (The audience in this case is other scientists.)

Large-scale utilization of nuclear fission power in our national economy does not seem possible unless "net gain breeding" of new fissionable material, such as $_{94}$Pu-239 or $_{92}$U-233, is employed.

The possibility of net gain breeding arises because admittedly somewhat more than two secondary neutrons are emitted per fission in some fissionable materials. One neutron per fission is required to maintain a chain reaction. If the over-all "neutron economy" is such that, after allowing for neutron leakage from the nuclear reactor and true parasitic neutron capture processes, more than one net neutron is still available to react with "fertile materials" like U-238 to form Pu-239, or to react with Th-232 to form U-233 in a similar process, then we may be able to produce more new fissionable fuel materials, Pu-239 or U-233, by "conversion" than we burn. If a reactor can be designed from both an engineering and a heat transfer standpoint, with enough margin to produce a net gain of Pu-239 or U-233 and allow for recycling and reprocessing losses, then in principle by recycling nuclear fuel and fertile materials we can look forward eventually to converting an appreciable fraction of the U-238 or Th-232 in the world into high-grade fissionable fuels. The consequent availability of hundreds of times the amount of nuclear fuel as compared with U-235 alone, and the effect of this upon over-all nuclear power economics, are obvious. A practical "net gain power breeder reactor" would be a tremendous step forward, even though one must recognize that a net gain breeder acts like compound interest and that the time required to double the amount of fissionable material will be long, even with net gains of say 10 per cent per cycle (J. R. Dunning, "Nuclear Power in the Future," *The American Scientist*).

Obviously, complex and difficult scientific ideas are being presented in this passage, but since the audience is composed of scientists to whom these ideas are familiar there is no attempt to avoid technical terms. The vocabulary is quite large, and full of scientific terms; no contractions or slang words appear. The structure of the sentences is usually complicated and the length considerable; these reflect the complexity of the ideas being dealt with. Grammatical usage in these sentences is conservative, with no liberties taken, such as the "everybody . . . they" that we saw in an earlier quotation. Finally, the tone of the passage is serious, factual, objective; no personal bias of the author with regard to the ideas presented can be detected.

For most of the writing and speaking you will have to do, both while you are in college and after you have graduated, you will find that *informal* English will be the more useful to you. Much of what you will read and most of what you will hear will be informal English, because it is the language that educated people use for most ordinary purposes. Informal English is commonly used in newspapers, most business letters, most magazine articles, most short stories and novels; it is spoken by radio and TV announcers and newscasters and by educated people as they go about their business. It is the informal variety of Standard English that you will usually hear in the classroom and, increasingly, from your friends outside the classroom.

You should, however, be able to use formal English, too. Most (though not all) of your textbooks will be written in formal English, and so will most research articles that are published in technical magazines in your major field. Some sermons and political speeches use formal English, though probably not so many as did thirty or forty years ago. You may seldom find yourself in a situation where you are called upon to speak at length in a strictly formal sort of English, but very likely, you will have to write it. The research or investigative papers that you will write in college are usually expected to be in an impersonal and formal style. If you are planning to enter a profession in which you must do research and publish your findings or present them orally, you will need to use formal English. If you are to become an engineer, most of your reports will be in a formal style.

As an educated man or woman, you should be able to use both varieties. Remember, however, that there is no clearly marked dividing line between the two, but rather a sort of sliding scale from the very informal to the very formal. You will have to decide what degree of formality or informality is called for by the situation, the subject, your purpose, and your audience, then use whatever degree seems to you most appropriate. When you have judged the degree correctly and have adapted your language accordingly, you will be speaking or writing good English.

EXERCISES

1. Which of the following passages would you label as Non-standard English? What things determine your decision?

(a) I like it, winter or summer. But I guess I like it the best when it gets really hot and they turn on the fire hydrants for a while and the little kids splash in the water. That's when the noise lasts till after twelve and, if you look out of the window, you can see a man in his shirt sleeves and his fat wife beside him, sitting out in front of the store in a couple of kitchen chairs. I know nobody's supposed to. But that's the way I like New York (Stephen Vincent Benét, "All Around the Town").

(b) Dorothea was sure that he had learned his little lesson. As long as Charles could remember, Dorothea had been sure of everything. She had been sure that she would be a great concert pianist. She had been sure, when she had been sewing Butterick patterns, that she could be a successful dress designer; and now she was sure that she could tell Elbridge Sterne ways to advance himself . . . (John P. Marquand, *Point of No Return*).

(c) "He's got the world beat . . . I've knew lots o' guys that had an alibi for every mistake they made; I've heard pitchers say that the ball slipped when somebody cracked one off'n 'em; I've heard infielders complain of a sore arm after heavin' one into the stand, and I've saw outfielders tooken sick with a dizzy spell when they've misjudged a fly ball. But this baby can't even go to bed without apoligizin', and I bet he excuses himself to the razor when he gets ready to shave" (Ring Lardner, "Alibi Ike").

(d) In imaginative writing the speculative organizing mind of the writer works with the data of perception. The process, if we can regard it for a moment so mechanically, still remains on the plane of sensation. But the sensations may cause certain powerful reactions which we describe generally as *emotions* (Herbert Read, *English Prose Style*).

(e) I was scared though. I knew Winder's temper, and he wasn't more than five steps off. When I'd talked the cigarette had bobbed in my mouth too, in spite of my trying to talk stiff-lipped; he'd know where it was. I made a swell target; he could judge every inch of me. When he didn't say anything, my back began to crawl. I wouldn't have thought I could feel any colder, but I did, all under the back of my shirt. Still, after the way he'd put it, I couldn't let that cigarette go either. I drew my own gun slowly . . . I wanted to squat, but it was no use with that cigarette. The best was to hold still and let the ash form (Walter Van Tilburg Clark, *The Ox-Bow Incident*).

(f) "Me?" the jailer cried. "Me get in the way of them Gowries and In-grums for seventy-five dollars a month? Just for one nigger? And if you ain't a fool you won't neither" (William Faulkner, *Intruder in the Dust*).

(g) You are hereby notified that the above-named plaintiffs have filed their petition in the above-entitled Court praying for judgment that the plaintiffs are the owners of the fee simple title to the real estate described in said petition; for judgment determining the heirs at law of Richard Roe, deceased, and the descent of the title to his interest in and to said real estate; that the Court determine all adverse estates or interests which are claimed in said real estate; and that plaintiffs' title thereto be quitted against you and each of you, and that you and all persons claiming by, through or under you be forever barred, enjoined, and excluded from any title, estate, or interest in, on, or to said real estate or any part thereof. . . . (Legal notice in a newspaper).

2. In the above passages which ones would you label formal writing? For what reasons?

3. In the passages quoted in "1" above arrange those which you have not already called Non-standard or formal, according to their degree of in-formality, beginning with the most formal. Explain why you have placed each passage as you have, being as specific as possible.

4. Select two editorials or columns from a newspaper and discuss the variety of usage and how it is achieved. What sort of audience is the writer aim-ing at, and on what do you base your opinion?

5. In one of your textbooks, find an example of formal writing; one of in-formal.

6. Make a list of common campus slang expressions which you hear during a week. What would their equivalents be in informal English? In formal English?

7. Arrange the following words and phrases in groups according to whether they are usually found in Non-standard, informal, or formal writing.

innuendo	hit the sack	hot rod
baby sitter	designate	cult
paleontology	groovy	perfidy
teen-ager	synthesis	explain
colloid	convey	pastoral
canine	bandwagon	take apart
ritzy	soap opera	antediluvian
a drunk	antithesis	sky high
fork it out	going strong	enthuse
squib	sure enough	rake-off
smog	sanctified	retrogression
alcoholic	generically	squelch
togetherness	fastidious	stuffed shirt
egghead	jalopy	Veep
semantics	cop	joint (meaning *house*)
snitch	undoubtedly	discriminating
endeavor	transfiguration	natural
prof	glommed	groan box
education	stiff (dead body)	wise guy
six-shooter	dough (meaning *money*)	fission
		drag strip

8. Arrange the following words and expressions in two columns, the formal words in one and opposite each formal word or phrase its informal equivalent: betrothed, teacher, keep, ocular defect, land reform, initiate, having many syllables, shortness, urban life, agrarian reform, earthly, differing, lunar eclipse, city life, maternal, retain, divergent, eclipse of the moon, terrestrial, begin, cease, polysyllabic, motherly, engaged, brevity, eye defect, pedagogue, stop.

3

CHOOSING AND TESTING
A THEME SUBJECT

If you are going to build something—a table, perhaps—you will not grab the first boards you can find and start sawing. On the contrary, since this kind of construction is an orderly process in which some things are done first and others next, a plan will be needed. You will begin by deciding on the kind of table and the material it is to be made of. Then you will draw a sketch of it, showing the exact size and shape, because you have learned from experience that it is easier to erase a line on a sketch and redraw it than it is to lengthen a board that has been sawed two inches too short. When your sketch is finished, and not until then, you begin the actual work of construction.

An analogy between building a table and writing a theme ought not to be pressed too far, since carpentry of this sort is chiefly a mechanical operation, whereas writing a good paper is not. Nevertheless, writing a composition is a process made up of various steps. These steps may not always occur in exactly the same order—in fact, you will sometimes be able to take several of them at nearly the same time. But in general the following description of the process will hold true:

The first step is to decide on a subject. Once you have done so, you must check the subject against what you know about it to be sure you have enough information available to discuss it properly. Next you must identify your audience and make sure that the subject is or can be made appropriate to that audience. Then, after making certain that the subject is the right size for the length of paper you plan to write, you decide on the central idea or main purpose so as to clarify what you are trying to do. When this is done, you assemble material—the ideas, incidents, examples out of which you will construct the paper. Then you make a sketch—that is, an outline—of the entire paper so that you can arrange (and rearrange) the material in what seems the best form for the purpose. Consulting the outline, you write a first draft of the theme. This version is not a finished product; it must be examined closely for defects of all kinds, the defects must be removed, and a clear final copy must be made. Though the finished paper, like a homemade coffee table, may not be a masterpiece that will be admired two centuries from now, you can nevertheless take satisfaction in having planned and written the theme in an orderly and efficient way. It should be a good example of the best work you are at present capable of doing.

All of these various steps in the process of planning and writing a paper will be discussed more fully in later chapters. The rest of this chapter will deal only with the first three steps: getting a specific subject, adapting it in various ways, and limiting it.

Getting a Subject

Whether it is English themes, the papers and examinations that you write for other courses, or the letters and reports that you may have to prepare after you have graduated, the problem of finding a subject to write about is usually not very difficult. If, ten years from now, you need to write a business letter, it is obvious that a specific situation, such as an overdue shipment or a need for information about prices, will have made it necessary for you to write the letter. You may need to think out the details of what you are going to say or how you are going to say it, but you will know the general subject that you must deal with. The same is true of term papers and of answers to examination questions in college. The subject will usually have been set for you by your teacher: perhaps a report on the causes of the Spanish-American War or an answer to the question, "What is meant by the 'laissez-faire' theory of economics?"

In your freshman English course the situation is usually not much different. You can almost certainly count on a measure of guidance from your teacher in selecting a theme topic. He will give you this help not because he wants to do your job for you but because usually he will want to organize the writing assignments in some kind of order. He will probably give you directions, more or less specific, for each theme you write, indicating at least the general nature of the subject he wants you to deal with.

But the main part of the job will still lie ahead of you. You will not be ready to begin writing until you have done some preliminary thinking to make the subject more specific. You must be sure that it fits within the limits of your own knowledge, you must adapt it to the particular audience you intend to address, and you must restrict it (or, less often, expand it) so that it will be suitable for the length of paper you plan to write.

Writing on Subjects You Know About

SJ 1   *Write on subjects that lie within your knowledge and ability*

Besides the many other reasons why you can be thankful you are living today instead of eighty or ninety years ago, you might consider the following theme topics that used to be assigned to high school students and college freshmen: "Evanescence of Pleasure," "Youth, Mammon, and Old Age," "The Superstitions of the Ancient Egyptians," "The Adaptation of External Nature to the Moral Constitution of Man." These topics—and dozens more of the same sort—were included in old textbooks on English composition and were inflicted on luckless students.

No one can write convincingly on a subject that he knows nothing about—and it is unlikely that college freshmen either then or now could do much with a subject like "The Adaptation of External Nature to the Moral Constitution of Man." Since your teacher has a good idea of what the average freshman can and cannot discuss with some authority, he will assign theme topics that he believes lie within the range of your knowledge and ability.

On the other hand, you should not expect him necessarily to give you subjects tailor-made for you alone. Sometimes, when you are lucky, an assigned topic will coincide neatly with your own knowledge and interests; at other times you may not be so fortunate. After all, there are other students in the class, whose interests will never be exactly the same as yours, yet the theme assignment ordinarily must be general enough or varied enough to meet the needs of these students as well as your own. Although your teacher will assign topics that he believes suitable for freshmen in general, you are an individual freshman and will usually have to make further changes in the subjects before they are entirely suited to *you.*

For example, your teacher would undoubtedly be safe in assuming that all the members of your English class know something about the general subject of education. All college freshmen have had at least a dozen years of it in grade school and high school and are now having their first experience with higher education. Perhaps your college English class has read and discussed several essays on education that have encouraged you to examine and evaluate the teachers and courses you had in high school as well as those you now have in college. Now, if your teacher offers a list of specific titles from which to make a selection, you probably will not have much trouble choosing one that accords with what you know. If the list contains titles like "High School English as Preparation for College English," "Studies versus Outside Activities," "My Opinion of Lecture Classes in College," and "A Comparison of High School Teachers and College Teachers," all you have to do is decide which subject you know the most about and are most interested in. All of them lie well within the range of your knowledge and experience.

But suppose your teacher, deciding instead to give you a more generalized assignment, simply asks you to write a paper in which you present your opinions on some aspect of education. What he is expecting, of course, is that you will frame for yourself a topic similar to those mentioned above, one that fits your own particular interests and experience and that you are therefore qualified to discuss. He does *not* expect you to write a philosophical essay in which you try to settle for all time the great problems of education, problems about which even experts have disagreed for centuries. Here is what happened when one student tried to discuss an aspect of education that he knew too little about:

The Need for Progressive Education

Objections and criticisms have been levelled at progressive education from its earliest days. "Our children don't learn the important foundations of knowledge—the teaching of Greek and Latin classics is ignored." "Progressive schools are sending to our colleges students who haven't even learned to spell." "Rude and uncivilized children are being turned out of these new-fangled schools." But what many of the most vehement foes of modern education fail to realize is that traditional schools have not met the needs of present-day society and that an adequate substitute must be found.

Old methods of education stressing the "three R's" and rigid discipline were established in our country's early days to create iron-willed and coldly calculating scholars or mould strait-laced ladies and gentlemen. But in today's society the need is not so much for grammarians living in an intellectual world as for citizens living in a world of tension and turmoil. Many school curriculums of the 18th and 19th centuries still exist today and have not changed enough to provide sufficient training for today's problems.

A student trained in a traditional school is filled with Latin verbs and dates of significant battles. He is too often taught facts independently of situations; he may know how to distinguish between a dangling participle and one correctly used, but not how to use this knowledge in speaking and writing more fluently. Such a student is not trained to get along with his next-door neighbor, vote for the best candidate for county treasurer, or keep himself in good physical condition, but rather to recognize right angles, dangling participles, and Greek verbs.

Contemporary America is a land of industry needing skilled mechanics and artisans, as well as doctors and lawyers. Contemporary American schools are still too largely occupied with producing doctors and lawyers and discouraging or neglecting the mechanics. Although the trend is to create a curriculum training hands as well as intellects, a student with a talent for carpentry often leaves school and becomes an apprentice rather than remain and graduate unprepared for his chosen profession.

The world of today requires a basic understanding of its people as well as a working knowledge of its industry. And here too the traditional curriculums are unsatisfactory. While a student learns the surface causes of World War II, he isn't taught to understand the years of German philosophy and thought that contributed to the war. Social studies in school are concerned with the "what happened" of history more than with the "why it happened." In order to become a true world citizen, the student must understand why people act as they do in addition to knowing the forms this action takes.

Progressive education is being introduced because of the insufficiency of traditional methods of education in preparing a youth to enter a world of industry and turmoil. The narrow old curriculum is being replaced by one broader and more liberal, one that emphasizes man's place and function in today's world rather than the world itself. But in order to meet the demands of contemporary society, the trend toward progressive education must continue until it has wiped out the unnecessary knowledge and thus renovated American schools.

This paper has an obvious fault: the author simply did not know enough about the subject to write convincingly on it. The paper raises many questions that the author has not answered: What, exactly, is meant by "progressive education"? What is a "traditional school," and is it true that a student who attends one (whatever it is) learns nothing but dates of battles and Latin verbs? Is it true that such a student will necessarily fight with the people next door, be a stupid voter, and become a physical wreck? The author has neglected to think carefully about the assigned subject—education—and then select an aspect of it that fitted his own knowledge and experience. As we glance through the theme, it becomes clear to us that the author is bluffing: he knows very little about "progressive education," still less about "traditional education," and nothing at all about the actual effects of these two systems on students trained under them.

When you are asked to write a theme, take a little time first to make sure that the subject fits within the limits of what you actually know through direct personal experience, through observing the experience of others, or through reading and conversation. Remember that writing is *communication*, an attempt to say something to someone else for a particular purpose. The one who reads what you write will naturally expect to have something communicated to him. But if he finds that nothing worthwhile is being communicated, that vague language is apparently being used to conceal a lack of knowledge, he is not likely to feel that you have dealt fairly with him.

EXERCISES

1. Which of the following general topics do you feel you have the background, interest, and ability to deal with in a composition?

(a) Electronics
(b) Baseball
(c) My High School
(d) Working One's Way through College
(e) These Small European Cars
(f) Choice Vacation Spots
(g) Jazz
(h) Debating in High School
(i) Being a Youngest Child
(j) Juvenile Delinquency
(k) Archery
(l) Summer Camps
(m) Women in Sports
(n) High School Clubs
(o) Hunting
(p) Fashion Illustration
(q) Learning Responsibility
(r) National Politics
(s) Teacher Certification
(t) High School (or College) Dramatics

2. Select five of the general topics in "1" that you decided you were competent to discuss; for each, write three specific titles which you could develop into themes of 500–700 words.

Choosing a Topic Appropriate to Your Readers

SJ 2   *Select a topic in which you can interest your readers*

Consideration of your readers has been discussed in a general way in Chapter 1. The matter needs to be discussed again here but in a more specific connection, for the next step in the writing process is to make sure that the subject you have chosen is one in which it seems likely that you can interest your intended audience. First, of course, you must be sure that you know who your audience is. Sometimes your teacher will specify a particular reader or group of readers as part of the assignment. At other times you may want to address your composition to the teacher himself. Or, perhaps most frequently, you may want to aim your themes at the other students in your English class; although they all have their own private interests and likes and dislikes, they are your own age, are freshmen like yourself, and therefore have much in common with you. Most of the things that interest you are likely also to interest your classmates, or can be so treated that your classmates will find them interesting.

Here is a good example of what can happen when a student forgets who his audience for a particular theme is. The assignment was simply to write a critical discussion of some problem that would be of interest to the other members of the class.

More Time Between High School Classes

In my high school we were allowed only three minutes to get from one class to another. I believe that more time should be allowed, since the average student just isn't able to get to his next class in three minutes and so is often tardy. For example, last year my first-hour class was woodwork, which met in the south end of the building, on the first floor; but my second-hour class was American history, which met in a room almost a half a block away on the second floor. Sometimes the woodwork teacher wouldn't excuse us until about two minutes after the bell had rung, since we had to put away the tools we had been using. This would make me late to my second-hour class because it took at least two minutes to walk to it.

Furthermore, we had to walk, not run. Running in the halls was forbidden. Once I was stopped by another teacher for running to my history class and had to go back again and walk all the way. That day I was three minutes late. When I arrived at our second-hour class late, the teacher would scold me for not being there on time. I finally had to quit stopping at my locker between first hour and second hour in order to save a little time.

We did have a rule at our school that allowed us, if we had not had time to stop at our lockers, to fill out a pass slip which would let us go back to our lockers after the class had started and get the material we needed. I did this sometimes, but it is a bad habit to get into because while you are gone from the room you miss some of the class discussion or some of the information the teacher gives about the next day's assignment. Often I found that I did not know that a test was to be given, since I had been out of the room when it was announced.

Whenever any of us came into a class late, we had to come in after school and make up time. Usually we had to stay in forty-five minutes, even if we had been only one or two minutes late. I had to go to work at three-thirty every school day. When I had to stay in to make up time for being late, I was late for work. Being late for work is all right once in a while, maybe, but when it happens two or three times a week the boss doesn't like it.

I am sure I was not the only one who got into trouble because only three minutes were allowed between classes; lots of us were late almost every day to certain classes which were located too far from the classes that met the hour before. Because the three-minute rule is unfair to many students, I believe it should be changed and that five minutes should be allowed between classes.

This theme is a weak effort in several ways, but perhaps its most obvious defect is that it discusses a particular problem in a particular high school, a problem in which most other college freshmen could not be expected to have much interest. Some of them may have come from little high schools that did not have corridors half a block long, so that even two minutes would have been plenty of time to allow between classes. Others may have attended high schools where five or ten minutes were allowed for students to get from one class to the next. And, after all, none of the members of the author's audience are in high school now, nor are they able to do anything about the situation being complained of (notice the last sentence of the paper, which seems to appeal for action). They may and probably do have a strong interest in whether the ten minutes allowed between college classes is time enough to get from one end of the campus to the other without a bicycle, but their interest in the interval between high school classes—especially at one certain high school which few or none of them attended—is likely to be slight. The author of this paper has, unfortunately, wasted his audience's time by discussing a topic that means little or nothing to them.

Now look at a more successful theme, written to fulfil the same assignment as the other one—a discussion of a problem interesting to the other members of the class.

Thanks for Not Very Much

Since my homeroom teacher had advised me that it would be wise to take senior English if I planned to go to college, I dutifully scribbled my name on the list with the rest of the students who were signing up for English 12. On my first day in this class I was unusually impressed by my teacher, an intelligent looking little woman with white hair and dark brown eyes accentuated by a pair of hornrimmed glasses. She informed us that the sole purpose of English 12 was to acquaint us with the sort of work we would be doing in college English classes. She went on to explain that she regularly talked with English professors and college students to keep up on the latest trends in college English teaching. I settled back comfortably and thought of how much this year of English would help me, how easy freshman English would be for me, and how proud my parents would be when I came home from my first semester of college with an A in English.

Our first assignment was to read everything there was in our literature books about the Anglo-Saxon period, then top this unit of study off with *Beowulf*. My teacher seemed to like this long poem, but I'll have to admit that I struggled with it as grimly as its hero did with the monster Grendel. With *Beowulf* behind us, we went on to Chaucer and the Middle Ages, to Shakespeare and the Elizabethan period, and on, period by period, through English literature until we reached the twentieth century. We learned dates and names, memorized a lot of poems and the titles and authors of still others—and finally wrote one 2,000-word research paper. It was the only paper we wrote all year. We studied grammar, learning such terms as "subjunctive," "retained object," "objective infinitive construction," and so on, and even learned to diagram sentences that contained these things. But we wrote only the one theme.

I wasn't aware then of any shortcomings in English 12. It certainly kept me busy all year and it did fill me full of facts about English literature and English grammar. I felt, at the end of the course, well prepared for freshman English at the University.

My first day in freshman English in college found me sitting in the front row with a smug look on my face. I could have answered any question asked about Milton, Browning, Keats, Shakespeare, or participles.

Our professor smiled and said, "This semester we shall be concerned only with writing themes." Everyone in the class groaned except me. I was too stunned to make a sound. Four home themes and five class themes later I was haggard, but my grades on themes had risen from C's to B's. We wound up the semester with a grand total of seven home themes, eight class themes and one extra-long paper. The total was about four times as much writing as I had done in my whole high school career, and because of my lack of earlier practice it was uphill work all the way.

Whether my English professor finally gave me an A for effort, or for my stubborn determination to improve my writing, or simply out of pity for me I'll never know. However, I went back home between semesters with my grade clutched tightly in my fist—and with a lot of interesting suggestions to give to my high school English teacher. I intended to make her understand that, although next year when I would take sophomore literature I would no doubt be glad for the training she had given me in English literature, she had certainly not prepared me for the sort of work that was expected of me in freshman composition. All the hours spent in diagraming sentences and memorizing grammatical terms had proved to be of little value to me. What she ought to have had us do in English 12 was write and write and write. I really intended to be pretty plain and tell her just how mistaken she was.

When I got to the high school she greeted me with a cheery hello and told a very bored class that she had had me in English 12 the year before. When she asked me what my grade in English was and I replied, she announced proudly to her class, "See what a big help English 12 is going to be to all of you! Dorothy couldn't have made that A without the sort of background she got in English 12. Isn't that right, dear?" I nodded helplessly.

The author of this paper has chosen a subject almost certain to interest all other members of her class. All of them will have shared her experience of making the transition between high school and college courses in English, and many will have had difficulties of one sort or another in adjusting to the expectations of a college teacher of English composition. A common fund of experience is shared alike by the author and her classmates that will insure interest in the subject.

EXERCISE

3. Which of the following topics are suitable for short papers (500–700 words) addressed to members of your English class? Give reasons for your choice.

(a) Boolean Algebra and Its Uses
(b) Pros and Cons of Fraternity Life
(c) Missile Guidance Systems
(d) My Home Town Newspaper
(e) How I Dig Clams
(f) How to Knit a Sweater
(g) The Day I Lost My Billfold
(h) What Should Be Done about Copied Themes

(i) My High School Didn't Prepare
    Me for College
(j) My Favorite Teacher
(k) Using a Geiger Counter for
    Prospecting
(l) How to Make White Sauce

(m) The Solar Battery
(n) How to Make a Sphygmoma-
    nometer
(o) Television Westerns Are Getting
    Worse

Making the Subject the Right Size

SJ 3   *Fit the subject to the length of your paper*

After you have determined that you know enough about the subject to do it justice and have made sure that it is appropriate to the interests of your readers, you should fit the subject to the length of theme you plan to write. You should keep in mind that the average freshman theme is not, after all, very long. Most themes run less than a thousand words, often no more than four or five hundred words. Printed in a book, a composition of this length would not take up much more than a page or two, if indeed that. You should therefore take care to see that your subject is neither so small that you will have to pad it to make a long enough composition, nor so large that you will need to write five or ten thousand words to do it justice. Actually, you are not likely to choose a subject that is too small. Sometimes you will apparently run out of things to say in a theme before you have written more than a page or two, but the trouble is seldom too limited a subject. Instead, what probably has happened is either that you did not know enough about the subject to begin with (that is, you failed to adapt it properly to the limits of your own knowledge); or you failed to see all the possibilities in the subject and made use of only a part of it.

You are far more likely to choose a subject that is too large. It is easy to make this mistake, because it seems much less trouble to skim lightly over the surface of a large subject, tossing off enough general and often unrelated remarks to add up to a paper of the required length, than it is to discuss a smaller subject thoroughly, telling your reader all he wants and needs to know about it. Here is a good example of what happens when the subject has not been trimmed to size:

Memories

My first in a series of memories occurred when my parents took me to the Alamo in San Antonio, Texas. Though I was only four years old, I can still picture this historical place and I have fond memories of it. I was told by my parents what this building stood for; my father said that many Texans had died in this place, fighting for what they thought was right. When I started to school and studied the battle of the Alamo, I realized even more what a wonderful memory that day had left on me.

At the age of seven I moved to New York with my parents, and the excitement of this move added another wonderful memory. I remember how thrilled I was the day we got on the train for New York, the center of the world. The train ride took much too long, as far as I was concerned, for I was anxious to reach this big city.

Arriving at Grand Central Station in New York City, I was amazed to find that buildings could be so tall. I must have looked rather funny to native New Yorkers, for I walked through the station and down Broadway with my head in the air looking at all the tall buildings. We went to a hotel for the night. Since this was the first time I had ever been in a hotel, I was quite excited. Several days later we moved into our first home in New York, and this too was quite thrilling. So you see, this trip to a new city left really wonderful memories in my mind.

At the age of nine, while living in Queens Village, New York, I started taking dancing lessons. All the girls I knew were taking these lessons, and I talked my parents into letting me do the same. I do not quite remember the first day I went to class, except that I was quite excited and a little scared. The night that really left an impression on me was the one of my first recital. It was held in a concert hall in New York City, and I was chosen to lead my class in the tap dance. I was wearing a blue and red dress and felt very proud of myself. I went through my dance very nicely after getting over a bad start. After my recital was over, my parents and I went to a restaurant for dinner and had a small party afterwards at our apartment. I think I shall never forget this day and the wonderful feeling of being in front of all those people, showing what I had learned.

When I was twelve, my parents and I moved to a town in northern New York, where I started in the seventh grade. I did not know then that this move would bring about a very sad memory. The first day I started to school I met a girl named Margaret Moore. After school that day Margaret invited me to her house for the afternoon, where I met her parents and her older brother, Billy, who was in the eighth grade. Peggy, as her friends called her, and I became the best of friends during the time I lived there.

When I entered high school, Billy was already a sophomore, and he and I started going together. Toward the end of my freshman year we had dated each other so much that all our friends considered Billy and me as practically going steady. The summer before I started my senior year in high school Billy left for college. Although by this time we hadn't been dating each other so often as before, we were still very good friends and wrote to each other often.

In the middle of my senior year, my parents and I moved again, this time to St. Joseph, Missouri, but Billy and I still wrote to each other. The day before Christmas, a year ago, I received a letter from Peggy, Billy's sister, saying that Billy had been killed in an auto accident. I was deeply shocked by this news. So you can see that this memory, which nothing can erase from my mind, is the saddest one of my life so far.

The assignment for this paper was one of those general topics mentioned earlier: "Write a theme in which you relate a memorable childhood experience." But notice what this student has done. Instead of narrating fully one particular experience, and telling us enough about it so that it seems real and important, the author has given us a galloping survey of nearly her whole life from the age of four—all in about seven hundred words. This isn't a theme, but instead a miscellaneous collection of possibilities for eight or ten themes. Look at it again to see what it includes: a trip to the Alamo, a train ride to New York, first impressions of New York City, the first night in a hotel, moving into a home in New York City, dancing lessons and a dance recital (with a celebration afterwards), moving to another town and making new friends, falling in love for the first time, the cooling of this affair, and the untimely death of the boy. If the author had wanted to include all these things in one good composition, she would have needed to write a small book.

Here is a look at a more successful paper written on the same general topic, a memorable childhood experience:

My First Encounter with Love

From the beginning, I'd better make the fact clear that my heart tumbled completely for the first time when I was at the innocent age of six. Now that you know there aren't any incriminating complications with college men, let me tell you about that tender moment when Dan Cupid first let an arrow zing my way.

The fellow victim was also a first-grader, one of the meanest, and therefore cutest, to be found in the school. Since he lived on the same block as I, our trysts were a simple matter of slipping out from under mother's watchful eye, sneaking along behind the bushes our neighbor had conveniently planted in a row, sprinting across another neighbor's yard, and heaving up the garage door. That is, that was my method of reaching the cool, dark shadows inside the garage. Even then, Tom knew what most boys know: namely, that if you sit still long enough the girls will come to you. So he merely dropped a hint each day, as we added our one and one and got three, that he would be playing in the garage that night after school. Almost before he could get there, I would come bouncing in, full of tender expressions such as "Tom, will you quit throwing dirt at me?"

But in fairness to my ego, I must tell you that the feeling was mutual. It was Tom who proposed and Tom who was saving up his dog pictures to hang on the walls of our home-to-be. For my part, I saved up playing cards I found on the sidewalk in the hope that I'd find a full deck, with which Tom and I could spend a companionable evening some cold winter night when our children were grown and gone.

I gave up my hit-and-miss search for cards, however, when I discovered how romantic Tom was. It's not every six-year-old who can kiss like THAT. And I know, because we spent three straight evenings in that garage testing our mothers' love.

And that brings me to the most memorable events of our courtship —my two spankings. Either my mother must have remembered similar guilty experiences from her own younger days, or she just didn't like to have me sneaking off for three nights in a row. Anyway, the last two of those nights, I was given lessons in the evils of boys—with a hairbrush. For one night, through one spanking, my love stood the test; but after the second, my mother's logic began to penetrate. After all, was seeing Tom for a few guilty hours in that cold, dark, dusty garage worth a spanking every night? I'd never had a spanking before, and could I let Tom now disrupt my home life for all the years I was stuck with it before we could be made one? I had a practical mind at that age; so when Tom walked another girl home the next day, I could figure out for myself that it wasn't worth it. For a year, or till I was at least seven, I was a bitter old-maid.

Now, though I have forgotten those trying, dark, lonely days without my lover, I still see the lesson I learned—that boys mean trouble, at any age or in any clime—being re-enacted almost daily on the campus. But, come to think of it, I might as well be six again; for when I see Cupid aiming his arrow, I hurry to place myself in the line of fire; and then I go through the same trials and tribulations all over again.

This paper, though it is nearly as long as the other one, covers only a few days or weeks of the author's life rather than a dozen or more years. Instead of telling about eight or ten unrelated incidents, it describes a series of happenings so closely connected with one another that we feel they make up a single experience. More than that, whereas the first paper is so vague and general that we don't get a clear impression of any of the things it tells about, this one includes details that make the experience seem more real: how the appointments were made, the route to the garage, the plans for a future home, the experimental kissing, the unfortunate ending of the love affair.

Remember, then, that it is very important for you to limit the size of your subject according to the scale of treatment you plan to give it. Though it is possible that you might choose too small a subject and have to pad it, it is much more likely that you will make the opposite error and choose a topic too big to be discussed adequately in the time and space you have available. Either mistake will produce bad results. A composition that has been padded will waste your reader's time and exhaust his patience; one that tries to present a 5,000-word subject in 500 words will do exactly the same. Either way, you lose—and so does your reader.

EXERCISES

4. The following topics are of various types, some very general, some more specific and suited to papers of 2,000 to 5,000 words, and some very specific and suitable for short papers of 500 to 700 words. Arrange the topics in three columns: (a) those which would require a book to develop; (b) those which would require 2,000 to 5,000 words to develop; and (c) those which could be used as subjects for short 500- to 700-word papers.

The Best Pet I Ever Had	Swimming
Dogs	Friendship
Cocker Spaniels	Climbing Pike's Peak
A Trip to the Ocean	College Life versus High School Life
Vacations I Have Had	How to Prepare for an Exam
First Sight of the Ocean	The Fall of Ft. Sumter
Education in a Rural High School	My First Summer Job
Mountain Climbing	How to Develop the Crawl Stroke
The Amoeba	Labor Unions
The Civil War	How the Airplane Strike Ruined My
Social Life in High School	Vacation
How to Raise Tomatoes	American Education
Strikes Are Un-American	My First Impression of College
My Best Friend	Halloween Has Changed
My Favorite TV Program	How to Change a Tire

5. Limit each of the following general subjects, first by selecting an aspect of each which could be developed in a term paper of 2,000 to 5,000 words; then further limit each subject by selecting one particular aspect of it which would be suitable for a 500- to 700-word paper.

Example: Rockets

        Rocket Development in Germany During World War II

        The Psychological Effects of the Buzz Bombs

(a) College Sports

. . . .
. . . .

(b) National Parks

. . . .
. . . .

(c) Hobbies

. . . .
. . . .

(d) Virus Diseases

. . . .
. . . .

(e) Recreation

. . . .
. . . .

(f) Winston Churchill

. . . .
. . . .

(g) Television

. . . .
. . . .

(h) Movies

. . . .
. . . .

(i) Politics

. . . .
. . . .

(j) Atomic Age

. . . .
. . . .

4

SELECTING MATERIAL
FOR A THEME

In the last chapter we looked at the first steps in the process of writing a theme. If you were to follow these steps in order, you would now have a subject to write about, you would have made sure that you know enough about it to discuss it fully, you would have identified your audience and considered whether the subject would interest them, and finally you would have made sure that the subject is the right size for the scale of treatment you intend.

Assembling Material

The next step in the process is to assemble the material—the ideas, reasoning, examples, incidents, details—out of which you will make the actual theme. Students often complain that they cannot find enough to say when they try to write a theme. It is true of course that neither freshmen nor anyone else can find something worthwhile to say on every subject. But if you have tested a particular subject in the way suggested in Chapter 3, making sure that it falls within the range of what you actually know, all you need do to find something worthwhile to say is examine your own mind. Material is there, waiting to be used. A short listing of the main sources of what you know may help to make you more aware of the kinds of material available to you.

1. From direct personal experience—things that have happened to you and things that you have done—you have gained a very large store

of information, attitudes, habits that you draw on constantly in the ordinary course of living.

2. You also have available a closely related body of material that you have gathered through a somewhat specialized kind of experience: observing, looking at the world around you and what is in it. The impressions derived in this way are recorded in your memory.

3. A third source of your knowledge is people—family and relatives, friends and acquaintances, employers and teachers. By knowing them well you have come to know a good deal about human beings in general, their thoughts, emotions, habits, and reactions. All these people, but especially your parents and teachers, have constantly added to and enriched your store of knowledge. With their help, you can draw on the accumulated experience, observation, and formal education of many other people.

4. One other great source of knowledge is written language. Much of what you have learned since you began to attend school has resulted from your ability to read. Reading makes available to you a wide selection of human knowledge on almost all subjects about which men have thought. Your college textbooks, the newspaper you read, the magazines, the novels or biographies, all add to your knowledge by informing you of the ideas, feelings, and actions of innumerable other people, American or foreign, living, dead, or even imaginary.

Except for research assignments, when your teacher asks you to write a theme he is expecting you to draw on this vast reservoir of material that lies ready and waiting in your mind. A strictly autobiographical subject, such as an unusual job or an unfortunate blind date, is not likely to tempt you into writing about things that lie outside the range of your own knowledge and experience. Such topics are obviously personal and require you to write simply and directly of what you did, what happened to you, and what the effect or impression on you was.

On the other hand, a subject that calls for an opinion on some problem or question—for example, freedom of speech or the quality of television programs—may lead you, if you are not careful, into making large generalizations which suggest that you are an authority on the particular problem and have the answer that all the rest of the world has been looking for (the theme on "The Need for Progressive Education" in Chapter 3 is a good example). This is not the way in which your teacher expects you to deal with the subject. Rather, he wants you to view the topic through the lens of your own experience and describe, say, your attitude toward an example of censorship with which you are familiar (censorship of certain kinds of comic books or certain movies, perhaps), or your conclusions after watching all the TV programs on one channel during three or four hours in a row on a given night. Handled this way, these subjects lie well within your ability. You will not only be presenting your opinions of the subjects, *but you will be including the evidence from your own experience which has led you to form these opinions.* And since you are the person best qualified to speak of your own experience you will be on safe ground; you will know what you are talking about and will have an excellent chance of convincing your readers that your opinions are well founded.

EXERCISES

1. Which of the following general subjects do you know something about? Radio, hunting, fishing, dancing, automobiles, flying, sewing, weaving, outdoor cooking, camping, airplanes, trains, gardening, outdoor sports, baking, knitting, horses, birds, fossils, magic, music, small-town politics, cats.

2. Take one of these general subjects that you know something about and suggest three specific theme topics that you could write on competently with the knowledge you now have.

3. From the standpoint of your own experience criticize eight of the following subjects. That is, which ones are good subjects for you and which aren't? Why?

Adopted	Camping, Canoeing, and Coming Home
The Sea and I	My First Fight
How We Celebrate Christmas	We Go to the City
	Our Family Hero
Rifle Range	I Do My Own Sewing
Relaxation? Read	My First Job
Grading Systems	A Turbine Generator
The English Movie	Religion and the College Student

4. Which of the following subjects call for an account of experience or observation and which are largely concerned with expression of opinion?

Our Old Car	Sensible Fashions for Men and Women
An Airplane Ride	How to Take a Picture
Is Voting a Right or a Privilege?	Is Television Improving?
	A Part-time Job
Choosing a Shotgun	Socialized Medicine Is Inefficient
The High School I Went To	My First Fish
	Army Life Is Good for a Man
I Don't Need English	My First Date

Getting a Central Idea

MAT 1 *Clarify your subject by deciding first on a central idea*

With a proper subject well in mind, you are ready for the next step in the process of writing a theme: you should bring your subject more clearly into focus by deciding what the central idea of the whole paper will be. This step is important because, though you have a suitable topic and have subjected it to preliminary testing, you need to know its exact limits and precisely what you intend to do with it, what the purpose or main point of the paper is to be. For example, if you are writing a theme on censorship, specifically censorship of your college newspaper, you should make sure in your own mind exactly what your own attitude toward censorship is, whether favorable, unfavorable, or some position in between. Once this attitude is clear in your mind, you will know more surely what you want to communicate to your readers and whether you want to bring about changes in their thinking about censorship or simply inform them of your views. Or, if you are writing a paper in which you plan to give your reactions to college registration, you should begin by deciding what your main impression was after registering for college classes; this will clarify your thoughts and help you communicate to your readers exactly what you want.

Take a moment to look at this theme:

Big Time Football, the Curse of Colleges

I guess the biggest complaint against big time football is the amount of time that it takes from other things. A player, if he is good, is expected to spend twenty-four hours a day thinking of nothing but football. When a student spends so much time on athletics, he is going to have to sacrifice something else. Generally it is his studies that he sidesteps. When and if the athlete graduates and gets his degree, all he has learned to do is to carry a football or block tacklers. He will be a complete loss in the job he takes after he graduates, unless of course he takes a coaching job.

When the student starts his first football practice, he generally has a surprise coming to him. College football is a lot different from football in high school. In high school a player can enjoy the game, and if he is good enough he can switch around and play several positions. College football is a hardboiled business, work and not play. And a player is given one position, which he must perfect and keep through his whole college career.

The alumni have gained power over the coach and team that seems sometimes to let them run things. If the coach hasn't been winning as regularly as the alumni think he should, they can often get him fired. The alumni are one of the main factors causing professionalism in college football. The colleges pay young men to play for them. Of course, it usually isn't out-right pay such as real professionals get for playing, but it might as well be. Colleges and universities give scholarships to pay for tuition, books, room and board, and sometimes add a little more for spending money. If colleges are going to pay athletes to come and play for them, why don't they classify these young men as professionals and let them earn really big money? This way, the alumni could scour the country for young men who can play football well, and stop worrying about whether they can read and write.

Big time football has a few good points too. It gives a student a chance to develop his body and keeps him from becoming a bookworm. It also gives him a chance to let off steam and stay out of trouble. Playing football in college should develop fair mindedness and sportsmanship in the athlete, if the coach allows it. The football scholarships that are given to young men offer them a chance for an education that many of them probably wouldn't have otherwise. Of course, this aid is of no value if all the athlete does is play football and does not study.

Probably the most obvious of the many weaknesses in this paper is that, after we have read it, we feel confused. We can't tell either what the writer's purpose is or what his real attitude is toward college football. The title leads us to expect an attack on college football, and in fact this is just what we get—until the last paragraph. Near the end of the theme the writer suddenly seems to change sides and lists several advantages of playing football in college. We feel annoyed with him because, after leading us to expect one point of view, he has suddenly intruded a totally different one and has failed to explain the shift.

In contrast, look at the following paper, in which the writer knows from start to finish what he is trying to do—and does it:

The Truth about Snakes

Ever since the unfortunate beginning, in the Garden of Eden, of our relationship with snakes, we have nourished an enmity against all snakes, a hatred that has turned into unreasoning fear. Why? What is there about snakes that makes them such terrifying creatures? Is it because they crawl on the ground? We don't seem to mind this same habit in a human baby. Perhaps the snakes' habit of sticking out their tongues frightens us; but we think the same action amusing in little girls. Or possibly it is their sinister hissing when they meet us unexpectedly; but geese make a similar sound without frightening us very much.

I think that the main reason for our fear of snakes is our ignorance of them. We are afraid of what we don't understand. But just as we aren't born with a fear of death, neither are we born with a fear of snakes. A small child handles a snake as he would a kitten or a puppy, completely without fear. As we grow up, however, we hear gasps of revulsion when snakes are mentioned; we pick up weird and frightening beliefs about them; we develop an entirely new and fearful attitude toward snakes.

Especially we develop the notion that, since some snakes are dangerous, just to be safe we should regard all snakes as dangerous, and we therefore shy away from all contact, sight, or even mention of snakes. But why? It is true that some snakes are potentially dangerous —but so is a slippery bathtub, a stepladder, an automobile. Do we avoid taking baths because we are afraid we might slip and hurt ourselves? Or do we refuse to ride anywhere in an automobile, preferring instead to walk because we think we will be safer?

I have just learned in a zoology course that there are about 3,000 kinds of snakes in the world, but of these only about 250 are venomous. According to species, then, only one snake in twelve is poisonous; and, according to the number of snakes that people are likely to encounter, only one in twenty-five is venomous. Besides, many of these don't have enough venom to affect a human being seriously. As to death from snakebite, consider the following figures that our zoology teacher gave us the other day. We have about 175,000,000 people in this country, many of them often tramping through land filled with water moccasins, copperheads, rattlesnakes, and coral snakes; yet only 100 of us die annually from snakebite. In the same length of time, about 30,000 Americans are killed in automobile accidents!

In the face of these facts, we have nevertheless convinced ourselves through ignorance, stubbornness, and superstition that snakes are repulsive and dangerous creatures. Many false beliefs still exist about snakes: that they are slimy; that some of them swallow their young alive to protect them from danger and regurgitate them when the danger has passed; that they have yellow blood; that one kind can suck the milk from a cow; that another can put its tail in its mouth and roll like a hoop; that the bite of a poisonous snake means sure death. There are hundreds of similar superstitions about snakes, all of which make good stories but poor science. Some of these notions are actually dangerous, such as the belief that in case of snakebite the use of antivenin will bring complete recovery, or that large doses of whiskey will counteract the poison. But even a slight overdose of antivenin may kill the patient, and whiskey only stimulates the heart to beat faster and pump the poison more rapidly throughout the body.

What should we believe, then, about snakes? Should we avoid them all just to be on the safe side? Should we fear them all? The answer, obviously, is no. We should try to replace superstition with fact and ignorance with knowledge. Snakes are merely our fellow creatures on this earth, often in fact beneficial to us as in their control of rodents. We should learn to understand their habits, their potentialities, and their limitations. We should recognize their good side as well as their bad and appreciate or at least tolerate their presence in the scheme of creation.

The author of this theme, you will notice, has a clearly apparent purpose: to persuade us that many of our beliefs about snakes are false and that we should develop a more intelligent attitude toward these creatures. He tries to explain our fear of snakes, he discusses the extent to which snakes are dangerous to humans, he lists a number of superstitions about snakes, and finally he tells us what he believes a rational attitude toward snakes should be. Throughout the paper, he has kept his purpose well in mind, and all the material he has brought in has a direct bearing on the main point—that for our irrational fear of snakes we should substitute an informed opinion of them, recognizing them as fellow creatures. When we have finished reading the paper, we feel that the author knew what he was about. As a result, we probably have learned some things that we hadn't known and perhaps are somewhat better disposed toward snakes than we were before reading the paper.

MAT 2   *State the central idea in sentence form*

When you have decided on the central idea of your paper, write it down in the form of a complete sentence. Using a complete sentence for this purpose, rather than just a phrase, has the advantage of making you round out the idea more fully so that you can see exactly what it is and how complex it is. For instance, you will not find it very helpful to jot down merely "Censorship of our college newspaper" or "My experiences during registration"; neither of these is specific enough to help you much in deciding what material to select and how to plan the paper. Instead, you should write down something more definite, like "Although our college newspaper is censored occasionally, I believe that this supervision is necessary," or "Registering for classes, though not easy, was not nearly as confusing as I had been told it would be." Notice that sentences like these are one-sentence condensations of an entire theme. A good, purposeful statement of this sort will help you to keep your eye steadily on whatever it is that you want to accomplish in the paper. It will make clear to you both the aim of the paper and the limits of the subject, and so will help you do an intelligent job of selecting the material you need.

EXERCISE

5. Following are subjects which might be possible for you. For each of five make a statement of a central idea (in a single complete sentence) that you think you could present in a theme.

How to Train a Pup   The 4-H Club
A Trip to the Dentist   Family Reunions
Blind Date   Hot Rods
Graduation   The Girl (Boy) Who Laughed at Me
A Friend in Need   My Favorite Childhood Game
Pro Baseball   Fire
My Best Friend   A Joke on Me

Selecting Material

MAT 3   *Select only relevant material*

The next step in the writing process is to select the best and most effective items of material for your theme. Keeping in mind the central idea of the paper, the audience you are intending the paper for, and the particular needs of this audience—what they already know or don't know about the subject, what their attitude (if any) toward the subject is likely to be—you should *think* about the subject to bring to the front of your mind the things you know about it, then jot down these items so that you can make a selection from them. An example will demonstrate this step.

Assume that the assignment is to write a character sketch of 800 to 1,000 words. You decide, after some thought, to write about a boy you knew in high school whose imagination and capacity for mischief made him the most skillful and amusing teller of tall tales that you have known. You have a subject, then, and you know that you are qualified to discuss it, since you were well acquainted with the boy. Because you are going to emphasize only this one special talent of your friend rather than write a complete history of his life, you believe that the subject is the right size for a theme of the assigned length. You believe also that, although the rest of your English class (in this case, your audience) did not know this boy, they will be interested in hearing about him since apparently everyone who knew him found him interesting and likable. Your job will be to choose and present material that shows his main talent to the best advantage.

Next, you compose a central-idea sentence to guide you. After consideration, you come up with this: "The most gifted liar I've ever known was a high school friend whose imaginative but harmless lies were a wonderful source of entertainment to his classmates." This sentence will remind you not only that the paper is to concern itself with this one aspect of your friend's character but also that you want to get across to your readers the special nature of the boy's gift—that he was liked and admired because his prevarications were always amusing, never mean or harmful. In other words, the sentence will help you keep to your main subject and establish a consistent tone or point of view.

You write at the top of a sheet of paper your central-idea sentence, and then begin to jot down things you remember about the boy. The list may include items like these:

CENTRAL IDEA: The most gifted liar I've ever known was a high school friend whose highly imaginative but harmless lies were a wonderful source of entertainment to his classmates.

John's father a garage owner
John's outline in American history class
Incident of the missing microscope in biology class
Incident of the borrowed skillet
John a born liar, but improved with practice
His lies always amusing, never mean
His report on teen-age drinking (his best performance)
John's part in the senior play
Had a frank and innocent-looking face
John's romance with the beauty queen
What John is doing now
John's hobby—amateur radio
Incident of the wrecked motor scooter
John's report on *Julius Caesar*

When you get all these things down and begin to figure out how much space it will take to tell about them, you realize that you have much more material here than you can possibly use if you are to write a paper within the assigned limits of 800 to 1,000 words. Since you will obviously have to leave some of these incidents and observations out, the question is which ones to cancel. Here your central-idea sentence will be useful; it will serve as a testing device by reminding you of the main point that you want to get across to your readers—that John's main talent was prevarication, which he exercised skillfully and entertainingly.

So, looking at your list again, you examine each item to see whether it would really help to accomplish your purpose. As you study the list, you realize that there are two kinds of items here: general observations about John's background, personality, and appearance; and various examples of John's behavior. In the first group there are several items which, it seems to you, will certainly have to stay, because they are general observations about John himself which your readers will need if they are to understand the boy's character. You decide, then, to use the items about John's being a born liar, and about his innocent and frank appearance (your readers will want to know what he looks like so that they can form a picture of him in their minds). You also decide that what John says he is doing now might be a good detail with which to end the paper; you leave it in. And you obviously want to make the point that his lies were entertaining rather than harmful. On the other hand, it becomes clear to you that neither the occupation of the boy's father nor the boy's interest in amateur radio has anything to do with the main point of the theme; you strike them out.

Next, turning to the second kind of items on the list, examples of things that John did, you count eight different incidents—not only more than you have room for in the paper but more than you will really need to get your point across. After a little study you decide that you cannot afford to leave out the incident of the report on teen-age drinking, because it was perhaps his greatest success. His brief romance with the beauty queen, although it is a good story, is not directly concerned with his ability to tell whoppers; the incidents about the lost microscope and the report on *Julius Caesar,* also good stories, really concern other sides of the boy's personality more than the one you are concentrating on. All three of these you scratch out. You are left, then, with four incidents besides the story of the report on drinking: the outline John turned in, in his American history class, the tale of the borrowed skillet, John's performance in the senior play, and the incident of the wrecked scooter. Examining these four closely, you remember that the scooter incident was very complicated and decide not to use it, since you will not have enough room for it. The incident about the senior play, though it would not take long to tell, is really not a very good example of John at his best; you draw a line through it, too.

Now your list looks this way:

CENTRAL IDEA: The most gifted liar I've ever known was a high school friend whose highly imaginative but harmless lies were a wonderful source of entertainment to his classmates.

~~John's father a garage owner~~
John's outline in American history class
~~Incident of the missing microscope in biology class~~
Incident of the borrowed skillet
John a born liar, but improved with practice
His lies always amusing, never mean
His report on teen-age drinking (his best performance)
~~John's part in the senior play~~
Had a frank and innocent-looking face
~~John's romance with the beauty queen~~
What John is doing now
~~John's hobby—amateur radio~~
~~Incident of the wrecked motor scooter~~
~~John's report on *Julius Caesar*~~

You have four pieces of general information about John still on the list, and three examples of him in action. This is enough material, you decide, for a paper of the assigned length. Besides, you are sure that it is all good material for your purpose, since you have tested it to see whether it is related directly to the main idea of the paper and whether it will create in the minds of your readers the impression of the boy that you are trying to communicate.

The next step in the process of writing this theme is, of course, deciding on the best order in which to arrange these separate items so that you can present them to your readers as clearly and effectively as possible. That is, you need to make an outline of some sort to guide you as you set about the actual writing of the theme. We will not discuss outlines in this chapter, however, because the subject deserves a chapter to itself. We will consider outlines in detail in the next chapter, where the outline for the paper we have been talking about will be presented. (The paper itself can be found in Chapter 8.)

EXERCISE

6. Select a theme topic, either one of those suggested in Exercise 5 (p. 48), or another one that you feel you can write on. State in one complete sentence the central idea you would like to develop in a theme. Next make jottings for the theme (as was done on page 49) of all the ideas and facts you might use to develop the central idea. Then edit by striking out the items you decide not to use. Indicate which ideas you excluded because they did not bear on your central idea.

The Best Kind of Material to Use

The main principle that should guide you in selecting material is relevance to the main idea or purpose of the paper. But you should be guided also by two other principles: you should distinguish clearly between fact on the one hand and opinion or judgment on the other; and you should use specific and concrete details. The best way to demonstrate the importance of these last two principles is to show you a paper in which the author neglected to take account of them.

The Best Teacher I've Ever Had

At the beginning of my junior year in high school, a new teacher appeared on the faculty to teach chemistry and applied science.

The new man was an admirable person. From the day he came, to the day two years later when he left, he was beyond any doubt the most popular man in the school system, liked by everybody not only in the high school but in the entire community as well. He wasn't really exceptional in appearance, but he did have an unusual personality.

He conducted his classes in such a manner that he put the rest of the teachers to shame. If there was ever any dissension among students during his class, he always handled it adequately and made those who were responsible for the disturbance feel ashamed of themselves.

Usually he made his classes so interesting that we all paid perfect attention and marvelled at his intelligence. I know I did, for the simple reason that he was beyond all doubt the most intelligent man I have ever met. He could do anything.

He had no favorites when it came to grading, for all of us were the same in his eyes unless we proved ourselves otherwise. However, if some of us did fall behind in class, he would take all the time necessary to help us get caught up.

Enemies were something he didn't have to worry about; he had none when he came, he made none during his stay, and he left none behind when he moved to another town.

One can't really appreciate this man without knowing him, but since I knew him well I can truthfully say that he was the best teacher I've ever had.

You probably will agree that this theme is a pretty dull effort. It is of course poorly organized, poorly thought through, and in general poorly expressed. But its dullness is mainly the result of the writer's failure to realize the difference between fact and opinion and his failure to use specific and concrete details.

FACT AND OPINION

MAT 4   *Distinguish carefully between fact and opinion*

Let us consider first the difference between fact and judgment, or opinion. Look again at the first two paragraphs of "The Best Teacher I've Ever Had." The sentence that makes up the first paragraph states facts: "At the beginning of my senior year in high school, a new teacher appeared on the faculty to teach chemistry and applied science." The time of this new teacher's first appearance, the actual appearance of a new teacher on the high school faculty, and the subjects for which he would be responsible—these are facts, not opinions. They are facts because they are things that really happened or conditions that really existed; there can be no argument about them. The author is simply reporting occurrences or circumstances and is not expressing any attitude or point of view toward them.

Now look at the sentences in the next paragraph. The first sentence, "The new man was an admirable person," is opinion or judgment, not fact. Here the author is not reporting an actual occurrence, but rather is telling us what his attitude toward the teacher is. Or, to put it differently, the author has examined a great many facts about the man—things the teacher has actually done and said—and, on the evidence of these facts, has passed judgment, has arrived at an opinion of the man.

We are not concerned here with whether or not this teacher really was an admirable person; he may well have been. The point is that when, in our reading, we run across a definite expression of opinion like this, there are certain expectations aroused in us that we feel deserve to be satisfied. Our curiosity is stimulated; and we naturally expect, since the writer has taken the trouble to arouse our curiosity, that he will go on at once to satisfy it by telling us *why* he feels as he does, *why* he holds this particular opinion. We feel we are entitled to see some evidence so that we can ourselves check the accuracy of his conclusion.

MAT 5   *Support opinions with suitable evidence*

In the paragraph we are looking at (the second of the theme), the first sentence leads us to expect that the sentences following will give us evidence for believing that this teacher was an admirable person. But the next sentence merely presents another opinion or judgment: "From the day he came, to the day two years later when he left, he was beyond any doubt the most popular man in the school system, liked by everybody not only in the high school but in the entire community as well." Perhaps this teacher was the most popular man in the school system, and perhaps everybody in town (with not a single exception) did like him. The trouble is that when we read the next (and last) sentence in the paragraph, we find that we have been given no evidence to prove the teacher's popularity. Instead, we are presented with still more opinions: "He wasn't really exceptional in appearance, but he did have an unusual personality." The whole paragraph leaves us dissatisfied. The rest of the theme, which consists almost wholly of more opinions, strengthens this feeling. Because the author has apparently been unaware of the difference between opinion and fact, and has presented opinions throughout the paper as though they were actually facts, he has failed to persuade us to share his admiration for the teacher.

You should not get the idea that there is anything wrong about expressing opinions; on the contrary, you are and always will be expected to give your opinion, in class and out of class, during college years and after graduation, in writing and in conversation. The important thing is for you to know when you are reporting a fact ("Professor Greenlaw often gives us tests without advance notice") and when you are expressing judgment or opinion ("Professor Greenlaw is not fair"). And it is just as important that you remember always to back your opinions with some of the main facts that led you to form them. Otherwise, you will have small chance of convincing someone else that your views are well founded.

EXERCISES

7. Which of the following are facts? Which are judgments?

The Nile is the longest river in the world.
The Russians are doing a better job of education than we are.
The population of my home town is 3,873.
Football should be abolished on college campuses.

Belonging to a sorority or fraternity helps a student get good grades in college.

Football plays a prominent part in campus life at most American colleges and universities.

Blister rust is a parasite which attacks white pine forests.

Kansas is known as the *Wheat state*.

Alaska will be a big asset to our country.

America has produced no great literature in the Twentieth century.

Our high school coach was a big man with twinkling eyes.

People who live in small towns are happier than those who live in cities.

Many boys growing up today dream of flying in rockets.

We have no right to try to stake out a claim on the moon.

Young people today are more frivolous than their parents were.

8. Following are some paragraphs taken from student themes. Which ones are expressing judgments? Which ones are simply reporting facts? Are there any which do both?

(a) Jim and I seemed to have a type of mental telepathy between us. There have been many times when I have been lazily dreaming of doing something, when along would come Jim, wanting to do the same thing. At other times our mental telepathy has been a real aid to us, in helping each other out of embarrassing situations and aiding one another during formal discussions.

(b) Engines have also undergone radical changes since the first car. The first engines had low horsepower and were of relatively simple design. The engine designs have varied from four to eight cylinders and in rare cases to twelve cylinders in line. The eight-cylinder engine known as the V-8, consisting of two banks of four cylinders, seems to be the most popular at this time. Horsepower has increased rapidly and radically since World War II.

(c) The San Blas native is not a handsome fellow. Generally, men and women are very small. Their heads are large, which sometimes make them look top-heavy because of their short necks. One of the most common events among the Indians is the birth of an "albino" boy, which they call "boy of the moon." Weak in bodies, disproportioned, their skin a milky white with yellow streaks, the albinos caught our attention continually.

(d) We waded out to the middle of the lake to our blind—a small concrete blind camouflaged with grass and straw. My father left me in the blind while he and my grandfather went out in front to put out the decoys. They set up about twenty-five wooden ducks, just enough to attract attention, and then climbed into the blind to wait. By this time dawn was approaching, shooting pink and yellow streaks of light through the gray eastern sky. And with the coming of dawn, the ducks were on the move. I could hear their quacking and chattering in the gray morning as they prepared for the day's long journey south. Just as the tip of the sun crept over the horizon, a large flock of ducks rose off the lake far to our left and disappeared in the distance. I knew it wouldn't be long now.

(e) I think that eventually there will be no segregation in the United States, but I don't think it will come about in time for us to see it happen. If I were asked my views of the segregation issue I could not give any definite answers without contradicting myself. About all that I can say about segregation is that I am for it and at the same time against it.

SPECIFIC AND CONCRETE DETAILS

MAT 6   *Use specific and concrete details for clear and vigorous writing*

Now let us consider the importance of specific and concrete details in good writing. Another of the reasons why you probably found "The Best Teacher I've Ever Had" so dull is that the paper contains almost no material of this sort. Here, for example, is the last sentence of the second paragraph again: "He wasn't really exceptional in appearance, but he did have an unusual personality." How much does this sentence really tell us about the teacher's appearance and personality? Almost nothing at all. Instead of getting a description of what the man really looked like, we are told only that he didn't look "exceptional"—which helps us about as much as though the writer had informed us that the man had only two legs and one head. Instead of being presented with some specific evidence about the man's personality, we are informed merely that his personality was "unusual"—a term so broad that it might include the personalities of anyone from Hamlet to Hitler.

The lack of specific and concrete detail throughout the theme makes it impossible for us always to be sure of what the author is talking about. And since we find in the paper nothing that interests us, we condemn it as dull.

Here, by way of contrast, is a paper that does make effective use of specific and concrete material:

Sam

I suppose that most people from average families would agree with me that life with Sam Carlin would be anything but serene. This idea crept up on me as soon as I met the young man.

It was a bright, cheerful April day, that day when I went home with Sara Carlin to meet her family. Sara was a cute redhead who occupied the seat next to me in eighth grade math. I'm not one to pass quick judgment on schoolmates, but from the day Sara and I discovered our mutual dislike of eighth grade math and of the prim schoolmarm who taught it, I knew that our relationship showed promise of blossoming into the sort of friendship one looks back at with nostalgia. Now, as the school year was drawing to a close, that promise had been fulfilled and I was looking forward eagerly to becoming friends with the rest of the Carlins.

Sara was the oldest of the five Carlin children. I met the other clan members in order. Mary, Dorothy, and Danny all seemed to be affectionate children—well-fed and apparently at peace with the world. Then I met Sam. I looked from Sam to the rest of the Carlins and my eyes traveled back to Sam. No change. My original impression had been accurate. Standing before me was a bony awkward lad of six years. The copper-toned hair of the older Carlins was replaced here by a tousled, carrot-hued mop. His right arm was in a sling, and perched on his freckled nose was a pair of glasses with a personality all their own. They were of the often-seen, round, silver-rimmed variety, but Sam had somehow managed to bend the nose piece which connected the two lenses. As a result of this mutilation, Sam appeared to have one eye almost in the middle of his right eyebrow and the other resting on his left cheek. I cautiously greeted him, and something about the toothless grin he gave me in return told me that this was no ordinary six-year-old.

Mrs. Carlin was all too happy that evening when Sara and I offered to take over her duties. The mother of five growing children doesn't get many chances for an evening "on the town." Mr. Carlin dutifully agreed to show her a big time, and Sara and I were left alone with our charges.

Dinner was a fairly calm experience. Sam had learned to eat fairly well with his left hand. He even managed to score direct hits on poor Dan with several spoonfuls of mashed potatoes. No one seemed to be even faintly surprised by his conduct; the idea seemed to be to dodge and keep eating. It was obvious that the tile walls of the Carlin breakfast room served for more than mere decoration. Finally we finished eating, scraped the potatoes off the walls, and went upstairs.

Bathtime rolled along smoothly until Sara and I were tucking Danny into his bed. Suddenly, over the roar of water splashing in the bathtub, we heard a piercing cry of, "It's stuck! It's stuck and I can't get it off!" We raced to the bathroom door, only to discover that it was locked from inside. No amount of screaming would bring Sam to the door; he seemed to be frozen to that faucet.

We beat the door, we kicked, we screamed, and the water rushed on. I turned to Sara, all hope gone. Suddenly the flash of an idea lighted her blank face and she whispered, "The trellis!" Almost before the words had left her lips we were outside the house viewing the situation.

The Carlin residence was a two-story house with a porch in front.

The bathroom window was directly over the porch roof and a trellis led up to it from the north side. The structure didn't appear to be very strong, and since I was lighter than Sara, I was elected to make the ascent.

The trip wasn't what could be called pleasure climbing. The roses which covered the trellis weren't without thorns and the whole structure was weaker than we had supposed. A total of three boards splintered under my feet. Finally I triumphantly strode onto the porch roof, unhooked the screen, and, giving Sara the encouraging look of a hero about to rescue a damsel in distress, threw up the window.

There was Sam, seated comfortably on the edge of the tub, still screaming as the water level neared the top. When Sam saw me he stopped screaming, turned around, and calmly shut off the water. I remained on my hands and knees, my head protruding through the window and my mouth wide open. Sam looked at my position critically and remarked soberly, "That's a silly way to get in here."

Since that night Sam has broken five more bones, attempted to flush an innocent kitten down a toilet, refilled a ditch dug by street repairmen, and run away from home twice.

In spite of Sam's mischief, his long-suffering family still love him. Only recently I learned that Mrs. Carlin had offered to become Den Mother for a pack of Cub Scouts. When I expressed amazement that such a busy woman could spare the time, she gave me a sad, tired smile and explained, "Sam wanted to be a Cub Scout and none of the other Den Mothers would take him, so—."

When you have finished reading this paper you have no doubt who Sam was, what he looked like, what his main characteristics were, what he did on this one occasion, and what the author's attitude toward him was. The picture is in focus. As a result, you find the theme clear and interesting.

The use of specific and concrete material—material that, by helping the reader see and feel and understand, makes a piece of writing meaningful and interesting—is a lesson that everyone must learn who wants to have people read what he writes. It is a lesson that professional authors learn early, for if the public neglects to read what they have written they rarely become professional authors.

EXERCISE

9. Read again the paragraphs from student themes in Exercise 8, on page 55. Which ones make good use of specific examples or concrete details to support other statements in the paragraphs? Which ones do not? Rewrite the latter to improve them.

5

ARRANGING THEME MATERIAL
EFFECTIVELY

After you have jotted down a list of ideas, examples, and other material for a theme and have selected the items most directly related to your central idea, the next step is to arrange these items in an appropriate order. This step is necessary for two main reasons.

First, the items on your list will almost never be in the best order, if indeed they are in any discoverable order at all, for you jotted them down just as they occurred to you. If you are to write the theme efficiently, you obviously need to be sure where to begin, where to go after you have begun, and where to end. You need a plan of operation. And, though it may often be simple and unpretentious, the plan should be written down so that you can keep it before you and consult it as you compose your paper.

Second, in writing a paper you are concerned mainly with transferring something that is in your mind to the mind of someone else, and making this transfer as complete as possible. It is not enough that your reader merely grasp the separate ideas that you are trying to communicate to him; you want him also to be aware of and understand the *relationships* that you see among these various ideas, and the *relative importance* of each idea. Otherwise, he has understood only a part of what you were trying to say to him. Suppose, for example, that you have written a paper on what you believe are immoral or antisocial tendencies in certain movies. If your reader understands merely that you are opposed to the sympathetic presentation of crime, brutality, and debauchery on the screen and fails to see that you regard some one of these as much more serious than the others, you have failed to communicate your full meaning to him. Or you would accomplish only a part of your purpose if your reader did not understand that you think movies about crime and movies about brutality are different aspects of the same tendency. If you carefully organize the material in your paper, you will make more certain that your ideas are fully understood.

Ways of Organizing Material

There are probably at least a dozen separate and recognizable patterns in which a writer can arrange what he has to say. There would not be much point in trying to list for you all these separate patterns, let alone their combinations, since they will not all be equally useful to you. Two of them, however, are especially important, and you should know about them.

The first of these is arrangement by *chronology,* by the order in which things have happened or are done. This is the pattern of organization that you will use when you tell a story—an account of a fishing trip, of your first formal dance, of being rushed by a fraternity or sorority. You will also employ this pattern when you are describing a process or operation, such as how milk is pasteurized or how a bird dog is trained. It is one of the most commonly used patterns, and it is also one of the easiest to use because the events or steps you are telling about are already in this order: first one thing, then the next, and so on to the end. Here is an example of chronological arrangement from the work of a professional author. It is an account of an incident in the gang warfare in Chicago during the 1920's; the structure of the paragraph is determined simply by the order in which events took place.

> In 1926, the O'Banions, still unrepentant despite the loss of their leader, introduced another novelty in gang warfare. In broad daylight, while the streets of Cicero were alive with traffic, they raked Al Capone's headquarters with machine-gun fire from eight touring cars. The cars proceeded down the crowded street outside the Hawthorne Hotel in solemn line, the first one firing blank cartridges to disperse the innocent citizenry and to draw the Capone forces to the doors and windows, while from the succeeding cars, which followed a block behind, flowed a steady rattle of bullets, spraying the hotel and the adjoining buildings up and down. One gunman even got out of his car, knelt carefully upon the sidewalk at the door of the Hawthorne, and played one hundred bullets into the lobby—back and forth, as one might play the hose upon one's garden. The casualties were miracu-

lously light, and Scarface Al himself remained in safety, flat on the
floor of the Hotel Hawthorne restaurant; nevertheless, the bombard-
ment quite naturally attracted public attention. Even in a day when
bullion was transported in armored cars, the transformation of a sub-
urban street into a shooting gallery seemed a little unorthodox (Frederick Lewis Allen, *Only Yesterday*).

The following passage describes a process—rocket propulsion—by
telling what happens inside a skyrocket after the fuse has been lighted.
Again, organization is determined by the sequence of happenings.

On firing, what happens is this:
Heat from the fuse ignites the surface of the powder on the walls
of the cone-shaped blast chamber. The powder does not explode, but a
continuous combustion takes place very rapidly, releasing large quantities of gas at high temperature. Considerable pressure builds up instantly in the chamber, since the hot gas is formed at a much faster
rate than it can easily escape through the restriction at the nozzle. The
net effect is to eject a stream of gas at great velocity, directed backward. This thrusts the rocket forcibly in the opposite direction.
As the fuel burns, the blast chamber rapidly enlarges, but the restriction at the nozzle continues to keep the pressure high and guides
the escaping jet. The rocket takes off with a tremendous swish, emit-
ting a stream of sparks and fire, and flies until the fuel is completely
consumed. Then an arrangement at the top of the tube fires the
"stars" and the bursting charge in which they are packed (G. Edward
Pendray, "Reaction Motors: How They Work and Some Experiments
with Them").

Of course, you will also have to write other kinds of themes besides
narratives or descriptions of processes. Probably many of your composition assignments will require you to discuss ideas or present opinions.
In this sort of paper, since it is not made up of a series of events, you
will have to use a pattern of arrangement that is based on the various
relationships among the ideas that you are presenting. We might list
many kinds of such patterns—cause and effect, comparison, contrast,
general to specific, definition, and others—all of them useful in special
situations. Some theme topics will lead you, almost without your thinking about it, to use one of these particular patterns. For instance, if you
are writing a paper on the differences between jet and turboprop airplane engines, or between New Orleans jazz and Chicago jazz, you
will almost automatically use contrast. If your paper is an attempt to
show the reasons why there is very little juvenile delinquency in your
town, you will probably use either the pattern of cause to effect or of

effect to cause. That is, you will tell what conditions in your town discourage delinquency (the *causes*) and lead up to the statement that there is little delinquency there (the *effect*); or, reversing the order, you will begin with the fact that young people in your town behave themselves and then list the reasons for their good behavior.

These patterns, which are largely determined by the particular subject you are writing on and by your purpose, are relatively specialized in their uses. There is another pattern, however, that has a wide general usefulness when you are writing about ideas and opinions. It is the pattern of *increasing importance*, or *climax*. In using this pattern, you arrange your material so that the most important idea, opinion, or example comes *last*, and the others lead up to it in order of increasing importance.

Here is a paper in which the order of climax has been used:

The Trouble with Advertising Is . . .

If the big advertising moguls wonder why more people don't buy the particular brands of soap and coughdrops and foundation garments that they are plugging, they ought to take a closer look at some of their own advertising. The faults of much current advertising are exemplified by the inevitable toothy girls grinning brainlessly from the back covers of magazines, by moaning voices complaining of sluggish livers and nagging pains in the small of the back, and by cynical claims that a certain kind of face cream will give a fifty-year-old woman the skin of a girl of twenty. Monotony, vulgarity, and dishonesty are hardly the most attractive baits to offer to prospective customers.

Take monotony, for instance. In spite of the time and money spent by public relations people to create clever and original advertisements, there is a deadly sameness in most ads. Pick out a given product and there will be half a dozen words used to describe it in nearly all the ads, regardless of the name of the manufacturer. Cigarettes are milder, smoother, filtered, cool, easy drawing. Soaps wash cleaner, purer, whiter, and make clothes smell sweeter. Automobiles are more powerful, smoother riding, luxurious, economical, distinctive. And it is a rare advertiser indeed who dares to promote his product without including a picture of a beautiful and mostly unclad girl smiling vacantly into space. It doesn't matter whether the product being advertised is piston rings, lingerie, or aircraft engines, the girl (I often think the *same* girl) is always there baring her teeth and legs at us. It's not hard to skip over an advertisement when we've already read the same words and seen the same vapidly smiling female dozens of times.

The chief offenders against ordinary good taste are advertisers of products that are supposed to improve our health. In order to sell this sort of merchandise, sponsors of TV programs seem to believe that they must first make us feel sick. Perhaps this line of thinking lies behind the horrible moist sneezes and rattling consumptive coughs that rend the air waves—followed inevitably by a tragic voice asking, "Are *you* suffering from a cold?" If I'm not, I don't want to be depressed by these sea lion noises; if I am, I've got enough troubles of my own without hearing about other people's. And then there are the peddlers of remedies for various internal disorders—acid indigestion, constipation, and insufficient liver bile. I don't know why it is, but TV commercials for this sort of product often seem to come at mealtime, and they always seem to me vulgar. If I've had my dinner interrupted by a graphic description of an ailing liver or of inefficient human plumbing, I'm not in a very friendly mood toward the makers of a certain kind of liver pills or stomach-sweetener. Though my liver may have been shirking its duty and my stomach be churning like the witches' cauldron in *Macbeth*, I'll steel myself to put up with both rather than subsidize such advertisements by getting the products they are promoting.

Finally, I am appalled by what appears to me to be callous disregard for honesty in much of the advertising business. Having been brought up to believe that truth is better than falsehood, and honesty better than dishonesty, I regard this manhandling of truth and honesty as the most serious offense committed by modern advertising. It is true that the government has forbidden the more obvious lies such as, "One bottle of Lohocla immediately cures cancer, backaches, cavities, and baldness." But there remain plenty of examples of more subtle kinds of dishonesty. A magazine advertisement showing a picture of a girl wearing a girdle—a girl with a figure that obviously needs no girdle—will say, "No other girdle whittles away so many inches." A cigarette ad will claim that "Willies are milder, smoother." Perfume ads insist that "A drop of 'Jungle Lust' perfume will make you irresistible." The truth is that no girdle whittles away inches; a girdle simply puts the inches somewhere else. The cigarette ad fails to tell us what Willies are milder or smoother than (an old rubber boot? wood chips? marijuana?). And the perfume ad neglects to mention the unfortunate fact that some of us girls, no matter what perfume we use, are simply not the irresistible type. If people are naïve enough to believe these advertisements, and apparently some are, they will be disillusioned by the inches that aren't whittled, the cigarette that isn't milder, and the perfume that doesn't attract so many men that a girl has to beat them off with a baseball bat. The end results of this sort of advertising are, first, that the consumer feels cheated; and second, that he becomes cynical toward claims made in advertisements. Since these reactions are not the sort that encourage further purchases of the same product, the advertiser loses too.

It seems to me that the advertising business might wake up and look at some of its shortcomings realistically. Perhaps the big companies are already satisfied with the amount of soap and cigarettes they are selling. But if they want to sell more products, and the fact that they spend so much on advertising suggests that they do, they might consider whether a satisfied customer is one who has been bored by monotony, offended by uncouth sounds and hospital-room details, and deceived by glittering half-truths. A little more variety, a little good taste, and a little more honesty in the use of language would, I think, be welcomed by all of us.

You will notice that in the first paragraph the author mentions three complaints against advertising: monotony, vulgarity, and dishonesty. The first of these she considers the least important, since all it arouses is boredom. The second, vulgarity, she regards as more important because it offends against good taste. The third, dishonesty, is in her opinion the most serious complaint of all.

This arrangement is effective for a good reason. Suppose that the order of the three main points contained in the theme above had been reversed, the most important first and the least important last. As you went through the paper, you would be impressed by the significance of the first point, since it is plainly a major criticism. When you found the second less important than the first, you would feel a sort of letdown, as though the author had failed to live up to what she had promised earlier. Then, when you discovered that the third point was even less important than the second, you would have a definite feeling of disappointment. Your interest in the paper would have lessened steadily as you read through it, so that at the end your attention would have wandered. The author would have been using not the order of climax, but that of anticlimax.

Kinds of Outlines and How to Make Them

Outlines are not an end in themselves, to be read for their own sake, but only a means to an end. They are, first, a convenience to you, the writer, helping you to plan the structure of your paper and relate your ideas properly to one another so that when you begin to write you will know what to say and when to say it. Second, if you have constructed a good outline and made effective use of it, both your reader and you will benefit from the result. He will understand more readily and more completely what you have said, since you have taken pains to arrange your ideas for his convenience; and you will gain the satisfaction of having your ideas fully understood.

It is a common mistake to think that all outlines, even those for short papers, must always be elaborate affairs several pages long, with Roman numerals, capital letters, careful indentations, and so on. The degree of elaborateness depends mainly on three things: the length of the paper, the complexity of the organization, and the way in which your own mind works. If a paper is going to run well over 1,000 words, you will probably need a fairly detailed outline. You will have so much material that you will usually need to work out your plan with some completeness to be sure of getting everything in, and in the right place. For a short paper of 500 words or so, though it needs to be planned just as carefully as the longer one, you will seldom need such a full outline. Even a short paper, however, should be outlined in detail if its subject is one that demands a rather complicated plan of organization —for example, a carefully reasoned argument for or against a required course in foreign language. On the other hand, if the pattern of organization you are using is based on the time relationship, the outline may be more simple, even for rather long papers, since the order of the various events has already been determined for you. In any case, the way you think must be taken into account. Some people have the ability to organize fairly large blocks of complicated material in their minds and to work this material into a paper with the help of only a few casual notes. At the other extreme, some need rather complete and carefully arranged notes to write a well-planned short paper on a considerably less complicated subject.

Most freshmen belong to neither of these two extremes. Probably you will be able to write most short papers with the aid of only informal outlines, but you will usually need fuller and more carefully prepared outlines for long papers.

EXERCISE

1. Which of the following subjects probably require a formal outline; which an informal?

(a) The Day I Kept House
(b) Pros and Cons of Entrance Examinations
(c) My Job as Stage Manager
(d) How to Make Pizza
(e) Shyness Is Often Mistaken for Snobbery
(f) Our Trip to _____
(g) The Effect of Television on My Reading Habits
(h) A Visit to the Planetarium

   (i) How to Put on Stage Make-up
   (j) Civil Defense Is Essential
  (k) Politics Is a Respectable Business
   (l) The Fight to End Polio
 (m) Broken Homes Lead to Juvenile Delinquency
  (n) An Account of a Rocket Launching

THE INFORMAL OUTLINE

AR 1   *Use an informal outline for most short papers*

For a handy example of the informal outline, the kind that will ordinarily serve for short papers, we can draw on the material of the last chapter. You remember, in connection with planning the paper about the boy who lied so imaginatively, that there was a list of various items that might go into the theme and that, after examination, some were canceled. The list of remaining items can be converted into a serviceable informal outline simply by deciding the order in which the items ought to appear, then numbering accordingly. The finished work sheet would look like this:

> CENTRAL IDEA: The most gifted liar I've ever known was a high school friend whose highly imaginative but harmless lies were a wonderful source of entertainment to his classmates.
>
> ~~John's father a garage owner~~
> 5. John's outline in American history class
> ~~Incident of the missing microscope in biology class~~
> 4. Incident of the borrowed skillet
> 1. John a born liar, but improved with practice
> 3. His lies always amusing, never mean
> 6. His report on teen-age drinking (his best performance)
> ~~John's part in the senior play~~
> 2. Had a frank and innocent-looking face
> ~~John's romance with the beauty queen~~
> 7. What John is doing now
> ~~John's hobby—amateur radio~~
> ~~Incident of the wrecked motor scooter~~
> ~~John's report on *Julius Caesar*~~

The informal outline, as you can see, is a fairly simple matter. All it shows, really, is what you plan to include and what order you want each item to appear in. It does not, as a rule, show in detail the particular relationships that exist between one item of material and another.

EXERCISES

2. Following are some theme topics that you might feel qualified to write on, or that might suggest other topics to you:

College English and High School English
Professor _____ Is a Fair (or Unfair) Grader
What Athletic Scholarships Do to Amateur Football
Men Are Stronger than Women
Some Aspects of Juvenile Delinquency
Radioactive Fallout and the Nation's Health
TV Is Smothering Imagination
Segregation and Integration
What Scouting Does for Boys (or Girls)
How TV Westerns (or some other type of program) Annoy Me
My Quiet Brother and My Noisy Brother (or sister, or friend)
Airplane Travel Is Fun
Today's Teen Agers Are Conformists
Jazz Music and Classical Music
A Tour through Mt. Vernon (or some other historical site)
My Case against Men (or Women)

(a) Select five topics (either from the list above or others which may occur to you) which you feel qualified to develop with an informal outline.

(b) Select five topics (either from the list above or others which may occur to you) which you feel qualified to develop with the use of a formal outline.

3. Select two of the subjects in 2a above and make a preliminary informal outline for each by doing the following:

(a) Write a tentative central-idea sentence.

(b) Put down all the ideas and facts that you can think of which might be used to develop the topic.

(c) Cross out those that you decide are not pertinent or necessary for developing your idea.

(d) Arrange those that are left in the order in which you wish to develop them.

THE TOPIC OUTLINE

AR 2   *Use a topic outline for longer papers and for complex theme material*

If the material of your paper requires you to work out these relationships clearly and be reminded of them as you write the paper, you should make a formal outline. One kind of formal outline is the "topic" outline, so called because each item is expressed as a "topic," a word or phrase, never a complete sentence. You will find it by far the most useful sort of outline when either the amount or the complexity of your theme material makes an informal outline inadequate.

As an example, here is the topic outline prepared by the author of the theme on advertising quoted on pp. 62–64.

CENTRAL IDEA: Modern advertising would be more effective if it were less monotonous, less vulgar, and, above all, less dishonest.

  I. Monotony of many advertisements
      A. Similar wording
          1. Cigarette ads
          2. Soap ads
          3. Automobile ads
      B. The ever-present smiling girl
      C. Resulting boredom of consumer
 II. Vulgarity of some advertisements for medicines
      A. Offensive noises in ads for cold remedies
      B. Offensive images in ads for medicines to cure internal disorders
      C. Resulting disgust of consumer
III. Dishonesty of some advertisements
      A. False claims
          1. Ads for foundation garments
          2. Ads for cigarettes
          3. Ads for perfumes
      B. Disillusionment of consumer
          1. Feeling of having been cheated
          2. Cynicism toward claims in ads
 IV. Need for reform in advertising methods
      A. Much present advertising offensive
      B. Much present advertising ineffective
      C. More sales from improved methods

Perhaps the best way to show you how to make a topic outline is to try to reconstruct the steps taken by the writer of this one. The assignment for the theme was to write a criticism of some aspect or aspects of modern advertising; the length was to be from 500 to 1,000 words, and the paper was to be addressed to the other members of the class.

The author, having the general subject, the approximate length, and the audience already determined for her, began by searching her mind to determine her attitudes toward advertising. As she thought about the matter, she realized that she had, in the course of her experience, seen and heard thousands of advertisements. Most of them, she decided, had made no impression on her at all; some had struck her as clever or amusing; and a considerable number had annoyed her in one way or another. She would use the last group in her paper.

Her next step was to draw up a tentative central-idea sentence: "Certain aspects of modern advertising irritate me." Although this sentence indicated in a general way the approach she intended to use in discussing the subject, she knew she would have to make it more specific later as her ideas became clearer.

Sorting through her memories and impressions again, she began jotting down things that occurred to her. Here is the list that resulted:

CENTRAL IDEA: Certain aspects of modern advertising irritate me.
Exaggerated claims for perfumes
Misleading ads for cigarettes
Billboards blocking view in country
Signs on sides of farm buildings
Whiskey ads try to convince you that your social standing depends on serving Old Fireball.
Conformity in dress and habits encouraged by advertising
Smiling girls in bathing suits usually around
Women in ads always perfectly made up, hair never in curlers, even in bed or at breakfast
Almost no women over twenty-seven or twenty-eight appear in ads
Never a homely man or woman in ads
Awful coughs and sneezes in radio and TV ads for cold cures
We're the first generation in history whose noses can't bear the smell of perspiration
Vulgar advertisements for liver remedies, laxatives, etc.
False claims in ads for foundation garments
Similarity of wording in ads for same type of product—soaps, cake mixes, perfumes, cars, cigarettes, etc.
Monotony of much advertising
Deceptive advertising for ways to lose fat
Disgusting advertisements for goo to keep false teeth from clicking or falling out in public
Falsity of ads for hair restorers
People cheated by false advertising

When the author had finished this list, she realized that she had managed to turn up far more material than she would need for her paper. She saw, too, that some of the items on the list were facts ("Billboards blocking view in country"), some were opinions ("Monotony of much advertising"), some were large generalizations ("People cheated by false advertising"), some were specific details ("Signs on sides of farm buildings"); and finally some items were in sentence form, whereas others were expressed as phrases. A lot remained to be done before the list could be turned into a theme.

Studying the list carefully, the author next tried to group items whenever possible. She found that most of them concerned three general criticisms of advertising: false claims, sameness of content and devices, and vulgarity. Tentatively numbering these as I, II, and III, she went through the list again, putting the appropriate numeral before each item in these three categories. Then, to make the grouping clearer she recopied the list in this way:

CENTRAL IDEA: Certain aspects of modern advertising irritate me.

I. False claims
   Exaggerated claims for perfumes
   Misleading ads for cigarettes
   Whiskey ads try to convince you that your social standing depends on serving Old Fireball
   False claims in ads for foundation garments
   Deceptive advertising for ways to lose fat
   Falsity of ads for hair restorers
   People cheated by false advertising
II. Sameness of content and devices
   Smiling girls in bathing suits usually around
   Women in ads always perfectly made up, hair never in curlers, even in bed or at breakfast
   Almost no women over twenty-seven or twenty-eight appear in ads
   Never a homely man or woman in ads
   Similarity of wording in ads for same type of product—soaps, cake mixes, perfumes, cars, cigarettes, etc.
   Monotony of much advertising
III. Vulgarity
   Awful coughs and sneezes in radio and TV ads for cold cures
   We're the first generation in history whose noses can't bear the smell of perspiration
   Vulgar advertisements for liver remedies, laxatives, etc.
   Disgusting advertisements for goo to keep false teeth from clicking or falling out in public

Three items on the original list wouldn't fit under any of these heads: "Billboards blocking view in country," "Signs on sides of farm buildings," and "Conformity in dress and habits encouraged by advertising." Besides, some on the new list had only a slender relationship to the heading they had been placed under. For instance, the second item under "Vulgarity" might be an interesting enough observation, but unless it were rephrased to indicate the vulgarity of ads for underarm deodorants, it would not fit in here. She decided to cancel it. Also, as she looked at the material under "II" she saw that the second, third, and fourth items, though in one sense they contributed to "Sameness," really made up a separate category of their own: lack of realism in ads. She was amused by this tendency in advertising but could not honestly say that she felt as strongly about it as she did about the other three categories. So she canceled these three items too. By then the list looked like this:

CENTRAL IDEA: Certain aspects of modern advertising irritate me.

I. False claims
Exaggerated claims for perfumes
Misleading ads for cigarettes
Whiskey ads try to convince you that your social standing depends on serving Old Fireball
False claims in ads for foundation garments
Deceptive advertising for ways to lose fat
Falsity of ads for hair restorers
People cheated by false advertising
II. Sameness of content and devices
Smiling girls in bathing suits usually around
~~Women in ads always perfectly made up, hair never in curlers, even in bed or at breakfast~~
~~Almost no women over twenty-seven or twenty-eight appear in ads~~
~~Never a homely man or woman in ads~~
Similarity of wording in ads for same type of product—soaps, cake mixes, perfumes, cars, cigarettes, etc.
Monotony of much advertising
III. Vulgarity
Awful coughs and sneezes in radio and TV ads for cold cures
~~We're the first generation in history whose noses can't bear the smell of perspiration~~
Vulgar advertisements for liver remedies, laxatives, etc.
Disgusting advertisements for goo to keep false teeth from clicking or falling out in public

As she studied the revised list, she noticed that the last item under "II" was an opinion for which the other two items provided support. To show this relationship, she drew a line through the main heading for "II" ("Sameness of content and devices") and moved the last item

("Monotony of much advertising") up to take its place. Turning to "I," she tried to find a new heading that would stand in the same relation to the items beneath as "Monotony of much advertising" did to the items under it. She decided finally on "Dishonesty of some advertising" as a clearer substitute for "False claims." The heading of "III" she expanded first to "Vulgarity of some advertisements." But, reflecting that perhaps not many people in her audience had noticed the little ads for false-teeth glue, she changed the heading again to "Vulgarity of some advertisements for medicines" and canceled the last item under "III," since it did not really concern medicines, where as the two that remained did.

At this point she saw that there were two items left under both "II" and "III," but that under "I" there were still seven. Because this put "I" out of proportion, she decided to do some more canceling, striking out the items concerning whiskey, ways to reduce, and hair restorers. The other items (perfume ads, cigarette ads, foundation garment ads, and the reference to people being cheated) she kept because she felt they would be of more concern to her audience.

She recopied the list again to see what it now looked like:

CENTRAL IDEA: Certain aspects of modern advertising irritate me.

I. Dishonesty of some advertisements
   Exaggerated claims for perfumes
   Misleading ads for cigarettes
   False claims in ads for foundation garments
   People cheated by false advertising
II. Monotony of many advertisements
   Smiling girls in bathing suits usually around
   Similarity of wording in ads for same type of product—soaps, cake mixes, perfumes, cars, cigarettes, etc.
III. Vulgarity of some advertisements for medicines
   Awful coughs and sneezes in radio and TV ads for cold cures
   Vulgar advertisements for liver remedies, laxatives, etc.

By this time, the author realized that the seriousness of the criticisms she was making pointed up the inadequacy of her central-idea sentence. The sentence plainly needed to be revised, since the three charges she was leveling at advertising had broader implications than just one person's irritation. After she had looked thoughtfully at her notes, it seemed to her that, assuming she was a reasonably average consumer, there must be many other people who objected to the same aspects of advertising. It also seemed clear that their hostility was exactly the opposite reaction from the one that the advertisers had hoped for. Consequently, advertising should be more effective if these faults were eliminated. She then revised her central-idea sentence to read: "Modern advertising would be more effective if it were less dishonest, less monotonous, and less vulgar." On second thought, she changed the position of the adjectives, since the present order did not seem to her the most effective. Using the pattern of climax, she made the sentence read: "Modern advertising would be more effective if it were less monotonous, less vulgar, and, above all, less dishonest." She also renumbered the three sections in her tentative outline to correspond with the revised order.

By this stage in the process, it had already become clear to the author that an informal outline would not be enough. She would have to use a formal outline that would show the relationship and relative importance of the ideas within each of the main divisions. Taking up the section on monotony first, she made one subdivision for similarity of wording and another for the smiling girls. But, since the first of these included a number of specific examples which she wanted to make sure of using in her paper, she added three subdivisions under it to accommodate the most important examples. The section was then in this form:

    I. Monotony of many advertisements
      A. Similar wording
        1. Cigarette ads
        2. Soap ads
        3. Automobile ads
      B. The ever-present smiling girl
      C. Resulting boredom of consumer

Then, checking this part of the outline against her central-idea sentence, she decided that she should add a third point to relate the material clearly to the main emphasis of the theme. Because she intended to argue in her paper that the faults of advertising impair its effectiveness, she wrote "C. Boredom of the consumer" to underline the result of the monotonous devices used by advertisers. She rewrote the second and third sections of the outline in the same way, so that they looked like this:

    II. Vulgarity of some advertisements for medicines
      A. Offensive noises in ads for cold remedies
      B. Offensive images in ads for medicines to cure internal disorders
      C. Resulting disgust of consumer

    III. Dishonesty of some advertisements
        A. False claims
            1. Ads for foundation garments
            2. Ads for cigarettes
            3. Ads for perfumes
        B. Resulting disillusionment of consumer
            1. Feeling of having been cheated
            2. Cynicism toward claims in ads

Finally, to round out the discussion and drive home the main point, she added a fourth main division:

    IV. Need for a reform in advertising methods
        A. Much present advertising offensive
        B. Much present advertising ineffective
        C. More sales from improved methods

The outline was complete, and the author was ready to begin writing the paper.

EXERCISES

4. Select two of the subjects in Exercise 2b (p. 67) and make a formal topic outline for each by doing the following:
  (a) Write a central-idea sentence
  (b) Put down the facts, ideas, and examples which you might use to develop the topic.
  (c) Arrange these in groups which are related.
  (d) Eliminate those which don't seem pertinent or necessary.
  (e) Decide what order each group might be discussed in and write headings for each group.
  (f) Make a topic outline showing exactly how you would develop your paper.

5. Following are some rough outlines on several general subjects. For each rough outline do the following things: (a) Cross out those points that don't seem relevant to the general subject. (b) Arrange the other points in groups that belong together and give each a heading. (c) Arrange the groups in the most logical order for use in a theme. (d) Write a central-idea sentence which would indicate the purpose and content of the theme.

  (a) *Extracurricular activities*
      Coke dates
      Bull sessions
      Work on the campus paper
      The spring formal
      Letters home

Time spent in the infirmary with flu
Oversleeping
Pep club
Football games
Homecoming committee
Study hall
Pep rallies
Library work
Firesides
The track meet
(b) *A college freshman's first semester*
Shyness
Placement tests
New friends
Summer job
Independence at last
Adjustment
Class schedule
Orientation
Counselors
Living with strangers
High school preparation
Eagerness
Living with many people
Naïveté
(c) *Our shrinking world*
Super highways
Radio
Modern appliances
Leisure time
News networks
Television
Guided missiles
Monopolies
Jet planes
Air travel
Modern architecture
Rockets
High-speed automobiles

THE SENTENCE OUTLINE

AR 3   *Use a sentence outline when unusually precise planning is called for*

You may sometimes be called upon to write one other important type of formal outline: the sentence outline. It differs from the topic outline mainly in that each separate point is expressed not by a word or a phrase but by a grammatically complete sentence. The topic outline, as we mentioned before, will ordinarily prove adequate for organizing most of your more complex papers, ones that can't be planned with the help of only an informal outline. Once in a while, though, you may have to write a paper in which, as you organize it, you need to see the exact limits of each point. Here a sentence outline will be useful; for when you are forced to express each idea as a complete sentence, you must necessarily round the idea out fully. The difference is that between writing "Boredom of consumer" and "The consumer is bored by the monotony of advertisements," or between "The ever-present smiling girl" and "A smiling girl is pictured in nearly all advertisements."

Sometimes also your instructor may ask you to write a sentence outline either because he wants you to profit from the discipline in organizing material that this exercise offers or because he wants to see more exactly what you are including within each separate point in your outline. The phrase "Ads for perfumes" will probably be clear enough to you, for you know what ideas it represents in your mind; after all, you are the one who is writing the paper. Your instructor, however, if he is to criticize your outline intelligently, may sometimes need a fuller statement of your ideas than the words or phrases of a topic outline can provide.

You go about making a sentence outline just as you do a topic outline, except that you must think more carefully about the exact meaning and limits of each point, and you must of course express each point as a sentence. To make clear the difference between these two kinds of outlines, here is an example of each. As a special exercise, the instructor had asked that both a topic and a sentence outline be prepared for the paper. (The theme written from the outlines appears in Chapter 8.)

Topic Outline

CENTRAL IDEA: For a successful marriage, the partners must agree as to the value of money and material possessions, must like most of the same things, must be tolerant of each other's faults, and must be genuinely in love rather than merely infatuated.

   I. Same attitude toward money and material possessions
     A. Agreement to live within means
     B. Willingness to work together for things they want
  II. Same preferences and interests
     A. In reading, music, etc.

    B. In other ways of spending leisure time

III. Attitude of mutual toleration

    A. Certainty of faults in both partners

    B. Possibility of correcting some faults

    C. Toleration of faults that can't be corrected

IV. Real love, not infatuation

    A. Is primarily spiritual

        1. Physical attraction temporary

        2. Spiritual bond permanent

    B. Is based on respect, admiration, understanding

    C. Provides securest foundation for successful marriage

        1. Encourages unselfishness

        2. Makes minor personal differences insignificant

        3. Reconciles differences in religion

            a. Change of faith

            b. Toleration of other's faith

Sentence Outline

CENTRAL IDEA: For a successful marriage, the partners must agree as to the value of money and material possessions, must like most of the same things, must be tolerant of each other's faults, and must be genuinely in love rather than merely infatuated.

  I. The partners in a successful marriage should have the same attitude toward money and material possessions.

    A. They should agree to live within their means.

    B. They should be willing to work together for the things they want.

 II. The partners in a successful marriage should have many of the same preferences and interests.

    A. They should have similar tastes in such things as reading and music.

    B. They should enjoy the same ways of spending leisure time.

III. The partners in a successful marriage should show an attitude of mutual toleration.

    A. Both partners will have some faults.

    B. Each may be able to correct some of his or her own faults.

    C. Faults in one partner that can't be corrected must be tolerated by the other.

IV. Partners in a successful marriage must above all be genuinely in love, not just infatuated.

    A. Real marital love is more a spiritual bond than a physical attraction.

        1. Physical attraction will ultimately weaken.

        2. A spiritual bond will last throughout life.

    B. Love is based on mutual respect, admiration, and understanding.

    C. Love provides the most secure basis for a successful marriage.
      1. It brings out the best in one's character by encouraging unselfishness.
      2. It makes minor personal differences seem insignificant.
      3. It can even reconcile differences in religion.
        a. One partner may adopt the other's faith.
        b. Each partner may tolerate the other's faith.

EXERCISES

6. Turn again to Exercise 4. Change one of the topic outlines that you wrote for that exercise into a sentence outline.

7. The following groups of sentences represent ideas to be developed in an expository paper, but they are not arranged in any definite order. Some of the sentences represent main ideas, some subordinate ideas. Write a covering central-idea sentence, then rearrange the sentences in each group so as to make a logically developed outline.

(a) Today we have something very different from free enterprise.
At one time there was little government interference with business practices.
Big manufacturers make use of price-fixing schemes.
Government controls have now reduced the ups and downs of business cycles and the threat of depressions.
America once had free enterprise.
Free enterprise is a system of economics in which there is a minimum of control and a maximum of opportunity.
In the first century of our existence as a nation the laws of supply and demand were in control.
Competition has now been reduced by law so that supply and demand no longer operate.
Industry is so big that only those people with huge assets can enter into many businesses.
Today instead of a free-enterprise system we might say we have a safe-enterprise system.
Once a man could go into any business he liked.

(b) Today most young people are politically informed.
If eighteen-year-olds must fight for their country they should have the privilege of voting for their government.
Many eighteen-year-olds now carry positions of responsibility.
Citizens should be allowed to vote at eighteen years of age.
We draft boys at eighteen years.
Eighteen-year-olds often accept the responsibility of marriage and family.
There is no logical reason for waiting until twenty-one.
We don't allow citizens to vote until twenty-one in our society, but we expect them to act like adults.

Eighteen-year-olds can be convicted of major crime and sent to prison.

Many eighteen-year-olds have positions of responsibility in school and the community.

Eighteen-year-olds have proved they are as well prepared for voting as their elders.

(c) Many practical steps can be taken to prevent or alleviate motion sickness.

Repeated movements in several directions cause more trouble than those in a single direction.

Motion sickness starts in the balance organs.

Don't drink carbonated beverages when going up in an airplane.

For those who can't avoid motion sickness by other means, there are new drugs available.

Women are more susceptible to motion sickness than men.

You should bend your head back and hold it very still.

Small canals carrying liquid and located close to the ears send messages to the vomiting center in the brain.

Other parts of the brain receive messages.

You should sit where you can see the horizon.

Nerve cells in the part of the brain that keeps you alert cause yawning.

Other centers cause a feeling of depression or cold or perspiration.

You should stick to your regular diet.

You should try to breathe fresh air.

Characteristics of Outline Form

The sample outlines just quoted illustrate various aspects of outline form about which there is general agreement. Some of these are no doubt familiar to you already; others you may not have known about. To guide you in making good outlines of your own, the most important of these characteristics are listed and explained briefly below.

CENTRAL IDEA

AR 4   *Head every outline with a central-idea sentence*

It is always wise to write the central-idea sentence at the top of the outline so that you will be able to refer to it constantly, both while you are checking and testing the points in the outline and while you are writing the paper. Any precaution you can take to make sure that you stick to your subject is well worthwhile; this is one.

OUTLINE SYMBOLS

AR 5   *Use standard outline symbols*

One of the standard usages of outlining is a particular system of numbers and letters to indicate divisions of varying importance. There is no special reason why this system is better than another one that you might invent for yourself, except that people have reached a general agreement on this particular one, as they have on red and green lights to control traffic. When you construct an outline you should mark the main divisions of the paper with Roman numerals; the next most important divisions, under each Roman numeral, with capital letters; the next, under the capital letters, with arabic numerals; and the next, under the Arabic numerals, with small (lower-case) letters. The system works out like this:

    I. A main division of the whole paper
      A. One of the main divisions of "I"
      B. Another of the main divisions of "I"
        1. A main division of "B"
        2. Another main division of "B"
          a. A main division of "2"
          b. The last main division of "2"
        3. The last main division of "B"
      C. Another main division of "I"
      D. The last main division of "I"
   II. A second main division of the entire paper
     (And so on.)

INDENTING

AR 6   *Indent outline headings to show their relative importance*

Notice that the most important divisions in an outline are placed farthest to the left, and the least important ones farthest to the right. Notice too that *all* Roman numeral divisions are placed at the same distance from the left-hand margin, all capital-letter divisions a little farther from the left, and so on. If you were to draw a straight vertical line through the first Roman numeral and extend it to the bottom of the page, it would go through all the other Roman numerals; and so for the other letters and numbers: each separate kind forms a straight line, one symbol below the other. The reason for this practice is that here is an easy way to remind you that all divisions of the outline that have the same kind of numbers or letters are equally important.

PUNCTUATING AND CAPITALIZING

AR 7   *Follow standard practice in punctuating and capitalizing outline headings*

Here is a list of the most common ways of using capitals and punctuation marks in outlines:

(a) Put a *period* after each number or letter.
(b) Begin each separate heading with a capital, even though it consists of only one or two words.
(c) In a topic outline, do not put a period at the end of the headings.
(d) Use a period at the end of headings in a sentence outline, since each heading is a sentence. (If the sentence should be in the form of a question, then of course you would use a question mark instead.)

The first three of these rules are not inflexible. Your teacher may prefer that you use some other system (no periods after numbers and letters, periods after the headings in a topic outline, etc.), but he will tell you if he does. The important thing is to use a consistent plan of punctuating and capitalizing throughout the outline. Don't put periods after some headings in a topic outline and omit them after others.

NUMBER OF MAIN DIVISIONS IN AN OUTLINE

AR 8   *Be sure that Roman numerals are used to designate only main divisions*

A student will sometimes ask his instructor, "How many Roman numerals do you want me to use in this outline?" The instructor can't answer the question; only the student himself can. The number of main divisions in a paper depends partly, of course, on the length of the paper, but also on the complexity of the material. Only the student can say how many main headings there will be, for only he knows what he is going to present in the paper. In general, however, most student papers of less than a thousand words will have probably not more than four or five main divisions. A number larger than this in a short paper almost always means either that the subject is too large and that the main ideas are going to be treated too briefly, or that the writer has confused main divisions with minor. That is, he has used Roman numerals for several points that actually should have been marked with capital letters or Arabic numerals.

EQUAL RANK FOR DIVISIONS OF EQUAL IMPORTANCE

AR 9   *Be sure that outline divisions having equal importance are given equal rank*

Although this point has already been suggested in the discussion of outline symbols and indenting, it is worth making again: Divisions that have the same importance should be numbered with the same kind of symbols—Roman numerals for main divisions of the paper, capital letters for the next most important divisions, and so on. The writer of the following excerpt from a student outline has forgotten this rule:

> CENTRAL IDEA: Intercollegiate football should be de-emphasized.
> I. Interferes with players' studying
>   A. Long practice sessions
>   B. Out-of-town trips
>   C. Physical exhaustion
> II. Encourages unethical practices
>   A. Illegal inducements to enroll at a college
>   B. Secret subsidies from alumni
>   C. Encourages unsportsmanlike conduct

You will notice that "C" under "II" is more important than the other capital-letter headings and should be numbered "III," since it is on a par with "Interferes with players' studying" and "Encourages unethical practices."

PARALLEL STRUCTURE FOR HEADINGS OF THE SAME RANK

AR 10   *Use parallel structure for outline headings of the same rank*

Another way to remember that points of the same rank are of equal importance is to use the same sort of grammatical structure in order to indicate the relationship. This is called parallel structure. (See also Chapter 9.) For instance, note the following:

> CENTRAL IDEA: Although there are some disadvantages in living at a fraternity house, these are outweighed by the advantages.
>
> I. Disadvantages
>   A. Costs a lot
>   B. Crowded living conditions
>   1. Everyone sleeps in the same dormitory.
>   2. Have to eat in shifts
>   3. Three or four people in room when you're studying
>   C. Noisy
> II. There are many advantages.
>   A. Good food
>   B. Often have house dances on weekends
>   C. Brothers help you with your studies.
>   D. Personal advice
>   E. Make many friends

The trouble with this outline is that "I" is a noun, "II" a sentence; "A" under "I" is a verb phrase, "B" is a noun phrase, and "C" is an adjective. The same sort of confusion is seen in the Arabic-numeral points under "B" and in the capital-letter headings under "II." A corrected version of the outline looks like this:

> CENTRAL IDEA: Although there are some disadvantages in living at a fraternity house, these are outweighed by the advantages.
>
> I. Disadvantages (noun)
>   A. Expensive (adjective)
>   B. Crowded (adjective)
>   1. Sleeping arrangements
>   2. Eating facilities   (noun phrases)
>   3. Study conditions
>   C. Noisy (adjective)
> II. Advantages (noun)
>   A. Good food
>   B. House dances
>   C. Help with studies   (noun phrases)
>   D. Personal advice
>   E. Friendships

Notice, though, that whereas *all* Roman-numeral points should be in the same form (here both are nouns), the headings of lower rank need not be in the same form throughout the whole outline, but only within their own sequence. That is, "A," "B," and "C" under "I" must share the same form, whether verb phrase, noun, prepositional phrase, adjective, or whatever else (here they happen to be adjectives). The headings of the same rank under "II," however, need not be in the same form as those under "I," but they must themselves be alike (here they are all noun phrases).

In general, this question of parallel structure becomes a problem only when you are writing a topic outline. The headings of a sentence outline must by definition all be sentences.

SINGLE SUBHEADINGS

AR 11   *In general do not use single subheadings in an outline*

Ordinarily when you make an outline you are *dividing* your subject. That is, when you write

> I. My duties as a summer farmhand
>   A. Harvesting wheat
>   B. Plowing stubble
>   C. Feeding the cattle
>   D. Mending broken fences
>   E. Repairing farm machinery

you have divided or broken up the first statement into its parts. "A" through "E" add up to "I"; they are the particular jobs that made up your duties. Because you are dividing, you should not as a rule list only one subhead anywhere in an outline. When you divide something, you come out with at least two parts: you can't divide something into *one*.

Here is part of an outline that shows faulty division:

> CENTRAL IDEA: Comic books should be censored more strictly.
>
> I. Harmful tendencies in comic books about crime
>   A. Criminals glamorized
>   1. Law officers belittled
>   B. Criminal techniques shown
>   1. Ways of breaking and entering
>   2. Ways of opening safes
>   3. Ways of escaping pursuit by police
>   4. Ways of murdering

Depending on how fully the author intends to treat the matter, "A" could be expanded to read "Criminals glamorized at expense of law officers," or "1" could be made a separate heading, equal in importance to "A":

    B. Law officers belittled

Once in a while in drawing up an outline you may not want to divide a particular heading but instead want to *support* it with an example. If you need to remind yourself to bring in the example when you write your paper, you might want to use a single subhead—perhaps something like this:

    CENTRAL IDEA: During the flood, amateur radio operators performed valuable services.

    I. Reported needs of stricken area
      A. Blankets and clothing
      B. Food and uncontaminated water
      C. Medical supplies and help
        1. Rumor of typhoid epidemic
    II. Helped victims communicate with relatives outside stricken area

Remember, though, that this sort of situation will be exceptional; as a general rule, you should not use single subheads.

INTRODUCTIONS AND CONCLUSIONS

AR 12   *Use meaningful headings rather than "introduction" and "conclusion"*

It is not particularly helpful to write an outline like this:

    CENTRAL IDEA: From the automotive engineer's point of view, present American automobiles are not well designed.

    I. Introduction
    II. Larger and heavier bodies than desirable
      A. Difficult to park in traffic
      B. Difficult to get in garage
      C. Difficult to drive on narrow roads
      D. Difficult to handle on muddy roads
    III. More powerful engines than desirable
      A. Excessive gas consumption
      B. Excessive speed for present highways
    IV. Fewer safety features than desirable
      A Seat belts needed

B. Padded dashboards needed
C. Flexible steering columns needed
V. Conclusion

If the introduction and conclusion contain material important enough to justify ranking them as main divisions of the paper, they should be treated like the other main divisions; that is, the main idea contained in each should be stated, just as for the other Roman-numeral headings. The words "Introduction" and "Conclusion" will not by themselves prove very helpful to you in an outline. One of course will tell you that you are going to begin and the other that you are going to end, but neither lets you know *how* you are going to begin or end.

If the material in the introduction and conclusion is not important enough to justify ranking these sections as main divisions, the best thing to do is simply to omit them from the outline. Remember that not everything in the finished paper should appear in the outline; otherwise, the outline would be as long as the paper. Many details you will necessarily have to hold in your mind. This is the way to treat a simple introduction or conclusion, one that is not a main division of the paper.

Turn back to p. 68 and look again at the outline for the theme on advertising; then compare it with the theme itself (pp. 62–64). Notice that the introduction, which simply states the problem that the theme will discuss, does not appear in the outline. On the other hand the conclusion, which sums up the arguments presented and makes an appeal for action, is an important part of the paper and so is listed in the outline as a Roman-numeral division. (The same practice has been followed in the outline for "Blueprint for a Successful Marriage," pp. 77–78.)

Building good formal outlines is not easy, especially if you have not learned previously to think clearly and systematically, for outlines demand this kind of thinking. Remember, though, that an important test of an educated man or woman is the ability to think clearly and logically. If you lack the ability and fail to develop it, your chances of surviving in college are not good. But you *can* develop this ability. Every course you take in college, including your course in freshman English, will help you do so. Making good outlines not only helps you write good papers; it helps you learn to think in the way that an educated person and college student must.

EXERCISE

8. The following outlines are faulty for one or more of the following reasons: punctuation, indenting, items of equal importance not given equal rank, lack of parallel structure, inexact central-idea sentence, single subheads that should be combined with another heading. Criticize three of the outlines, pointing out the faults; then rewrite the outlines, correcting the faults.

(a) *City Life versus Country Life*

CENTRAL-IDEA SENTENCE: City life and country life both have advantages and disadvantages.

I. City life more complex
   A. Advantages
      1. Many cultural opportunities
      2. Great choice in shopping
      3. Many things to do.
   B. Hard to Know People
   C. Transportation difficult and time-consuming
   D. Country life more simple.
      1. Chance to know people more easily
      2. Transportation no problem
      3. Housing inexpensive
      4. Not many cultural opportunities
      5. Shopping possibilities limited

(b) *Excessive Speed on the Highways*

CENTRAL-IDEA SENTENCE: There are many solutions to high-speed driving.

I. Excessive speed may take your life.
   A. Most highways are not designed for high-speed driving.
      1. Two lanes
      2. Narrow shoulders
   B. Too many curves for high speeds
      Most drivers are not capable of high-speed driving.
II. There are many solutions to high-speed driving.
   A. Construction of turnpikes
      1. Set a maximum speed for all highways
      2. Eliminate sharp turns and blind spots.
   B. Check on drivers
      1. Radar
      2. Have cars checked by highway patrol
   C. State speed laws
      1. Minimum
      2. Maximum
   D. Federal law requiring all cars to have seat belts.

(c) *Movie Colleges versus Real Colleges*

CENTRAL-IDEA SENTENCE: Movies never picture colleges as they really are.

I. Colleges in movies are always of the Ivy League type.
   A. Stately buildings covered with vines
   B. Populated by all-American type of men and women
   C. Everybody belongs to a fraternity or sorority.

      D. Accurate view of college is never seen.
        1. College life is portrayed as a bowl of cherries.
        2. The possibility of study is ignored.
        3. Intellectual students are objects of ridicule.
   II. A real college is vastly different.
      A. Study is the keynote.
      B. Students are common guys and girls trying to learn.
      C. Life at college is work, not fun and frolic.

(d)   *Should Physical Education Be Compulsory?*
      CENTRAL-IDEA SENTENCE: Physical education should not be a compulsory subject.

   I. Introduction
   II. Good points of physical education
      A. Physical
        1. Mental
   III. Bad points of physical education
      A. Physical
      B. Mental
      C. Others
   IV. Conclusion

(e)   *The Trouble with Being a Woman*
      CENTRAL-IDEA SENTENCE: Though a woman can choose a career or marriage, she must always remember to be the ideal woman.

   I. Though there are good things about being a woman, they are tinged with disadvantages.
   II. A woman loses independence in marriage.
      A. A man doesn't submit any of his independence to a woman.
      B. A man insists upon having his own way.
      C. A woman isn't the final judge in her own home.
   III. A woman can choose a career rather than a family.
      A. Her opportunities are limited.
      B. Hard to rise to important positions.
   IV. A woman must always be gentle, sweet, and obedient.

(f)   *Weather Superstitions*
      CENTRAL-IDEA SENTENCE: Old superstitions about the weather are no longer believed.

   I. Ground Hog Day
   II. First Snowfall
   III. Lightning striking twice in same place
   IV. Rainbow at night, rainbow in morning
   V. Present weather predictions
      A. Modern equipment
      B. No basis for old superstitions

6

BEGINNING AND ENDING
A THEME

Many of the compositions you will write in freshman English will be so short (300–500 words) that you need pay little attention to particular ways of beginning and ending them. If you have limited the size of subject carefully and planned the arrangement of material, it is usually enough simply to begin with the first item and end with the last.

Probably, however, you will also write a number of longer papers in your English course, ones running to 1,000 words and sometimes more; and papers required of you in other courses almost always will be over 1,000 words. In writing these longer papers, which usually will be fairly complex in content and structure, you should give some thought to exactly how best to get the paper under way and how to round it off satisfactorily. The particular methods you choose will depend on several things, chiefly subject, purpose, and audience. But to help you in deciding, this chapter will list and illustrate a number of the most effective and most commonly used ways of beginning and ending. Several examples of ineffective ways of beginning and ending often found in student papers will also be shown.

What a Good Beginning Should Do

A good beginning should do two things: gain the attention and interest of the audience and get the discussion of the subject under way.

Ordinarily, you can afford to take the attention and interest of your

89

audience for granted only when you are writing for a specialized group of readers on a subject that you know in advance is close to their concerns. In such cases, even if the paper is to be fairly long and complex, you can safely move at once into the presentation of your subject. A good example is the paper in which Dr. Jonas E. Salk announced the discovery of polio vaccine. His article, addressed to other physicians, began:

> Investigations have been underway in this laboratory for more than a year, with the objective of establishing conditions for destroying the disease-producing property of the three types of poliomyelitis virus without destroying completely their capacity to induce antibody formation in experimental animals. The success of experiments in monkeys with vaccines prepared from virus produced in tissue culture and referred to briefly elsewhere led to the studies now in progress in human subjects. It is the purpose of this report to present the results obtained thus far in the investigations in man . . . ("Studies in Human Subjects on Active Immunization Against Poliomyelitis").

Notice that this opening simply assumes that the audience will be interested. Dr. Salk introduces his subject by presenting factual background information and stating clearly the purpose of his report. He was perfectly safe in launching at once into his subject, for the mere mention of it was all that was necessary to awaken the keenest interest among the physicians who were his audience.

Ordinarily, however, you will be writing for less specialized audiences than the one addressed in this article and, to communicate your thoughts fully and effectively, will need to take steps to arouse interest. The following quotation from an essay giving the author's impressions of China, seeing it again thirty years after his last visit, provides a good example of an opening that tries to gain the reader's interest:

> Westerners once loved Peking not only for its beauty but also for the astonishing advantages they enjoyed there. In one quarter of the city they were rulers; at their feet they saw a nation of traders and artisans; and on their whims depended the coolies' hope of life—if they all took a ricksha the runner would die within a year from heart trouble; if they all went on foot, he would die within a week of hunger. I traveled in China thirty years ago, when it was in a state of anarchy, and I had a lordly status. I now told myself: "This time I'll be cut down to my right size." Not at all. The privileges accorded the tourist have, if anything, increased (Alfred Fabre-Luce, "Chinese Journey").

The specific and rather startling observations about the high status once enjoyed by foreigners in Peking, the author's expectation that such conditions would have changed under the Communist regime and his surprised discovery that they have not, all serve to arouse our interest and curiosity. Notice also that this paragraph is closely related to the rest of the essay, providing an appropriate introduction to the author's impressions of a tour through Red China.

Effective Ways to Begin a Theme

When we examine the opening paragraphs of a considerable number of published articles, we see that certain methods of beginning are used more often than others and that they can be classified roughly into a number of categories. Illustrated below are some of the most frequently used kinds of openings. As you read through the list, keep in mind that we are not dealing with rules or formulas to cover all the possible ways to begin a piece of writing, but rather suggestions. You must choose the particular method or combination of methods that you think best suited to your subject, your purpose, and your audience.

INCIDENT

BE 1 *Begin with an interesting incident related to the subject*

One of the most frequent ways of beginning is to present an interesting incident that has a direct bearing on the subject to be discussed. An example is the opening paragraph of an article on a coal-mine disaster:

> One afternoon a few years ago William E. Rowekamp and a few other coal miners, their day's work done, were sitting around underground at the bottom of the shaft of the Centralia No. 5 mine, waiting for time to go "on top" and home, when all at once a foul cloud of coal smoke and powder smoke billowed from the mouth of the Main South Entry, the main tunnel leading southward into the mine workings. An ex-GI asked, "What is it, Uncle Bill?" Rowekamp, an old coal miner and an officer of the local union, knew the lad was nervous so he said only, "It could be several things." But Rowekamp knew what it was—an explosion. Somewhere far back in the catacomb of entries and crosscuts and rooms, somewhere among the fifteen-odd miles of active tunnels or the hundred-odd miles of abandoned workings, an explosion had occurred, and this cloud of smoke was the backwash of the tornado of flame and blast. Rowekamp had no way of

knowing it then but one hundred and eleven men were dead or dying (John Bartlow Martin, "The Blast in Centralia No. 5").

The author has chosen in his first paragraph to describe the dramatic moment of the explosion, confident that it will at once gain the interest of his readers as well as lead directly into the main part of the article, which discusses the background and the effects of this explosion.

EXAMPLE OR INSTANCE

BE 2   *Begin with an example illustrating an important aspect of the subject*

Another useful way to begin is to offer an example or instance that illustrates an important aspect of the subject. Here is the beginning of an article that points out the dangerous rate at which this country's underground water supplies are being used up. The author presents a specific and interesting example of one way in which this resource can be increased.

> On the giant King Ranch which stretches over the arid Gulf plain of Texas, the Klebergs, who own the ranch, have built a 1500-acre lake with the intention of pouring the water down a rathole. Near the dam that holds this vast pond, they have drilled a deep well. The water from the lake is piped to the well, filtered to remove silt, and pumped down the well to spread through the water-bearing sands deep in the earth. Here the water is held without evaporation and moves under the million acres of the ranch to replenish the hundreds of windmills that pump water for the livestock (Grant Cannon, "Refilling Our Wells").

STARTLING OR PROVOCATIVE STATEMENT

BE 3   *Begin with a startling statement about the subject*

One of the simplest yet most effective ways to begin is to make one or more statements about the subject that surprise the reader or excite his curiosity, statements that the rest of the essay will attempt to explain or justify. The first sentence in the passage just quoted is an example, and others are easy to find. The opening sentence of an essay by a Frenchman on "Love in America" is a curiosity-provoking statement that the remainder of the essay tries to explain:

America appears to be the only country in the world where love is a national problem (Raoul de Roussy de Sales, "Love in America").

QUESTIONS

BE 4   *Begin with questions about the subject that the rest of the paper will answer*

Especially when your purpose in a paper is to explain something or to argue for or against a certain point of view, you will find that questions make effective openings. The questions should be phrased in such a way that they clearly demand answers and thus arouse the reader's curiosity; and they should bear directly on the main idea of the paper, which should for the most part consist of detailed answers to the questions.

Alan Paton, the South African novelist, begins an article about the race problem in his country this way:

> Is the white man in South Africa really in a dilemma? Or is he merely being arrogant, selfish, and domineering, as so many of his critics think he is?
> Is he in a tragic dilemma? Or is he in a comic dilemma, like the monkey who has put its paw into the hole in the gourd, and will be caught because he is too greedy to let go? Or is the monkey's dilemma perhaps comic only to those who are not monkeys? ("The White Man's Dilemma").

QUOTATION

BE 5   *Begin with a quotation related to the subject*

Sometimes you will find that a quotation closely related to your subject can provide an effective beginning. Here is an example taken from an article lamenting that book reviews and literary criticism in America have become so polite:

> "I have had great pleasure in reading Jean-Paul Sartre's latest novel," said Francois Mauriac not long ago, pausing a moment before adding the stinger, "—and in finding that it was extremely bad."
> This openly malicious flick by a Nobel Prize winner at one of his leading contemporaries is merely the most recent instance of how much saltier the literary life is in France than over here, where a suffocating decorum tends to deaden and flatten almost everything printed and publicly said about books and their authors (Richard Hanser, "A Plea for Literary Mayhem").

COMPARISON OR CONTRAST

BE 6   *Begin by comparing or contrasting a part of the subject with something else*

A comparison makes an effective beginning when you are trying to explain something difficult or technical like the operation of an internal combustion engine or the formation of a moving image inside the picture tube of a television set. By comparing the subject with something already familiar to your readers, you can lead them more easily from the known to the unknown and help them to understand difficult ideas and processes.

Here is an example of this kind of opening, quoted from an article that explains in non-technical language the role played by catalysts in modern industry:

> Did you ever try to burn a lump of sugar with a match? You can't. But place some cigarette ash on it, and you can. Nothing happens to the ash; it merely makes the chemical reaction of burning possible.
> As sugar burns in the presence of ash, so a host of fundamental reactions take place in the presence of substances called catalysts. All chemical reactions involve changes in the reacting materials; the peculiarity of a catalytic reaction is that the catalyst which promotes it is not changed at all ("Chemistry's Secret Agents," *The Lamp*).

Contrast has the advantage of gaining the reader's attention by placing two strikingly unlike things side by side. This short beginning paragraph does this and also states the main idea of the essay:

> Mankind has the technical ability to reduce the toll of sickness and poverty throughout the world to an extent never dreamed of even a few decades ago. Yet we teeter on the brink of self-destruction by allowing population growth to outstrip economic advance (Frank W. Notestien, "Poverty and Population").

Although there are many other good ways, and combinations of ways, to begin papers besides those just listed, you are likely to find the ones suggested here the most useful in your longer papers.

Ineffective Ways to Begin a Theme

Unfortunately, student papers often illustrate less successful ways of beginning; knowing in advance what some of the most frequent of these are, you should be able more easily to avoid them in your own compositions.

AN APOLOGY OR COMPLAINT

BE 7   *Do not begin with an apology or a complaint*

A student who begins his paper with an apology for his lack of knowledge or for having failed to consider his subject previously is, quite obviously, off to a bad start. He is, in effect, informing his readers at the outset that what he is about to say is not worth very much. Notice, for example, the effect of the following opening paragraph from a theme:

> Are athletic events, as they are established today, beneficial to an institution of higher education? It is my opinion that they are not. I have not done any research on this subject and I have not even thought much about it before, but I do know what my opinion is and how it was formed. Therefore, I would like to set down in this paper some of the things that have helped me to form the opinions I now hold.

Though it is certainly not this student's intention, he appears to be advertising the fact that his opinion has been hastily formed and is poorly founded.

The sort of complaint contained in the following beginning paragraph may be heartfelt but it is not likely to make a very favorable impression on a reader:

> I really don't see why we have to write themes in this course. Writing themes is hard work for some people, and I am one of those people. However, since I have to write a theme, I might as well get started. It isn't going to be any good, but here goes.

OBVIOUS STATEMENT

BE 8   *Do not begin with an obvious statement*

Another kind of weak beginning for a paper is a sentence that says something obvious, something the reader must already know and does not need to be told. Here are two examples:

Both high school and college football have their advantages and disadvantages. Some of the advantages are important and some are not; the same is true of the disadvantages.

※　　　※　　　※　　　※　　　※

Everyone needs an education and everyone gets one, though there are all kinds of educations that people can get.

IRRELEVANT MATERIAL

BE 9   *Do not begin with irrelevant material*

A paper should not begin with material that has little or no apparent relation to the subject that is to be discussed. One variety of this fault of irrelevancy is failure to see where the subject really begins. A familiar example is the sort of autobiograpical paper that begins with the first meeting and subsequent marriage of the student's parents, then proceeds leisurely through the birth of several children until finally the student himself arrives on the scene. But this fault can occur in other kinds of papers as well; look at this opening paragraph of a theme on the advantages of golf as a sport for people of all ages:

Authorities tell us that golf is a game which originated in Holland. It was first played on the ice, the goal being a stake instead of a hole in the ground. Then, in the fifteenth century, Scotland discovered the game and gradually changed it into its present form. In the late nineteenth century golf was still virtually unknown in America.

The background information is interesting enough but unfortunately it has nothing directly to do with the subject to be discussed.

OVERGENERALIZATION

BE 10   *Do not begin with too many generalizations or with one that is too broad*

Generalizations, particularly expressions of opinion that stimulate curiosity, are often useful to begin papers with, but it is possible to have too much of a good thing. A weak opening will result either from using too wide a generalization or from using too many generalizations. Here is an example of the former:

Education, no matter what it concerns or how well or how poorly it is carried out, always is a benefit to the people being educated.

The trouble with this generalization is that it takes in too much territory; the student who wrote it would have a very difficult time trying in the rest of the paper to demonstrate the truth of his first sentence.

The other fault, using too many generalizations, is illustrated in this opening paragraph:

> The wonder and satisfaction in looking for the silver lining is that this lining can nearly always be found. No matter how gloomy and dreary things appear there is usually something pleasant about the situation. However small that "something" is, the pleasure it conveys to those who search for it is real and gratifying. The ability to rise above the clouds and view the silver lining is one which not everyone possesses.

DEPENDENT OPENING SENTENCE

BE 11   *Do not begin with a sentence that depends grammatically on the title*

Though it is not a faulty beginning in the same sense as the others that have been listed, the opening sentence that depends grammatically (or "leans," as some teachers say) on the title is usually considered not advisable. Here are several examples:

> *The Big Wheel*
> This kind of college student actually started his fabulous career when he was very young, learning at an early age that if he yelled long enough he would always get his own way.
>
> ❀   ❀   ❀   ❀   ❀

> *What Is a Good Driver?*
> Very few people actually know the answer to this question although nearly everyone believes that he himself is a good driver.
>
> ❀   ❀   ❀   ❀   ❀

> *The Sort of Girl I Want to Marry*
> She doesn't need to be just like the girl that married dear old Dad, but I certainly could do a lot worse than that.

The fault illustrated in these opening sentences does not involve the nature of the material itself, as do the other defective beginnings that have been mentioned; rather, it is a violation of a generally accepted convention, like a breach in manners. Because it is generally regarded as a defect, you will be wise to avoid it.

EXERCISES

1. Prepare an informal outline for any three of these theme topics and for each write an effective opening paragraph:

One Person I Disliked
The Case for (against) Comics
My One Talent
Collecting Fossils (Rocks, Butterflies, Scale Models, etc.)
Model Airplanes
Skiing as I Do It
My Introduction to Music (Art, Science, Religion, Literature, Poetry, etc.)
Roller Skating (or Ice Skating)
My Exhibit at the Science Fair (4H Fair, County Fair)
Building a Campfire
Raising Guppies (Turtles, Parakeets, Siamese Cats, Dachshunds, etc.)
Trout Fishing
The Kind of Book I Like Best
I Was a Soda Jerk (Clerk, Stenographer, Cook, etc.)

2. Examine two magazines and find two beginnings in each which you feel are effective. Explain why you think they are good.

3. Study the following beginnings and give your opinion of their effectiveness:

(a)   The life of Heinrich Schliemann is the story of the poor minister's son who at the age of seven dreamed of finding a city, and who thirty-nine years later found not only the city but treasure such as the world has seldom seen (C. W. Ceram, "The Man Who Found Troy").

(b)   Have you ever wondered what you would say if you were suddenly called upon to defend the human race?
Suppose you were invited to participate in a great debate or, better still, a mock court trial called for the purpose of deciding whether the human species had justified its right to survive—whether, on the basis of its virtues and weaknesses, it was actually entitled to the gift of life. Suppose your job was that of attorney for the defense. How would you go about collecting your evidence? What witnesses would you call? What arguments would you use? (Norman Cousins, "Don't Resign from the Human Race").

(c)   Chatting with a college man is supposed to be fun. So when we asked our College Board Members to ask five college men, "What do you think of a young woman's combining career and motherhood?" we thought we were giving our reporters (1) a pleasant assignment, (2) a good excuse for a coffee date. And since this is a question of current importance to college women, we were also looking for thoughtful answers (Marybeth Little, "Are College Men Boys?").

(d)   There is something to be said for a bad education. By any standards mine was deplorable; and I deplored it for years, in private and
in public. I flaunted it as if it were a model, a kind of cultural Purple
Heart which both excused my deficiencies and lent luster to my mild
achievements. But as time goes on I murmur against it less. I find
that even ignorance has its brighter side (Phyllis McGinley, "The
Consolations of Illiteracy").

4. Criticize the following openings from student themes. Tell why you
think they are good or bad.

(a) From a student paper called "What's a Good Driver?":

A few short years ago a man named Henry Ford became a father.
There was nothing really so startling about that. It happens all the
time. But Ford was a little different from the usual father. His offspring was an industry, an industry that changed the motto "Get a
horse!" to "Get a Ford!" Everyone knows how important Ford's contribution to the automobile industry has been and how great it has
been to mankind. What would our civilization be without the automobile? But Ford and others like him created the greatest depopula-
tor of the world since the invention of war—the American driver.

(b) From a paper on choosing an occupation:

This is a very poor group of subjects to write on; at least it is for
me. I have chosen the one on occupations because I think I know
more about it than any of the rest, but that isn't much.

(c) From a paper on the student's high school English class:

"A doubtful throne is ice on summer seas." These words are the
first that come to mind when I think of my English class when I was
a sophomore in high school. My teacher quoted the line at least two
hundred times, to give an example of a metaphor. Although there
must have been other quotations to exemplify similes, they did not
impress me as vividly as the "doubtful throne" phrase, for I don't recall them.

(d) From a theme in which the author discusses her curiosity. It is called
"Curiosity in Me":

Every human is an individual. Curiosity is inherent in everyone.
There are also individual differences in every human. These differences cause the trait of curiosity to differ in different people.

(e) From a paper called "Johnny Busia":

"Know Johnny Busia? Sure do. Why, everybody in Alaska knows
good old Johnny." Yes, just about anybody you ask does know "good
old Johnny"; for of all the fabulous old-timers left in the land of the
setting sun, of all the men who staked their lives in the rush of '98,
of all the grimy prospectors who went "clean mad for the lust called
gold," the one who tops them all is Johnny Busia.

(f) From a student paper describing a hunting experience:

My father, my grandfather, and I arrived at the lake an hour before sunrise that cold fall morning. As I stepped out of the car, clad

in hip boots, heavy hunting clothes, and cap, I trembled with excitement and anticipation. For this was the day I had eagerly awaited for three weeks—my first duck hunt.

(g) From a paper called "A Bad Boy":

This topic states that this boy is bad. I guess he was, for the boy was me.

What a Good Ending Should Do

The most obvious, though perhaps not the most helpful, way to answer the question of what an effective ending for a paper should accomplish is simply to say that it ought to bring the paper to an end. It should leave the reader feeling satisfied that you have said all you intended and needed to say and therefore have stopped.

Effective Ways to End a Theme

Of the many good ways of ending longer papers, we list five that you may find particularly useful. But remember that your decision on how to end a paper must always take into account your purpose, the nature of the material you have presented, and the way in which you have presented it. Choosing a way to end a composition is emphatically not a matter of applying a rule but of using good judgment.

MOST IMPORTANT POINT LAST

BE 12   *End with the most important point*

In many papers that deal with ideas rather than events and incidents, an effective way to end is to arrange your ideas in order of increasing importance and stop when you have presented your last and most important idea. (See Chapter 5, pp. 62–64.) This is the method used in a short essay on what the author calls "the fifth freedom," "the freedom to be one's best." After the opening, the essay presents three "misunderstandings," which, in the opinion of the author, are causing us to lose this freedom, then three courses of action that he believes will restore it to us. The third and most important of these brings the essay to an end.

Finally, we can expose our children to the best values we have found. By relating our lives to the evidences of the ages, by judging our philosophy in the light of values that history has proven truest, perhaps we shall be able to produce that "ringing message, full of content and truth, satisfying the mind, appealing to the heart, firing the will, a message on which one can stake his whole life." This is the message that could mean joy and strength and leadership—freedom as opposed to serfdom (Seymour St. John, "The Fifth Freedom").

SIGNIFICANCE OF THE SUBJECT

BE 13   *End by stating the significance of the subject*

When you especially want to impress your readers with the importance of your subject, you can end with a paragraph that states clearly the significance of the subject and thus drives the point home. This method is used to end an article about a young American scientist who received a fatal dose of radiation while working with radioactive material.

> Louis Slotin was not a great or famous man, and he has been in his grave now for almost eight years. Yet his story has seemed worth telling, and not only because nuclear radiation, which kills without being seen or felt, is more terrifying than need be, just because it is so mysterious. It has seemed worth telling also because it is a story of human bravery and sacrifice, qualities which may yet save a civilization threatened with destruction by the very weapons Louis Slotin helped to make (Stewart Alsop and Ralph E. Lapp, "The Strange Death of Louis Slotin").

RESTATEMENT OF MAIN IDEA

BE 14   *End by restating the main idea*

You can end longer papers effectively by restating the main idea in the final paragraph, thus unifying your discussion and impressing the main point upon the reader. An article on insects begins with this paragraph.

> In the white shale of eastern Kansas, in the coal layers of Pennsylvania, in sedimentary rock formed below volcano-ringed lakes in Colorado, scientists have found fossil insects, some more than 100 million years old. Insects were part of the world prehistoric men knew just as they are part of our modern world with its television and jet planes and atom bombs. And in this modern world, as in the epoch of Neanderthal Man, insects have traits and abilities completely beyond those of men.

It ends by repeating, in the last sentence, the idea expressed at the beginning of the essay:

The lists of science today include something like three-quarters of a million kinds of insects. They are still, as they were in the days of Linnaeus, the most varied in form of all the animals. And they still possess within their infinitely diversified bodies capacities not found in any other creatures—not even in man (Edwin Way Teale, "Those Phenomenal Insects").

APPEAL FOR ACTION

BE 15   *End with an appeal for action*

Often the papers you write in freshman English will be criticisms of particular situations, such as the presence or absence of an honor system on your campus, or the way in which student elections are conducted. Ordinarily when you write a paper of this sort, pointing out things that you think are wrong with the situation being discussed, you really are suggesting that something be done to improve matters. An effective ending, then, is an appeal to your readers to take action, to do whatever you think necessary to remedy the situation. In an article listing the great scientific discoveries likely to result from the exploration of outer space, an astronomer argues that Russia's present superiority in this field has resulted from a policy of more generous support for basic research than we have had in the United States. He ends his essay with an appeal to the American people:

> Meanwhile, the American people should give wholehearted support to a full-scale space program. We can be sure that the scientific discoveries and new inventions made in the course of our efforts to attain space flight will more than pay the cost. Success is within our view. Our scientists merely need the respect, confidence, and support of governmental leaders to make the greatest adventure of all history a reality (Donald H. Menzel, "The Astronomer's Stake in Outer Space").

SUMMARY

BE 16   *End with a summary if your paper is fairly long or contains difficult material*

The summary is an effective means of concluding certain kinds of papers, but inexperienced writers use it more often than they should. The purpose of a summary is to present briefly and clearly the main points that have been made so as to fix them firmly in the mind of the reader. In a theme only three or four pages long, a summary at the end is not very complimentary to the reader's intelligence, since it suggests that he is not bright enough to remember what he has just read.

Generally speaking, end with a summary only when a paper is fairly long or presents complicated ideas that the reader may have trouble keeping clear. As an example, one rather long essay ends with a systematic summary, even numbering the main points to keep them distinct in the reader's mind:

> One might sum up the situation in a series of propositions: (1) The Age of the Common Man has begun. (2) Despite all the gains that it may legitimately claim, they are threatened by those confusions which arise when the common denominator is consciously or unconsciously allowed to function as a standard of excellence. (3) The dominance of mass media almost exclusively under the control of those who are little concerned with anything except immediate financial gain does tend to debase taste. (4) Ultimate responsibility for the future rests with the thinkers and the educators whose most important social task at the moment is to define democratic culture in some fashion which will both reserve a place for uncommon excellence and, even in connection with the largest masses, emphasize the highest rather than the lowest common denominator (Joseph Wood Krutch, "Is Our Common Man Too Common?").

Because the ending provides the final chance for you to make your views clear, or to persuade your readers to agree with the ideas or attitudes you have presented, you should take special pains to use the most appropriate and most effective endings that you can devise.

Ineffective Ways to End a Theme

Several kinds of ineffective endings often found in student compositions are listed below to help you avoid mistakes of this sort.

APOLOGY

BE 17   *Do not end with an apology*

Just as an apology does not make a strong opening for a theme, it also is a weak and unemphatic ending. An apology at the end has the effect of undercutting all that you have said in the rest of your paper. Here as an example is the final paragraph from a paper that tried, over-ambitiously, to discuss the advantages of education.

This paper was not intended to prove any particular point or to disprove anything either. Instead, it has merely tried to discuss something related to education. I haven't thought very much about education in this particular way before, but I do think education is important, and I hope you do too.

NEW IDEA OR AFTERTHOUGHT

BE 18 *Do not end with a new idea or an afterthought*

The last paragraph of a composition is not the place to bring in a new idea unrelated to the rest of the paper, or to add another detail or notion that you have just thought of. The obvious reason is that you will arouse the curiosity of the reader, but because you are at the end of the paper you will not be able to satisfy his desire to know more. The result is a feeling of disappointment. Here is an example of a new and unrelated idea wrongly introduced; the paragraph ends a theme that criticizes the influence of television on children:

> Theoretically, after a child has spent six or seven hours in school he ought not have to take a great deal of homework home with him for the next day. In practice, however, most children don't spend their time wisely in school and so need three or four hours in the evening to do their lessons. There is no doubt at all that television programs lure children away from necessary homework. As a result, their grades go down because either they don't do their work or they don't turn it in on time. This difficulty leads to two other questions: Is homework wrong? Or is the school's system of grading wrong?

If material of this sort is important enough and closely enough related to deserve being included, it should be brought in at the appropriate place in the paper; if it does not meet these tests, it should be omitted.

INCONCLUSIVE ENDING

BE 19 *Do not end a paper inconclusively*

There is a kind of ineffective ending that is difficult to define exactly, because it takes many forms. The main fault of such an ending is its failure to conclude; although the writer has obviously said all he is going to say, the reader feels that the paper seems unfinished. Examples will help to make this error clear. The first is the final paragraph of a theme called "If I Were a Parent."

Parents should try to understand their children, try to find out why they behave as they do, try to help them overcome their bad habits and encourage them in their good habits. They should make their children feel free to come to them with their troubles, knowing that they will find understanding and help. All of these things help to make good parents. There are also a lot of other characteristics that good parents should have but I won't take the time to discuss them.

Here is the ending of a theme on segregation, a topic that the student probably did not know enough about.

I think that eventually there will be no segregation in the United States, but I don't think the end of segregation will come about in time for us to see it happen. If I were asked my views of the segregation issue, I could not give any definite answers. About all that I can say is that I am for it and at the same time against it.

UNNECESSARY SUMMARY OR RESTATEMENT

BE 20   *Do not end a short and uncomplicated paper with a summary*

A summary or restatement is a useful way to end a long and complex paper. To end a three- or four-page theme with a summary suggests that the reader is not bright enough to remember what he has just read. Here are two examples of unnecessary summaries. Both come from papers of about 500 words, and both papers deal with uncomplicated subjects, the first with a student's reasons for majoring in pharmacy, the second with the advantages of living in a small town.

In summary, let me say that I have chosen to major in pharmacy because (1) pharmacy offers good working conditions, (2) pharmacy is a profession that pays quite well, (3) pharmacy offers job security, and (4) pharmacy deals with chemistry, which is one of my easiest subjects. In the preceding paragraphs I have tried to present these reasons in detail.

Using my home town of Blue Springs as an example, I have tried to show some of its good points and some of its bad ones. I think that the good points far outweigh the bad, and for this reason I repeat that I believe a small town is a better place to live than a big city.

Remember that not all the papers you write will need a distinct introduction and conclusion. (In fact, both of these words have been intentionally avoided throughout this chapter, simply because they often suggest something more elaborate than "beginning" and "ending" do.) Many of your papers in freshman English probably will be under 500 words and seldom will call for special attention to particular ways of beginning and ending. Longer papers usually will need this attention, but you will not necessarily have to devote main headings of your outline to the beginning and ending or use several pages in your paper to present each of them. The ways of beginning and ending effectively that have been suggested in this chapter can be managed as successfully in three or four sentences as in three or four pages. The length of a beginning or ending usually depends much more on the length and complexity of the paper than on the particular method used.

EXERCISES

5. Examine two magazines and find two endings in each which you feel are good and tell why.

6. Study the following endings and give your opinion of them:

(a) So, after four years of seeing everything there is to see in big-time college football—victories, defeats, publicity, hospitals, championships, and bowls—of being known as a "football player" rather than a human being, of seeing myself and my teammates misrepresented and misquoted by sportswriters who seldom attempted to know the players personally, of playing in a 97,000-seat stadium in which my nonplaying student friends were forced to sit in the end zone, of having my natural desire for physical exercise corrupted and commercialized, of giving up pleasant afternoons in favor of kicking and rolling in the dust and muck of the practice field—I have decided that big-time football is a poor bargain for the boys who play the game (Allen Jackson, "Too Much Football").

(b) American women have so much that they can teach us "backward" Chinese females. But I make bold to suggest that perhaps we Chinese women can teach them something in return—something they have forgotten (Helena Kuo, "American Women Are Different").

(c) The days were golden, the nights were dim and strange. I still recall with trembling those loud, nocturnal crises when you drew up to a signpost and raced the engine so the lights would be bright enough to read destinations by. I have never been really planetary since. I suppose it's time to say good-bye. Farewell, my lovely! (E. B. White, "Farewell, My Lovely!").

(d) This uncanny stability is simply a matter of shape. Whenever anything is wrong, the airplane by that very fact presents a different side of itself to the onrushing air. Since its shape is designed with just that idea in mind, the air will create on the new shape a new force, and the new force rights the airplane (Wolfgang Langewiesche, "Why an Airplane Flies").

7. Criticize the following endings from student writing:

(a) From a theme on a student's high school English preparation:

It seems as though high school instructors nowadays are more interested in maintaining a good income, better working conditions, and a good retirement plan than they are in teaching. There always seems to be more controversy over Johnny running down the stairs than over Sam's grade on the last test. All in all, I shall have to admit that if I were running that particular school there would be some changes made.

(b) From a paper in which the student describes the difficulties he had in getting together all his supplies for his first semester in college:

I made so many trips back to the book store for exchanges and for buying more supplies that after a while every clerk in the store knew me. Whenever I went by a clerk she would ask if I was sure I had everything I needed this time. I think that the only lady who did not mind seeing me again was the one at the cash register.

(c) From a paper in which the student has described a prisoner named Frank Brackens, his background, appearance, and behavior:

I pity Frank Brackens. I don't condone the things he has done, but I can understand why he did them. Every crime that he committed was for him personal revenge. He possibly could have been a great athlete, for he has the coordination, speed, endurance, and intelligence. Instead he is a menace to the society which spawned him.

(d) From a paper that describes a visit to the San Blas Islands off South America:

It had been very interesting to discover that scarcely seventy-five miles from the Panama Canal, in the route of world trade, still exists a people whose origin dates back many centuries before the discovery of America. These people have preserved the purity of their race and have retained unchanged the ancestral traits that have been handed down through the ages.

(e) From a paper in which the student gives reasons for deciding to attend his home-town university:

While I was still in high school I and several friends would go to the University gymnasium at night and work out on the bars and rings. We would hardly be there more than a few minutes before we would be put out of the building because we were not university students.

7

WHAT PARAGRAPHS
ARE FOR

The old saying that "the paragraph is the composition in miniature" is not entirely true, for certain problems of organization and development cannot be dealt with in so small a unit. Still, much can be said for this notion. Most of the problems that you face in writing an entire paper also confront you each time you write a paragraph, and a student who consistently writes good paragraphs is likely to be able to combine them into good papers. The paragraph, therefore, deserves unusually close study.

If your experience has been typical, your junior high and high school English texts talked about paragraphs in much the same way that cookbooks talk about cakes: assemble the ingredients, follow directions —and a good cake (or paragraph) is bound to result. There *are* principles (if not rules) to guide you in writing good paragraphs, but there are no recipes. Good paragraphs cannot be produced mechanically. You do need to know the principles, however, and the best way to discover them is to learn what paragraphs are intended to do, and how they do it. In this chapter, we will look closely at the paragraphs of several good writers to see what can be found out about their methods of paragraphing and the purposes that their paragraphs serve.

Paragraphs as Punctuation

To show you how much we depend upon the division of material into paragraphs when we read, let us look at a selection in which the paragraph divisions have been left out. Here is a passage from *A Farewell to Arms,* Ernest Hemingway's famous novel about World War I. The story is told by the main character, Lieutenant (or, in Italian, "Tenente") Frederic Henry, an American who had volunteered as an ambulance driver with the Italian army, which was then fighting the Germans and Austrians in Italy. Henry has been seriously wounded by the explosion of a mortar shell and has been carried by one of his men, Franco Gordini, to a dressing station for emergency treatment. As he is lying on the ground waiting for his turn, he speaks to Gordini:

"How are you, Franco?" "I am all right." He sat down beside me. In a moment the blanket in front of the dressing station opened and two stretcher-bearers came out followed by the tall Englishman. He brought them over to me. "Here is the American Tenente," he said in Italian. "I'd rather wait," I said. "There are much worse wounded than me. I'm all right." "Come come," he said. "Don't be a bloody hero." Then in Italian: "Lift him very carefully about the legs. His legs are very painful. He is the legitimate son of President Wilson." They picked me up and took me into the dressing room. Inside they were operating on all the tables. The little major looked at us, furious. He recognized me and waved a forceps. "Ça va bien?" "Ça va." I have brought him in," the tall Englishman said in Italian. "The only son of the American Ambassador. He can be here until you are ready to take him. Then I will take him with my first load." He bent over. "I'll look up their adjutant to do your papers and it will all go much faster." He stooped to go under the doorway and went out. The major was unhooking the forceps now, dropping them in a basin. I followed his hands with my eyes. Now he was bandaging. Then the stretcher-bearers took the man off the table. "I'll take the American Tenente," one of the captains said. They lifted me onto the table. It was hard and slippery. There were many strong smells, chemical smells and the sweet smell of blood. They took off my trousers and the medical captain commenced dictating to the sergeant-adjutant while he worked. "Multiple superficial wounds of the left and right thigh and left and right knee and right foot. Profound wounds of right knee and foot. Lacerations of the scalp (he probed—Does that hurt?—Christ, yes!) with possible fracture of the skull. Incurred in the line of duty. That's what keeps you from being court-martialled for self-inflicted wounds," he said. "Would you like a drink of brandy? How did you run into this thing anyway? What were you trying to do? Commit suicide? Anti-tetanus please, and mark a cross on both legs. Thank you. I'll clean this up a little, wash it out, and put on a dressing. Your blood coagulates beautifully." The adjutant, looking up from the paper, "What inflicted the wounds?" The medical captain, "What hit you?" Me, with eyes shut, "A trench mortar shell." The captain, doing things that hurt sharply and severing tissue—"Are you sure?" Me—trying to lie still and feeling my stomach flutter when the flesh was cut, "I think so."

Even though an interesting story is being told, you probably find this hard to read. In the first place, everything is jammed together so that you are not always sure who is talking. In the second, you find this solid block of words tiring to your eye and mind since it runs on and on without a break. You have no opportunity to pause a moment and get your bearings before going on again. And finally, you can't tell how the author wants you to group the events described, which ones he wants you to see together and which ones separately.

Now read the passage once more, printed this time as Hemingway wrote it, with the paragraph divisions shown:

"How are you, Franco?"

"I am all right." He sat down beside me. In a moment the blanket in front of the dressing station opened and two stretcher-bearers came out followed by the tall Englishman. He brought them over to me.

"Here is the American Tenente," he said in Italian.

"I'd rather wait," I said. "There are much worse wounded than me. I'm all right."

"Come come," he said. "Don't be a bloody hero." Then in Italian: "Lift him very carefully about the legs. His legs are very painful. He is the legitimate son of President Wilson." They picked me up and took me into the dressing room. Inside they were operating on all the tables. The little major looked at us, furious. He recognized me and waved a forceps.

"Ça va bien?"

"Ça va."

"I have brought him in," the tall Englishman said in Italian. "The only son of the American Ambassador. He can be here until you are ready to take him. Then I will take him with my first load." He bent over. "I'll look up their adjutant to do your papers and it will all go much faster." He stooped to go under the doorway and went out. The major was unhooking the forceps now, dropping them in a basin. I followed his hands with my eyes. Now he was bandaging. Then the stretcher-bearers took the man off the table.

"I'll take the American Tenente," one of the captains said. They lifted me onto the table. It was hard and slippery. There were many strong smells, chemical smells and the sweet smell of blood. They took off my trousers and the medical captain commenced dictating to the sergeant-adjutant while he worked. "Multiple superficial wounds of the left and right thigh and left and right knee and right foot. Profound wounds of right knee and foot. Lacerations of the scalp (he probed—Does that hurt?—Christ, yes!) with possible fracture of the skull. Incurred in the line of duty. That's what keeps you from being court-martialled for self-inflicted wounds," he said. "Would you like a drink of brandy? How did you run into this thing anyway? What were you trying to do? Commit suicide? Anti-tetanus please, and mark a cross on both legs. Thank you. I'll clean this up a little, wash it out, and put on a dressing. Your blood coagulates beautifully."

The adjutant, looking up from the paper, "What inflicted the wounds?"

The medical captain, "What hit you?"

Me, with eyes shut, "A trench mortar shell."

The captain, doing things that hurt sharply and severing tissue— "Are you sure?"

Me—trying to lie still and feeling my stomach flutter when the flesh was cut, "I think so." (Ernest Hemingway, *A Farewell to Arms*.)

This time you find that the passage reads easily and smoothly and that it is entirely clear. The conclusion to be drawn from this exercise is that you may, if you wish, think of paragraphing as a sort of punctuation. That is, when you see a period in the middle of a page of writing, you know that the author is telling you that he has ended a part of his thought. The words between this period and the one before it are, in the author's mind, a unit which he wants you to read and understand together. In the same way, the indention that marks the beginning of a paragraph is a sign that the author wants you to consider what follows, up to the next indention, as a unit also. The paragraph may be a single word, a phrase, a sentence, or many sentences totaling several hundred words. The point is that the writer, in the hope of making clearer to you what he is saying, of communicating his ideas to you more fully, has divided or "punctuated" his words into the units we call *paragraphs*. When he decides to end one paragraph and begin another, he does so because, in his judgment, this is an important way in which he can help you to understand him better.

What Paragraphs Do

It is neither possible nor useful to list all the specific reasons why a particular writer may decide to begin and end his paragraphs as he does. Paragraphing is a highly individual matter depending, among other things, on the material being presented, on the writer's purpose, and on his notion of the needs of the readers he is addressing. We can, however, discover some of the more important purposes that paragraphs serve and use them as general guides. Since most of your themes are likely to be either narratives (stories, anecdotes, incidents) or expositions (presentations of facts, ideas, opinions), it will be best for us to center our attention on these two kinds of writing.

PARAGRAPHS IN NARRATIVE

If you look again at the selection from *A Farewell to Arms,* you will notice at once that each time a different person speaks, Hemingway begins a new paragraph. Paragraphing dialogue is a practice followed by nearly all writers, for it has the clear advantage of helping the reader to remember who is speaking. It is an especially obvious example of paragraphing used as punctuation.

Now let's examine some of the other paragraphs in the selection, ones that don't consist entirely of reported conversation. Look at the three paragraphs that begin " 'I am all right' "; " 'Come, come,' he said"; and " 'I have brought him in.' " The first of these marks the end of Henry's wait for medical treatment, since the Englishman has made arrangements to have him admitted to the tent at once. The second paragraph concerns the taking of Henry into the station. The third deals with the time between his entry into the station and the beginning of treatment. Notice the principle at work here: these three paragraphs represent three separate stages of the action—waiting outside, being carried in, and waiting for treatment. By paragraphing each of them separately, Hemingway has helped us to see more clearly the course of the action: the order in which the events happened, and the change of scene from outside the station to inside it. If these paragraphs, with the snatches of dialogue that connect them, had been printed solid with no paragraph divisions, the effect would have been much less clear.

The longer paragraph that begins " 'I'll take the American Tenente' " groups a number of related incidents and details. It tells first of Henry's being placed on the table, and of his sensations—the feel of the table, the smells of blood and chemicals; then comes the monologue of the doctor as he works, a speech ended by the question of the adjutant. Like the three paragraphs just analyzed, this one deals with a stage of the action, but the stage is not so clearly defined as those in the other three paragraphs; the examination and treatment continue for several paragraphs beyond this one. Perhaps the best explanation of Hemingway's decision to let the adjutant interrupt and thus end the paragraph is that he feels the paragraph at that point has done what he wanted it to do. He has included a variety of details in the paragraph because he wants us to see them together and thus gain a certain impression: the sharp contrast between the highly personal concern of the wounded man and the impersonal, professional attitude of the doctor as he goes about his job. Although for Henry this is a unique and extremely painful experience, for the doctor it is simply another incident in a day's work. When Hemingway feels that he has made this clear to us, he lets the adjutant break in, and begins a new paragraph. The remaining paragraphs in the selection are dialogue again, reinforcing the contrast just presented and advancing the action.

Perhaps the most important thing that this analysis of the selection has shown is that *each paragraph is regarded by the author as a unit.* All the items or details within a particular paragraph are related to one another more closely and more clearly than they are to the material in the paragraphs on either side. The contents of a given paragraph have something in common that justifies the author in wanting his readers to consider the paragraph a distinct unit, separate in some way from the rest of his material.

Our analysis also suggests a number of general principles to guide the writing of paragraphs in narrative:

PAR 1   *When reporting dialogue, begin a new paragraph to show a change of speaker*

PAR 2   *Begin a new paragraph to mark a change of scene in narrative*

PAR 3   *Begin a new paragraph to emphasize a change in the course of the action*

PAR 4   *Use a separate paragraph to group related events or details in narrative*

Nevertheless, not every writer will always paragraph narrative according to these principles. For, as was said a few pages back, paragraphing is an individual matter that cannot be completely reduced to rules.

We might be able to add a few more principles to the list if we analyzed more paragraphs either by Hemingway or by other writers; but these four, together with the over-all principle of unity, are the most important in narrative. They account for so many paragraphs in stories, novels, histories, and other narrative forms that you can safely assume that they will be useful guides for paragraphing your own narrative compositions.

PARAGRAPHS IN EXPOSITION

Like narrative paragraphs, those in expository writing may be thought of as a sort of punctuation also. We can illustrate some of the specific purposes they serve by analyzing another selection as we did the one by Hemingway. We will use a selection from an essay on Babe Ruth written by Paul Gallico a few years after the Babe's retirement from baseball. The excerpt is rather long because we need a varied sample of paragraphs to analyze. To make it easier to refer to particular paragraphs, numbers have been used.

(1) This is perhaps the greatest truth about the Babe—that no matter how phony or drippingly sentimental the situation in which he found himself might be, whether it was the outcome of natural instincts on his part to be kind or whether it was as carefully stage-managed as the first visit of a cub columnist to the home of a particularly vicious prizefighter, Ruth was always the honest and sincere element in the situation. He, if no one else, believed in it and played it up to the hilt, not ever for his own personal gain or glory or to build up an elaborate false character to be sold to his public, but because he believed that that was the kind of person he was. His generosity and his affections were just as Gargantuan as his appetites.

(2) Consider for instance the brilliantly phony plea to Babe Ruth made by his friend Senator Jimmy Walker at a baseball writers' banquet at the close of a season during which Ruth had been a particularly bad boy, had broken training, had quarreled with Miller Huggins, his manager, had been fined and suspended and sent home, had, in short, acted the part of a spoiled, willful, naughty brat.

(3) The Senator rose to speak in a banquet hall filled with tough, hard-boiled, worldly-wise baseball-writers whose daily job it is to peddle treacle about the baseball heroes and soft-pedal the sour stuff, baseball managers, perhaps as tough and hard a group of men as there is in sports, celebrities of every kind; and he made a personal plea to Babe Ruth to reform himself and behave because he owed it to the dirty-faced kids in the streets who worshipped him; the Babe, he said, had a great responsibility to the youth of the country and he must not shirk it!

(4) It was maudlin; it was in some ways cheap and tear-jerking. But, as I have suggested, it was likewise brilliant, and the brittly hard, cynical Senator of the State of New York knew what he was do-

ing. Because Ruth robbed it of all cheapness, of all sensationalism, or everything that was vulgarly maudlin, by getting to his feet and, with tears streaming down his big, ugly face, promising the dirty-faced kids of the nation to behave—for their sake. And then he kept his promise. He was never in trouble again. From that time on he began to learn a little about moderation and restraint. Nor did it make him any the less a picturesque character, because he never went sissy or holy on the boys. He retained all of his appetites and gusto for living. He merely toned them down. He learned what every celebrity in the United States eventually must learn—to perform his peccadillos in strict privacy if possible. Formerly Ruth had perpetrated his right out in public.

(5) Ruth's baseball record is a remarkable one and deserves inclusion even in such an informal estimate of him as this. He has an all-time total of 708 home runs and 723 homers, adding those he hit in World Series. He holds the record for the most home runs hit in one season: namely, 60, scored in 1927 in a season of 151 league games. He likewise holds the world's record for the total number of bases on balls during a playing career, 2,036, an indication of what the opposing pitchers thought of him. For twelve years he led his American League in home runs hit, and for eleven years hit forty or more out of the park each season. There are dozens of other minor records that one could dig out of the files and the record-books, all connected with his prodigious hitting, such as runs batted in, runs scored, extra base hits, and so on; but they still remain dusty figures and reveal nothing of the manner of his making these numbers—numbers which in two or three generations will be all that will remain of George Herman Ruth, except legend.

(6) For he played ball on the same enormous scale on which he lived his life, intensely, fervently, and with tremendous sincerity and passion. It was impossible to watch him at bat without experiencing an emotion. I have seen hundreds of ballplayers at the plate, and none of them managed to convey the message of impending doom to a pitcher that Babe Ruth did with the cock of his head, the position of his legs, and the little, gentle waving of the bat, feathered in his two big paws.

(7) And, curiously, no home run that Ruth ever hit managed to hint at the energy, power, effort, and sincerity of purpose that went into a swing as much as one strike-out. Just as when he connected the result was the most perfect thing of its kind, a ball whacked so high, wide, and handsome that no stadium in the entire country could contain it, so was his strike-out the absolute acme of frustration. He would swing himself twice around until his legs were braided. Often he would twist himself clear off his feet. If he had ever connected with that one. . . .

(8) Every move that Ruth made brought some kind of answering sound from the crowd in the stands. Each swung strike left a trail of

laughter, but backed by a chorus of respectful and awed "Ooooooooohs" as the audience realized the power that had gone to waste and the narrow escape the pitcher had had. Ruth's throws to home plate from the outfield, or to a base, so accurate that the receiver never had to move a step from his position to receive them, always brought ripples of incredulous laughter, the "I'm seeing it, but I don't believe it" kind.

(9) And of course his home runs brought forth pandemonium, a curious double rejoicing in which the spectator celebrated not only Babe's feat and its effect upon the outcome of the game, but also his excellent luck in being present and with his own eyes beholding the great happening. There must be an enormous amount of fetishism in our hero-worship of successful athletes, and seeing Ruth hit a home run always seemed to have definitely a stimulating effect upon the people, almost as though by having been there when it happened, some of the magic stuck to them. Behind the autograph craze which sends the crowd clamoring around Ruth and other celebrities for signatures there is pure fetishism, with the touch of the signature of the great one desired for a talisman.

(10) Because Ruth will always be one of the great success stories, the fairy tale come true—From Rags to Riches, or the Orphan Who Made Good. It is one of the favorite fables of our democracy, and when it comes to life as it sometimes does in startling places, we are inclined to regard the lucky character as more royal than royalty.

(11) We apply the titles of Kings and Queens to our successful athletes, as expressions of a belief in their fortunate birth, anointed and under a lucky star. Thus Ruth was always and always will be the King of Swat, a distinct and royal personage to whom the ordinary rules of life do not seem to apply. For among the other blessings with which he was apparently showered when he entered this world—blessings which, it is true, were not apparent at the time—was the gift of being able to deliver where there was something important at stake, when it meant the most, when the greatest number of eyes were upon him. We admire this trait greatly, and all our fictional heroes are endowed with it. They always come through at the right time, just as Ruth hit his home run for the sick boy the day he promised to do so (Paul Gallico, "His Majesty the King").

The first paragraph in the selection deals entirely with one trait of Babe Ruth's character—his deep and unaffected sincerity—and is expressed in a series of generalizations which the author needs to support with specific evidence if he is to make the point of the paragraph clear and convincing to us. Paragraphs 3 and 4, accordingly, present an important incident from Ruth's career to illustrate his sincerity. The purpose of the second paragraph is simply to build a bridge between the generalizations of paragraph 1 and the illustrative incident told of in paragraphs 3 and 4. It shows us the relationship between what has gone before and what is to follow, and gives the background information that we need to understand the incident. This sort of paragraph, common in expository writing, is called *a transitional paragraph,* since its purpose is to connect the paragraphs on either side of it. The third paragraph begins with the incident itself and tells only of the Senator's speech. The fourth paragraph, though still concerned with the incident, presents a different part of it—the Babe's reaction to the speech—and goes on to tell what influence this episode had on Ruth's career. In this way, the material of paragraphs 3 and 4 is tied in with that of paragraph 1; we are now ready to agree with the author's statement that Ruth was an unusually sincere man.

Since all four of these paragraphs are closely connected (generalizations, transition, supporting evidence), they could have been written as a single long paragraph if the author had wanted to do so. The result, however, would have affected us quite differently; we would have found it harder to follow the development of the author's thought because we would have lacked the benefit of the indentions, which mark the main shifts in the development.

Up to the end of paragraph 4, the essay has dealt mostly with Babe Ruth's character and background. From this point on, the essay discusses Ruth as a ballplayer. Paragraph 5, therefore, which introduces this section, presents a series of statistics about the Babe's professional career to show us how outstandingly successful he was. But, since statistics by themselves are likely to strike most readers as abstract and dry, Gallico follows this paragraph with others that try to bring the statistics alive and give us the feeling of what it was like to watch this great player in action. The sixth is again a transitional paragraph, bridging the gap between the statistics and the descriptions of Ruth batting and throwing. Paragraph 7 shows us a picture of Ruth swinging and missing; the next paragraph tells us about the crowd's reactions to his strikeouts and to his incredibly long and accurate throws; and the ninth paragraph, after mentioning the way spectators greeted Ruth's home runs, goes on to offer an explanation of the reaction and of the man's great popularity, thus tying the series of paragraphs together and leading into the more general discussion of Ruth's greatness in the last two paragraphs of the selection.

The eleventh paragraph, which discusses Babe Ruth's right to the title "the King of Swat," leads directly into the conclusion of the essay, a detailed example of his ability "to deliver where there was something important at stake." The short tenth paragraph might have been combined with the eleventh, since both deal with the same subject—Babe Ruth as a great popular hero. The most likely reason why the author has made it a separate paragraph is that he believes the two statements in it are important, for they sum up and explain Ruth's great appeal for the American public. Wanting to make these statements stand out so that we will realize their importance, Gallico has paragraphed them separately and in this way attracts our attention to them. This is another device often used in expository writing: making a separate paragraph out of an especially important sentence or two in order to emphasize them for the reader.

On the basis of this analysis, we can now make a few summarizing statements about purposes served by paragraphs in exposition.

PAR 5   *Use a paragraph to mark a transition in expository writing*

Occasional paragraphs, usually rather short ones, are used to indicate relationships between paragraphs on either side. They are called *transitional paragraphs.*

PAR 6   *Use a short paragraph for emphasis*

Sometimes a separate paragraph is made up of one or two sentences that contain ideas that the writer thinks particularly significant.

PAR 7   *In general, use paragraphs in exposition to mark stages in the development of your thought*

Most expository paragraphs contain material that the writer wants us to see as a unit, material related to the paragraphs on either side but also in one way or another different from the material in adjoining paragraphs. The author, sensing this difference and wanting us to be aware of it also, "punctuates" the material for our convenience by putting it into a separate paragraph. The difference may be the result of the author's introducing and developing a single distinct idea, as in the fifth paragraph of the Gallico selection, which develops the statement that "Ruth's baseball record is a remarkable one. . . ." Or the difference may be due to the author's desire to combine two or more ideas that in his opinion are so closely related that they need to be placed together in the same paragraph; an example is paragraph 9, which describes the way the crowd behaved when Ruth hit a home run, analyzes their behavior, and goes on to discuss the nature of hero worship.

PAR 8   *Paragraphs in exposition should be unified*

More often than not, the unity of an expository paragraph is emphasized by a generalization (or "topic sentence") that indicates the purpose of the paragraph or summarizes its thought, though sometimes the generalization is in a nearby paragraph instead. Occasionally such a generalization is lacking, but in this case the material and purpose of the paragraph are so distinct that a suitable generalization could easily be supplied; that is, the generalization is implied rather than stated directly.

DESCRIPTIVE PARAGRAPHS

Perhaps most description is embedded in paragraphs that contain other kinds of material, usually narration but sometimes exposition. There are, however, occasional paragraphs of "pure" description. Here, for example, is a paragraph (not among those already quoted) in which Paul Gallico describes Babe Ruth's appearance:

> He is six feet in height, or close to it, with an unshapely body that features a tremendous, barrel-shaped torso that tapers down into too small legs and an amazingly fragile and delicate pair of ankles. But his head is even more remarkable. It is enormous, too large even for his big bulky frame. His eyes are brown, small, and deep sunk, but clear and bright. His nose is flat and pushed in. Nobody did it for him; it grew that way. It gives him a quaintly appealing porcine look, emphasized by the little, glittering eyes. His mouth is large and thick-lipped and featured by fine white teeth. His hair is a dark brown, almost black, and crisp and curling.

Notice that this paragraph is made up entirely of related details, related not only because they all refer to the same man but especially because they all point to one conclusion: that Babe Ruth was far from handsome. The structure, in other words, is that of an expository paragraph; its purpose is furnishing supporting evidence for several generalizations made in the paragraph just before:

> . . . George Herman Ruth is not sculptured after the model of the hero. He is one of the ugliest men I have ever known. He was kneaded, rough-thumbed out of earth, a golem, a figurine that might have been made by a savage.

Sometimes descriptive material is woven into a narrative pattern, as in this passage describing the preparations being made by a group of Confederate soldiers to hang three Union captives:

There were twelve or fifteen men with their horses, and at that moment three others rode up and dismounted. In the light of a pine-knot that a negro held up she could see that they were Confederate cavalry. Some of them had gray uniforms, some no coats. On two horses and on an old mule she saw men, and at the same moment saw that their uniforms were blue. The clothes of all three were dirty and torn, two of them wore caps. They were not astride but, with the men cursing at them, were trying to stand up in the saddles. A soldier who was trying to throw ropes over the boughs of a post-oak swore at the negro for not holding the torch higher. The flare of the pine-knot struck all around, and even from that distance she could hear where birds flew upward from the trees around. Meanwhile the officer who directed the hanging was stepping back and forth, giving orders and cursing at the prisoners. He was a middle-aged man in a better uniform than the rest, and wore a black felt hat with the wide brim turned straight up in front. He looked in a fury, and then, as the preparations neared completion, grew quieter, until finally he stood motionless, watching relentlessly what went on. The officer's silence affected his men, who were now silent, looking at him, at the men on the horses, and at the tree limbs above where the ropes were being thrown. In the moment of stillness Sallie Bedford heard the little noises in the grass near her, the small innocent life going on, and faintly a bird calling, far down toward the end of the avenue (Stark Young, *So Red the Rose*).

At times descriptive material makes up a large part of a paragraph in which both expository and narrative methods have been combined. Here is an example:

I looked up with interest at the new face in the lantern-light. He might have stepped out of the pages of "Jesse James." He wore a sombrero hat, with a wide leather band and a bright buckle, and the ends of his moustache were twisted up stiffly, like little horns. He looked lively and ferocious, I thought, and as if he had a history. A long scar ran across one cheek and drew the corner of his mouth up in a sinister curl. The top of his left ear was gone, and his skin was brown as an Indian's. Surely this was the face of a desperado. As he walked about the platform in his high-heeled boots, looking for our trunks, I saw that he was a rather slight man, quick and wiry, and light on his feet. He told us we had a long night drive ahead of us, and had better be on the hike. He led us to a hitching-bar where two farm-wagons were tied, and I saw the foreign family crowding into one of them. The other was for us. Jake got on the front seat with Otto Fuchs, and

I rode on the straw in the bottom of the wagon-box, covered up with a buffalo hide. The immigrants rumbled off into the empty darkness, and we followed them (Willa Cather, *My Antonia*).

Notice that the second sentence of the paragraph is a generalization, which is supported by descriptive details, but that a time relationship controls most of the rest of the paragraph.

We can say, then, that as a rule descriptive paragraphs are organized on the pattern either of expository or of narrative paragraphs, or some combination of the two.

Remember that the decision to begin or end a paragraph at a certain point is not made according to hard-and-fast rules, nor on the other hand is it made by flipping a coin. Rather, it is based on the writer's clear awareness of what he wants to say and how he can best say it in order to lead his readers to a full understanding of his ideas and the relationships among them. Your English teacher will sometimes disagree with your paragraphing, saying you should have begun a new paragraph at one place or should not have done so at another. You should realize that when he makes such criticisms he is not penalizing you because you have broken certain "laws." Instead, he is telling you that he, as a skilled and practiced reader, believes that you have misjudged some of the relations of your ideas and the effect that a certain arrangement of ideas into paragraphs will have on your reader.

The next chapter will help you further by showing in more detail the characteristics of good paragraphs.

EXERCISES

1. Examine the following selections. What does each paragraph accomplish and why did the author begin and end each paragraph where he did? Can you find a generalization which covers each paragraph? If it isn't stated explicitly, can you write the implied generalization which covers each paragraph?

    (a) An oak tree may seem a world in itself. It may have hundreds of organisms of dozens of kinds that depend on it for food; it may give support to Spanish moss and other epiphytes; protection to birds that nest in its branches. The leaves that it drops decay, and the characteristics of the litter of oak leaves may determine the kind of soil organisms, and the direction of soil development.

    But this complex of organisms does not form a community. It is not an intelligible unit of study. If we start to analyze the relationships of the various organisms associated with the oak tree, we find ourselves constantly led away from that association into some larger grouping. The caterpillars that feed on the oak leaves are developmental stages of a butterfly that gets food from the goldenrod in a clearing. The birds nesting in the oak tree forage through the nearby forest, and their behavior cannot be understood in terms of the tree, but only in terms of the forest. Similarly, we find that the association of organisms in the soil depends not so much on the fact that they are under an oak tree, as on being part of the oak forest.

Our biotic community, then, is the forest, not the association in the tree. The complex of organisms making up the forest does form an intelligible field of study, where the events and relationships can be understood with only casual and occasional reference to external phenomena. The range of the birds nesting in our particular tree depends on the relations with birds in neighboring trees, on the "territory" in the forest that is available for each family. The kind of food that they are able to gather depends on a selection from the kinds available in the forest. The number of caterpillars of a given kind eating the leaves of the oak tree depends on the density of population of that particular species in the forest, which is a matter of balance of parasites, climatic relations, and so forth. The characteristics of the forest as a whole can be related to the regional climate, to the physical and chemical factors of the general environment. The climate within the forest can be understood in relation to the density and the size of the trees. The forest constitutes a biotic community (Marston Bates, *The Nature of Natural History*).

(b) The most remarkable man I have ever known in my life was my uncle Edward Philip Leacock—known to ever so many people in Winnipeg fifty or sixty years ago as E. P. His character was so exceptional that it needs nothing but plain narration. It was so exaggerated already that you couldn't exaggerate it.

When I was a boy of six, my father brought us, a family flock, to settle on an Ontario farm. We lived in an isolation unknown, in these days of radio, anywhere in the world. We were thirty-five miles from a railway. There were no newspapers. Nobody came and went. There was nowhere to come to. In the solitude of the dark winter nights the stillness was that of eternity.

Into this isolation there broke, two years later, my dynamic Uncle Edward, my father's younger brother. He had just come from a year's travel around the Mediterranean. He must have been about twenty-eight, but seemed a more than adult man, bronzed and self-confident, with a square beard like a Plantagenet King. His talk was of Algiers, of the African slave market; of the Golden Horn and the Pyramids. To us it sounded like the *Arabian Nights*. When we asked, "Uncle Edward, do you know the Prince of Wales?" he answered, "Quite intimately"—with no further explanation. It was an impressive trick he had.

In that year, 1878, there was a general election in Canada. E. P. was in it up to the neck in less than no time. He picked up the history and politics of Upper Canada in a day, and in a week knew everybody in the countryside. He spoke at every meeting, but his strong point was the personal contact of electioneering, of barroom treats. This gave full scope for his marvellous talent for flattery and make-believe.

"Why, let me see"—he would say to some tattered country specimen beside him glass in hand—"surely, if your name is Framley, you must be a relation of my dear old friend General Sir Charles Framley of the Horse Artillery?" "Mebbe," the flattered specimen would answer. "I guess, mebbe; I ain't kept track very good of my folks in the old country." "Dear me! I must tell Sir Charles that I've seen you. He'll be so pleased." . . . In this way in a fortnight E. P. had conferred honours and distinctions on half the township of Georgina. They lived in a recaptured atmosphere of generals, admirals and earls. Vote? How else could they vote than conservative, men of family like them? (Stephen Leacock, "My Remarkable Uncle").

2. Following are some passages with the paragraph indentations omitted. Indicate where you feel paragraphs should begin, and give reasons for placing them as you do.

(a) Scientists have generally adopted the name "tsunami," from the Japanese, for the misnamed tidal wave. It ranks among the most terrifying phenomena known to man and has been responsible for some of the worst disasters in human history. What made the 1946 tsunami especially notable was that a number of oceanographers happened to be in the Pacific (in connection with the Bikini atomic bomb test) and were able to observe it at first hand. It became the most thoroughly investigated tsunami in history, and from it came the development of an effective new warning system by the U. S. Coast and Geodetic Survey. A tsunami may be started by a seabottom slide, an earthquake or a volcanic eruption. The most infamous of all was launched by the explosion of the island of Krakatoa in 1883; it raced across the Pacific at 300 miles an hour, devastated the coasts of Java and Sumatra with waves 100 to 130 feet high and pounded the shore as far away as San Francisco. The ancient Greeks recorded several catastrophic inundations by huge waves. Whether or not Plato's tale of the lost continent of Atlantis is true, skeptics concede that the myth may have some foundation in a great tsunami of ancient times. Indeed, a tremendously destructive tsunami that arose in the Arabian Sea in 1945 has even revived the interest of biologists and archaeologists in the Biblical story of the Flood. One of the most damaging tsunamis on record followed the famous Lisbon earthquake of November 1, 1755; its waves persisted for a week and were felt as far away as the English coast. Tsunamis are rare, however, in the Atlantic Ocean; they are far more common in the Pacific. Japan has had fifteen destructive ones (eight of them disastrous) since 1596. The Hawaiian Islands are struck severely an average of once every 25 years (Joseph Bernstein, "Tsunamis").

(b) Only the light at the top of the stairs was lighted, but the switch was just beside the door. There was a smell of fresh floor wax from the living room, and a moist smell in the dining room from Nancy's potted plants. "Charley," Nancy said, "isn't it a lovely house?" "Yes, it's a swell house," Charles said. Nancy had taken off her evening wrap and was straightening her hair by the mirror. "I know it's got outs about it," Nancy said, "but don't forget one thing. You and I did this by ourselves, without any so-and-so to help us. I suppose you think it's a corny thing to say, but that's why it's a nice house." Of course, the appearance of any house depended on one's state of mind, and now he was feeling more cheerful. "And now come in and look at the living room floor," Nancy said. "Do you want a glass of milk before you go to bed?" The last thing he wanted was a glass of milk, but then Nancy had known that he had taken a drink after dinner (John P. Marquand, *Point of No Return*).

3. Criticize the paragraphing in the following student theme, saying why you think it is good or bad. If it is not good, make the revisions you think necessary to improve it.

Uncle Walter

One of the kindest men I have ever known was my Uncle Walter. He wasn't my uncle but ever since I could talk I knew him as Uncle Walter. He was better than an uncle in many ways as he was always there when I needed someone to talk to.

We lived in the country and Uncle Walter and his wife Mabel lived directly across the road from our house. When my brothers and I were small we often went to Uncle Walter's and played in the swing tied in one of the great cedar trees growing in his yard. If he wasn't busy in the fields he would push the swing for us; and when we tired of that he would tell us stories about the surrounding countryside's history.

He told us there had once been a town where we lived and he showed us where the old school house, blacksmith shop, and saloon had been located. We often went to the old graveyard that was in a corner of one of his fields and looked at the epitaphs on the grave markers. He once took us to a high cottonwood tree on the banks of Slate Creek and showed us where three horse thieves had been hanged.

Occasionally we would go to the Chisholm Trail, which was one-quarter of a mile away, and hunt for arrowheads while he told us stories so vividly that we could almost imagine ourselves taking part in them.

Whatever we did together was always fun, whether hunting, fishing, fixing fence, or shucking corn. In the winter he would pull my brothers and me on a sled behind his horses, with the snow from the horses' hooves flying in our faces. Uncle Walter introduced me to many of the beauties of nature. It was he who first showed me a nest of baby rabbits nestled in the green grass of a small grove of trees behind his house. One evening when my younger brother cut his forehead and my parents took him to the doctor, we sat on the open porch of Uncle Walter's house and he pointed out some of the constellations to us. At the time I didn't realize how fortunate I was, but now as I look back I realize my brothers and I were three of the luckiest boys on earth to have known Uncle Walter.

One day while I was at school Uncle Walter had a heart attack. He was in bed for two months, but he always kept busy and interested in what was going on. When I visited him in the hospital the day before he passed away, he asked me about the World Series and said he would soon be out of bed to see it.

That was Uncle Walter, always cheerful and kind even when he knew death was just around the corner. Since he has died our neighbor has destroyed the grave stones and plowed up the old grave yard, but the memories of Uncle Walter will never be destroyed. You can't destroy memories of a great man.

8

WRITING GOOD
PARAGRAPHS

The last chapter tried to give you a somewhat different point of view toward paragraphs from the one you may have had, a point of view based on the notion of paragraphs as a sort of punctuation intended, like other devices of punctuation, to help the writer communicate his ideas clearly and effectively. Now we need to look at some of the problems you will encounter in writing good paragraphs.

The first of these problems is how to develop a paragraph, how to find what to say in a paragraph and how to say it. Actually, paragraph development is mainly an aspect of the process of gathering and selecting material. That is, in order to develop a paragraph, you must first have something that you want to say and know with some exactness what it is. This process has already been discussed in Chapter 4, but we need to consider it again, this time specifically as it relates to the development of paragraphs in narrative and in exposition.

Developing Narrative Paragraphs

When you are composing paragraphs in a narrative, two circumstances make the job a little easier than it would be if you were writing an expository paper: the main principle of organization (the order in which things happened) is already known to you; and you have a definite story to tell. That is, you know pretty clearly what you want to say, as well as the order in which you want to say it.

Two problems remain, however, that you must pay particular attention to when you write narrative paragraphs. One concerns the best sort of material to use in developing narrative paragraphs; the other, proper grouping of material into paragraphs.

USING SIGNIFICANT DETAILS

PAR 9   *Use significant details to develop paragraphs in narrative*

In writing a narrative you must remember that you want to make the account as clear and real to your readers as possible. This means that you can seldom be satisfied simply with giving the bare outline of what happened; you will need to write paragraphs that include plenty of details, the sort that will bring the story alive for your readers.

Here are some student paragraphs that suffer from a lack of enough significant details:

> Fortunately, my choice of fraternities narrowed to only two, but somehow I was halfway pledged to both of them. While I was in one I seemed to favor it the most; as soon as I reached the other, I changed my mind.
> The rushing committees of both houses gave me sales talks at such a prodigious rate that only when I was alone could I do any constructive thinking. When two days had passed, I finally reached a decision and pledged the fraternity of my choice.
>
>   ❈   ❈   ❈
>
> The only trouble was that we were not ready for a cloudburst. I have no idea how much rain fell, but it was a lot and we were just not prepared to cope with it. Our camp was a mess. It took us all the next day to repair the damage.

Notice in the first two paragraphs that the experience of fraternity rushing is presented in such general terms that we never get a clear idea of such significant matters as the good and bad points of the two fraternities, the nature of the sales talks, the men who made these talks and the circumstances under which they were made, and finally the particular house that the writer chose and the reasons why he chose it. Lack of details cripples the other paragraph also; the results of the cloudburst are not described in enough detail to present a clear picture.

Contrast with these paragraphs the following student theme, in which details have been effectively used in developing narrative paragraphs:

To Catch a Fish

Ever since I was a small boy I have enjoyed fishing. My dad owns eighty acres of grassland that is cut into two jagged pieces by the muddy, winding Rattlesnake Creek. This stream is the home of one of the most delectable foods that nature has to offer, the channel catfish.

Summer nights spent fishing here had given me relaxation, peace of mind, and pleasant memories; but they had never seemed to supply me with many catfish. I was getting something good for the soul but nothing fit for the frying pan. My problem seemed ridiculously simple: to outwit a mere fish.

But, as I exhausted every possible strategy, I decided that the problem was not so simple. The "mere fish" was outwitting me. I had unsuccessfully tried every kind of bait that I could think of: blood bait, frogs, earthworms, crayfish, minnows, and even grasshoppers. I had tried bank line, trot line, rod and reel, and flyrod in every combination; but none of them worked consistently. I had tried fishing on moonlit nights and dark nights, on nights when the barometer was rising and nights when the barometer was falling. It made no difference. My conclusion was that successful fishing depended on some mystic power which I obviously lacked.

After a typically unsuccessful evening of fishing last summer, I decided that the fish "just weren't hungry." I had begun packing my tackle in the trunk of the car when I saw a battered old pickup bouncing toward me. It came to a jerky stop beside me and discharged a friendly looking old man dressed in dirty striped overalls and a faded blue shirt. "Had any luck?" he asked.

I replied that I hadn't and expressed doubt that anyone could catch fish on such a night. "They just aren't biting," I said.

Instead of answering, he grinned and pulled a bulging gunny sack from the back of his truck. It was full of catfish! Before I could ask how he had caught them, he said, "Guess I'll try it again tomorrow night. Like to go along?" I jumped at the chance. At last I could learn an expert's secret of success.

The next evening we met as planned. I had a rod and reel, a bundle of bank lines, and several jars and cans of assorted baits; he had only two cane poles, one of which he handed to me, and a bucket of frogs. "Frogs are best this time of year," he explained. I didn't believe him, for I had tried frogs only the night before and hadn't had even a nibble on them. Then I saw how he fastened them by threading the hook and leader through their hind legs so they would seem to be actually swimming through the water. Maybe frogs really would work.

We walked over to the bank. I was just about to throw in my line at a deep-looking spot when the old fellow stopped me. He proceeded to test the depth by sticking his pole in the water; it was only two feet deep. I wondered why I had never thought of finding the deep holes this way. Finally, I found a good hole and, standing on the edge of the bank, began fishing. I was stopped again. "You'll never ketch any that way," he said. "Them fish can see you there as plain as day. Get farther back from the bank." Another reason for my previous failures had been disclosed. I saw that it was necessary to use my head even if I was only trying to outwit a catfish.

Two hours later the old man's gunny sack again contained a fine mess of fish; and I had caught some of them! From now on, fishing could be more than an enjoyable experience in the open air for me. At last I could have a good time and eat it, too.

The use of significant details in narrative paragraphs will help you to gain and keep your reader's interest as well as enable you to communicate fully what you have to say. The story you are telling will come alive. It will seem as significant and interesting to your reader as it did to you when you decided to write about it.

GROUPING MATERIAL INTO NARRATIVE PARAGRAPHS

Besides taking care to use details effectively in developing narrative paragraphs, you must be sure to study the nature of your material to see how it can best be arranged into paragraphs—what to include within a single paragraph, and when to end it and start another. We talked about this in the last chapter when we analyzed the Hemingway selection to discover the main purposes of narrative paragraphs, but some examples of student paragraphs that are defective in this respect may help you to guard against the difficulty.

PAR 10   *Do not use fewer paragraph divisions than your material requires*

The following excerpt from a theme shows too few paragraph divisions; the writer has ignored distinct changes in the movement of the story, each of which ought to have been marked by a new paragraph.

> What a shock Thanksgiving vacation was to me! This long-awaited first trip home from college could hardly have been more of a surprise and, in some ways, a disappointment. Even though I expected some changes in my family, my friends, and myself, I hardly imagined that three short months could bring about such remarkable differences. When my parents met me at the train station I was full of college experiences that I knew they would want to hear all about as we drove the twenty miles to our house. Unfortunately, I didn't get a chance

to tell them anything about myself. It seems that my younger sister, Polly, has been running around with a girl my parents don't approve of and has been staying out too late for a girl of fifteen. Nearly all the way home I had to listen to a catalog of Polly's misdemeanors and my parents' worries about her. Because she and I have always been very close, my parents wanted me to talk to her and make her realize that they have her own best interests at heart. Well, Polly was waiting for us at home, and after the first excited greeting we went upstairs to her room so we could talk and catch up on the last three months. It wasn't long until I discovered that I don't know my sister as well as I thought. We had both been doing entirely different things for three months, living in totally different environments, associating with different people. It was almost like talking to a stranger. She kept talking about high school clubs and her own friends and a dreamy sixteen-year-old she has been dating, all of which suddenly struck me as childish. Forgetting about the heart-to-heart talk my parents wanted me to have with Polly, I found myself anxious to talk about myself and what I had been doing. But it was hard: my sister hasn't the faintest idea where Watkins Hall and the University Library and the Campanile are; or who Carol Jameson and President Dougherty and Mother Williams are; or how grim chemistry labs can be and how distinguished Professor Maximilian looks. Conversation that is mainly definitions and explanations can get pretty boring. The next day I found myself involved in another boring conversation, and again it came as a surprise to me. About ten girls from my high school class got together that afternoon but we didn't seem to have anything in common to talk about any more. We spent a couple of hours telling the latest jokes we had picked up, but I'm afraid I found the time passing slowly and dully. We couldn't even discuss current events, for we had all been too busy leading our own self-centered little lives to notice what had been going on in the world around us. I finally said goodbye rather self-consciously and drifted away feeling dissatisfied.

As you will see, the long second paragraph should be divided in three. The sentence beginning "Well, Polly was waiting for us at home" should start a new paragraph, and the one that begins "The next day I found myself" should begin another. In both cases, a new part of the story is presented; each of the divisions should accordingly be marked with paragraph indentions.

PAR 11   *Do not use more paragraph divisions than your material requires*

The next excerpt shows the opposite fault: too many paragraph divisions. Instead of grouping related details and parts of the action within paragraphs so that the reader can follow the progress of the story easily, the writer has used many little paragraphs without much regard to the relations among details and thus has increased the difficulty of reading.

I didn't want to make this trip in the first place, for I had planned a ten-day leave to the States.

Unfortunately, I was not given any choice in the matter. I had just reconciled myself to the idea when I noticed on the base operations board that our aircraft would be none other than the one everybody called "Unlucky Lady."

This plane was a C-119, commonly known as a flying boxcar. We had had this ship assigned to us for nearly a year but it still hadn't flown more than four hundred hours. Some mechanical difficulty was always occurring just about at takeoff time.

I knew for sure now that I would not enjoy the trip.

When the time came to board the ship I looked with distrust at the big pot-bellied craft and its two huge engines. Nevertheless I entered with the ten other passengers and settled myself uneasily in a bucket seat.

The hatch was slammed shut and we taxied out to the approach strip. There the co-pilot revved up the engines while the pilot checked the instruments and obtained takeoff clearance from the control tower.

The engines sounded fine to me as we sped down the runway and took to the air.

We circled the field once, then headed northeast over the Caribbean Sea. Everything seemed to be going smoothly. I started to relax with the book I had brought with me to pass the time. We had been airborne about an hour when it happened.

The port engine started sputtering; one glance at it told us what was wrong.

The engine had developed an oil leak, which caused a tremendous amount of thick black smoke to stream behind us. We all crawled to that side of the ship and were staring worriedly out the portholes when suddenly the ship turned on its side and went into a steep dive.

All the passengers, including me, were thrown heavily to the floor. I was so shaken up that at first I didn't realize that the abandon-ship siren was howling. We had been issued parachutes before we boarded the ship but none of us had his on. I didn't bother to look for my own parachute but just grabbed the one nearest me.

I was so scared (mostly of having to jump, I think) that it seemed like hours before I could get my chute buckled. I was making my way to the forward jump hatch when the engine finally took hold again. I don't know what magic the pilot had worked, but we pulled out of the dive and started back toward land.

I could sense that the men around me were praying that this lopsided plane would make it back to the base.

It would be a useful exercise for you to rewrite this theme, improving the paragraphing.

EXERCISE

1. Where, in your opinion, should the paragraph divisions come in the following excerpt from student writing? Give reasons for your choices.

The formerly inefficient enrollment procedures at my University have been greatly aided by the installation of electronic computing equipment. Just how those procedures have been aided is at present hard to determine; however, there are several possibilities. One is that the machines have made confusion more mechanical and more efficient. Another is that those students who are running the machines are getting their calculus problems done without working too hard. Still another possibility is that someone in the University got a big kickback from the manufacturer on the sale of the machines. It is true, though, that there are advantages to the new system. For instance, English classes did not meet for nearly two days because the machines did not have class information ready. Even now, five days after enrollment, teachers in most departments do not have lists of persons supposed to be in their classes. The enrolling itself was designed to be very efficient, I am sure. But it did not work that way. In certain areas bottlenecks developed and personnel were swamped while in other areas workers had nothing to do. Most of those who were scheduled to enroll at 11:00 or 1:30 were caught in long lines when lunch time was declared and all the workers left for at least an hour. Thus those poor students trying to finish enrollment faced two choices: go to lunch and lose their place in line, or do without lunch. Those who left and lost their place became bitter toward the administration because they had to wait another two hours in the afternoon; those who stayed became even more bitter because they were famished by the time they were completely enrolled. Enrollment was confusing this semester, but for next semester the administration is thinking about getting more machines. This addition will undoubtedly make enrollment even more confusing.

Developing Expository Paragraphs

Both in your freshman English class and in your other courses in college, you will be called on to write a great many more expository paragraphs than narrative paragraphs. You will probably find that in general it is harder to manage paragraphs in exposition than in narrative, because most narrative paragraphs have a single principle of organization —the time relationship—whereas expository paragraphs are organized according to a greater variety of relations among the ideas they contain.

METHODS OF DEVELOPING EXPOSITORY PARAGRAPHS

To make more clear exactly how a writer develops paragraphs in expository prose, let us analyze several paragraphs from the passage already quoted from Paul Gallico's essay on Babe Ruth:

> This is perhaps the greatest truth about the Babe—that no matter how phony or drippingly sentimental the situation in which he found himself might be, whether it was the outcome of natural instincts on his part to be kind or whether it was as carefully stage-managed as the first visit of a cub columnist to the home of a particularly vicious prizefighter, Ruth was always the honest and sincere element in the situation. He, if no one else, believed in it and played it up to the hilt, not ever for his own personal gain or glory or to build up an elaborate false character to be sold to his public, but because he believed that that was the kind of person he was. His generosity and his affections were just as Gargantuan as his appetites.

The three sentences in this paragraph are all *generalizations,* statements of the author's opinions about one aspect of Babe Ruth's character. All three say nearly the same thing but in different words. The method of development used is *repetition,* although the first sentence contains a *comparison.* This paragraph looks ahead to the ones that follow, for the author understands that we will not be content to accept these generalizations on trust but will want some evidence to support them.

> Consider for instance the brilliantly phony plea to Babe Ruth made by his friend Senator Jimmy Walker at a baseball writers' banquet at the close of the season during which Ruth had been a particularly bad boy, had broken training, had quarreled with Miller Huggins, his manager, had been fined and suspended and sent home, had, in short, acted the part of a spoiled, willful, naughty brat.

This paragraph, which consists of a single sentence, is as we noted earlier, a *transitional paragraph* linking the first one with the third and fourth. It consists mostly of background details that we need to know if we are to understand fully the incident told of in the next two paragraphs.

> The Senator rose to speak in a banquet hall filled with tough, hard-boiled, worldly-wise baseball-writers whose daily job it is to peddle treacle about the baseball heroes and soft-pedal the sour stuff, baseball managers, perhaps as tough and hard a group of men as there is

in sports, celebrities of every kind; and he made a personal plea to Babe Ruth to reform himself and behave because he owed it to the dirty-faced kids in the streets who worshipped him; the Babe, he said, had a great responsibility to the youth of the country and he must not shirk it!

The over-all method of development here is *example,* but we find *descriptive details* about baseball writers, the author's opinion of these men (a *generalization*), and *narrative facts* (the report of the Senator's argument).

It was maudlin; it was in some ways cheap and tear-jerking. But, as I have suggested, it was likewise brilliant, and the brittle, hard, cynical Senator of the State of New York knew what he was doing. Because Ruth robbed it of all cheapness, of all sensationalism, or everything that was vulgarly maudlin, by getting to his feet and, with tears streaming down his big, ugly face, promising the dirty-faced kids of the nation to behave—for their sake. And then he kept his promise. He was never in trouble again. From that time on he began to learn a little about moderation and restraint. Nor did it make him any the less a picturesque character, because he never went sissy or holy on the boys. He retained all of his appetites and gusto for living. He merely toned them down. He learned what every celebrity in the United States eventually must learn—to perform his peccadillos in strict privacy if possible. Formerly Ruth had perpetrated his right out in public.

Like the paragraph just before, this one is composite, partly expository and partly narrative. It is developed by *generalizations, narrative facts, descriptive details*—and, toward the first of the paragraph, by *contrast* (the difference between the cynical Walker and the naïve Ruth).

Ruth's baseball record is a remarkable one and deserves inclusion even in such an informal estimate of him as this. He has an all-time total of 708 home runs and 723 homers, adding those he hit in World Series. He holds the record for the most home runs hit in one season: namely, 60, scored in 1927 in a season of 151 league games. He likewise holds the world's record for the total number of bases on balls during a playing career, 2,036, an indication of what the opposing pitchers thought of him. For twelve years he led his American League in home runs hit, and for eleven years hit forty or more out of the park each season. There are dozens of other minor records that one could dig out of the files and the record-books, all connected with his prodigious hitting, such as runs batted in, runs scored, extra base hits, and so on; but they still remain dusty figures and reveal nothing of the manner of his making these numbers—numbers which in two or three generations will be all that will remain of George Herman Ruth, except legend.

This paragraph begins with a *generalization* broad enough to include nearly all the rest of the material presented; the generalization is developed by a series of statistics (*facts*). The last half of the last sentence, which contains not more facts but opinions of the author, leads directly into the paragraphs that follow, pointing out that mere dry statistics fail to give a real picture of Ruth's greatness; the next four paragraphs bring the statistics alive by showing us the Babe in action.

We could go on to analyze the remaining paragraphs in the selection, or we could quote and analyze paragraphs by other writers besides Gallico. For our purposes here, however, the five we have looked at can be considered a typical enough sample to suggest several conclusions.

First, a variety of specific methods may be used to develop expository paragraphs: *repetition, comparison, contrast, details, examples, illustrations, facts, generalizations.* A little further analysis would allow us to add to the list such others as *cause, effect, definition, inductive reasoning, deductive reasoning.* Expository paragraphs can be, but certainly need not be, developed by any one of these methods alone. As a matter of fact, paragraphs in which two or more methods are combined are much more often seen than ones developed by a single method.

Second, good expository paragraphs, as we have already seen in the last chapter, are unified in their content and purpose, often having a "topic sentence" that emphasizes this unity. But narrative, expository, and descriptive material may all be combined within the same paragraph if the writer's purpose calls for such a combination and if the material is closely related.

Finally, if we try to reconstruct Gallico's reasons for developing his paragraphs in the particular ways he did, we must conclude that, as he wrote, his attention was fixed firmly on *what he wanted to say and how he could best say it to the sort of readers he was writing for.* He was trying to do the best job he could of communicating his ideas to a definite audience. If he had used a key term that he thought would be unfamiliar to his readers, or had used a familiar term in a special sense, he would have devoted a paragraph to defining it. If he had thought that his readers would get a clearer notion of Ruth's character by seeing it compared with that of some other famous ballplayer, he might have written a paragraph developed entirely by comparison.

PAR 12 *Concentrate less on specific methods of para-graph development and more on what you want to say and how you can best say it to your readers*

THE DANGER OF OVERGENERALIZING

PAR 13 *Do not overgeneralize; support generalizations with appropriate material*

Paragraphs made up entirely of generalizations are not uncommon in good writing, but nearly always they are either preceded or followed by other paragraphs containing the supporting material on which they depend. The first four paragraphs quoted from Gallico earlier in this chapter furnish an example. Many student writers compose not only paragraphs but sometimes entire themes of generalizations, forgetting to include the necessary supporting material. This habit of overgeneralizing is, in fact, one of the most frequent and most serious weaknesses in student writing. Here is a typical example:

The Purpose of an Education

Acquiring an education is a process that never stops. Obviously, since a human being can't know everything or do everything, one of the most important things an education should do for him is to make him realize what is worth learning or doing. He has to know what is possible, what is worth trying even when it seems impossible, and what is not worth doing. Since he must realize that he can never be completely right about anything, he must be awake to new ideas and he must be able to evaluate them intelligently.

A good education helps a person to understand the viewpoints of other people and groups of people and makes him realize what is going on in the world around him. Of course, sympathizing with everyone's point of view not only is not possible but even is not right. But most people have never heard of many interests and opinions present in the world. It is important to know enough about enough things to realize what the world is really like and what a person can do himself to improve the worst parts.

An education should teach a person to think for himself. In fact, the whole idea of a good education is the unending collection of facts, ideas, and opinions, and studying and thinking about them to decide their importance and relationship.

An education should teach a person how to take full advantage of his potentialities and opportunities. Not everyone is born with the same abilities; not everyone has the same amount of good luck or the same amount of reward for effort. Everyone can do something useful and everyone can accept the seeming insignificance of his own accomplishments.

To sum up, I believe that a good education is one that will enable a person to live a life satisfying to himself and as useful as possible to the world, fulfilling his possibilities as far as circumstances permit and understanding what life is about.

The author of this paper has tried to discuss a large and important subject but the result is unsatisfactory. Every paragraph in the paper is composed entirely of generalizations, each of which might have served as the nucleus of a paragraph or even a series of paragraphs. Because of overgeneralizing, the paper is hard to understand and tiresome to read; we feel that we are unable to come to grips with whatever it is that the writer actually means.

EXERCISE

2. In two of the following three paragraphs explain what part each sentence has in accomplishing the purpose of the paragraph. (In order to answer this question you will need to decide what the purpose of the paragraph is and what main idea the paragraph is developing.) The sentences have been numbered in order to help you in discussing them.

(a) 1. The migratory habits of the ant armies follow a rhythmically punctual cycle. 2. The *Eciton hanatum* species, for example, wanders nomadically for a period of 17 days, then spends 19 or 20 days in fixed bivouac. 3. This cycle coincides precisely with the reproductive cycle of the tribe. 4. The army goes into bivouac when the larvae, hatched from the last clutch of eggs, spin their cocoons and, now quiescent, approach the pupal stage. 5. At the end of the first week in permanent camp, the queen, whose abdomen has swollen to more than five times its normal volume, begins a stupendous five- to seven-day labor and delivers the 20,000 to 30,000 eggs of the next generation. 6. The daily foraging raids, which meanwhile have dwindled to a minimum, pick up again as the eggs hatch into a great mass of larvae. 7. Then, on about the 20th day, the cocoons yield a new complement of callow workers, and the army sets off once more on its evening marches (T. C. Schneirla and Gerard Piel, "The Army Ant").

(b) 1. All this is very interesting, but what about the primary objective, the development of a better technique for studying colds? 2. We cannot yet, unfortunately, report success. 3. Much effort has been devoted to cultivation of the cold virus in fertile hens' eggs, by each of several different techniques that have proved useful with other viruses. 4. No unequivocal success has been attained. 5. Nor have we succeeded in inducing colds in experimental animals. 6. We have tried rabbits, rats, mice, guinea pigs, hamsters, voles, cotton rats, gray squirrels, flying squirrels, hedgehogs, pigs, chickens, kittens, ferrets, baboons, green monkeys, capuchin monkeys, red patas monkeys and a sooty mangabey. 7. People have told us that they have observed that such-and-such an animal develops colds in captivity when in contact with human colds. 8. Such clues we have followed up, but in vain. 9. The "colds" in these animals have either not been reproducible or have seemed to be due to bacteria rather than to a true cold virus (Christopher Howard Andrews, "The Common Cold").

(c) 1. But most colleges fortunately have a philosophy different from this. 2. In most colleges, athletes must pass their courses or run the risk of probation and ineligibility. 3. In these colleges much time is spent on the guidance of athletes in an attempt to keep the men on an even keel. 4. At Columbia, for instance, nearly all of the coaches have professorial rank and attend faculty meetings, where athletic policy and academic problems are both discussed. 5. The coaches are educators, and many of them are student counselors. 6. Most colleges attempt to orient the student, athletically, by organizing an extensive intramural sports program, which ordinarily enlists the support of most of the students in games for fun, not for dollars. 7. The thoughtful freshman will put athletics into reasonable balance with his other activities (Robert U. Jameson, "How to Stay in College").

Developing Paragraphs from an Outline

To make the discussion of paragraph development more specific and therefore more helpful to you, we will look at the way in which outline headings are expanded into paragraphs. As examples for analysis, we will use two of the outlines and themes quoted earlier in this book, since you are already familiar with them.

DEVELOPING PARAGRAPHS FROM AN INFORMAL OUTLINE

As our first example, let's look at the theme written from the informal outline quoted on p. 66 of Chapter 5. First, here is the outline:

CENTRAL IDEA: The most gifted liar I've ever known was a friend of mine in high school whose highly imaginative but harmless lies were a wonderful source of entertainment to his classmates.

1. John a born liar, but improved with practice
2. Had a frank and innocent-looking face
3. His lies always amusing, never mean
4. Incident of the borrowed skillet
5. John's outline in American history class
6. His report on teen-age drinking (his best performance)
7. What John is doing now

Now read the first paragraph of the theme to see what relation it has to the outline:

Genius at Work

John was born with the ability to tell incredible lies in a really convincing manner, a gift much less common and a great deal more useful than the proverbial silver spoon. The talent of lying proficiently is one that is almost impossible to acquire, even through constant practice; it takes a certain amount of genius to lie as John did, without blushing, without faltering, and without getting trapped by one's own inventiveness. I would not, however, want you to think that John hadn't practiced. On the contrary, he had seventeen years of diligent practice behind him. Yet, confirmed liar though he was, John didn't look the part. His honest, straightforward manner and appearance made it impossible for anyone to associate him with the slick, oily characters usually thought of in connection with dishonesty. From looking at his thatch of red hair, his ginger-snap freckles, and his wide, innocent, blue eyes framed by hornrimmed glasses, it would seem ridiculous even to suspect that anything John said was not the gospel truth.

You will notice here that the paragraph develops not one but *two* of the headings in the outline. The first half of the paragraph is developed by a series of related generalizations. The second half begins with a generalization ("Yet, confirmed liar though he was . . .") and is developed by a combination of other generalizations and descriptive details.

It would have been possible to begin a new paragraph with the words "Yet, confirmed liar though he was . . .", because there is a shift here to a description of the boy's face. But the author had a good reason for writing this material as a single paragraph: his feeling that the material was so closely related that we should see and consider it together. Everything in the paragraph is introductory, preparing us for the picture of the boy that follows—generalizations about him and his special talent, and the contrast between this talent and his appearance. In the author's opinion, this contrast would be more apparent to us, and therefore more effective, if the two contrasting elements were placed side by side in the same paragraph.

Here is the second paragraph:

> John's lies were never mean. He lied for the love of the art itself, and for his own and his friends' amusement, such as the time he talked the home economics teacher into giving him a skillet from the foods laboratory. His story was that some equipment had been stolen from the journalism darkroom and that there was nothing in which negatives could be washed. John used the skillet for the conventional purpose, however, and hamburgers were sold for eighteen cents apiece that day in journalism.

This paragraph begins with two related generalizations, the second one ending with the words "his friends' amusement." The rest of the paragraph consists of a specific example (a brief narrative) to support the statements. Again, two headings in the outline have been treated in a single paragraph because they are closely related. Actually, the generalizations at the beginning of this paragraph contain the central idea of the whole paper. The author could have paragraphed them by themselves for emphasis but decided instead to support them with a short example to satisfy our desire for evidence to back them up.

Here is the third paragraph:

> At other times, John put his talent to work in various academic emergencies. When he was studying American history under a teacher about whom it was said that she weighed outlines rather than read them, he handed in an outline that must have weighed nearly a third as much as a new-born child. It was packed with interesting information, such as the somewhat surprising fact that England lost the Battle of New Orleans in the War of 1812 because the British troops wore high-laced black boots which took them so long to put on in the mornings that they were always late for a battle. The same outline also advanced the theory that the American Colonies revolted against King George III because the colonists objected to the King's un-American habits: the King was known to eat raspberry jam on mashed potatoes, and to spend an hour after lunch hanging by his knees from a low branch in the garden at Buckingham Palace. Either John presented his explanations with remarkable persuasiveness or the rumors circulating about the history teacher were true, because the outline was returned to him with an "A" on it, while less imaginative—and shorter—outlines came back with "C's."

The author has developed this paragraph exactly as he did the one before: a generalization supported by a detailed narrative example. It is represented in the outline, however, by only one heading, number 5, since the incident described is separate from those mentioned in headings 4 and 6.

We should read the next three paragraphs together:

Perhaps the most brilliant performance of John's career occurred in his American government class during his senior year. Because the semester was nearly over, the students in the class, including John, were desperately trying to raise their grades a notch or two by giving oral reports, worth five credit points each, on some topic of current interest. There was nothing unusual about the way John delivered his report; in fact, he was not an especially good speaker on such occasions, since his voice was not very loud and he always fell into a sort of singsong way of speaking when he was in front of a class. But the content of the report was electrifying. The other reports, taken usually from *Time* or *Newsweek* and inevitably concerning taxes, foreign aid, or Russia, regularly put us to sleep. But not John's report.

Material for this particular report, John informed the teacher and the class, had been taken from an article on teen-age drinking in a certain large midwestern city. (John said that for obvious reasons the city could not be identified by name.) The article, he added, had appeared in the April issue of the *Reader's Digest,* a copy of which he held in his hand. He then presented his audience with an alarming set of statistics. According to studies made during the past three years by Dr. Manuel Hernandez, the noted sociologist and criminologist, sixty per cent of the students at one of the large high schools in this city were confirmed alcoholics; of the remaining forty per cent, twenty-seven per cent drank frequently, or "socially," as John put it; five per cent drank only occasionally; and the last eight per cent were teetotalers.

Following this general information about the alcoholic content of the student body at this unfortunate high school, John presented several typical case histories, among them the unhappy case of Joe X. Joe had been drinking heavily since eighth grade—starting with rye and bourbon whisky—and now, a senior in high school and an incurable alcoholic, he had turned to vanilla extract, bay rum, and rubbing alcohol. After several more examples of the same sort, John summarized the findings of Dr. Hernandez, walked to his desk and sat down, beaming out of his thick glasses while the teacher (who must have had some pretty awful notions about the sinfulness of modern youth) nodded with an air of "Well, this is just the sort of thing you can expect nowadays" and recorded five more points by John's name in the gradebook. If any of us in the class had had sharp enough eyes, we would have seen that the table of contents of the April *Reader's Digest* from which John had apparently been reading mentioned neither teen-age drinking nor Dr. Hernandez.

These three paragraphs, mainly narrative, are represented in the outline by only one heading, number 6, and tell of only a single incident. Why did the author paragraph this material as he did? Two obvious reasons come to mind: first, if he had not divided the incident, the paragraph would have been unusually long and difficult to untangle. Second, the paragraph would have been several times longer than any of others in the paper and therefore out of proportion with the rest.

But the author had other and better reasons for his paragraphing here, reasons based directly on his material. The first of these paragraphs begins with a generalization that all three paragraphs support. The material in the first one, however, is introductory. The next paragraph introduces us to the report itself—first the background information about subject and sources that the boy gave the class, then the statistics. At this point the author began a new paragraph because the nature of the material changes from general to specific, from statistics and background details to the specific example of the imaginary Joe X. This paragraph, telling of the dramatic high point of the report and going on to conclude the whole incident, is closely tied together by the chronological relationship: the details are presented in the order in which they happened.

Finally, here is the concluding paragraph:

> Just what John is really doing now, no one quite knows. He recently moved to San Francisco and has sent back word that, after working for a while in an opium den in Chinatown, where he lighted the pipes of addicts, he had taken a position with a fish cannery, counting the sardines that go into each tin. There's a strong suspicion among his old friends, though, that actually he is just a freshman at Stanford, happily lying his way toward a bachelor's degree.

This paragraph, like the third in the theme, develops just one heading in the outline (number 7). It begins with a generalization, supports the statement with narrative facts, and concludes with a sentence that makes a sharp and amusing contrast with the boy's reports of his activities.

After this analysis, you can see that one heading in the outline does not automatically result in one paragraph. Some headings do, some do not. This happens, in part, because an informal outline usually shows only the main points to be discussed and the order in which they are to be taken up. This kind of outline seldom does much to show the particular bearing of one heading on another.

We can make one other observation as a result of our analysis of this paper. Throughout, the author has made effective use of *specific* material to develop the points in his outline. Paragraphs containing generalizations include also plenty of evidence to support the generalizations. Paragraphs that are primarily narrative (like the fifth and sixth) include enough significant details to interest us in the incident being reported and to let us follow it easily and clearly.

DEVELOPING PARAGRAPHS FROM A FORMAL OUTLINE

Now let us examine a topic outline and the theme based on it. We will use the outline called "Blueprint for a Successful Marriage," quoted in Chapter 5. Instead of a detailed analysis, it will be enough simply to quote the theme and to note, in the right-hand margin, the methods by which each paragraph has been developed and the relation between outline headings and paragraphs. Here is the topic outline:

> CENTRAL IDEA: For a successful marriage, the partners must agree as to the value of money and material possessions, must like most of the same things, must be tolerant of each other's faults, and must be genuinely in love rather than merely infatuated.

 I. Same attitude toward money and material possessions
  A. Agreement to live within means
  B. Willingness to work together for things they want
 II. Same preferences and interests
  A. In reading, music, etc.
  B. In other ways of spending leisure time
 III. Attitude of mutual toleration
  A. Certainty of faults in both partners
  B. Possibility of correcting some faults
  C. Toleration of faults that can't be corrected
 IV. Real love, not infatuation
  A. Is primarily spiritual
   1. Physical attraction temporary
   2. Spiritual bond permanent
  B. Is based on respect, admiration, understanding
  C. Provides securest foundation for successful marriage
   1. Encourages unselfishness
   2. Makes minor personal differences insignificant
   3. Reconciles differences in religion
    a. Change of faith
    b. Toleration of other's faith

Blueprint for a Successful Marriage

	Methods of Development	*Basis in Outline*
Though I'm still a spinster and obviously have no first-hand experience of marriage to qualify me to speak as an authority on the subject, I don't expect to remain a spinster forever. In fact, if all goes well, people will begin calling me "Mrs." just three months from now, for I plan to be married in January. For this reason, I've been doing some serious thinking about marriage lately and have rather definite ideas on what it takes for a marriage to be a success. I'll be the first one to admit that these ideas are only theory so far, but I hope soon to put them to the test.	Generalization and facts	Introduction (not in outline)
It seems to me that before entering into a marriage contract the persons involved should ask themselves four questions: Do we have the same attitude toward money and material possessions? Do we like the same things? Are we willing to be tolerant of each other's shortcomings? Is our attraction to each other based on something deeper than infatuation?	Generalizations, questions	Introduction (not in outline)
No doubt there are other important questions too—religious belief, for example—but these four are the ones that concern me most. I think that if the right answers can be made to these four questions, other problems, including most differences of religion, will work themselves out. (Perhaps I feel so sure of this because my own parents are of different faiths, yet their marriage is a very happy one.)	Generalizations, example	Introduction (not in outline)
The first question may seem unromantic and perhaps not very important, but I don't think it should be ignored. Both partners in a marital enterprise must realize that their standard of living should not be above		

	Methods of Development	*Basis in Outline*

their income. Failure to agree on this has broken up many marriages, including several that I know of myself. One of these was the marriage of a young schoolteacher and a girl who, in spite of her husband's small salary, insisted on dressing extravagantly, driving a new convertible, and trying to furnish their apartment like a New York penthouse. Before they had been married a year, the man was deeply in debt, had lost the car, had lost the furniture—and had lost his wife, who divorced him with his full and, I suppose, relieved consent.

Generalizations, example

I. Same attitude toward money and material possessions
   A. Agreement to live within means

Probably most young couples have to start out on fairly slender budgets; but, instead of this being a disadvantage, I think that it should strengthen the marriage if both husband and wife agree to live within their means. That is, by starting on a small income and working their way up together, they should be drawn more closely to each other by the need for cooperation. A couple who, during their first year of marriage, are able to afford a European honeymoon, a new house, a new car, and a two-oven electric range would not, it seems to me, have nearly so much incentive as less wealthy couples to work together closely as a team and so strengthen their relationship.

Generalizations, reasoning, example

   B. Willingness to work together for things they want

The second question, "Do we like the same things?" is more complicated than the first, since it involves more. For any marriage to be successful, I think the partners must share the same tastes and enjoy the same kinds of experiences. A person who likes to read the works of Tolstoi and listen to Beethoven's string quartets will find little in common with someone who never reads anything more difficult

	Methods of Development	*Basis in Outline*

than a movie-fan magazine and listens only to popular music. Two such people would find it hard to talk about anything more profound than the size of last month's water bill. But, besides similar tastes in such things as reading and music, the two partners should also enjoy doing the same things together during leisure time. If people can't play together, there won't be much joy in working together. The woman who feels that she belongs in exclusive hotels and night-spots will soon find herself bored with a husband who prefers to spend his vacations fishing for trout on a secluded stream high in the mountains.

[Methods of Development: Generalizations, examples,*]*

[Basis in Outline: II. Same preferences and interests
  A. In reading, music, etc.
  B. In other ways of spending leisure time*]*

Now for the third question, "Are we willing to be tolerant of each other's shortcomings?" Though it may be easy enough to answer "yes" to this question, I'm sure that living up to the answer must be one of the most difficult things a husband or wife has to do. No matter how well suited two people are, each will find in the other some traits or habits that are displeasing. Since it is likely that neither partner suspected the existence of most of these traits before marriage, both will probably feel somewhat disillusioned when they first discover that their ideal is not perfect after all. If the marriage is to last, however, I believe that each person must learn to accept the failings of the other. It's true that often when a person sees that one of his habits or actions is annoying his partner, he can correct whatever it is that is causing the trouble. A wife, for instance, might start leaving bridge parties earlier in order to have dinner ready on time, or a husband might

[Methods of Development: Generalizations, examples*]*

[Basis in Outline: III. Attitude of mutual toleration
  A. Certainty of faults in both partners*]*

	Methods of Development	Basis in Outline

stop going to stag poker parties every Saturday night so that he could take his wife dancing instead. But sometimes there are attitudes or habits, developed usually over many years, that seem impossible for some people to change. My father, for example, good husband though he is, is completely oblivious to the problem of keeping a house tidy. The garbage in the sink could be piled nearly to the ceiling before it would occur to him to wrap it and carry it outside to the garbage can. And I'm afraid that he's one of those men who just can't see an ashtray; most of his cigarette ashes go on the floor, and his cigarette butts either in the sink or out the front door, where they make the sidewalk look like the entrance to a poolhall. This failing of his has annoyed my mother for twenty years now, but she has learned to accept it philosophically as a necessary evil and is even able to joke about it. Little faults like this one must be overlooked by each partner, for both will have them. If two people care enough for each other, it won't be hard to do.

This point brings me to the last and, for me, most important question: Is the attraction based on something deeper than infatuation? Before discussing it, let me define what the word "love" means to me. I think of love between man and wife, the sort of love that really lasts, as primarily a sort of spiritual bond. The physical attraction, though it is important, is of less value in the long run than this spiritual unity, for it is less permanent. It is bound to lessen somewhat through the years, whereas the other should become stronger. A marriage founded on temporary infatuation is

Basis in Outline (right column):

B. Possibility of correcting some faults
C. Toleration of faults that can't be corrected

Methods of Development (for last paragraph): Generalizations, definition

IV. Real love, not infatuation
    A. Is primarily spiritual
      1. Physical attraction temporary
      2. Spiritual bond permanent

	Methods of Development	Basis in Outline

likely to fall apart as soon as Saturday night's gaiety fades into Monday-morning blues. Orchids were meant for moonlight: they wilt quickly in the steam over the kitchen sink.

Genuine love, in my opinion, is based upon the mutual respect, admiration, and understanding which develop as each partner learns to know the other's mind and very soul. It brings out the best in a person's character by causing him to put the wishes and best interests of the other before his own; concern for oneself becomes secondary. It takes precedence over material concerns, tastes and preferences, annoying habits, and differences of opinion. It can even reconcile differences in religious belief, either by causing one person to join the church of the other or by making possible a spirit of toleration toward each other's faith, realizing that both worship the same God. If this sort of love forms the basis for a marriage, the husband and wife need not doubt its stability.

Generalizations (summary) — for the paragraph beginning "Genuine love":

B. Is based on respect, admiration, understanding
C. Provides securest foundation for successful marriage
  1. Encourages unselfishness
  2. Makes minor personal differences insignificant
  3. Reconciles differences in religion
    a. Change of faith
    b. Toleration of other's faith

My ambitions are high: this is the sort of love that I hope for in my own marriage. — *Statement of fact* — (Not really in outline; paragraph for emphasis)

Of the paragraphs in this theme that are represented in the outline (all, that is, but the first three and the last), paragraphs 6 and 7 each develop a complete Roman-numeral division (II and III). But paragraph 4 develops only "A" under "I"; and paragraph 5, "B" under "I." The eighth paragraph develops "IV, A" and its subdivisions; while the ninth paragraph includes "B" and "C" under "IV," together with the subdivisions of "C" and of "3."

When you are working from a topic or sentence outline, you will almost certainly begin a new paragraph whenever you come to a Roman-numeral heading, for these headings indicate the main divisions of your paper, the main stages in the development of your thought. But it would not be accurate to say that you will necessarily develop everything within a particular Roman-numeral division in a single paragraph. Sometimes you will; at other times, the nature of the material or the impression you want to create will lead you to use two or more paragraphs to develop a Roman-numeral division.

The successful developing of paragraphs from headings in an outline, whether an informal outline or a formal topic or sentence outline, depends on your knowing clearly what you want to say, and on your judgment as to how you can most clearly and effectively arrange your material for readers. The same is true of the methods of development that you use to expand points in your outline into finished paragraphs: you must know what you want to say, what impression or effect you want to make on your readers, and what their reactions are likely to be if you say it this way or that way. If you believe your readers will be confused unless you define a key term, by all means define it; if you believe they already know the meaning of the term, don't define it—you would be wasting your time and theirs. If you think a contrast or a comparison or an example will make your meaning clearer to your readers, use it; if you think it will not, don't use it.

You are the judge. You will decide wrongly sometimes, and your English teacher will tell you when he thinks you have made a mistake. But every time these mistakes are pointed out to you, you should be less likely to make them again.

Relating Sentences within Paragraphs

PAR 14 *Relate sentences within paragraphs so that the thought moves without interruption from one sentence to the next*

When you group sentences together into a paragraph, you do so because in your mind you see some kind of relationship among them and want your readers to see it too. Indenting the first word of the opening sentence is a sign to your readers that you believe this relationship exists. But the indention alone is not enough; it merely puts you under the obligation to prove to your readers that there really is a connection among the sentences that has justified your placing them in a separate paragraph. To help demonstrate this connection, you must be careful to relate each sentence to the ones on either side of it, tying them all together into an ordered structure.

RELATING SENTENCES IN NARRATIVE PARAGRAPHS

In narrative paragraphs, the difficulty is lessened because the time relationship provides a means for binding the sentences together: first one thing happens, then the next, and so on. You must be sure, though, to keep the events and actions you are telling about in the order in which they took place, and to furnish your readers with occasional reminders of this order. The following paragraphs from a student paper telling of a duck-hunting trip show careful attention to the order of the events told of and to expressions (italicized) that help us to follow the course of the story.

As we crawl into our blind, all is quiet save for the intermittent quacking of a lonely mallard on a pond half a mile away. This lazy, rhythmic sound almost hypnotizes me, and I am almost asleep *when the hollow thumping of distant guns brings me back to reality.* It is time to shoot, but still too dark to shoot accurately. *Suddenly,* five tiny jet-propelled teal flash by in front of us and disappear into the western sky *before we can even raise our guns. Soon* they are back; and, taking an unpredictable turn, they drop down to the water far out from the blind. They are out of range, but they will serve as living decoys for the bigger ducks we hope will come along.

Five minutes later we see what we have been waiting for. A good-sized flock of mallards is swinging toward us from the east. *Now* they are directly over us, but too high to shoot. We crouch motionless in the blind, not daring to look up at them, for nothing will frighten them away as surely as the sight of an upturned face. We can only listen to the beating of their powerful wings *as they pass overhead.*

When we can no longer hear them, we take a cautious peek over the edge of the blind to see where they have gone. They are west of us and coming back. *This time* they are lower. The safety on my gun clicks off. The ducks are well in range *now;* I can even see the glistening green of the drakes' heads. It is time to shoot. *As soon as we rise in our blind,* the ducks flare straight up into the air. I hurriedly point my gun at them, pull the trigger, and miss. Now, take your time and make this one good! I pick out a big drake and make sure my gun is swinging with him *before I shoot.* He folds *suddenly* in mid-air, pauses *for a moment, then* plummets down into the water. *By now,* the other ducks are out of range; but there are three fine mallards lying on the water.

RELATING SENTENCES IN EXPOSITORY PARAGRAPHS

In good expository paragraphs, the sentences must be clearly related to one another so that together they make up an orderly unit in the development of the writer's thought. Otherwise, the reader will have a feeling of dislocation, of unpleasant surprise, somewhat as though he were going down a flight of stairs and suddenly discovered too late that one step was missing, so that he landed with a jolt on the next one down. Here is a paragraph from a student theme which gives us this impression; notice especially the "missing step" between the first and second sentences.

> From the player's point of view, any football game is dangerous, and there is even the chance that it may be fatal. Most high school coaches are careful to insist on good sportsmanship; winning is important, but clean play is more important. In college football the philosophy often seems to be "Win at any cost," and if this means breaking the leg of the other team's right halfback, just be sure that you are hidden on the bottom of a pile of players when you do it.

When the fault was pointed out to this student, he revised the paragraph to show the relationships that he had intended but had forgotten to express in the first version. Besides having to add two or three transitional phrases, he also found it necessary to supply one completely new sentence.

> From the player's point of view, any football game is dangerous, and there is even the chance that it may be fatal. *On the whole, however, I think that the sort of football played in college is much more dangerous than the game as it is played in high school. I say this chiefly because* most high school coaches are careful to insist on the rules of good sportsmanship; winning is important, but clean play is more important. In college football, *on the other hand,* the philosophy often seems to be "Win at any cost," and if this means breaking the leg of the other team's right halfback, just be sure that you are hidden on the bottom of a pile of players when you do it.

Relating Paragraphs

PAR 15   *Relate each paragraph clearly to those on either side*

Just as the sentences within a paragraph should have a clear bearing on one another, so the separate paragraphs that make up a whole composition should all be related. Again, as with sentences in narrative paragraphs, the time relationship helps to make clear the connection of one paragraph with the next in narrative writing; the reader knows that events are being presented in the order in which they happened. But you need to take special care to relate the paragraphs in your expository writing, since the order in which the separate paragraphs appear depends on a greater variety of relationships. If you do not indicate these relationships clearly, you place yourself at a disadvantage. Your readers must try to figure them out for themselves—if they can, and if they are willing to take the trouble. Usually, what is called for is a sentence, a phrase, sometimes just a word to serve as a transition between two paragraphs, linking them together either by some sort of reference to ideas that have already been presented or by some indication that a definite plan of organization is being followed ("in the first place," "next," and so on).

Here is a student theme in which the transitions have been italicized so that you can identify them easily.

The Trouble with Being a Woman

I suppose it sounds wonderful to be a woman. We can influence men, bear children and create homes, have careers, and always be admired and protected simply because we are women. But in spite of these apparent advantages, our world is a good deal narrower than a lot of men seem to realize.

Let's examine first the common belief that women influence men— the notion that behind every great man there stands a woman who has inspired him to be great. Well, there's Josephine, who no doubt influenced Napoleon a great deal. But does she get credit for her husband's accomplishments? He went out and conquered nations and got himself in all the history books, while she stayed home and embroidered his shirts. There's Socrates, certainly a great man, and who knows how much his wife Xantippe may have contributed to his greatness? But today he is called the father of philosophy and the wisest of the ancient Greeks, while poor Xantippe has become known merely as a nagging wife. There's the poet Milton, the author of *Paradise Lost*. It's hard to believe that his wife had nothing to do with his career, yet she is best known today for the fact that after Milton had been married to her for awhile he wrote a pamphlet in favor of divorce.

The same sort of situation exists today. We women advise, humor, and inspire men, and the men go out to write treaties or sell life insurance—and take all the credit. If a wife attempts to break the pattern and do something on her own for which she can get the credit, combining a career with a family, the man frowns sternly and puts his foot down: "A woman's place is in the home." And there we must stay, washing diapers and wiping noses and cooking meals, burying our ambitions and sacrificing our independence to the will of our husbands.

Since a woman gives up so much of her independence to her husband, it would seem only fair to let her control things in the home. It's true that today there are probably more women who are the boss at home than there were a few years back, but as a rule the man still has the last word. When the refrigerator stops keeping food cold, he's the one who decides whether to buy a new one or to have the old one repaired. When Junior wants the car for a date, it's his father he asks, not his mother. When Susan needs a new dress, it's her mother who helps her pick it out; and it's her father who pounds the table and shouts about living within the family budget. The man's opinion nearly always rules.

If a woman decides that marriage would cost her too much of her independence and chooses a career instead, she finds the cards stacked against her. Medicine, law, journalism are all considered primarily male territory. It is difficult for a woman to break into a field such as journalism. If she does manage to get a beginning job on a newspaper, each advancement must be made by a clear show of her superiority. A man can move from cub reporter to city editor by a combination of luck, the right friends and a little brains, but a woman must rely on her ability alone if she wants to be anything but editor of the society page. In the medical profession, a woman is no longer looked on as an unnatural female, but just let her try to specialize in anything except female ailments or children's diseases. After all, what man stricken with appendicitis or pneumonia would trust himself to the hands of a woman doctor?

But the hardest thing of all about being a female, I think, is the effort to fit into the hallowed mold of true-blue womanhood. We are expected to attend teas and open-houses (ordeals that men can nearly always avoid), and not only suffer through them but smile sweetly to everyone while tottering on three-inch heels. We coeds must be in the house at 10:30 on week-nights, wake up in the morning fresh and demure, and refrain from making loud noises in public. Men can stay out all night or hitch-hike across the country; women must keep their reputations unblemished and take trains. And not only must we keep sweet and good and obedient, but we must like it.

So, as you can see, our lives are mapped out for us. We can marry and submit to the (we hope) benevolent dictatorship of a husband; or we can choose a career and for the rest of our lives fight uphill for adequate recognition. But whichever we choose, we must grin and bear it and always stand firmly on our pedestal as representatives of Sacred Womanhood. It's a man's world, all right.

Paragraph Length

PAR 16   *Paragraphs should be varied in length*

The question of how long paragraphs ought to be has been answered indirectly in various parts of this chapter and the one before: paragraphs should be long enough to do what the writer wants them to do—and no longer. But this advice should be made a little more specific.

The length of any paragraph depends mainly on its purpose, the kind of material it presents, and the writer's judgment of the needs of his audience. Paragraphs whose main purpose is emphasis will necessarily be short—ordinarily no more than a sentence or two. Transitional paragraphs will seldom be much longer, for their purpose is to bridge the gap between two main stages of the discussion being presented. Paragraphs in dialogue will often be short also, sometimes no more than a single word ("Yes," "No," "When?" etc.). Paragraphs whose purpose is to describe an action or series of actions, a scene, a person, and so on, will usually be somewhat longer because their success depends in large part on an accumulation of related details. Expository paragraphs that are intended to present a stage in the unfolding of the writer's thought will usually be even longer.

Ordinarily, paragraphs in narrative (especially if dialogue is included) will average considerably shorter than paragraphs in expository writing. For example, the fourteen paragraphs that make up the selection from Hemingway's *A Farewell to Arms,* quoted on pp. 109–111, average about thirty-two words each. The longest paragraph contains 162 words; the shortest, two. There are two main reasons why narrative paragraphs are often fairly short. One, many readers find long speeches tiresome, so that paragraphs containing dialogue are usually short. Two, what is called *narrative movement,* the sense of things happening in order, is slowed down by too many long paragraphs. Rather short paragraphs are more likely to give the reader an impression of action taking place; and narrative, of course, is a presentation of some sort of action.

Paragraphs in exposition (leaving out those intended for transition or emphasis) are usually longer than those in narrative because they present not action but a group of related ideas. They embody a sizable division of the author's thought. As an example, the 11 paragraphs quoted earlier from Paul Gallico's essay on Babe Ruth range from 62 to 192 words, the average being 118.

In developing paragraphs, whether expository or narrative, you must always take into account your estimate of the needs of your readers. Suppose you have begun a paragraph with a sentence like "It was the usual collection of magazines that you expect to find in the office of a small-town dentist," or "A boy is seriously mistaken if he thinks that all he needs to do to guarantee his future success in business is pledge the right fraternity." You must realize that your readers will want to be shown some evidence to support the statement. The *amount* of support it needs (that is, how long the paragraph will be) depends on what you think will satisfy your readers that the statement is well founded. When you have included what seems to you enough support, end the paragraph.

Few students write paragraphs that are too long. Short, underdeveloped paragraphs, however, are one of the most common faults in freshman themes. Such paragraphs are usually the result of failing to realize that generalizations must be supported adequately.

In three of the better themes quoted in this chapter, the paragraphs have been fully developed, the generalizations properly supported. The following figures on the length of paragraphs in these papers might be of interest to you:

Theme	*Longest Paragraph*	*Shortest Paragraph*	*Average Length*
"Genius at Work"	202	83	143
"Blueprint for a Successful Marriage"	379*	18	133
"The Trouble with Being a Woman"	168	53	116

* This paragraph (the seventh) could and possibly should have been split in two. It is fairly long and does have a place where it could logically be divided.

You should not think that all your own paragraphs must fall within the word limits of the paragraphs in these papers. But you can get from these figures some general notion of the fullness of treatment that is ordinarily called for in student paragraphs, as well as the considerable range in length that may exist. And, since most of the paragraphs in these papers happen to be expository, remember that when you write a narrative composition the paragraphs may average somewhat shorter than these.

EXERCISE

3. The four following excerpts from student writing are faulty from the standpoint of paragraph construction. Some are underdeveloped. Some are too general and lack sufficient specific supporting material, or they show poor organization and no central idea. Some are perhaps all right in themselves but lack proper transition between paragraphs. Read each selection through, then choose three and criticize the paragraph construction of each. The paragraphs in each selection have been numbered for ease in discussing.

(a) 1. Perhaps the first big business venture I was ever involved in consisted of catching snakes for sale to the public. I say *big* only because it was big to me and my partner, for certainly there is no great demand among most people for snakes. However, wise for our eleven years and filled with dreams of success, we embarked upon our adventure without the slightest thought of failure.

2. Now in order to sell or trade snakes you must first have the snakes, so off we went to the nearest lake to catch some merchandise. This was not as hard as you might think, because if you are quick with your hands you can pick snakes right out of the water as your partner turns over the flat rocks they hide under.

3. This occupation is not without its adventure, for sometimes you find more than just water snakes. We did our hunting where a kind of water moccasin lives, which, being unaccustomed to being pushed around, is inclined to be a little indignant. The fastest I think I ever saw a human being move was when my partner turned over a rock and found three copperheads. He stared at the copperheads and the copperheads stared back. My partner left in a hurry.

(b) 1. About one-thirty last night four pledges were in Pat Allen's room having a bull session on affairs in general. Someone said, "You know, it certainly is a perfect night. I hope the night of our walk-in is as pretty." Somehow this gave all of us the same idea at the same time. We would take an active for a walk-in. The only active handy was an unfortunate soul sleeping on a couch on the second floor.

2. Very carefully all of the pledges were awakened in the dorm and directed downstairs. We had to be very quiet because the actives sleep on the third floor. The plans were set: Harrison and Jeffries would tie his feet. Allen and Lamb would try to cram a gag into his mouth before he could scream. Tucker and I would barricade the dorm door.

3. Everything went off perfectly—nothing broken and no unnecessary noise. The victim was able to tear the gag loose about halfway down the stairs, but fortunately we have no light sleepers in the house.

4. We parked him in the car and blindfolded him. At two-thirty we started driving around town to confuse him. Then on the other side of a town about sixteen miles away we let him out of the car. We raced back to the house to unhook the telephones so the line would be busy.

5. At seven-thirty this morning our victim walked in the front door. He had walked a mile to a farm house, where he was taken in

and allowed to sleep in the living room. The farmer had brought him to the fraternity house when morning came.

6. I'll bet a dollar we'll pay for our prank this evening, but it was worth it.

(c) 1. Both high school and college football have their advantages and disadvantages.

2. High school football is more of a sport in the true sense of the word than is college football. College football is more a job or business and is run like a big machine. It is almost all work and no play. In high school, football is nothing but a game to enjoy. The boys who make up the team usually know each other personally. They are usually friends and see each other off the field as well as on it. In college football, players may never learn more about a teammate than his name. This certainly doesn't help the spirit of college football.

3. Any football game may be dangerous or even fatal to its players. But on the whole college football is much more dangerous than is high school football. High school football is based much more on sportsmanship than college football. This difference will be more evident from watching a college game carefully and following every play closely. No one can help seeing the dirty playing done by members of both teams. There is some dirty playing in high school, but not on such a large scale. It is usually frowned on by high school coaches, while it is often taught and admired by college coaches.

4. If it is true that football is a game to emphasize sportsmanship and teamwork, high school football is more successful than college football.

5. Football in college is much more of an entertainment than it is in high school, for college football is considered big time. There is a selection of good players from all over the country in the college sport, while in high school there is just a small selection of inexperienced players from a certain town or a district in a town. The coaches and players are also much more skilful in college than in high school. As a result, the college game is usually more interesting to spectators.

(d) 1. People go to movies for entertainment. They go because they like to see other persons having the kind of trouble that happens in real life. Some persons go to movies because they have heard that the picture is worth the time and money involved.

2. Some persons go to movies to see their favorite movie star. To them it doesn't make any difference what the picture is, as long as their favorite actor plays in it.

3. Some people go to movies for relaxation. They have a chance to forget about the business deal they are trying to conclude with another large business firm. They have a chance to see the trouble other people have and to laugh at what they say or do.

4. Some people like to see a movie two or three times. I can understand seeing a picture twice, but seeing it for a third time seems a

waste of time. When you see it for a third time you know almost exactly what is going to happen.

5. Some persons go to movies because they have nothing better to do. They go because it is a change in their daily routine. Going to a movie makes time seem to pass faster than it really does.

9

WRITING
GOOD SENTENCES

In this chapter we will be concerned mainly with ways to make sentences *effective*. We will have to use various grammatical terms, since it is not possible to discuss sentence elements and their relationships without having names to call these things by.

Making the Meaning Clear

The most important single aim of any kind of communication is clearness. No matter how important your ideas may be, if they are expressed in ambiguous or muddled sentences they are likely to go unappreciated because of not being understood. In this section, we will consider several things that help to produce clearness:

1. Clear reference of modifying elements
2. Clear pronoun reference
3. Accurate subordination
4. Exact comparisons
5. Accurate parallelism
6. Consistency
7. Accurate word order

CLEAR REFERENCE OF MODIFYING ELEMENTS

SEN 1   *The sentence element that a modifier refers to must be clear*

The position and wording of certain kinds of modifiers can confuse the meaning of a sentence, sometimes causing a humorous reaction that is both unintended and unwanted. For instance:

> Flying at an altitude of 21,000 feet, the long string of cars looked like a procession of ants.
> Exhausted by the long wait at the airport, sleep came at once to the three children.

SEN 1 A   *Avoid dangling participles*

Both of these sentences begin with what are usually called *dangling participles*. That is, the introductory phrases "Flying at an altitude of 21,000 feet" and "Exhausted by the long wait at the airport" seem to modify something in the main clause that logically they cannot. In the first sentence, we get the impression that the string of cars is flying four miles above the ground; and in the second, that sleep is exhausted. True, in sentences like these the confusion of meaning is usually momentary rather than lasting; an average reader, after a little analysis, can tell what the intended meaning is. Meanwhile, though, the construction has drawn more attention to itself than the writer intended; and, since the error is often amusing, the attention has been of the wrong kind.

A participial phrase of this sort at the beginning of a sentence will appear to modify the first noun or pronoun (usually the subject) in the main clause. One way to revise such faulty constructions, therefore, is to put the right noun or pronoun in this position:

> Flying at an altitude of 21,000 feet, we saw far below us a long string of cars that looked like a procession of ants.
> Exhausted by the long wait at the airport, the three children fell asleep at once.

Such sentences may be revised in other ways, too:

> As we were flying at an altitude of 21,000 feet, we saw below us a long string of cars, like a procession of ants.

From an altitude of 21,000 feet we saw a long string of cars, like a procession of ants.

The three children, exhausted by the long wait at the airport, fell asleep at once.

The three children, who were exhausted by the long wait at the airport, fell asleep at once.

SEN 1 B *Avoid dangling gerunds and infinitives*

Other phrases containing non-finite forms (see Chapter 12) may cause the same sort of trouble. Here is a dangling gerund phrase:

In setting a new local record for the 100-yard dash, a muscle in Harrison's right thigh was strained.

To avoid giving the impression that the leg muscle set the record, we could revise the sentence this way:

In setting a new local record for the 100-yard dash, Harrison strained a muscle in his right thigh.

Here is a dangling infinitive phrase, with a possible revision:

To get through enrollment as quickly and painlessly as possible, your instructions must be absolutely clear.

REVISION: If you are to get through enrollment as quickly and painlessly as possible, your instructions must be absolutely clear.

SEN 1 C *Avoid unclear elliptical clauses and prepositional phrases*

Elliptical clauses (those in which the subject or verb or both must be understood from the rest of the sentence) and prepositional phrases may both cause this kind of difficulty:

ELLIPTICAL CLAUSE: While cruising along the turnpike at 75 miles an hour, a small black dog unexpectedly trotted from behind a bridge support.

REVISION: While we were cruising along the turnpike at 75 miles an hour, a small black dog unexpectedly trotted from behind a bridge support.

PREPOSITIONAL PHRASE: As a high school sophomore beginning to go on dates, mother expected me to accept more responsibility.

REVISION: As a high school sophomore beginning to go on dates, I was expected by my mother to accept more responsibility.

Sometimes the trouble is mainly the result of inexact word order:

Wings flapping leisurely, we watched a large flight of geese go over the blind.
REVISION: We watched a large flight of geese, wings flapping leisurely, go over the blind.

There is nothing wrong in itself with using elements of this sort to begin sentences. Here are examples of these modifying phrases that are clearly related and therefore effective:

At last we gained the Platte. Following it for about five miles, we saw, just as the sun was sinking, a great meadow, dotted with hundreds of cattle, and beyond them an encampment of emigrants (Francis Parkman, *The Oregon Trail*).

Living at close quarters, the father and mother quarreled constantly, and the boy had to witness these quarrels (Edmund Wilson, *To The Finland Station*).

EXERCISE

1. Some of the following sentences lack clarity because of dangling modifiers. Copy those sentences which you feel have this kind of fault; underline the part that is unclear; rewrite the sentence correcting the error.

(a) Eating our lunch by the side of the Lincoln Highway, the traffic was a steady roar in the background.

(b) Having been frozen for two hours, Dr. Amos said I was lucky not to lose my toes.

(c) Made void by many violations, the treaty seems nothing more than a scrap of paper.

(d) Our house was burned down while away for the weekend.

(e) Having fallen from the roof, a spinal injury kept my father in bed for months.

(f) George carefully selected the painting for his fiancée with the blues predominating.

(g) The Red Cross is offering a course in the latest methods of civil defense in the armory.

(h) Though only an amateur, his instructor felt he should compete with professionals.

(i) Kitchen duty was the hardest to take when in the army.

(j) Having spent three years on the island, the natives were very familiar to us.

(k) Not being used to handling a boat, it nearly tipped over.

(l) To build model railways, an infinite amount of patience is necessary.

CLEAR PRONOUN REFERENCE

SEN 2   *The antecedent of a pronoun should be clear*

The usual definition of a *pronoun* is that it is a word used in place of a noun; though this is not a perfect definition, it will serve our purposes here while we discuss pronoun reference. The noun that a given pronoun refers to (that is, is substituting for) is called the *antecedent* (from a Latin word meaning "something that goes before"). And, since the pronoun depends on the antecedent for its meaning, it is obvious that a reader must be able to identify the antecedent clearly and quickly. In the following sentence from a student theme, the unclear reference makes it impossible to figure out the exact meaning:

> Her mother told her that, because she had been out so late the night before, she would have to refuse the invitation.

This sentence might be revised in either of these ways, depending on what is meant:

> Her mother, having been out late the night before, told her she was too tired to accept the invitation.
>
> Having been out late the night before, she was told by her mother that she would have to refuse the invitation because she was too tired.

In most sentences, the antecedent will be the noun that most nearly precedes the pronoun. In the following sentence from a student paper, however, the noun in this position plainly cannot be the antecedent:

> I have reason to believe that my fear of snakes may be only a quirk in my own mind, which is nevertheless shared by most girls.

The trouble here is that the student seems to be saying that *her mind* is shared by most girls. The sentence can be made clear in this way:

> Although most girls are afraid of snakes, I have reason to believe that my fear of them may be only a quirk in my own mind.

In this version a clear antecedent, "snakes," has been supplied.

SEN 2 A *Provide clear antecedents for "it," "this," "which"*

Three pronouns in particular, "it," "this," "which," need to be watched carefully, for it is easy to use them with vague or even non-existent antecedents, as in the following sentences:

> The Indians used to believe that when there was a ring around the moon there would be rain. Today of course it is known to be only a superstition.
> REVISION: Today of course this belief is known to be only a superstition.

> In Mark Twain's *Life on the Mississippi* it tells how Twain learned to be a steamboat pilot.
> REVISION: In *Life on the Mississippi* Mark Twain tells how he learned to be a steamboat pilot.

> We young people today have much greater educational opportunities than were available a generation ago. For our own good and that of our society we should take advantage of this.
> REVISION: For our own good and that of our society we should take advantage of these opportunities.

> The late Bernard DeVoto was, among other things, novelist, historian, conservationist, literary scholar, political ghost writer, teacher, lecturer, professional gadfly, and the ultimate authority on the dry martini cocktail, which made him one of the most versatile men of our time.
> REVISION: . . . a variety of talents which made him one of the most versatile men of our time.

SEN 2 B *"You" and "they" are acceptable as indefinite pronouns only in the most informal writing*

In very informal writing, both "you" and, less often, "they" can be used as indefinite pronouns; they contribute to a relaxed, conversational tone. When this is the effect wanted, the words are useful; but they should be used sparingly. In the following sentence, "they" would probably not strike most people as objectionable:

> In the more sophisticated circles nowadays they are serving plates of hors d'oeuvres that include such delicacies as fried silkworms and grasshoppers, rattlesnake meat, preserved baby bees, and chocolate-covered ants.

"You" is sometimes used as an informal equivalent of "one," as in:

You don't look a gift horse in the mouth.

The following passage from E. B. White's essay glorifying the Model T Ford shows this use of "you" as an indefinite pronoun:

> First you bought a Ruby Safety Reflector for the rear, so that your posterior would glow in another car's brilliance. Then you invested thirty-nine cents in some radiator Moto Wings, a popular ornament which gave the Pegasus touch to the machine and did something god-like to the owner. For nine cents you bought a fanbelt guide to keep the belt from slipping off the pulley ("Farewell, My Lovely!").

EXERCISE

2. In some of the following sentences the pronoun reference is not clear. Copy those sentences which are faulty in this respect, underlining the faulty pronoun. Then rewrite the sentence correcting the error.

(a) In the chemistry lab they approximate actual research conditions.

(b) Everyone feels spring is a time to relax, which makes it hard for the teachers.

(c) Henrietta told Martha that she had never been fair to her.

(d) If you want to get ahead in business you will have to learn to compromise.

(e) The rocket ignited but did not leave the ground, which is exactly what I had thought would happen.

(f) They say the cold war could go on for years.

(g) John's brother told him he couldn't hope to get on the first team.

(h) In one of the reference books on fungi, it said that fungi spores have been known to live in the stratosphere.

(i) If you don't put our old car in the garage on cold nights, it won't start in the morning.

(j) After the gas tank is filled an official seals it so you can't add any gas during the race.

(k) The African people are being motivated by a desire to throw off foreign domination, which makes an explosive situation.

(l) His whole attitude toward his neighbors was undergoing a change; it was a new experience.

ACCURATE SUBORDINATION

SEN 3   *Use subordination to show exact relationships and relative importance of sentence elements*

Subordination, in grammar, means putting the thought of a sentence element in a form that reduces its importance in the sentence it occurs in. That is, "The Russians launched their first sputnik in the autumn of 1957" is an independent clause that can properly be punctuated as a sentence. The following versions have been subordinated; that is, they have been reduced in importance below the level of an independent clause and so cannot be punctuated as sentences. (See also the discussion of period faults, pp. 242–245).

> When (although, because, after, until, before, etc.) the Russians launched their first sputnik in the autumn of 1957,
> The Russians, launching their first sputnik in the autumn of 1957,
> The first sputnik, which was launched by the Russians in the autumn of 1957,
> The first sputnik, launched by the Russians in the autumn of 1957,
> The first sputnik having been launched by the Russians in the autumn of 1957,

Sentence elements are subordinated for two main reasons: to show exact relationships between the subordinated elements and another part of the sentence; and to let the reader know that the idea contained in the subordinated element is less important than some other idea in the sentence. Failure to subordinate produces this sort of thing:

> I was out hunting with my father last weekend and suddenly two pheasants flew out of a patch of weeds and they came straight towards me. I blazed away at them almost pointblank but I missed them both and my father was very amused.

This style is tiresome because the ideas are presented as though they were all equally important, and they have no more relation to one another than beads that happen to have been strung on the same string. Such writing obscures the exact meaning of what is being said and also shows a lack of thought and consideration that will certainly prejudice a reader unfavorably. Here is a revision of the passage:

> When I was out hunting with my father last week, two pheasants suddenly flew out of a patch of weeds and came straight toward me. Although I blazed away at them almost pointblank, I missed them both, to the great amusement of my father.

In this version, the two most important ideas are seen to be the sudden flight of the two pheasants and the writer's failure to hit either of them; these ideas are stated as independent clauses. The other ideas, being less important, have been reduced below this level and have been introduced by words that show specific relationships between these ideas and those of the main clauses.

The ability to use subordination effectively is one of the surest marks of a good style, for it shows that the writer has carefully weighed his ideas for their relative importance, has studied them to see what their relationships are, then has put them in a form that makes clear to the reader both the relative importance and the relationships. In the following sentence, the wrong idea has been subordinated:

> One evening we were having a barbecue in the back yard, when our dog grabbed a three-pound sirloin off the grill.
> REVISION: One evening, when we were having a barbecue in the back yard, our dog grabbed a three-pound sirloin off the grill.

In the next sentence a relationship needs to be indicated between the two ideas:

> Karen has always been regarded as a scatterbrain and she is a good friend of mine.
> REVISION: Although Karen has always been regarded as a scatterbrain, she is a good friend of mine.

SEN 3 A   *Avoid overusing "so" as a connective between main clauses*

A common error in student writing is sticking two independent clauses together loosely with a "so" rather than subordinating the less important clause by introducing it with a more exact connective. Actually, sentences that use "so" in this way are uncommon in good writing except when conversation is being reported. Here is an example in which the use of "so" weakens the expression:

> Some of the people I wanted to see weren't in, so I decided to come back that afternoon.
> REVISION: Because some of the people I wanted to see weren't in, I decided to come back that afternoon.

SEN 3 B   *Do not use too much subordination*

Finally, although subordination is indispensable for clear communication, it can be overdone; over-subordination makes the following sentence too complicated:

On my trip home for vacation I sat next to a man who talked constantly about his farm, which had once been owned by a governor of Indiana, who was a distant relative of whom he seemed very proud.

EXERCISE

3. Most of the following sentences suffer from improper subordination, either too little, too much, or subordination of the wrong element. Rewrite those sentences which you feel can be improved.

(a) We have had the Salk vaccine for protection against polio for several years and there are still many people who haven't been inoculated.

(b) Most of the high school graduates today have not had to work and they fail to understand the conditions that existed in America during the depression.

(c) Jim was not an exceptional student but he made good grades and was able to pass the tests and he worked very hard to reach his goal.

(d) We were put on an army plane. The plane took two hours to fly to Tokyo.

(e) Some people must be careful not to exercise because of heart trouble. Some exercise can be beneficial to the average person.

(f) Gerald spends hours studying at the library and in his room and his grades are improving.

(g) He coached the team through three losing years and the alumni demanded his dismissal.

(h) American people spend a very small part of their income on education, so they have little reason to complain of their schools.

(i) Scientists say the Grand Canyon underwent many changes. Many layers of rock were deposited. At one stage the canyon area was a great plain. The stream known as the Colorado River meandered across this plain.

(j) I am an optimist and I have a friend who is in a constant state of depression, so the controversy of pessimism versus optimism is one of our favorite topics.

(k) Engineering is a highly technical profession, so a proficient engineer must have extensive training in many skills.

(l) Last summer we were hiking through the Olympic Mountains when we came across a grizzly bear.

EXACT COMPARISONS

SEN 4   *Express comparisons accurately*

Poorly expressed comparisons interfere with clear communication. The obvious error of comparing two things that cannot logically be compared is shown in this sentence:

Graham Greene's detective stories are much better than Mickey Spillane.

REVISION: Graham Greene's detective stories are much better than those of Mickey Spillane, or . . . than Mickey Spillane's.

In the original sentence, stories were being compared to a *man;* the revision compares stories with other stories.

An error in logic makes this comparison unclear:

The future of the world seems to weigh more heavily today on atomic scientists than on any people.

Since the wording appears to suggest that atomic scientists aren't people, the sentence should be revised like this:

The future of the world appears to weigh more heavily today on atomic scientists than on any other people. (Or, perhaps more accurately, . . . than on most other people.)

Another common error in comparison, frequent in relaxed conversation but regularly avoided in writing and in careful speech, is a mixture of two degrees of comparison, the comparative and the superlative, with the former construction left unfinished.

When it came to the habits of Indian tribes in the Rocky Mountains and the great deserts of the West, Jim Bridger knew as much if not more than anyone else.

The following is a correct but awkward revision:

When it came to the habits of Indian tribes in the Rocky Mountains and the great deserts of the West, Jim Bridger knew as much as, if not more than, anyone else.

Less cumbersome is this:

When it came to the habits of Indian tribes in the Rocky Mountains and the great deserts of the West, Jim Bridger knew as much as anyone else, if not more.

EXERCISE

4. In the following sentences are examples of poorly expressed comparisons. Copy those sentences which contain such examples and underline the faulty comparison. Then rewrite the sentences so as to correct the error.

(a) Portland streets are harder to get around in than San Francisco.
(b) Babe Ruth's batting record was better than Mel Ott.
(c) The day Russia launched her first Sputnik was one of the most significant, if not the most significant day in the 1950's.
(d) Baseball is as popular, if not more popular, than football in our area.
(e) Americans worry more about Strontium 90 than the Russians.
(f) My friend Timothy studies harder than any student I know.
(g) Journalism has a basic story form which is used more often in reporting news than any form.
(h) The sheriff's routine police duties are less tiring than the police chief.
(i) Their area is as crowded, if not the most crowded area in town.
(j) More boys in the dormitory voted for Helen than the other girls.

ACCURATE PARALLELISM

SEN 5   *Use parallelism accurately*

Parallel structure, in rhetoric, means that two or more elements that are being used together must have the same grammatical form. For instance, in the following sentence there are two examples of parallelism:

> The new ships must be *fast, manageable,* and *seaworthy;* that meant *longer, less beamy* and *lower-built* ships (T. S. Bindoff, *Tudor England*).

The phrase "fast, manageable, and seaworthy" consists of three parallel adjectives, all serving as subjective complements (predicate adjectives); the phrase in the second clause, "longer, less beamy and lower-built ships," is a similar series of adjectives except that this time all three are in the comparative degree and all modify a following noun.

In the sentence:

> Drake brought back *a ship laden with precious metals and a mind stored with potent memories (Ibid.).*

parallelism is shown in the two phrases "a ship laden with precious metals" and "a mind stored with potent memories." Each phrase consists of a noun modified by a participial phrase.

In the following sentence, the noun phrases "the exertions" and "the sacrifices" are in one parallel construction; another is made up of a series of verb phrases, each modified by a prepositional phrase:

> When the world wars came, the people of the liberal democracies could not be aroused to *the exertions* and *the sacrifices* of the strug-

gle until they *had been frightened by the opening disasters, had been incited to passionate hatred, and had become intoxicated with unlimited hope* (Walter Lippmann, *The Public Philosophy*).

Generally speaking, parallel structure is used for ideas that are of the same level of importance. Putting these ideas in the same grammatical form underlines for the reader their equal importance and in this way helps him to grasp the meaning more completely.

SEN 5 A   *Do not use parallel form for unequal ideas*

Using parallel form for ideas that are not equally important may confuse or mislead the reader. The following two sentences from student themes are examples of this fault:

> Putting on a hat, a raincoat, and *a burst of speed,* he raced out the door and splashed toward the barn.
> REVISION: Putting on a hat and raincoat, he raced out the door and splashed toward the barn.
> The reasons were good enough to make his answer cautious, his manner polite, and *his friends surprised.*
> REVISION: To the surprise of his friends, the reasons were good enough to make his answer cautious and his manner polite.

SEN 5 B   *Use parallel structure for ideas having equal importance*

The opposite error, not using parallel form for comparable ideas, is usually the result of hurried or careless writing. It is seen in this sentence:

> Stanley Kowalski, a main character in Tennessee Williams' play *A Streetcar Named Desire,* likes to drink beer, play poker, and bowling.
> REVISION: Stanley Kowalski, a main character in Tennessee Williams' play *A Streetcar Named Desire,* likes to drink beer, play poker, and bowl.

SEN 5 C   *Elements joined by correlative conjunctions should have parallel form*

Correlative conjunctions (both . . . and, not only . . . but also, either . . . or, neither . . . nor) by their very nature link two sentence elements that must be kept in parallel form. Here are several examples of correct usage:

> A valley glacier is nourished not only by the snow that falls directly upon it in the zone of accumulation, but also by great masses of snow that avalanche onto it from steep slopes along its course (L. Don Leet and Sheldon Judson, *Physical Geology*).
>
> As a final resort, we can either impose limitations on the amount of water pumped from the underground or restrict the uses to which ground water can be put (*Ibid.*).
>
> He suddenly appears unannounced in Ophelia's chamber; and his appearance and behaviour are such as to suggest both to Ophelia and to her father that his brain is turned by disappointment in love (A. C. Bradley, *Shakespearean Tragedy*).

Common errors in parallelism that result from the careless use of these patterns are illustrated in the following sentences:

> After watching him cheerfully put up with a solid hour of heckling, I decided that he was either very good-natured or he was wonderfully self-controlled.
>
> REVISION: After watching him cheerfully put up with a solid hour of heckling, I decided that either he was very good-natured or he was wonderfully self-controlled [parallel independent clauses].
>
> OR: . . . that he either was very good-natured or was wonderfully self-controlled [parallel verb-plus-complement phrases].
>
> OR: . . . that he was either very good-natured or wonderfully self-controlled [parallel adverb-plus-adjective phrases].
>
> Every car on Low-Dollar Dave's lot not only had been owned by an elderly schoolteacher, but no car had been driven over forty miles an hour.
>
> REVISION: Not only had every car on Low-Dollar Dave's lot been owned by an elderly schoolteacher, but no car had been driven over forty miles an hour [parallel independent clauses].
>
> At the end of the first week, my new boss told me that he was impressed both by my eagerness and clumsiness.
>
> REVISION: At the end of the first week, my new boss told me that he was impressed both by my eagerness and by my clumsiness [parallel prepositional phrases].
>
> OR: . . . impressed by both my eagerness and my clumsiness [parallel noun phrases].

EXERCISE

5. Some of the following sentences contain examples of faulty parallelism. Some have incomparable ideas in parallel form; others have comparable ideas which are not in parallel form. Underline all the examples of faulty parallelism which you can find and rewrite the sentences in which they are found so as to correct the error.

(a) Municipal police departments have the task of protecting people against law violators and to make the country safe for law-abiding citizens.

(b) Maria was either a fabulous liar or she was the most popular girl in her senior class.

(c) I had a feeling of accomplishment and that those long hours of practice had not gone to waste.

(d) His report was about a tribe of South American Indians and how to sail a boat down the Amazon.

(e) The buildings were clean, sparkling, and had been built of island stone.

(f) The Navajos operate a coal mine, maintain a high-grade ram herd, run a low-cost housing project, and a flourishing Arts and Crafts Guild is managed by them.

(g) The question was not only out of order, but we felt it was not clearly stated.

(h) Some resemble medieval religious songs, others are like love songs, and still others having the quality of a marching song.

(i) This kind of reporting calls for diligence, ingenuity, and having breadth of vision.

(j) An open-book exam is usually much more difficult than to take an objective test.

(k) The reporter working on such a story is not only a social historian but he must have writing skill.

(l) He appeared in an old sweater, a rumpled hat, and an obvious daze.

CONSISTENCY

SEN 6   *Aim at consistency in sentence structure*

You should try to avoid various inconsistencies or undesirable shifts in construction. Some of these cause serious confusion of meaning, others cause less. But you should do your best to find and correct all of them before you put a paper in final form.

SEN 6 A   *Avoid unnecessary shifts in person*

One of the most obvious kinds of inconsistency is a shift in person:

> One may be trying to read a dull chemistry assignment, when in bursts your roommate offering to beat you at table tennis.
> REVISION: You may be trying to read a dull chemistry assignment, when in bursts your roommate offering to beat you at table tennis.

OR: A student may be trying to read a dull chemistry assignment, when in bursts his roommate offering to beat him at table tennis.

SEN 6 B *Avoid shifts in number*

Another obvious inconsistency is a shift in number:

The men wear white sombreros, fancy embroidered shirts, tight jeans, elaborately decorated boots, and the standard hand-gun slung low on his hips.
REVISION: . . . slung low on their hips.
OR: The typical man wears a white sombrero, an embroidered shirt, tight jeans, elaborately decorated boots, and the standard hand-gun slung low on his hips.

SEN 6 C *Avoid unnecessary shifts in tense*

In the following sentence the error is an unnecessary shift in tense:

The alarm goes off at the correct time and John arrives at the Student Union by seven o'clock, but he was due for a surprise.
REVISION: . . . but he is due for a surprise.
OR: The alarm went off at the correct time and John arrived at the Student Union by seven o'clock, but he was due for a surprise.

SEN 6 D *Be consistent in sequence of tenses*

One aspect of consistency in tense is what is called *sequence of tenses;* that is, what tense forms are appropriately used after what other tense forms. The problem can be made rather complicated, as you would find if you were to try explaining the exact differences in meaning between "I would have liked to visit Mexico last summer" and "I would like to have visited Mexico last summer." Since this book tries to center on the most common writing problems rather than to be all-inclusive, the following general comments and illustrations will be enough for our purposes. They should help you to avoid significant errors in tense sequence:

1. If a verb in the past tense or past-perfect tense is used in the independent clause of a sentence, a past-tense or past-perfect-tense verb is usual in the dependent clause.

Caroline was (past tense) ill with flu when Christmas vacation ended (past tense).

Caroline had been (past-perfect tense) ill for a week when her parents arrived (past tense) for a visit.

2. But if the dependent clause expresses a general truth, a present-tense verb can be used.

George unfortunately forgot (past tense) that lacquer is (present tense) highly inflammable.

3. A present infinitive ("to stay"), rather than a past infinitive ("to have stayed"), is used after a past or past-perfect verb.

He wanted to stay (not: to have stayed) home Saturday.
He had wanted to stay (not: to have stayed) home Saturday.

4. If a present-tense verb is used in the independent clause, the verb of the dependent clause may be in any tense.

Everybody expects that the Globetrotters will win (future tense).
My biology teacher says that few insects are (present tense) really deadly to man.
Joe insists that he has invented (present-perfect tense) a foolproof system for winning at poker.
She swears that I never gave (past tense) her my pin.

SEN 6 E   *Avoid needless shifts in tone*

Inconsistency may result from a marked shift in the tone or degree of formality of a passage. This fault seldom causes real obscurity of meaning, but it can interfere with clear communication by directing the reader's attention to the error and away from what is being said. Here are two examples:

She did not weep at her mother's funeral. Instead, she showed real guts.
REVISION: . . . Instead, she showed real courage.

Other inconsistencies of expression are hard to classify except under the heading of miscellaneous mixtures. Here are three such garbled sentences:

To criticize the athletic program as a whole would have to be taken up by someone else, for I don't pretend to be an expert.
REVISION: Criticizing the athletic program as a whole would have to be done by someone else, for I don't pretend to be an expert. (Other revisions are possible.)

The girl I want to marry will have to be the sort that would rather spend most of her time being a good mother to her children, and not to see how many social engagements she could attend in one day.

REVISION: The girl I want to marry will have to be the sort that would rather spend most of her time being a good mother to her children than see how many social engagements she can attend in one day.

The pharmacist that I have given you the hours he works gets one hundred dollars a week.

REVISION: The pharmacist whose work schedule I have just described gets one hundred dollars a week.

EXERCISE

6. The following sentences contain examples of shifts in construction or inconsistent construction. Pick out all the examples you can find of this kind of error and rewrite the sentences correctly.

(a) Looking at the picture, one sees Soyer as a small, gay, good-humored, and intelligent man, and you are immediately anxious to know more about him.

(b) As a college student a person should be aware of the differences between high school and college; therefore, you should be able to write about it intelligently.

(c) A woman can take more mental punishment than men can.

(d) The only way Russia could insure our inability to retaliate would be to destroy all our supplies of nuclear weapons and in so doing she would have to use a device of sufficient power to endanger herself. This is a fine mess for Russia to be in.

(e) If I knew in advance that Foster would be my boss, I would have been more tactful in talking to him.

(f) When flies bite, when joints ache, and if it rains on Easter it will rain seven Sundays thereafter are examples of other rain superstitions.

(g) If Mansfield and Nicoletti managed to reach first base, we would now have the head of the batting order coming up.

(h) The hospital would have telephoned us during the morning if his condition changed.

(i) A driver must also show his crash helmet at this inspection because if a sports car should roll during a race, you would be a dead duck without a helmet.

(j) I imagine most people have met an extremely intelligent person and have been awe-struck by them.

(k) The film comes in boxes of twenty-five sheets each and had to be loaded with great care.

(l) It is incredible from a woman's standpoint that all she has to do is flutter her eyelashes, or a mild flirtation will work for the least expensive of gifts she desires.

ACCURATE WORD ORDER

SEN 7 *Use accurate word order*

In English a modifier is usually placed as near as possible to the element it modifies. This rule is not absolute but it holds true most of the time. Failure to observe this principle often causes a lack of clearness as in the following sentences from student papers; faulty word order has garbled the intended meaning:

> The energy in the body produced by food is measured in calories.

The sentence can be misread to mean that the body is produced by food.

> REVISION: The energy produced in the body by food is measured in calories.
> The West Virginia turnpike traffic is composed of 75 per cent trucks.

The difficulty here is that the traffic on this road seems to consist of nothing but trucks, and of fractional trucks at that!

> REVISION: Seventy-five per cent of the West Virginia turnpike traffic is composed of trucks.
> I believe that all this caution is not necessary.

This sentence in its present form suggests that no caution at all is necessary.

> REVISION: I believe that not all this caution is necessary.
> OR: I don't believe that all this caution is necessary (more informal).

The next sentence could have two possible meanings:

> There is one more common complaint.
> REVISION: There is one complaint more common (that is, one commoner complaint).
> OR: There is one additional common complaint (if this is the meaning intended, "more" will have to come out of the sentence).

The question of where "only," and similar words, such as "ever," "even," "just," etc., should be put in a sentence has roused a good deal of argument. Some people insist that such a word must always come just before the element it modifies, but others say that it is usually more idiomatic (that is, more in keeping with established word patterns in

English) to put the word right before the verb of the sentence, whether it modifies the verb or not. Some people argue that in a sentence like "He only bought two tickets" the true meaning is that (to paraphrase) he *merely purchased* two tickets, and did not do anything else. The test of this argument is whether, when hearing or reading "He only bought two tickets" anyone would actually misunderstand in this way. Such a possibility is unlikely. Native speakers of the language would interpret the sentence, logically or not, to mean "he bought two tickets" (not three, not four). The same would be true of sentences like "She just left a nickel for a tip" and "no one even said a word"; the sentences will be clearly understood.

Sometimes separating one of these words from what it modifies results in an awkward sentence, as in this example:

> Whether or not Hemingway's *The Old Man and the Sea* will become a classic, time only will tell.
> REVISION: . . . only time will tell.

On the other hand, in this sentence from a novel by Graham Greene, the "only" sounds natural and unobjectionable:

> A bright feminine voice said: "But what is the young housewife to do if her table only seats four?"

You should by no means get the impression that "only" and similar words regularly come before the verb rather than before the word modified. On the contrary, the latter position is much more frequent, especially in writing; and though it may sometimes be awkward or less emphatic, it can never be called actually wrong. The point is that there is no ironclad rule that requires you always to put "only," "ever," "just," "even," etc., just before the word they modify. Usually this will be where you place them; but sometimes you will have a more vigorous sentence if you place them elsewhere. You must use your own best judgment.

Here are examples of "only," the most frequently used of these words, placed just before what it modifies:

> The British legionaries and auxiliaries were rated equal or second only to the Illyrians as the finest troops in the Empire (Winston Churchill, *History of the English Speaking Peoples*, Vol. I).
> Yet even if our sea communications with the bulge of Brazil were assured, we should still be only better prepared to conduct the passive defense. Our bases, including those leased by Britain in 1940, are

good only for our passive defense; they cannot be used for the active defense of South America (Walter Lippmann, *U.S. Foreign Policy: Shield of the Republic*).

EXERCISE

7. In most of the following sentences, faulty word order has garbled the intended meaning or resulted in a lack of clarity. Rewrite the sentences to make them more clear.

   (a) Nearing us the man held out his hand, who had literally called off the dogs.

   (b) When I was almost within reaching distance of him again he moved away.

   (c) I arrived so that I could check my gear about an hour before the show began.

   (d) Every girl practically has a sense of humor.

   (e) During the tornado the house was destroyed on the corner.

   (f) All the concern for radioactive fallout is not justified.

   (g) Will you only go as far as the corner?

   (h) They were pictured as very devoted men to their duties and jobs.

   (i) Then we drive some wooden stakes beside the pins called laths.

   (j) He sees Dalton knock the packages out of the arms of a small young woman with long blonde curls and a pale blue dress that just matches the color of her eyes in an effort to get acquainted.

   (k) His resignation only came because he did not have proper support.

   (l) The Dead Sea Scrolls were merely discovered by sheerest accident.

Varying the Structure of Sentences

Good writing does not use the same sentence patterns over and over again but instead varies sentence types, sentence length, and the arrangement of sentence elements. A style that lacks these characteristics becomes monotonous and gives the impression either that the writer is careless and does not notice that he is getting tiresome, or that his ability to write is severely limited—in short, that he is clumsy and unskilled. These reactions hinder full communication; they produce hostility rather than interest.

To make the discussion of sentence variety in this section fully understandable, we should first get clearly in mind the usual grammatical classification of sentences. There are four main types: Simple, compound, complex, and compound-complex. A simple sentence is one that includes only one independent clause, as in this example:

The day was the coolest August 24 on record.

The subject of the independent clause is "day" and the verb is "was"; there is no other clause, dependent or independent, in the sentence.

A simple sentence may be fairly long and complicated because of the presence of various modifiers and other elements below the rank of a clause:

> For early Romantic writers beginning with Byron, the favorite symbol was the Haunted Castle—inaccessible, lonely, dwelled in by a young aristocrat of fabulous lineage, a Manfred seeking absolution for an inner sense of guilt, but wholly contemptuous of humankind (Malcolm Cowley, *Exile's Return*).

Here the subject is "symbol" and the verb "was." The structure is still that of a simple sentence.

A *compound* sentence is one made up of two or more independent clauses (the sentence must *not* contain a dependent clause). Here is an example:

> A bright red European sports car stood at the curb, and a thin, blond young man was lounging near it, glancing toward the house from time to time.

There are two independent clauses here: the subject of the first is "sports car" and the verb is "stood"; the subject of the second is "man" and the verb is "was lounging."

A *complex* sentence contains one independent clause and one or more dependent clauses:

> After the Congressman had finished speaking, the crowd silently dispersed.

There is one dependent clause in this sentence ("After the Congressman had finished speaking") and one independent (the rest of the sentence). Here is a more complicated example:

> Humphrey was an enormously talented composer, who died at the early age of twenty-seven, before he had time to show whether he was going to be an original genius or merely a very clever imitator of the dominant styles of the day (A. K. Holland, *Henry Purcell*).

In this sentence the independent clause is "Humphrey was an enormously talented composer"; there are three dependent clauses, the first of them beginning "who," the second "before," and the third "whether."

A *compound-complex* sentence is, as you might expect, a combination: it must have at least two independent clauses, making it compound; and one or more dependent clauses, making it complex. The sentence may be fairly short, like this one:

> If he is called upon to review a book by Joyce or Eliot, he will say certain things he believes to be accurate: they are not the things lying closest to his heart (Malcolm Cowley, *Exile's Return*).

Or it may be considerably longer and more involved:

> There is his personality, as revealed in chance interviews or as caricatured in gossip; there are the values that he assigns to other writers; and there is the value placed on himself by his younger colleagues in those kitchen or barroom gatherings at which they pass judgment with the harsh finality of a Supreme Court—John X has got real stuff, they say, but Jonathan Y is terrible—and they bring forward evidence to support these verdicts (*Ibid.*).

The first of these sentences contains two independent and two dependent clauses; the second contains five independent clauses and four dependent.

SEN 8 *Use variety of sentence types*

As mentioned before, a skillful writer uses all four of these sentence types, not in any certain order or set pattern but instead mingling them almost unconsciously as he puts his thoughts on paper. He may find, however, in looking over his first draft that he has unknowingly written a series of simple or complex sentences that, by their similarity of form, turn the reader's attention away from what is being said and direct it instead to the repetitious way it is said. The writer will then revise some of the sentences in the passage so as to break up the pattern and make the form more varied. Here, for example, is a series of seven sentences; the sentences have been numbered so they can be more easily referred to:

> (1) To American writers of my own age, or at any rate to those who went abroad in 1921, the author who seemed nearest to themselves was T. S. Eliot. (2) Essentially the picture he presented was that of the local-boy-makes-good. (3) He was born in St. Louis; he was in the class of 1910 at Harvard, where he took courses that anyone might have taken and belonged to three or four undistinguished

clubs; he continued his studies at a French provincial university and got a job in London. (4) Now, ten years after leaving Cambridge, he was winding himself in a slow cocoon of glory. (5) But his glory, his making good, was not in the vulgar sense of making money, making a popular reputation: in 1921 the newspapers had never heard of this clerk in Barclay's Bank. (6) His achievement was the writing of perfect poems, poems in which we could not find a line that betrayed immaturity, awkwardness, provincialism or platitude. (7) Might a Midwestern boy become a flawless poet?—this was a question with which we could not fail to be preoccupied (*Ibid.*).

Sentences 1 and 2 are complex, sentence 3 is compound-complex, sentence 4 is simple, sentence 5 compound, sentence 6 complex, and sentence 7 compound-complex. The result is a pleasing variety of sentence form.

EXERCISE

8. Analyze the following passages from the standpoint of variety by making a chart which will show for each passage: (a) sentence type (simple, compound, complex, or compound-complex; (b) sentence length; (c) sentence beginnings. Your teacher may ask you to fill in the chart for one or more of the passages, or for all of them. After you have completed the chart make use of the information you have tabulated by writing a short paragraph of analysis for each passage showing how variety has been achieved. The sentences have been numbered for your convenience.

EXAMPLE

Passage No.	Sentence No.	Sentence Type	No. of Words	Type of Beginning Phrase
A	1	compound-complex	23	Prep. phrase ("For a time")
	2	simple	6	
	3	etc.		
	4			
	5			
	6			
B	1	simple	4	Subject ("I")
	2	etc.		

(a) 1. For a time I watched the picture, and I realized that I had been ignoring a part of our life that everybody knows. 2. I was interested in the characterization. 3. The girl, known as Her or She, was a blonde, very pretty but completely unvoluptuous because these are Family Pictures. 4. Sometimes she wore a simple gingham dress and sometimes a leather skirt and boots, but always she had a bit of a bow in her hair and her face was untroubled with emotion or, one might almost say, intelligence. 5. This also is part of the convention. 6. She is a symbol, and any acting would get her thrown out of the picture by popular acclaim (John Steinbeck, "How to Tell the Good Guys from the Bad Guys").

(b) 1. I was never stage-struck. 2. I have known dramatists who wandered in every night to the theatre in which their play was being acted. 3. They said they did it in order to see that the cast was not getting slack. 4. I suspect it was because they could never hear their own words spoken often enough. 5. Their delight was to sit in a dressing-room during the intervals and talk over this scene or the other, wondering why it had fallen flat that night or congratulating themselves on how well it had gone, and watch an actor make up. 6. They never ceased to find the theatrical gossip of the day absorbing. 7. They loved the theatre and everything connected with it. 8. They had grease-paint in their bones (Somerset Maugham, *The Summing Up*).

(c) 1. Afterwards, of course, there were endless discussions about the shooting of the elephant. 2. The owner was furious, but he was only an Indian and could do nothing. 3. Besides, legally I had done the right thing, for a mad elephant has to be killed, like a mad dog, if its owner fails to control it. 4. Among the Europeans opinion was divided. 5. The older men said I was right, the younger men said it was a damn shame to shoot an elephant for killing a coolie, because an elephant was worth more than any damn Coringhee coolie. 6. And afterwards I was very glad that the coolie had been killed; it put me legally in the right and it gave me a sufficient pretext for shooting the elephant. 7. I often wondered whether any of the others grasped that I had done it solely to avoid looking a fool (George Orwell, "Shooting an Elephant").

(d) 1. This job of boat steering required exquisite skill. 2. Even before the small whaleboat was launched, Comstock had to coil the harpoon line properly in the tub which stood at his boat's prow—a task which might take several hours, for one kink could be fatal. 3. This line was about two hundred fathoms long. 4. If the chase of a harpooned whale developed into heroic proportions, the lines from six different boats would be joined, and the agonized whale might sound nearly a mile in the distance; but always when he surfaced there would be that gadfly harpoon in his side and that small boat trailing more than a mile astern (James A. Michener and Grove Day, *Rascals in Paradise*).

CHOPPY SENTENCES

SEN 9   *Avoid strings of short, choppy sentences*

The following passage from a student paper contrasts sharply with the passage from *Exile's Return* quoted on p. 181. The student has written six consecutive simple sentences, all nearly the same length. The result is an annoyingly monotonous sentence rhythm.

> You need the right equipment to train your own roping horse. You should try to keep the equipment as simple as possible. It may be fun no doubt to try all the many new gadgets on the market. They will only confuse the horse and make him difficult to handle. The only necessary equipment is a stout neckrope and a noseband. These things are the least cumbersome to work with and the least confusing to the horse.

The passage might be revised like this:

> You need the right equipment to train your own roping horse. Although it is no doubt fun to try the many new gadgets on the market, they will only confuse the horse and make him difficult to handle. You should keep the equipment as simple as possible. A stout neckrope and a noseband are all you really need, for these are the least cumbersome to work with and the least confusing to the horse.

The pattern now consists of a simple sentence, a complex sentence, another simple sentence, and a compound-complex sentence. And notice that besides being less choppy, the sentences (and the ideas they express) are now more closely knit.

STRINGY SENTENCES

SEN 10   *Avoid writing series of long, loosely constructed sentences*

The opposite fault from choppy sentences is long, flabby strings of clauses joined haphazardly, yet punctuated by their authors as sentences. They are the written equivalent of the conversation of the bore who speaks in one continuous sentence, tying all his ideas together with an endless series of "and-uh's." Here, taken from a freshman theme, is a specimen of the type:

> I believe that as government becomes more socialistic it becomes more centralized and more powerful and it also becomes more dictatorial too, and then the leaders of the government become more powerful and more dictatorial and the people get intimidated and the end result is totalitarianism.

Without attempting to pass judgment on the ideas of the first passage, we can nevertheless see that the sentence has been very carelessly put together. Here is a somewhat improved version:

> I believe that as a government becomes more socialistic it necessarily becomes more centralized and therefore more powerful. The greatly increased authority which then is automatically acquired by the leaders of the government soon reaches dictatorial proportions. Robbed of their former freedom, the people become intimidated— and totalitarianism results.

SENTENCE LENGTH

SEN 11 *Vary the length of your sentences*

There can be no very specific answer to the question "How long should sentences be?" Like paragraphs, sentences should be long enough to accomplish their intended purpose—and no longer. You have only your own judgment to help you in such matters but you can make that judgment increasingly reliable by studying the sentences you encounter in your reading. In general, the more formal the style, the longer the sentences; the more informal the style, the shorter the sentences. You may also find that a difficult subject presented in its full complexity will demand more complicated—and therefore longer—sentences. Simple ideas (or difficult ideas being dealt with for a general audience) usually are presented in shorter sentences.

Exactly what "longer" and "shorter" mean when you talk about sentences cannot be precisely stated. But if you study the sentence length in a page of good writing you will notice that the sentences vary considerably in length. Yours should do the same to avoid monotony. As an example, here are two paragraphs from an essay by Bertrand Russell; the number of words has been placed in parentheses at the end of each sentence.

Einstein was indisputably one of the greatest men of our time (11). He had in a high degree the simplicity characteristic of the best men of science—a simplicity which comes of a single-minded desire to know and understand things that are completely impersonal (32). He had also the faculty of not taking familiar things for granted (12). Newton wondered why apples fall; Einstein expressed "surprised thankfulness" that four equal rods can make a square, since, in most of the universes that he could imagine, there would be no such things as squares (35).

He showed greatness also in his moral qualities (8). In private, he was kindly and unassuming; toward colleagues he was (so far as I could see) completely free from jealousy, which is more than can be said of Newton or Leibniz (32). In his later years, relativity was more or less eclipsed, in scientific interest, by quantum theory, but I never discovered any sign that this vexed him (26). He was profoundly interested in world affairs (7). At the end of the First World War, when I first came in contact with him, he was a pacifist, but Hitler led him (as he led me) to abandon this point of view (34). Having previously thought of himself as a citizen of the world, he found that the Nazis compelled him to think of himself as a Jew, and to take up the cause of the Jews throughout the world (37). After the end of the Second World War, he joined the group of American scientists who were attempting to find a way of avoiding the disasters to mankind that are threatened as a result of the atomic bomb (38) ("The Greatness of Albert Einstein").

In contrast with the skillfully varied pattern of sentence length in this quotation, notice the tediousness of the pattern in the following excerpt from a freshman paper:

I started applying for scholarships and at length accepted one. I was gradually gaining confidence in myself during this time. The more self-confidence I had, the less I worried about college. When I finally graduated from high school, I had no more misgivings. In fact, I was actually looking forward to being a freshman again. My attitude was that since others had made the change, I could too.

Here is one way in which the passage might be improved by varying the sentence length (and of course the sentence structure as well):

Gradually gaining confidence in myself, I started applying for scholarships and at length was able to choose from among several that were offered me. The more my self-confidence increased, the less I worried about college. When I finally graduated from high school I had no more misgivings and in fact was actually looking forward to being a freshman again. My attitude was that since others had made the change, I could too.

VARYING SENTENCE BEGINNINGS

SEN 12   *Vary the beginnings of your sentences*

The characteristic pattern of sentence elements in English is subject-verb-complement. Although to avoid monotony of style a careful writer will introduce variations in this pattern, the majority of English sentences are organized in this way. The first word or two of a sentence is likely to attract the close attention of the reader. The reasons are several: The first word is distinguished by a capital letter, a pause has followed the end of the sentence before, and the reader's uncertainty as to what the new sentence is to be about will make him look closely at the beginning. Therefore, repetition of structure or wording at the first of a sentence is certain to be noticed. The student who wrote the following passage was clearly unaware that the repetitive pattern of his sentence beginnings distracts the reader from the sense of what is being said:

> He was born prematurely on August 21, 1941. He was underweight and so frail that the doctors doubted whether even an incubator would save him. He was the second son of his parents. He was to learn later that a brother, born two years before him, had died at the age of six weeks. He was destined to grow up, however.

The repetition of "He was" at the first of each sentence becomes a nuisance. Nearly every occurrence of "he was" could be retained, though, and the words made unobjectionable simply by locating them elsewhere in the sentence sometimes and using some other sentence element as an opener. Here is one way this might be done:

> Born prematurely on August 21, 1941, he was underweight and so frail that the doctors doubted whether even an incubator would save him. He was the second son of his parents. Later he was to learn that a brother, born two years before him, had died at the age of six weeks. He himself, however, was destined to grow up.

To see how sentence beginnings are varied, and how often they are varied, in good writing, you might turn back to the example just quoted from Bertrand Russell. The eleven sentences in the quotation begin like this:

1. Subject (Einstein)
2. Subject (He)
3. Subject (He)

4. Subject (Newton)
5. Subject (He)
6. Prepositional phrase (In private)
7. Prepositional phrase (In his later years)
8. Subject (He)
9. Prepositional phrase (At the end of World War I)
10. Participial phrase (Having previously thought of himself as a citizen of the world)
11. Prepositional phrase (After the end of World War II)

A little over half of the sentences begin with the subject; the rest begin in other ways to produce a pleasing variation from the normal pattern.

If you are to develop a clear and interesting manner of writing, you must learn to deal successfully with the various problems of sentence construction that have been discussed in this chapter. These matters deserve your closest attention, for they concern the fullness with which you are able to communicate your meaning. No one expects you to remember all these things all of the time while you are writing a first draft, but you *are* expected to read through the first draft and revise your sentences when necessary to repair omissions or oversights. And the more your writing skill increases, the fewer of these oversights and omissions will remain to be taken care of in revision.

EXERCISE

9. Some of the following passages are uninteresting for one or more reasons—choppy sentences, stringy sentences, or lack of variety in sentence beginnings and structure. Indicate which paragraphs you feel are uninteresting and why. Then rewrite the passages in a more interesting fashion, correcting the errors.

(a) The flag was put out. That was the signal for the speedboat pilots to begin the race. I was nervous. I watched my father get off to a slow start. It was my father's first speedboat race. I could see his face dripping with sweat. It was a close finish between the two top drivers, but I was more concerned with the last place finisher, my father.

(b) History is supposed to picture the influence women exert over men. Bathsheba was the inspiration of David's sin, but little is heard of her after the birth of her son. David went on to rule a kingdom while Bathsheba faded into obscurity. Napoleon was partly molded by Josephine, but he conquered nations while she no doubt embroidered his shirts. And the same holds today. We women advise, cajole, and inspire men, and the men go out independently to write treaties or sell life insurance.

(c) Falling in love is a pattern that begins when a child is born. Ideally, the child's parents give him all the affection and security he needs. They supply him with food and clothes, the symbols of love, and love itself. When he cries, he is given a bottle, and when he is wet his diapers are changed. Later his mother kisses him when he skins a knee and protects him from other children.

(d) When Antonia first came to the Nebraska frontier she was young, pretty, and eager to learn. She helped around home as much as she possibly could, then hurried to Jim Burden's farm for her daily lessons. She quickly learned to speak English as she and Jim walked across fields. She learned about the country in which she was growing up. She learned to adjust herself to hard work and getting along with different kinds of people. She had no difficulty adjusting, either. She enjoyed working out of doors. She was always bright and friendly to everyone. She was as much a part of the frontier as the sky and the uncultivated land.

(e) I had my first job of working for the athletic department the following Saturday. It was selling programs. I was to report at gate 17 any time before 11:30. I was expecting a small bundle, one to two hundred, but I was handed three hundred to sell. Not only did I fear I wouldn't sell this many. I could hardly lift them. I surprised myself by selling all three hundred. This was more than anyone else had sold in two years. I had made fifteen dollars and was looking forward to the next game.

(f) When mother offered to take me with her on her trip to the bank, I was so thrilled that I could hardly sit still during what seemed an endless ride downtown to a huge stone building with pillars that seemed to reach the sky, and I knew we were there at a real bank, when we pulled open the heavy front door with its gleaming handles and entered into another world which had a calm, cool, dignified air, almost as I had dreamed it would be.

(g) I first started to work for my dad in a service station. This is good outside work that takes much manual labor. I filled cars with gas, washed the windshields, swept the floorboards, checked the oil and water and put air in the tires. I also fixed flats, greased cars and washed them. I worked at the station for about four years. Then my dad sold out and we moved to Arizona.

(h) Many western movie plots are based upon town corruption. There are always a few upright citizens, but they are too meek to band together. It usually turns out that all the townspeople need is a leader. They get their leader by sending for help. They don't send for a dozen good men or the militia. They send for one man. He can capture the whole gang singlehanded. The hero never fails the poor townspeople. He goes right to work. About ninety minutes later he has captured the entire gang.

10

USING
THE RIGHT WORDS

The problem of choosing exactly the right words to express your meaning and communicate it fully and accurately is perhaps the most important in the entire writing process. Unless you choose your words well and use them carefully, you will inevitably fall short of saying what you want and being understood as you wish. In this chapter, we discuss a number of problems that concern word choice; we begin with one of the most troublesome problems of all: the temptation to use more words than are needed.

Wordiness

It is not true that the shortest way of saying something is *always* the best way. You should use as many words as you need in order to say exactly what you mean—*but no more.* The writing of most people, except skilled professional authors, nearly always contains unnecessary words that waste the reader's time. If, as the reader proceeds, the fault continues, he is likely to become impatient and give up.

INFLATED WRITING

WD 1 *Avoid inflated writing*

Student writing shows many specific kinds of wordiness, but two of them are especially annoying. The first may be called *inflated writing,* since the language has been blown up to dimensions considerably larger than the subject calls for. At its worst, it is not only inefficient but pompous and insincere as well. Here are examples taken from student papers, with possible revisions:

> He derives much pleasure from the reading of the written accomplishments of literate man, both prose and poetry.
> REVISION: He likes to read both prose and poetry.

> Sam is concerned primarily with the opportunities college can afford in the field of pure enjoyment.
> REVISION: Sam came to college to have fun.

> While much emphasis was put on the penmanship aspect of writing, the great art of spelling went relatively untouched.
> REVISION: Penmanship was emphasized more than spelling.

A particular variety of inflated writing is emotional description of nature, such as this:

> I could faintly see stars that were desperately trying to push their rays through a layer of stubborn clouds. Every now and then one of them succeeded and winked and flirted with me as if boasting of its accomplishment. It laughed too soon, for in the next minute it was once more hidden by an unsympathetic cloud and had to start again its never-ending, frustrating task.

It would not be entirely fair to the author of this passage to say that it could be boiled down to "Most of the time the stars were hidden by clouds." The writer is trying to sketch a picture and communicate an emotion, not merely convey bald information. But he tries too hard, gets too emotional, uses words carelessly and too abundantly. Students who write like this should look more steadily and more carefully at what they wish to describe, then write about it and their feelings toward it in words that are honest and faithful to the facts.

REDUNDANCY

WD 2 *Avoid redundancy*

A second frequent kind of wordiness is called *redundancy;* that is, unnecessary repetition of ideas. Here are some examples:

> The thought that he would ever attend college was startling and surprising to him.

REVISION: The thought that he would ever attend college was startling to him. ("Startling" and "surprising" mean nearly the same thing.)
OR: He was surprised at the thought that he would ever attend college.

Both the husband and the wife should have a mutual understanding of each other.
REVISION: The husband and wife should understand each other. ("Mutual" implies "each other.")

She was a typical teen-age adolescent. (An adolescent would necessarily be teen-age.)
REVISION: She was a typical teen-ager.
OR POSSIBLY: She was a typical adolescent.

In the following paragraph from a student paper, each sentence repeats in slightly different words the same idea:

> If someone were to ask me what I would do if war should come, I would not know how to answer the question. Many things would enter my mind, but I have not thought enough about this question before so that I could answer it. Realizing that I have never been faced with the actual situation of war, I do not know how I would react. I have had no experience with war and therefore any ideas I might have about it are completely unpredictable. I have never been sufficiently curious about war to do much thinking about it and what I would do if a war should break out and involve me in it.
> REVISION: I don't know how I would react if war should come.

Redundancy has several possible causes. Sometimes it is the result simply of hasty writing that has not been proofread. The sentence that uses both "startling" and "surprising" is an example. Sometimes, however, redundancy is caused by a writer's ignorance of the exact meanings of certain words—and his failure to look the words up in a dictionary. The sentence that recommends a mutual understanding of each other for husbands and wives is probably an example of such ignorance. The sort of redundancy that is seen in the paragraph about war is more difficult to cure, for it is the result of fuzzy thinking. The student who wrote that paragraph was going around in circles—and apparently was unaware of the fact. This kind of redundancy can often be avoided by the discipline of a good outline. If the content of the paragraph had been properly represented in an outline, the writer almost certainly would have seen that he was dealing with only a single idea and that one statement of it was enough.

MISCELLANEOUS WORDINESS

WD 3   *Avoid other kinds of wordiness*

Here are examples of other kinds of wordiness:

> Salaries in the field of government are not as high as in the field of business.
> REVISION: Salaries in government are not as high as in business.

> Generally, the men and women of this tribe are of a very small size.
> REVISION: Generally, the men and women of this tribe are very small.

> The mirror of the telescope is round in shape.
> REVISION: The mirror of the telescope is round.

> In the case of an athlete, if he flunks a subject he must make it up.
> REVISION: If an athlete flunks a subject, he must make it up.

> A liberal education is valuable for an engineer, both in a financial sense and in a social sense.
> REVISION: A liberal education is valuable for an engineer, both financially and socially.

You should draw two conclusions from this discussion of wordiness: know clearly and fully what you want to say; say it concisely—but not so concisely that you omit something that you need to say.

EXERCISE

1. In the following passages you will find many examples of wordiness. Rewrite the passages which you feel err in this way.

(a) I have often thought that if I could be granted a wish I would have Miss Horner transported to ancient Rome. Whisked back in the swirling eddies of time, her dissatisfied soul would flee the cares of modern existence to at last find peace in the grandeur of classic antiquity. There she would be content in an atmosphere of unspoiled splendor; she would delight in the pristine life; she would make an elegant Roman, and know sublime happiness. But alas, no magic can bring back times past. Alfreda Horner remains, with the rest of us, suspended in the illusion of present existence—a high school teacher in the twentieth century, born 2,000 years too late.

(b) Now that you know some of the symptoms of this terrible disease, televisionitis, perhaps you will want to know more about its terrible and ravaging effects. These effects are so terrible that, once infected and cured, a person is always in danger of succumbing again to the disease. To illustrate this fact, I remember one summer when I went without a TV set for a month. I was sure I was completely cured.

However, on my first night near a television set I was afflicted and watched TV until two o'clock in the morning. How I suffered from its renewed effects! Each reinfection after a temporary cure increases its dreadful effects.

(c) I hooked a seventeen-pound Northern Pike. We almost upset the canoe in the procedure of getting him landed.

(d) The money that had been stolen amounted to the vast sum of twelve hundred dollars; this money was also a total loss because it was not insured.

(e) While I worked on a dude ranch in Wyoming I had many various jobs. One of these jobs was that of the ranch chauffeur. This job required me to meet all trains and planes and deliver the guests safely to their cabins.

(f) I learned how to talk to people that I hadn't known too long and how to get along better with people. I learned how to be nice to people that I didn't care for too much. Chauffeuring requires a person to be the type that can get along with all types of people.

(g) The need for modern highways has been emphasized because of the horsepower and speed in modern cars of today.

(h) By graduation time last year I was finally reconciled to the fact that the institution of higher learning atop Mt. Oread in the city of Lawrence on the Kaw River was the only place for me.

(i) On August the ninth, in the year of our Lord nineteen hundred and forty-two, the joy (and, almost as often, the irritant) of our family life came into this world. She was so fat that the doctor had been convinced that she would be twins. As it turned out, there was only one roly-poly blackheaded butterball who was soon dubbed Sharon Lorraine Norris.

(j) Many people are killed each year by driving too fast, letting their car get out of control by excess speeding.

Repetition

Repetition of words can be either a vice or a device in writing. Properly used, it is a valuable means of directing the reader's attention to key ideas and impressing these ideas on his mind; it is also a useful way of tying together related ideas in a passage. Carelessly used, repetition can annoy a reader and interfere with effective communication.

EFFECTIVE REPETITION

WD 4   *Use repetition to unify a passage or to stress ideas*

In the following paragraph from Somerset Maugham's *The Summing Up*, notice the unifying effect of repeating "write," "writer," and "writing":

It is evident that no professional writer can afford only to write when he feels like it. If he waits till he is in the mood, till he has the inspiration as he says, he waits indefinitely and ends by producing little or nothing. The professional writer creates the mood. He has his inspiration too, but he controls and subdues it to his bidding by setting himself regular hours of work. But in time writing becomes a habit, and like the old actor in retirement, who gets restless when the hour arrives at which he has been accustomed to go down to the theatre and make up for the evening performance, the writer itches to get to his pens and paper at the hours at which he had been used to write. Then he writes automatically. Words come easily to him and words suggest ideas. They are old and empty ideas, but his practised hand can turn out an acceptable piece. He goes down to luncheon or goes to bed with the assurance that he has done a good day's work. Every production of an artist should be the expression of an adventure of his soul. This is a counsel of perfection and in an imperfect world a certain indulgence should be bestowed on the professional writer; but this surely is the aim he should keep before him. He does well only to write to liberate his spirit of a subject that he has so long meditated that it burdens him and if he is wise he will take care to write only for the sake of his own peace. Perhaps the simplest way to break the habit of writing is by changing the environment to one that gives no opportunity for the daily task. You cannot write well or much (and I venture the opinion that you cannot write well unless you write much) unless you form a habit; but habits in writing as in life are only useful if they are broken as soon as they cease to be advantageous.

Intentional repetition of individual words or phrases, as in the following two sentences, is a common way of stressing an idea for the reader:

He was a materialistic hero of a materialistic generation (Vernon Louis Parrington, *Main Currents in American Thought*, Vol. 3).
Distinction of manners and dress was gone, dignity and repose were gone, traditional standards were gone . . . (*Ibid.*).

INEFFECTIVE REPETITION

WD 5   *Avoid ineffective repetition*

Though certainly not the most serious fault in student writing, ineffective repetition is one of the most common. Repetition properly used draws the reader's attention to ideas that the writer thinks important and that deserve to be stressed. Improperly used, repetition draws the reader's attention to ideas that the writer did not mean to emphasize or to ideas that do not deserve such close attention.

Student writing shows four common sorts of unsuccessful repetition

—more often the product of carelessness than of a small vocabulary. First, and perhaps most frequent, is *excessive repeating of particular words*. It is illustrated in the following excerpts from freshman themes:

> As he began to grow and to learn to crawl and to stand up, his parents noticed that he seemed slow to understand what they said and to learn to talk.
> REVISION: As he grew and learned to crawl and stand up, his parents noticed that he seemed slow in understanding what they said and in learning to talk.

> Comic strips are written for many different purposes, but the main purpose of comic strips is to provide entertainment for different readers. Because different people enjoy different kinds of entertainment, there are many different kinds of comic strips.
> REVISION: The main purpose of all comic strips is to provide entertainment; but there is a great variety of them, since people differ widely in the kinds of entertainment they prefer.

A second kind of ineffective repetition is the *careless use of different forms of the same word* in the same sentence or in neighboring sentences:

> I never met anyone who didn't feel a warmhearted feeling for George.
> REVISION: I never met anyone who didn't have a warmhearted feeling for George.

> When our guest of honor failed to appear, none of us appeared to be discouraged.
> REVISION: When our guest of honor failed to appear, none of us seemed to be discouraged.

A third kind of objectionable repetition is *use of the same word in different senses*, as in these examples:

> The track manager keeps track of items issued to the athletes.
> REVISION: The track manager keeps a record of items issued to the athletes.

> It looks as if she has never tried to improve her looks.
> REVISION: It looks as if she has never tried to improve her appearance.

Finally, another kind of unsuccessful repetition involves *homonyms*— that is, words that are pronounced alike but that differ in meaning:

> When my father came home, he was pleased to see that his industrious son had been working hard all day in the hot sun.
> REVISION: When my father came home he was pleased to see that I had been working hard all day in the hot sun.
> (Other revisions are possible.)

The boar, with two of our arrows sticking in his shoulder, bore down on us like a diesel locomotive.

REVISION: The boar, with two of our arrows sticking in his shoulder, hurled himself toward us like a diesel locomotive.

EXERCISES

2. The following sentences contain examples of faulty repetition and examples in which repetition has been used effectively. Criticize the sentences. That is, indicate where you find repetition used ineffectively and where you find it used effectively. Rewrite those sentences which you find faulty so as to eliminate the ineffective repetition.

(a) One scene in this movie that proves to me that movies of this type should not be shown in public is the last scene of the movie.

(b) Certainly the government should seek some way to cure the public's addiction to tobacco, for certainly it isn't going to do any good to stop harmful advertising of tobacco if people cannot be cured of the addiction.

(c) Death is always more somber when surrounded by death. There is nothing so depressing as seeing a black procession in the fall nosing through dead streets, passing through dead leaves and dead trees, ending up at a cemetery where a dead body is lowered into dead ground.

(d) Perhaps the best thing about her is her sense of humor. She has a dry and witty sense of humor that will challenge the best.

(e) She has a personal interest in the personnel manager.

(f) Marie looks as if she's never looked at herself in a mirror.

(g) The trees around this lake were not large trees but they were pretty trees and the grass under them was velvet soft.

(h) Autumn is the time for loneliness. It is lonely to walk along and not hear the scurry of children at play, of disgruntled husbands cutting lawns. It is lonely for a mother to surrender her children to education. A row of empty picnic tables, an empty baseball field, a deserted amusement park—all are lonely.

(i) I knew the boys would be worrying by now and were probably out looking for me. It was very cold by now and I was riding as fast as my horse would carry me.

(j) Most of my math teachers would work several examples of the work we were to do for the next day and then give the assignment for work to be handed in.

3. The authors of the following passages have made use of frequent repetition. Find as many examples as you can in which you feel the repetition is used for a specific purpose, and explain what it contributes to the effect of the passage.

(a) The problem, the great problem, of our military planners is to organize and maintain armed forces capable of fighting *any kind* of war *anywhere.* We cannot afford not to prepare to fight any kind of war anywhere. This does not, of course, mean that all kinds of forces—strategic air, defensive air, tactical air, conventional land power, nuclear land power, should be maintained at great strength, ready instantly for war. It means, rather, that we must keep alive the art of fighting any kind of war anywhere in the world, that we must have at least cadre forces of many different types keyed to different missions, capable of expansion in case of war. We must have fire-fighting forces, police forces capable of taking the first shock, and a mobilization potential to raise more of the same after war starts (Hanson W. Baldwin, "Limited War," *The Atlantic Monthly,* May, 1959).

(b) Obviously, we do not know what the ultimate effects will be of the atomic weapons tests we have already conducted. I am not sure that we know what will be the ultimate effects of our methods of disposal of radioactive wastes. I doubt that we know what we are doing to the sea through the use of modern detergents and the fouling of its surface with oil. I am not sure that we know what we are doing with modern insecticides, which we employ quite recklessly in agriculture for our immediate purposes, giving little thought to their ultimate effects. We who call ourselves Christians must acknowledge responsibility in these matters, most of which are international in their implications (George F. Kennan, "Foreign Policy and Christian Conscience," *The Atlantic Monthly,* May, 1959).

(c) Another formative principle came to me from a phrase of Nietzsche's: "The poets? The poets lie too much." I was nineteen when the phrase stuck in my mind; a dozen years passed before it worked effectively, and I decided not to tell lies in verse. Not to feign any emotion that I did not feel; not to pretend to believe in optimism or pessimism, or unreversible progress; not to say anything because it was popular, or generally accepted, or fashionable in intellectual circles, unless I myself believed it; and not to believe easily. These negatives limited the field; I am not recommending them but for my own occasions (Robinson Jeffers, "Foreword" to *The Selected Poetry of Robinson Jeffers*).

Triteness

WD 6   *Use fresh, unhackneyed language*

The student who begins an autobiographical theme with the remark that he first saw the light of day on April 27, 19–, that he was a bouncing baby boy, and that his proud father cried the happy news from the housetops to all and sundry—the student who writes like this is likely either to have his readers yawning or to have them laughing at (not with) him before they have finished the first paragraph. Such writing is full of phrases that have been overused for years; their odor of staleness spoils the whole composition and causes readers to neglect or to under-rate the ideas or information being presented.

None of us can entirely avoid using trite phrases, especially in con-versation, but college students and other educated people should be careful not to let them become so numerous in their language that they attract attention. They should take special pains to keep trite phrases to a minimum in their writing, for, since writing (unlike conversation) can be revised and corrected, there is much less excuse for allowing objec-tionable phrases in written language than in spoken.

Four kinds of trite expressions are especially frequent in student writing. First are what may be called *set phrases:* first and foremost, last but not least, in closing let me say that, mad dash, wild ride, by leaps and bounds. A second kind is *overworked quotations:* never say die, sad-der but wiser, method in his madness, master of my fate, kill the fatted calf. Third are *over-used figures of speech,* often either *personifications:* Mother Nature, Mother Earth, grim reaper, Father Time; or *compari-sons:* fresh as a daisy, tired as a dog, slippery as an eel, strong as a bull, quick as a flash. Other stale figures also appear fairly often: burn the midnight oil, wheel of fortune, festive board, ladder of success, road of life. A fourth kind of trite expression is called *euphemism,* a device in-tended to gloss over an unpleasant or embarrassing fact by substituting vague or more pleasing language for the simple and direct word or phrase: pass away, summoned to the great beyond, pass the great divide, meet one's Maker (to die); inebriated, intoxicated, under the influence (drunk); memorial park (cemetery or graveyard); tavern, cocktail lounge (bar); unmentionables (underwear); regurgitated (vomited); ab-domen, tummy (belly). Some of the words that have been substituted for in this way are now actually little-used—undertaker, for instance, or belly (except when referring to animals). In many cases, however, the euphemism is pretentious and unnecessary; the simple verb "die," for example, is nearly always preferable to the fancier and longer ways of stating the same inescapable and familiar human fact.

The best way to avoid trite expression is to consider carefully what you really mean, what the experience really felt like to *you,* what the scene really looked like to *you;* then say what you have to say as honestly and directly as you can. For instance:

> I have always had a weakness for the fair sex.
> REVISION: I have always liked girls.

Tired but happy, our ears still ringing with the sound of thunderous applause, we wended our weary way homeward.

REVISION: As we slowly walked home along the dark streets, occasionally scuffling our feet a little from weariness, it seemed to us that we could still hear the enthusiastic clapping of the audience. We were tired, yes; but we were contented too, for we felt now that the weeks of hard work, the many late rehearsals, the endless memorizing of lines had been worth all they cost us.

Mother Nature had put on a frock of green.

REVISION: Spring had finally arrived; the trees and bushes had turned a bright, fresh green as their new leaves unfolded, and on the forest floor clumps of newly sprouted weeds and spring flowers contrasted with the brown of last year's vegetation.

EXERCISES

4. In the following paragraph pick out all the trite expressions that you can find. Then rewrite the paragraph using a fresh and direct means of expression.

In my humble opinion the average American college woman has a pretty mixed up idea of what the ideal man should be. After listening to some of the midnight gabfests at college I've come to the conclusion that what most of the girls are really concerned with is how good looking a guy is, whether or not he has a good line, how well fixed he is, and how he spends his money. The reason behind this concern with surface qualities may be that all girls want to go with someone the other girls will put their stamp of approval on. And somehow this mental image of the knight in shining armor has sprung up in the minds of countless thousands of coeds. A truly praiseworthy male must have the broad shoulders and muscles of a football player, the classic features of a Greek god (with a slight twinkle in the eye), a definite way with the ladies, and money to burn. This particular type is often referred to as a "perfect doll." A less wondrous individual, but still passable date material, is a "good guy," while at the bottom of the social ladder is the "cube" or "square," with whom no self-respecting girl would be caught dead.

5. Many—but not all—of the following sentences contain examples of triteness. Find as many as you can and rewrite the sentences, eliminating the trite expression by substituting a direct phrase.

(a) One acquires an education to learn to appreciate the finer things in life.

(b) Many of those men had been in the hills for over a year without seeing any kind of civilization except their own company and a few Koreans who lived in the abandoned bunkers on the ridge lines.

(c) His powerful body lumbers along on short squat legs.

(d) We rush madly from one activity to another and don't have time to appreciate any of them.

(e) How in the world is one expected to know beforehand that it takes simply ages to get to Lindsey Hall from Clark Annex?

(f) By starting at the bottom of the ladder of material success and working up together, a couple should be drawn closer together.

(g) I watched the movie hero prancing up a staircase, his trusty blade slapping from side to side.

(h) As the show progressed I began to feel as if butterflies were flying around in my stomach.

(i) Old round Mr. Sun was just peeking over the horizon when we started up the trail.

(j) Although he was worried for hours before the show, he appeared cool as a cucumber once it had started.

(k) After what seemed an eternity, a fire engine rounded the corner and pulled up before the burning shed.

(l) I guess Mortimer has really succumbed to Dan Cupid's arrow this time.

Idiom

WD 7 *Use exact idioms*

The word *idiom* refers to the typical patterns used in a particular language to express meaning. Russian, for instance, has no words for "a," "an," and "the," and does not ordinarily use the present tense forms of the verb "be"; the English sentence "The man is my friend" would be expressed in Russian as "Man my friend" (Chelovyek moy droog). Russians say, "With me new coat" (U menya novoyeh pal'to), but we would say, "I have a new coat." The omission of words for "the" and "is," and the use of "With me (is)" for "I have" are correct idioms in Russian, though they would be incorrect idiom in English.

Like all languages, English has many idiomatic expressions, combinations of two or more words that, whether or not they fit the usual rules of grammar and logic, have a specific meaning and must be used as they are. For example, we say that a person has *a* cold, or that he has *the* flu, or that he has pneumonia. Though there is no logical or grammatical reason why we use "a" with the name of one illness, "the" with that of another, and neither with the name of a third, it is incorrect (unidiomatic) to use a different pattern. In the same way we say that two nations are *at* war, or *in a* war, or declared war *on* each other. We *put up* some sandwiches, or *put up with* a nuisance, or *make do with* what we have.

Though such idioms at first make little or no sense to a foreigner learning English, people who have spoken the language from earliest childhood usually do not have much difficulty with most of them. Some idioms, however, often those containing prepositions, cause trouble even for many native users of English. A few examples are:

> We were tired with her tantrums and selfishness.
> REVISION: We were tired *of* her tantrums and selfishness.
>
> Twenty-seven men were initiated to our fraternity last year.
> REVISION: Twenty-seven men were initiated *into* our fraternity last year.
>
> George's sense of humor was so boisterous and caused so much commotion in a crowd that I was always glad that it was peculiar with him alone.
> REVISION: . . . peculiar *to* him alone.
>
> Although our date was for seven-thirty, I had to wait on her for thirty-five minutes.
> REVISION: Although our date was for seven-thirty, I had to wait *for* her for thirty-five minutes.
> (BUT: The clerk waited on me, is good idiom.)

Many of the most troublesome idioms are listed in Chapter 17. Your dictionary will also list idioms under the most important word in the phrase. Whenever you are in doubt as to the correctness of an idiom, or whenever your teacher marks one wrong on your themes, be sure to look up and learn the correct version.

EXERCISE

6. In the following sentences you will find some incorrect idioms. List all those which you feel are not correct and rewrite the sentence using the correct idiom. In case of doubt, consult your dictionary.

(a) My father is completely oblivious of household chores.
(b) I liked my job very much because there was more money involved and less hours to work.
(c) Shawnee Street has a personality opposite of that of Cherokee Street.
(d) There are two types of anti-freeze—that which has a alcohol base and that which has a ethylene base.
(e) The night that made the greatest impression with me was that of my first recital.
(f) Jeremy was bothered with his roommate's study habits.
(g) Fred returned to the farm and married up with Esther's sister.
(h) Genevieve acted oblivious to his affection.
(i) MacNeil tormented the neighbors by late parties.

(j) Cary was reconciled with his lonely existence.
(k) Wolverines are found in small quantities around the Great Lakes.
(l) The Jones boys have arisen socially in Carter High School.
(m) He is susceptible with any kind of flattery.
(n) The people who lived there were indifferent of the beauties of their valley.

Colloquialisms

WD 8   *Use colloquialisms only in appropriate situations*

Many people have the notion that any word or expression that a dictionary labels "colloquial" is incorrect and should not be used by educated writers and speakers. This view is mistaken. The label "colloquial" simply means that the word or expression so marked is more likely to be found in conversation and informal writing than in more formal situations; it is neither incorrect nor illiterate.

If the subject, the audience, and the situation call for an informal written style, a few colloquialisms are entirely suitable and in fact help to establish the informal tone that is wanted. Notice how the effectiveness of the following passage is heightened by the occasional use of colloquialisms (they have been italicized so you can easily identify them).

> Apparently the only people who are more prone to *splurging* when they get in a supermarket than housewives are the wives' husbands and children. Supermarket operators are pretty well agreed that men are *easy marks* for all sorts of impulse items and cite cases *they've* seen of husbands who are sent to the store for a loaf of bread and depart with both their arms loaded with their favorite snack items. Shrewd supermarket operators have put the superior impulsiveness of little children to work in promoting sales. The Indiana supermarket operator I mentioned has a dozen little wire carts that small children can push about the store while their mothers are shopping with big carts. People think these tiny carts are very *cute;* and the operator thinks they are very profitable. The small children go *zipping* up and down the aisles imitating their mothers in impulse buying, only more so. They reach out, hypnotically I assume, and grab boxes of cookies, candies, dog food, and everything else that delights or interests them. Complications arise, of course, when mother and child come out of their trances and together reach the check-out counter (Vance Packard, *The Hidden Persuaders*).

On the other hand, colloquialisms should nearly always be avoided in a formal style. In the following paragraph from a student research paper, where formal style is appropriate, the colloquialisms (again italicized) are a jarring note and should be eliminated.

> The terms of the Potsdam ultimatum were very favorably received by Japan's leaders. In the interim between the beginning of 1945 and the issuance of the ultimatum, Japan had realized that she was *licked,* and she had been trying to *finagle* a satisfactory separate peace with Russia. By this time Japan was concerned mainly with the threat of losing her status as a nation if the Allies demanded unconditional surrender; thus she was overjoyed when she found that the Potsdam Declaration promised that the surrendered Japan would remain a sovereign nation free to choose her own government and free to rule her own land. In spite of some *griping* by the War Minister, the war cabinet agreed to accept the terms of the Potsdam Declaration.

Slang

WD 9 *In general, avoid using slang in writing*

Words marked in the dictionary as slang are, unlike colloquialisms, regarded as non-standard. The creation of slang terms is usually an attempt to find a new way of expression, and slang is therefore often exaggeratedly imaginative—rubberneck, egghead, gorilla (gangster), hardboiled, hot rod. When the terms are newly coined they add color and liveliness to informal conversation and occasionally are valuable in writing when special effects are being aimed at. For example, the following paragraphs from a review of a novel about jazz musicians gain a certain amount of color and vigor from the intentional—and limited—use of slang:

> There is a school of thought that holds that bullfight bores are more deserving of ballbat anesthesia than jazz bores, but this school is wrong. A bullfight bore may re-enact Manolete's death spasms, but a jazz bore will replay the same Charlie Parker record, with contrapuntal commentary, until his woofer melts. The public ear has been grievously bent, and therefore any novel about jazzmen that is fresh, authentic and ungummed by cultism is an achievement.

> Playwright Garson (*Born Yesterday*) Kanin (rhymes with rain in), a jazz saxophonist during his knockabout days, has managed this much. His novel is cast in the form of a onetime saxman's fond, moody reminiscence of the hard-blowing early '30s. Jogged by a telephone call from one of his old partners, the narrator recalls the rise and fall of the combo they formed. The group begins as a trio, built around an astonishingly good young trumpeter. Then the saxman finds a pianist at a Harlem rent party, and the trio sounds even better as a quartet.

Bookings pick up, and with the addition of two more saxophonists and a drummer, the outfit seems on the point of blowing itself a big name ("The Lost Beat," *Time,* June 29, 1959).

In general, though, slang is rarely used in good writing, for besides being non-standard it has two other disadvantages. First, like trite phrases, it often stereotypes meaning and so fails to communicate clearly and precisely. For example, calling a girl a "slick chick" or a boy a "square" really does not tell anyone very much about these people. "Slick chick" is simply a general term of approval, just as "square" is a general term of disapproval. Since the reasons for these judgments are not apparent, the judgments actually do not say anything about the people who are being judged; but they do say something about the person using the terms: he approves of the girl, disapproves of the boy—and uses hackneyed terms to say so.

The other disadvantage of slang is that it goes out of date rapidly. It is as subject to changes in fashion as women's clothes. Dictionaries list some slang terms, and occasionally a slang term survives, becomes respectable and enters the language permanently, on an equal basis with other words (mob, gin, taxi, TV, radio, derrick are examples). Most slang never gets into dictionaries: it passes out of existence before dictionaries can record it. At the time this chapter is being written, "beatnik" slang is at the height of popularity among teen-agers around the country. Probably, by the time the chapter is printed and in your hands many of the following "beatnik" terms will already sound stale: cube, cat, cool, dig, crazy, nervous, monster (telephone), Squaresville, flipped, octopus, in orbit, pad, bug, calf.

Though colloquialisms will often be useful in your less formal college writing, you will rarely be justified in using slang in your papers; like other kinds of non-standard expression, it will be inappropriate to the style of writing expected of you.

EXERCISES

7. In the following sentences, identify which words and expressions are colloquialisms and which are slang. In case of doubt, consult your dictionary.

  (a) Bert departed with the evidence and left me holding the bag.
  (b) After the seed was paid for and the supplies ordered we managed only to break even.
  (c) Jones lived eighteen months in a shack in the desert.

(d) Gregory was miffed when his roommate continued to borrow his neckties.
(e) Geraldine had a real brain storm during study period.
(f) The professor will crack down on us if we don't get this paper in on time.
(g) Nick Olson's new recording is solid.
(h) Judge Fairweather perpetrated the biggest swindle in years.
(i) It was one of his usual corny jokes.
(j) The brass in the front office will have to approve your leave.
(k) I'd advise you to butter up the boss if you don't want to be bounced.
(l) What is Dolores's pitch this time?

8. From the following passage pick out all the colloquialisms you can find. Be able to discuss what effect they have on the passage.

This week we feel like soothing a bank, and are happy to report that, with the cooperation of one of our footloose subscribers, we are able to do so here and now. Our subscriber found himself in Rostov one day not long ago, he tells us, and called at the local bank to exchange some traveller's checks for rubles. The Russian bank clerk there took a look at the traveller's checks, which had been issued by the First National City Bank of New York, and then produced an enormous looseleaf notebook in which samples of foreign currencies of the world were neatly pasted up. Leaf by leaf, the clerk plowed through the notebook as our man looked over his shoulder, and at last came upon a First National City Bank traveller's check. He compared our man's checks with this, but there was one thing wrong: the check in the notebook had printed across it, in wide-spaced letters in red ink, "SPECIMEN." However, this subscriber of ours was nobody's fool. Noting the troubled look on the countenance of the Russian bank clerk, he endorsed his checks in a confident fashion and then, before the clerk could say anything, whipped out a red-ink ball-point pen and nonchalantly printed "SPECIMEN" across the face of each one. The clerk sighed gratefully, handed over the rubles, and our man went on his way, winding up in our office in due course and telling us this tale, thus enabling us to follow our aforementioned inclination this week. Stop worrying, First National City Bank of New York! That's the story behind those checks from Rostov you've been frowning over all these weeks. You needn't call in the F.B.I. Just relax and go back to counting your blessings (*The New Yorker*, Aug. 1, 1959).

Connotations of Words

WD 10   *Make accurate use of the connotations of words*

Many words have, besides their central meaning (called *denotation*), certain overtones that often are just as important as the central meaning in deciding whether or not a particular word should be used. "Horse," "steed," "charger," "palfrey," "nag," "plug," "hay-burner" all refer denotatively to the same species of four-footed animal—but obviously the words are not interchangeable. Each of them, except perhaps the first, has overtones, called *connotations,* that restrict its use and make it appropriate in some situations and not in others. You would not refer to a handsome thoroughbred Arabian stallion as a *nag,* nor would you (unless you were trying to be humorous) be likely to say that you went to a riding academy yesterday and rode an hour and a half on a *steed* or a *palfrey.*

It is true that not everyone will have exactly the same connotations for the same word, since the particular connotations that a word has for a person depend on his previous experience. "Dog" will have favorable connotations for someone who loves dogs, but the opposite kind for someone who was once severely bitten by a dog and now dislikes or fears them. Generally speaking, though, there is usually a large area of agreement on connotations. Such words as *mother, childhood, love, peace, patriotism* have favorable connotations for most people; just as *traitor, pig, filth, idiot, drunkenness* have unfavorable ones.

Effective writing makes careful use of connotations. Poetry provides one of the clearest examples, for a large amount of its effectiveness depends on a skillful use of connotations. You can see this if you contrast "Rime of the Ancient Mariner" with "Poem of the Old Sailor." Or contrast

> I've got a pain in my chest, and I'm in a stupor
>   As though I had swallowed poison
> Or taken a narcotic
>   A minute ago and am passing out. . . .

with the first four lines of the "Ode to a Nightingale" as Keats wrote them:

> My heart aches, and a drowsy numbness pains
>   My sense, as though of hemlock I had drunk,
> Or emptied some dull opiate to the drains
>   One minute past, and Lethe-wards had sunk. . . .

The same kind of awareness of the value of connotations is apparent in much advertising. Notice that cigar advertisements speak of "aroma," not "scent" or "bouquet"; on the other hand no advertiser of perfumes or women's underarm deodorants would mention the "aroma" of these products; instead, he would probably say "scent" or "fragrance."

Check your own writing carefully after the first draft is done to be sure that you have not used words with inappropriate connotations, as in the following sentences taken from freshman themes:

> I don't like to see women smoking; it's a man's habit. Women should remember they are women and always be *effeminate*.
> REVISION: . . . always be feminine.

> Then came the biggest surprise of all—*daddy* said I could take my car back to college with me.
> REVISION: . . . my father said I could take. . . .

> There, not three feet behind me, was the store manager *ogling* me suspiciously.
> REVISION: . . . glaring at me suspiciously (or, watching me suspiciously).

EXERCISES

9. For each of the following groups of words with the same denotative value, pick out those that (a) have the most favorable connotative value for you; (b) the most unfavorable. Then, select five of the groups and write sentences using the words in them so as to show their connotative value.

(a) Thin, slim, skinny
(b) Sleek, slick, silken
(c) Slavish, servile, menial
(d) Thrust, shove, push
(e) Jabber, chat, babble
(f) Insane, mad, crazy
(g) Influence, prestige, weight
(h) Average, medium, mediocre

(i) Everlasting, continual, endless
(j) Grand, magnificent, imposing
(k) Frighten, scare, terrify
(l) Falsehood, misrepresentation, lie
(m) Senile, old, elderly
(n) Vocal, fluent, glib
(o) Rich, affluent, loaded

10. In the following passages pick out the words that have connotative meaning for you. Then rewrite the passages trying to use more neutral words, ones that do not have connotative meaning.

(a) Northwestern Mutual agents find satisfying careers with this company, helping others achieve security. . . . By character, ability and training, you will find your Northwestern Mutual agent remarkably well qualified to help you with your protection and investment problems (The Northwestern Mutual Life Insurance Company, Milwaukee, Wis.).

(b) So last year they took seven-year-old Tommy out of . . . public school after watching him vegetate on a soda-pop diet of "life-adjustment" courses (*Time*, June 29, 1959).

(c) For men of action . . . here are watches that resist shock, storms, water. . . . Here are watches with precision-crafted, jeweled movements to mark every moment accurately, precisely, unfailingly. Here, too, are watches you'll be proud to look at, proud to wear—superbly styled with modern good taste (Bulova Watch Co.).

(d) Once upon a time (i.e., four years ago) professionally sentimental, consistently profitmaking Hollywoodsman Walt Disney built the zingiest, zowiest toy his fertile mind could imagine—and then invited others to come play with it. . . . canny Producer Disney has been reaping more tangible rewards. Since the opening, his dazzling, 61.2 acre carnival has taken in $48 million. . . . Such coin counting has spawned sincere flattery: imitation Disneylands are shooting up across the country (*Time,* June 29, 1959).

(e) You can't go back home to your family, back home to your childhood, back home to romantic love, back home to a young man's dreams of glory, and of fame, back home to exile, to escape to Europe and some foreign land, back home to lyricism, to singing just for singing's sake, back home to aestheticism, to one's youthful idea of "the artist" and the all-sufficiency of "art" and "beauty" and "love," back home to the ivory tower, back home to places in the country, to the cottage in Bermuda, away from all the strife and conflict of the world, back home to the father you have lost and have been looking for, back home to someone who can help you, save you, ease the burden for you, back home to the old forms and systems of things which once seemed ever-lasting but which are changing all the time—back home to the escapes of Time and Memory (Thomas Wolfe, "The Wind Is Rising and the River Flows," from *You Can't Go Home Again*).

(f) Much have I travelled in the realms of gold,
And many goodly states and kingdoms seen;
Round many eastern islands have I been
Which bards in fealty to Apollo hold.
Oft of one wide expanse had I been told
That deep-browed Homer ruled as his demesne;
Yet did I never breathe its pure serene
Till I heard Chapman speak out loud and bold.
Then felt I like some watcher of the skies
When a new planet swims into his ken;
Or like stout Cortez when with eagle eyes
He stared at the Pacific—and all his men
Looked at each other with a wild surmise—
Silent, upon a peak in Darien (John Keats, "On First Looking into Chapman's Homer").

Abstract and Concrete Words

WD 11   *Distinguish between abstract and concrete words*

Many nouns can be classified as either abstract or concrete. Abstract nouns are those that stand for *abstractions*—an idea or quality, something that you cannot detect with your senses. Examples are such words as democracy, government, honor, villainy, courage, kindness. Concrete nouns stand for things that you *can* detect with your senses—stone, girl, sedan, saucer, policeman, explosion, telegram.

WD 11 A *Be sure that the meaning you attach to abstract words is understood by your readers*

Both kinds of nouns are needed for clear and effective communication, but when you use abstract nouns you should take certain precautions. The very fact that nouns of this kind stand for things that cannot be touched or tasted or felt or heard or smelled makes it inevitable that there will be a good deal of disagreement about the exact meaning of many of them. "Success" means one thing to a physician, another to an engineer, still another to a crane operator. Other words, such as "individualism," "business," "labor," "morality," are likely to cause the same sort of difficulty. When you use words of this class in your writing, be sure that you make clear exactly what they mean to you so that your reader will not misunderstand.

WD 11 B *Use concrete words to help specify the meaning of abstract nouns*

A good way to clarify the meaning of abstract nouns is to support them with examples and details that narrow their meaning. Here you will find that concrete nouns, which are much less likely to be misunderstood, will be indispensable. Notice how in the following passage the meaning of the abstract noun "individualism" is limited and made clear by specific material and concrete language:

> Why does France produce so infinite a variety of individuals as the Curie sisters and Roger the Frog? It has become a cliché to say that the French are individualists and that it is their individualism that prevents stable, efficient government, saps the economy, and keeps France divided and weak. This is true and obvious, but what is rarely examined is the cause of French individualism.
>
> Surely individualism is not a biological phenomenon. It is highly unlikely, I would guess, that a French baby sent to America to be raised would grow up to start a new political party at the age of twenty-one. No, what is passed on from generation to generation is a mistrust of all authority, of society itself, and, above all, the conviction that a man must count only upon himself for his own salvation.

The French do not believe in the commandment, "Love thy neighbor." They say: "Keep a sharp eye on thy neighbor, for chances are he is up to no good."

Frenchmen for centuries have had to fight to defend their homes, their property, their freedom, not only against foreign neighbors but against their fellow Frenchmen. The extension of the domains of the Capetians from the Paris basin to the Atlantic, the Pyrenees, the Mediterranean, and the Alps was not a natural expansion but a man-killing conquest of peoples and territories that went on for some eight hundred years, punctuated by raiding parties from Africa, Britain, Scandinavia, Austria, and Germany. The most cruel of all wars—religious and civil conflict—completed the ravages of feudal and imperial wars that set Frenchmen against Frenchmen. Other countries have suffered from war and invasion, of course, but none has the bloody history of the French (David Schoenbrun, "Manners and Morals of the French," *As France Goes*).

EXERCISES

11. In the following passages from student themes, pick out all the abstract nouns you can find. Then rewrite one of the paragraphs in a more concrete style to make it more meaningful.

(a) The husband and wife should have a mutual understanding in a successful marriage. Each should know how the other feels about such things as religion, raising a family, and a philosophy of life. With this knowledge, each will be better able to approach problems in a manner which will not offend the other. In this way many an unpleasant argument may be avoided. With an understanding of each other's feelings, they may discuss their differences intelligently and arrive at a solution agreeable to both.

(b) The desire to know is embedded in the mind of every person. It is true that some people are more curious than others, but everyone wants to know about something. Each of us goes about the task of satisfying his desire to know in a different fashion. Some turn to reading as a means of finding what they want to know. Others talk with people who have the information they want, and still others get the information firsthand by actually seeing or doing the things about which they are curious.

12. In the following passages of student writing pick out all the concrete words you can find. Be able to explain what they contribute to the effect of the passage.

(a) My father, my grandfather, and I arrived at the lake an hour before sunrise that cold fall morning. As I stepped out of the car, clad in hip boots and heavy hunting clothes, I trembled with excitement and anticipation.

Soon we had loaded ourselves with equipment—shotguns, shells, decoys, thermos bottles of hot coffee—and began the hike through the woods to the lake. The frost-covered leaves crackled underfoot, and a biting northerly wind swept through the trees. Far off in the cold morning a train whistled.

(b) With each succeeding dive, I became more fascinated with the water-life. An old stump held scores of tiny fish. Small snails clung to odd, broadleafed plants. Rocks loomed in fantastic shapes, coated with mud and moss. And here, lying on its side, lay an old sunken boat, bearded and furry with plant life!

General and Specific Words

WD 12 *Distinguish between general and specific words*

A great many words can be classified as either general or specific. Abstract words, such as liberty, enthusiasm, loyalty, represent general ideas and may therefore be considered general words. Many concrete words, such as animal, people, flower, food, are general words also; they stand for classes of things, general groupings under which are many specific varieties (flower: daisy, lily of the valley, petunia, nasturtium, marigold).

There is no clear dividing line between general and specific words. Rather, words are more general or less general, more specific or less specific, on a sort of sliding scale, depending on the other words they are being compared with. For example, *policeman* is more specific than *officer* but more general than *police sergeant*, which in turn is more general than *Police Sergeant George Thorne*. Here are some other examples:

property	real estate	building	ranch house
music	sonata	piano sonata	"Moonlight Sonata"
man	college student	varsity athlete	pole vaulter
transportation	automobile	foreign car	Volkswagen

WD 12 A *Use specific words for greater clarity*

Textbooks sometimes contain sentences like the following, which are so full of general (and abstract) words that it is difficult if not actually impossible to tell what the author means:

The self-situational relationship is a highly important focus for education and guidance but has not been given systematic attention, together with emphasis on self-understanding and situational understanding.

Good writers can present material just as difficult or technical as that which apparently is in the sentence just quoted, but by using specific and concrete words whenever possible, they can communicate their meaning clearly. For example, here is a passage in which Thomas Henry Huxley describes the scientific system of classifying the animal kingdom —surely a difficult enough subject, yet his meaning is clear:

Those kinds which include no other subdivisions than the sexes, or various breeds, are called, in technical language, species. The English lobster is a species, our cray fish is another, our prawn is another. In other countries, however, there are lobsters, cray fish, and prawns, very like ours, and yet presenting sufficient differences to deserve distinction. Naturalists, therefore, express this resemblance and this diversity by grouping them as distinct species of the same "genus." But the lobster and the cray fish, though belonging to distinct genera, have many features in common, and hence are grouped together in an assemblage which is called a family. More distant resemblances connect the lobster with the prawn and the crab, which are expressed by putting all these into the same order. Again, more remote, but still very definite, resemblances unite the lobster with the woodlouse, the king crab, the water flea, and the barnacle, and separate them from all other animals; whence they collectively constitute the larger group, or class, *Crustacea.* But the *Crustacea* exhibit many peculiar features in common with insects, spiders, and centipedes, so that these are grouped into the still larger assemblage or "province" *Articulata;* and, finally, the relations which these have to worms and other lower animals, are expressed by combining the whole vast aggregate into the sub-kingdom of *Annulosa.*

If I had worked my way from a sponge instead of a lobster, I should have found it associated, by like ties, with a great number of other animals into the sub-kingdom *Protozoa;* if I had selected a fresh-water polype or a coral, the members of what naturalists term the sub-kingdom *Coelenterata,* would have grouped themselves around my type; had a snail been chosen, the inhabitants of all univalve and bivalve, land and water, shells, the lamp shells, the squids, and the sea-mat would have gradually linked themselves on to it as members of the same sub-kingdom of *Mollusca;* and finally, starting from man, I should have been compelled to admit first, the ape, the rat, the horse, the dog, into the same class; and then the bird, the crocodile, the turtle, the frog, and the fish, into the same sub-kingdom of *Vertebrata.*

And if I had followed out all these various lines of classification fully, I should discover that there was no animal, either recent or fossil, which did not fall at once into one or other of these sub-kingdoms ("A Lobster; or, The Study of Zoology," from *Discourses Biological and Geological*).

WD 12 B *Avoid overuse of general words*

We need general words in English to stand for the general ideas and classes of things that we must often discuss. But one of the commonest weaknesses in freshman writing is the tendency to be more general than necessary, to prefer words that range toward increased generality and to neglect to use enough words that range in the opposite direction. The reason is not hard to find: it is easier to write in general terms than in specific, to say "College life develops maturity," and let it go at that, than to say specifically what is meant by college life and maturity, and exactly what the cause-and-effect relation is that is claimed to exist between them. It is important to be specific to avoid misunderstanding; what one person means by college life and maturity will not necessarily be the same as the meaning that someone else attaches to these general terms.

EXERCISES

13. The following sentences are simple statements containing only general nouns. Rewrite the sentences, adding some more specific details.

(a) My friend likes sports.
(b) I attended school in a small town.
(c) His duties were monotonous, but not difficult.
(d) The prairie was covered with vegetation.
(e) A strange individual came to our door one day.
(f) Women may choose some careers.
(g) I like my home town because of the people.
(h) The farmers went about their work.
(i) She was an interesting individual.
(j) Following the game we had a celebration.

14. Arrange each of the following groups of words in an order that moves from general to specific.

EXAMPLE: Person, European, Englishman, Churchill

(a) Bee, insect, creature, queen bee.
(b) Beef, sirloin steak, meat, food.
(c) Paleontology, zoology, biological science, science, knowledge.
(d) Plant, carrot, vegetable, yellow vegetable.
(e) Entertainment, comedy, *Much Ado About Nothing*, drama.
(f) Bed, household equipment, furniture, bedroom furniture, spool bed.
(g) Ponderosa pine, conifers, trees, vegetation.
(h) Sport, 100-yard dash, track, outdoor sport, race.

(i) Upper-division course, education, "History 403," senior seminar, higher education.

Passive Voice Verbs: Uses and Abuses

WD 13   *Distinguish between active and passive voice forms of verbs*

Voice in English grammar refers to the relation between the subject of a sentence and the action or condition that is expressed by the verb. There are two voices, the active and the passive. If the verb of a sentence is in the active voice, the subject generally is the performer of the action indicated by the verb. Here are examples:

> On the third tee, Crawford drove his ball deep into the woods to the right of the fairway.
> The scorpion promptly stung him in the finger.
> The pilot circled the field three times before landing.

In the first sentence, the subject, "Crawford," performs the action expressed by "drove." Similarly, in the next two sentences "scorpion" and "pilot" are the doers of the action.

If the verb of a sentence is in the passive voice, the subject is usually then the receiver of the action, as in these sentences:

> The ball had been driven deep into the woods to the right of the fairway.
> He had been stung in the finger by a scorpion.
> The pilot was told by the tower to attempt a landing.

In the first example, the subject, "ball," is acted upon; the performer of the action is not expressed. In the second and third examples, "he" and "pilot," the subjects, receive the action; in both sentences, the performer of the action is expressed by a prepositional phrase.

EFFECTIVE PASSIVES

WD 13 A   *Use passive-voice verbs when the performer of an action need not be emphasized*

Although verbs in the active voice are more common than those in the passive, the latter voice has its proper uses. A passive voice verb may be used when the performer of the action is unknown or need not be mentioned; or when the writer feels that the receiver of the action needs to be stressed more than the performer. We can draw examples of these uses from Sir Winston Churchill's account of the execution of Mary Queen of Scots:

> In the early morning of February 8, 1587, *she was summoned* to the great hall of Fotheringay Castle. Accompanied by six of her attendants, she awaited the servants of the English Queen. From the neighbouring countryside the gentry gathered to witness the sentence. Mary appeared at the appointed hour soberly clad in black satin. In the quietness of the hall she walked with stately movements to the cloth-covered scaffold erected by the fireplace. The *solemn formalities were smoothly completed.* But the zealous Dean of Peterborough attempted to force upon the Queen a last-minute conversion. With splendid dignity she brushed aside his loud exhortations. "Mr. Dean," she said, "I am a Catholic, and must die a Catholic. It is useless to attempt to move me, and your prayers will avail me but little."
>
> Mary had arrayed herself superbly for the final scene. As she disrobed for the headsman's act, her garments of black satin, removed by the weeping handmaids, revealed a bodice and petticoat of crimson velvet. One of her ladies handed her a pair of crimson sleeves, which she put on. Thus the unhappy Queen halted, for one last moment, standing blood-red from head to foot against the black background of the scaffold. There was a deathly hush throughout the hall. She knelt, and at the second stroke *the final blow was delivered.* The awed assembly had fulfilled its task. In death *the majestic illusion was shattered. The head of an ageing woman with false hair was held up by the executioner.* A lapdog crept out from beneath the clothes of the bleeding trunk (*A History of the English Speaking Peoples,* Vol. II, *The New World*).

In all but the last of the italicized passages the performer of the action is not expressed. In the first, for example, it is unimportant who summoned Mary to her execution—some official, probably, who is of no great interest to us. The important thing is that Mary was directed to come to the great hall to meet her death. In the last passage the performer of the action ("the executioner") needs to be identified but the severed head of the Queen is clearly the center of attention in the grim scene. The agent, therefore, is expressed in a prepositional phrase, and "head" is made the subject of the sentence.

WD 13 B   *Use passive-voice verbs to help achieve an impersonal tone*

In certain kinds of business, governmental, and professional writing, which often must be objective and impersonal, the proportion of passive verbs will necessarily be higher than in other kinds. For instance, here is a short paragraph from a college textbook on geology; the passive verbs have been italicized.

> Several scales *have been proposed* to describe the size of various units, from large boulders to minute clay minerals. The Wentworth scale *is reproduced* in Table 5–1. Note that although the term clay *is used* in Table 5–1 to designate all particles below 1/256 mm in diameter, it *is* also *applied* to certain minerals. Since confusion may result unless a distinction *is made* between size and mineral, we must refer specifically to "clay size" or "clay mineral," unless the context makes it clear which *is meant* (L. Don Leet and Sheldon Judson, *Physical Geology*).

INEFFECTIVE PASSIVES

WD 13 C *Avoid overusing the passive voice; in general, prefer active-voice verbs for a vigorous style*

All six of the passive verbs in the passage just quoted can be justified; but those in the following sentences, which are taken from business correspondence, are unnecessary. Since they emphasize words that do not deserve such attention, these sentences become weak and ineffective.

> It is desired to acknowledge the assistance that you gave us.
> REVISION: We wish to acknowledge the assistance that you gave us.
>
> Acknowledgment is made of your letter of August 31.
> REVISION: We have received your letter of August 31.
>
> The question was raised by you when you visited our office.
> REVISION: You raised the question when you visited our office.

The same kind of ineffective passives are common in student writing:

> Studying was instinctively disliked and avoided by us.
> REVISION: We instinctively disliked and avoided studying.
>
> During my four years in the photography club many pictures for the school paper were taken and processed by me.
> REVISION: During my four years in the photography club I took and processed many pictures for the school paper.

Do not be afraid to use a passive verb when the situation calls for one —but make sure that this is the best way to say what you mean. Remember that active verbs, which help to create a vigorous style, should heavily outnumber passive verbs in most of the writing you do.

In this chapter, ten important problems of word choice have been discussed, problems that directly concern the effectiveness with which you are able to communicate what you want to say. With practice you will become increasingly aware of these problems and will be able, even when writing the first draft of a paper, to avoid many of the difficulties they cause.

But word choice is so complex and the problems it raises are so numerous that the wording of a first draft, no matter how carefully you have written it, always can be improved. Never prepare a clean, final copy of a paper without first having closely examined it for such blemishes as wordiness, triteness, and unnecessary passive verbs; and for such positive qualities as concrete language, careful use of connotations, and effective repetition. Care in these things leads to an efficient prose style.

EXERCISE

15. In the following passages find all the passive-voice verbs and say whether you think the passive is the effective voice to use in each instance. Give reasons.

(a) Few new types of machine parts were developed between 1815 and 1850. There was, however, a significant change in materials, as wooden machines gave way to iron. The boilers of early steam engines had sometimes been made of wood wrapped with iron bands —an outgrowth of the cooper's art of barrelmaking. But these boilers blew up under pressure. Iron boilers provided the solution. It was the same in many other fields, as can be seen by comparing the wooden works of an old clock with the metal parts of a modern timepiece.

The coming of the iron age was associated with the use of steam in power engines. All tools and machines are operated by some sort of power. Simple tools like hammers employ man power. Treadmills use man or animal power; wind and water mills use the force of wind or water currents. The steam engine did not at once supersede other power engines. Textile mills, for example, were long operated by water wheels—which is why American cotton factories as well as flour mills were located along the fall line of the rivers. The cars on the earliest railroads were pulled by animals and experiments were made with wind power. It seems strange to think of "sailing" a train, but this was actually tried in the 1830's. The steam engine, however, won out—once it was made of iron and fueled by coal. Other uses for steam engines also became apparent. During the 1840's, for example, steam presses replaced hand presses in printing establishments (Curti, Shryock, Cochran, and Harrington, *A History of American Civilization*).

(b) During Bligh's absence on this trip a number of the *Bounty* crew, survivors of the sixteen who had remained in Tahiti, were hauled back to England for trial. These were not the ringleaders, who by this time had settled on Pitcairn, but lesser figures who had been abandoned by Christian. At Tahiti one man had been murdered by a companion, who was then killed by the natives. The remaining fourteen were rounded up in March, 1791, by the twenty-four-gun frigate H.M.S. *Pandora*, under Captain Edward Edwards. The retributory arm of the British Admiralty had reached across the world to bring back for court-martial as many men as could be found of those who had stayed behind on the *Bounty* on that fateful April morning. But of course not even the determined *Pandora* could find the eight ringleaders (James A. Michener and Grove Day, *Rascals in Paradise*).

11

GETTING YOUR PAPER READY
TO HAND IN

Before the freshman English course has ended, your teacher will have spent a great deal of time reading and marking your papers. To economize his energy and so to help him do a better job of reading these papers, he will almost certainly ask that you follow a number of accepted procedures in preparing the final copy. They are designed to standardize the form of the paper so he can give all his attention to what you have said and how you have said it.

Typed Papers

Whenever you can, type your papers. Handwriting is seldom as easy to read as typing. But if you are not a good typist and make errors in typing that you would not ordinarily make in longhand, it is better not to type your work. Nor is it a good idea to have an expert typist prepare the clean copy of your papers; the finished paper, after the typist has made corrections and revisions in the manuscript, no longer represents your own unaided efforts but is really a collaboration between yourself and the typist. Turning in such a paper as entirely your own work is not honest. Remember that the reason for taking this course is to learn how to write well; to do this you need to have your mistakes pointed out and explained to you by your teacher.

If you do type your papers, you should always double-space them; you should leave wide margins (about 1½ inches) at the top, bottom, and both sides; and you should type on only one side of the paper. It is customary to center the title at the top of the first page, then leave four spaces before beginning the paper itself. Always use standard unruled white typing paper, 8½ x 11 inches.

Handwritten Papers

Always use paper that is a full 8½ x 11 inches, never the smaller sheets; it is very likely that your instructor will refuse to accept anything else. Be sure to write on wide-lined paper—sheets on which the ruled lines are at least ⅜ inch apart. Paper with narrower ruling not only will cramp your handwriting but it will leave no room for the corrections that your teacher probably will want you to add between the lines after he has read and returned the paper to you.

Most notebook paper has a ruled margin on the left side. Be sure not to write to the left of this line and be sure also to leave a margin at least equally wide at the right side of the page. Your teacher will need margins on both left and right to make references to errors and to comment on your paper.

Most teachers object to the use of paper ripped out of spiral-bound notebooks; it looks, and is, messy. It is better to use paper that has been punched for looseleaf binding. Some college and university English departments require the use of a special manuscript paper that has wide lines and often ruled margins on both left and right sides of the sheet.

Write all papers in ink; most instructors will refuse to accept papers written in pencil, since they are hard to read and usually look untidy. Black or blue ink is generally preferred to more exotic colors like green and lavender. And be sure to write on only one side of the paper— standard practice where manuscript is concerned.

Crowded, messy handwriting often makes a paper so hard to read that the reader can't properly judge its value. Your handwriting need not be beautiful or perfectly regular, but it must be legible. Don't write eccentrically or with a lot of curlicues. Form the letters carefully, making loops where they belong and no loops where they don't belong, and don't crowd the writing. A paper that is not easily legible is likely to be returned to you unread and penalized with a low grade. This is a defensive measure that your teacher is justified in taking to preserve his eyesight and patience.

Proofreading

After the final copy of a paper has been completed, be sure to proof-read it carefully for errors that you have missed seeing before or that have got in by accident when you copied from the rough draft. *This step is very important.* If an error appears in the version that you give to your instructor, he will have to mark it against you whether it was due to real ignorance or to carelessness. You can't afford to be penalized for mere carelessness.

It takes a while sometimes before students realize this. For example, almost half the spelling errors that appear in freshman writing may be the result of careless writing, not of ignorance. The student who writes "were" when he means "where" or forgets to add final *s*'s or -*ed*'s or writes "not" for "note" is not necessarily a poor speller, though his paper will come back to him littered with marks of "sp." More likely, he is a bad proofreader, and this is a different matter, actually much easier to treat than bad spelling.

Proofreading is a skill that can easily be learned by anyone with normal intelligence and eyesight. You need application and conscientiousness to master it, but the effort required is not superhuman and the dividends are highly rewarding. The problem should be approached systematically, as described below:

To begin, you should realize that there are many kinds of reading, depending on the material being read, the purposes for which it is being read, and so on. Sometimes you skim, seeking only the key idea in each paragraph; sometimes you look at every sentence but don't linger; sometimes you ponder almost every word; sometimes you go back and reread again and again until the idea emerges clearly. Students who are poor proofreaders generally are so because they don't realize that proofreading is a special kind of reading, quite different from the sort of reading they usually do.

Watch someone's eyes while he is reading normally. Notice that his eyes do not move smoothly, sliding without pause from one end of a line of print to the other, then repeating the motion with the next line. Instead, they move in little jerks, stopping three, four, or more times in traveling across each line. What this means is that in most normal reading the eye focuses on certain words—really, certain letters of certain words—and sees only these directly. Other letters, other words, are seen, we might say, out of the corners of the eyes, not directly. If a student proofreading his theme uses the eye movements that he em-

ploys in ordinary reading, he often will fail to see that he left the final
e off "white" or forgot to put a period at the end of a sentence or perhaps even left out one or more entire words. The reason is that he is not
seeing directly each word of each sentence and each letter of each word.
If he could really see what he has written, he would be able to identify
and correct a great many foolish mistakes.

The problem, then, is to control eye movements so that each word and
letter can be seen distinctly. The way to do this is to slow down the
motion of the eye as it travels across a line of writing. If it stops only
three or four times, of course many things in the line will not be seen
directly; but if the eye can be made to move more carefully and de-
liberately across the line, a great many more things in the line will be
clearly seen.

Several mechanical tricks can be used to slow the eye down and
cause it to remain longer on each line. First, since your tongue and lips
cannot form spoken words as rapidly as your eye can recognize them in
silent reading, try reading your papers aloud after the final copy is
ready. You will often catch many careless errors by this means, for you
will read more slowly and carefully. You will also often be able to catch
awkward wordings—unintended rhymes, unwanted repetitions of words
—that will strike the ear when they are spoken.

If your proofreading is still faulty, try covering with a piece of paper
all but the line that you are reading aloud; when you have read that line,
move the paper down so that the next line appears, and read it. In this
way your eye is forced to remain on one line at a time and cannot skip
on to the next until you are satisfied that you have read one line carefully.

If you are a really difficult case and are still having trouble, take a
pencil and place it lightly on each word of the exposed line in turn as
you read the line aloud. This is a rather drastic measure but it is guar-
anteed to force you to look at each word; and this, of course, is what
you want.

All of these devices are time-consuming, admittedly. But if you drill in
these ways regularly and conscientiously, you will soon be pleasantly
surprised at the improvement in your proofreading skill. You will develop new eye habits and will be able to "shift gears" more easily and
more successfully when you switch from normal reading to proofreading. Soon you will find that you can do without the pencil; next, you
can abandon the paper that you use to cover lines; and at last you
should be able to proofread silently. Though this sort of drill may seem

tiresome to you, don't underestimate its value; it offers a sensible and systematic way to clear up a disability that, if neglected, will cause you much trouble.

One more suggestion. Though some of your papers probably will have to be written in class—impromptu papers—others will be assigned for preparation outside class. Impromptu papers are written under pressure of time, and you will have to learn how to budget the minutes of a class period carefully so that you are able not only to write but to proofread a theme in about fifty minutes. Prepared papers can be written more leisurely, but you will find it wise to write the paper as soon as possible after it has been assigned. You can think of a number of obvious reasons why this is good advice, but there is another that may not occur to you: If you write the paper, then let it "cool off" for a day or two before giving it a final proofreading, you are much more likely to find such errors as omitted words. The reason is that you probably will have forgotten the exact way you expressed your ideas and so will be more likely to read what is actually on the paper than read from the recollection in your mind of what you thought you had written.

Endorsement of Papers

Because your teacher receives many themes and must not get them mixed up, he will give you instructions at an early meeting about the kind of identifying information that he wants you to put on each paper. No doubt he will want the pages numbered, and perhaps he will want your name at the top of each page in case the paper should come apart. He may want the paper turned in flat, he may want it folded in half from top to bottom with the writing inside, or he may ask that it be folded vertically, the long way. Pages of a theme of ordinary length should not be clipped, pinned, or stapled together. On the outside of folded papers your teacher will want your name and certain other information. The following endorsement is fairly typical:

Dorothy Rawson	(Your name)
English 101, 10 MWF	(Course, hour, days of meeting)
Mr. Johanson	(Instructor's name)
September 27, 19–	(Date)
Theme 2	(Theme number)

If the paper has been folded vertically (probably the most common practice), be sure that the folded or closed edge is to the left (like a book); then put the endorsement toward the top.

12

SENTENCE
UNITY

Getting an idea of sentence unity is your most important assignment in so far as correct grammar and punctuation are concerned. You must realize that some word units are complete sentences but that others are not, and you must be able to punctuate these different units suitably.

The typical written English sentence must have a verb form—and this verb form must be of one particular kind. "The house had been painted" fits this requirement of a typical sentence, but "the house having been painted" does not. The typical sentence must have an expressed subject. Notice the following expressions:

Evans reached third successfully. But neglected to touch second.
Evans reached third successfully. But he neglected to touch second.

The second part of the first expression is not a typical sentence: it lacks an expressed subject; the second part of the second expression fits in with the patterns of typical sentences. Furthermore, the typical sentence must not begin with a word that signals that what follows is not a sentence. Notice the following:

When the train finally arrived . . .
Then the train finally arrived.

In the first of these expressions, the word *when* signals the fact that the words following are not a sentence. The word *then* does not make the

225

same signal, and the second expression is a sentence. In general, the typical sentence has in it a verb form of the right kind, has in it an expressed subject, and does not have at the beginning a signal word that shows it is not a sentence. The rest of this chapter will explain these notions, one at a time.

Sentences are expressions that satisfy a general feeling for unity of expression. Correct punctuation of sentences often depends more on this feeling for unity than it does on strict logic. In accordance with general feeling for unity of expression, the words "the men working in the chemical division" do not make up a sentence, but the words "the men were working in the chemical division" do. People are commonly irritated by punctuation like the following:

> The men working in the chemical division. Were in favor of the plan.

They are similarly irritated when two sentences are put together without punctuation strong enough to set them apart, as in the following:

> Most of the men were strongly in favor of the plan, they were displeased by the delays in putting it into effect.

This punctuation—with a comma instead of a semicolon—violates the common feeling for formal sentence unity. Avoiding such mistakes, therefore, is simply common sense.

Explanations of English grammar usually start with a listing of the "parts of speech," traditionally eight in number. Knowledge of all of these, however, is not really necessary for an understanding of formal sentence unity. This book will postpone definition and discussion of most of these terms until later. Knowledge of verb and subject alone, along with some information about prepositions and conjunctions, is enough to lead you to notions of formal sentence unity.

In what follows, technical grammatical terms are used. Employing them is the most natural and most economical way of giving you explanations. But it is your main job to find out how words and other units really work, not merely to be able to give names for them. In following pages, this book will use the terms *finite* and *non-finite* in connection with verb forms. But your knowing these words is less important than your understanding how the forms work. Perhaps you can already see that the third form in the following does not fit with the rest:

> *were helping, is going, being called, had stopped, will begin.*

This latter knowledge is more important than knowing the technical terms *finite* and *non-finite*. This book will use the term *conjunctive adverb*. But your knowing that term is less important than your realizing that the third word in the following list does not signal the way the others do: *nevertheless, thus, although, still, however.* Bear in mind that knowledge of the names for various units is less important than knowledge of how they work.

Recognition of Verbs

Verbs are often defined in terms of their meanings as words that express action, being, condition, or situation. Certainly many words that express action are verbs: *explode, deliver, punish, erase.* But with these verbs are companion forms showing occurrence of action—"expressing action" in a broad sense—and these companion forms are not verbs: *explosion, deliverance* and *delivery, punishment,* and *erasure.* The idea of "being" is expressed by the verb *exist,* but it is also expressed by the companion noun *existence.* In the sentence "the milk seemed sour," all grammarians would agree that *seemed* is a verb, but it does not clearly express action, being, condition, or situation. It appears hard, then, to recognize certain words as verbs by their meaning alone.

Verbs are sometimes defined in terms of over-all function or use as words that make complete statements when joined with subjects. This statement is quite true, but it may not be very useful to you if you are not sure what a subject is and what makes a statement complete instead of incomplete. You may be able to *feel* the incompleteness of "a big fire at the Ellis Mills" as a statement and, on the other hand, the completeness of "a big fire occurred at the Ellis Mills," but if you cannot *feel* this difference at once the definition given in the first sentence of this paragraph is not very useful to you.

Use of patterns may help you to recognize verbs. Try inserting in the blanks the simplest form of the word being tested: we_____, you_____, they_____. If you can make sense with the two-word unit resulting, the word that has been inserted is probably a verb—at any rate a word that may sometimes be a verb. Try this pattern with *ask, send,* and *write.*

we ask	you ask	they ask
we send	you send	they send
we write	you write	they write

These little statements make sense of English, even though they do not tell what is being asked or sent or written. The words *ask, send,* and *write* are verbs. If you try the same pattern with words labeled as other parts of speech the result is nonsense:

we wood	you wood	they wood
we true	you true	they true
we soon	you soon	they soon
we with	you with	they with

These words are not verbs; they make no sense when inserted in the pattern.

EXERCISES

1. By using the pattern given in the section above (we _____, you _____, they _____), find out which of the following words might be called verbs: *admire, apply, avoid, blame, brilliant, change, constant, deny, emerge, fix, greed, impact, joyful, little, mouth, other, point, rash, savage, social, survive, treat, weird, zero.*

2. Find out which words in the following might be called verbs:

A Navy flier named Cribbs spotted three men on a sandbar in the Mad River. When he lowered his hoist, the men made the mistake of grabbing it together. Cribbs felt the helicopter being pulled into the river. Over the intercom he told his crewmen to shake them loose. The crewmen jerked the rope; two of the men fell off and Cribbs flew the third to high ground. His companions, unhappily, had been tumbled into the water. Cribbs went back, let down to about fifty feet, and dangled the hoist within reach of the closest swimmer. The man might have been a fish snapping at bait; in a moment the line tugged and the pilot pulled him up. The third man was picked up a mile down stream. . . . (David K. Dempsey, *Flood*).

Verb Forms: Finite and Non-finite

Parts of *to be* (*am, is, was, will be, have been, having been,* etc.) are verbs, as are parts of *to have* (*has, had, has had, having had,* etc.). Similar verbs—sometimes called *auxiliaries*—include *will, shall, would, should, can, may,* and *might.* These words are combined with other verb parts to build up a surprising number of different forms. For *turn,* for instance, we have the following: *has turned, had turned, has been turned, had been turning, is turned, were turned, will turn, might turn,*

*can turn, shall be turned, could be turned, may be turning, being turned,
having turned, to be turned.* Many forms have their own specific names;
for instance, *had been turning* is an active past-perfect progressive form.
But you do not need to know many terms like that. You do need to be
able to divide these forms into two main groups.

*The two main groups of verb forms are, first, finite forms and, second,
non-finite forms.* You can usually tell whether a form is finite or non-
finite simply by looking at it, just as you can tell a hammer from a
hatchet or a cup from a glass simply by looking at it. Each verb has
many finite forms—so many that it will be much easier to consider non-
finite forms first. *There are two main kinds of non-finite forms. One is
the infinitive.* Most infinitives look like the following:

to turn	to be turned
to have turned	to have been turned

Notice that *to be saved* looks like *to be turned;* it is made up in the
same way; it is therefore an infinitive, a non-finite form. *To have destroyed* looks like *to have turned;* it is made up in the same way. It is
an infinitive. *Have come* does not fit the pattern of the infinitive forms;
the pattern includes *to have turned* but not just *have turned. Have come*
is not an infinitive.

*Participles and gerunds make up the second of the two non-finite
forms;* except for the past participle, discussed later, participles and
gerunds are the same in form, although not in use. They look the same;
they are made up in the same way; they fit the same pattern. All gerunds
and most participles look like the following forms:

turning	being turned
having turned	having been turned

Is *being answered* a participle or gerund—and therefore a non-finite
form? It looks like *being turned;* it is made up in the same way. It is
therefore a participle or gerund, a non-finite form. On the other hand,
is *are speaking* a participle or gerund? The pattern given above does
not show the form *are turning;* since *are speaking* is not made up according to the pattern, it is not a participle or gerund.

*The infinitive and the participle and gerund are the only non-finite
forms. All other forms are finite.* If a verb form is not an infinitive or
a participle-gerund, it is a finite form. If you know the eight forms given
for *turn* and if you remember that forms that do not look like them are
finite, you can tell the difference between most finite and non-finite

forms. Is *to have retreated* finite or non-finite? It looks exactly like *to have turned;* it is made up in the same way. It is non-finite—an infinitive. Is *are wearing* finite or non-finite? Since it does not look exactly like any of the eight non-finite forms of *turn* and is not made up exactly like any of them, it is finite.

EXERCISES

3. Make up the eight non-finite forms for each of the following: *aid, call, earn, govern, increase, kill, need, prepare, risk, waste.*

4. Indicate which of the following forms are finite, which non-finite: *was abused, being banished, having captured, to have dealt, was feeding, will hunt, having been mailed, were parading, to be rejected, being sprayed, were wrestling.*

5. Pick out the finite and the non-finite verb forms in the following:

The conspirator forced his way between the President and his wife. Mrs. Lincoln's laughter dissolved in confusion. She saw the young man towering above her, but she did not know who he was or what he wanted. The major saw a cloud of smoke and, without understanding, jumped up and tried to grapple with the intruder. Booth dropped the derringer and pulled out his knife. The major laid a hand on his arm, and the assassin's arm went high in the air and slashed down. Rathbone lifted his left arm to counter the blow, and the knife sliced through his suit and flesh down to the bone. (Jim Bishop, *The Day Lincoln Was Shot*).

Subjects

As the word *subject* is commonly used, only finite verbs have subjects. Many grammarians have tried to use meaning and function to define *subject*. The subject has been called the most important thing spoken of in the sentence. But in "the Japanese attack on Pearl Harbor brought the United States into World War II," *attack* is the subject, and the attack was hardly more important than the United States or than World War II. The subject has been called the person or thing about which something is said. But in "the table was upset by the puppy," it is hard to see that something was said about the table but not also about the puppy. The subject has been called the doer of the action, but in "the wood had been cut unevenly by the carpenter," *wood* is the subject, although it is not the doer of the action. The subject has been defined as what acts or is acted upon. But in "the erratic course of the plane was followed by the anxious observers," the subject is *course*, something that neither acted nor was acted upon very noticeably. These conventional definitions of the term *subject* usually lead to the right conclusion, but they are not entirely accurate and complete.

It is best not to try a complete definition of the term *subject* and to look on it simply as a necessary unit in the structure of the typical English sentence. *You can usually find the subject by taking out the finite verb (either without or else with the words closely accompanying it) and forming a question composed of* who *or* what *and that finite verb.* Answering this question will give you the subject. In "the accident occurred in the afternoon," ask yourself the question "who or what occurred (in the afternoon)?" The answer, of course, is "the accident," and *accident* is the subject. In "the name of the street has been changed to Elmwood Avenue," the word *name* answers the question "who or what has been changed?" and is the subject. In "doubt about the witness's identification hurt the prosecutor's case," the word *doubt* answers the question "who or what hurt?" and is the subject.[1]

EXERCISES

6. Pick out the finite verbs in the following. Find the subject for each one.

(a) The telephone had stopped ringing when Marcia returned to the room.

(b) The other miners in the group had remained in the main gallery and were rescued later.

(c) Since the television set had broken down during the fight, we did not know the outcome until later.

(d) A new clutch had been installed on the truck, but evidently some minor adjustments were needed.

(e) The authorities were planning new buildings to accommodate the increasing enrolments.

(f) A short hair-do is often convenient for a busy college girl.

(g) The book was issued in an attractive gold and red binding.

(h) Boats were sent out to pick up the survivors swimming around.

(i) Several industries have recently left Plainville, and the mayor's committee is discussing steps to remedy the situation.

(j) Unlicensed dogs are rounded up by the city dog catcher to be disposed of later.

[1] Answering a question made up of *who* or *what* and a finite verb will not always give you the subject. If the question "who or what was given?" is asked about the sentence "the child was given a dime," the answer is likely to be *dime* instead of *child,* the subject. The question "who or what was taught?" may lead to the idea that *algebra* instead of *they* is the subject in "they were taught algebra." The method recommended here does not work well with sentences showing this pattern, but it seems the best and easiest general way to pick subjects.

Subject and finite verb are the key parts of the typical sentence. Without a subject or without a finite verb one does not have a formally complete sentence (although he may have a group of words that expresses a meaning satisfactorily). Solving most grammatical problems involves finding subject and finite verb first. Often other sentence parts may be ignored. You will find it valuable to use the following pattern in solving grammatical problems:

Subject	Verb

The check came back because of insufficient funds.

check	came

The relief pitcher helped his own cause by hitting a home run.

pitcher	helped

Troublesome Subject Patterns

Some kinds of subjects need special explanation:

1. In "the car and the truck have both been repaired," the answer to the question "who or what have been repaired?" is *the car and the truck;* in this sentence the subject is composed of two items joined with *and.* Subjects with two or more items so joined are compound subjects. *Chemistry and trigonometry* is a compound subject in "chemistry and trigonometry are given during the second semester."

2. In "either the department head or the course instructor will sign the class card," the answer to the question "who or what will sign?" is *either the department head or the course instructor,* another subject composed of two elements.

3. Often words like *he* and *they* and *who* and *which* are subjects. In "they had been called at six o'clock," *they* answers the question "who or what had been called?" and is the subject. In "Jones gave a different account about what was said at the meeting," the word *what* is the subject for *was said.*

4. The subject may be a non-finite verb form; *swimming* and *to cut* are the subjects in "swimming after a heavy meal may be dangerous" and "to cut the wood before noon was impossible."

5. Sometimes the subject is a whole group of words; in "that Kane would command the party had been decided several weeks before," the subject for *had been decided* is the whole foregoing group of words (*that Kane would command the party*).

Words and groups of words that serve or might serve as subjects are called *substantives*.

EXERCISES

7. Pick the finite verbs in the following. Find the subject for each one:

(a) Neither the captain nor the mate was told about the breakdown until later.

(b) Members of the ground crews as well as the pilots are given periodical physical examinations.

(c) How to hook up the radio apparatus was a mystery to the survivors.

(d) From September 25 to October 10 is the period for filing drop and add slips.

(e) What he was to do with the discarded junk puzzled the stage manager.

(f) Being snubbed in this way by an old friend hurt Betty very much.

(g) To win the state open tournament three years straight is a notable achievement.

(h) This tractor along with its various attachments is for sale for $900.

(i) By ten o'clock on election night we usually know who has been elected.

(j) Both the Campbells and their friends were invited to the reception.

8. Pick out the finite verbs in the following passage. Find the subject for each one.

Nobody could cope with such a situation, but the mayor did his resourceful best. He ordered airplanes equipped with loud-speakers of great power to fly over the self-beleaguered city and to explain what the source of the great stampede had been. Every morgue and hospital in the city and its environs was mobilized. All bridges and tunnels were instantly cleared for the transport of the injured, as Manhattan's hospitals could not handle five percent of the casualties. Police, using pistols with little ceremony, brought to a partial halt the epidemic of looting that occurred in the early afternoon. People were commanded to take the equivalent of air-raid shelter and to stay there. . . . Army Ordnance then tried its supersecret, twenty-four-inch rockets. Careless fusing caused one of these to explode at a low level, destroying the upper stories of the Metropolitan Life Insurance Building. . . (Philip Wylie, *Opus 21*).

9. Make up five sentences twelve or more words in length to illustrate each of the following kinds of subjects: (1) compound (composed of elements joined with *and*); (2) composed of elements joined by *or* or *nor*; (3) *who, which, what,* and similar words; (4) non-finite verb forms; (5) larger bodies of words.

Past Participles

It is not hard to take apart the sentence "the policeman killed the hold-up man" and find that *killed* is the finite verb and *policeman* the subject. Any reader of English knows from this sentence that the policeman has done the action indicated. But in "the policeman killed by the bandits lay where he had fallen," the policeman has been killed. In this second sentence *killed* is no longer a finite actional verb; instead, it is a non-finite past participle, the participial form omitted in the discussion of non-finite forms above. With single-word verb forms ending in *-ed* (*burned, divided, forced,*) and similar verb forms suggesting past time (*bound, bought, eaten*) you may be uncertain whether the form is finite or non-finite. When the substantive most closely connected with the verb form shows who or what has done the action indicated, the form is finite: the house *burned* to the ground, the truck *forced* its way through the drift, they *learned* the signals quickly. When the substantive most closely connected with the verb form shows who or what has received the action indicated, the form is a non-finite past participle: a *burned* child, the manuscripts *burned* in the fire were invaluable, a *forced* and implausible solution, a light truck *forced* off the bridge in the collision, an easily *learned* verse, a lesson quickly *learned*.[2] For *turn*, then, and for *force*, there are five participles: *turning, being turned, having turned, turned, having been turned; forcing, being forced, having forced, forced, having been forced.* Unlike the other participles, the forms *turned* and *forced* are identical with finite forms.

EXERCISES

10. In the following, determine whether each italicized form is a non-finite past participle or a finite past tense; the men *obeyed* the captain's order; he *walked* to the corner; the watch *repaired* by the jeweler; a poorly *executed* sketch; the hypothesis *accepted* by the majority; elective courses *recommended* for engineers; the goods *damaged* in the fire; the plan *decided* on at the meeting.

11. Reread the paragraphs quoted in Exercises 2, 5, and 8. Which verb forms in *-ed* are finite past tenses; which are non-finite past participles?

---

[2] This is a general statement, and like all general statements, it has exceptions. In "a newly arrived visitor," the meaning is that the visitor has done the arriving, but the form *arrived* is a non-finite past participle. Such situations, however, are uncommon and unlikely to cause you trouble.

Phrases

A phrase is a group of words that does not contain both subject and finite verb. It may contain either the subject of a finite verb or the finite verb itself, but it does not contain both.

Note the following: *having enough money, being advised to take economics, having called his office, to detect the enemy planes, to be caught in the act.* These have no finite verbs and no subjects; they are phrases.

Note the following: *the plane being on time, the bills having been paid, this resignation to take effect immediately.* In these the substantives (*plane, bills, resignation*) look like subjects, but the verb forms are all non-finite. Hence these groups are phrases.

Note the following: *in the afternoon, on the table, after the game, over the bridge.* The words *in, on, after,* and *over* are prepositions. In general, a *preposition* is a word joining a following substantive to the rest of a sentence in some relationship like place, circumstance, or time. You will find it easy simply to note that prepositions include the words given above and such others as *through, at, for, before, beyond, after, under, into, to, around, across, beneath, toward, during, up,* and *down* (although many of these words have other functions as well).

If a phrase begins with a non-finite verb form (like *having enough money, being advised to take economics*), it may be called a *non-finite verb phrase.* If a phrase begins with a preposition (like *in the afternoon, on the table*), it is called a *prepositional phrase.* These two kinds of phrases are quite common, but there are other kinds of phrases.

EXERCISES

12. Indicate which of the following groups of words are phrases: *before the raid started, until dawn came, the food having spoiled, when the ice melted, beyond the blue horizon, having been seriously injured, during the fourth period, in all three outfield positions, the telegram having been delayed, to be given additional privileges, having been given first aid, to tie the score in the sixth inning, and there were other changes, were asking many questions, the flour to be sold at discount.*

13. Pick out prepositional phrases among the groups of words given in Exercise 12. Pick out non-finite verb phrases.

14. What phrases do you find in the following? Specifically, what prepositional and non-finite verb phrases do you find?

By evening, Christian was exhausted. He hadn't ridden a bicycle for years and in the first hour or two he had gone too fast. Also twice during the day shots had been fired at him, and he had heard the bullets snipping by, past his head, and had driven himself frantically out of danger. The bicycle was wavering almost uncontrollably all over the road as he slowly pushed into the square of a fair-sized town at sunset. He was pleased, dully, to see that the square was full of soldiers, sitting in the cafes, lying exhausted and asleep on the stone benches in front of the town hall, tinkering hopelessly with broken-down Citroens in an attempt to get them to move just a few more kilometers. Here, for a few moments, at least, he would be safe (Irwin Shaw, *The Young Lions*).

Clauses

A clause is a group of words that contains both subject and finite verb. In "the men were waiting outside the pay office," there is a finite verb, *were waiting,* and a subject, *the men,* and the group of words is consequently a clause. "And the paint supplies were stored nearby" is a clause because it contains a finite verb, *were stored,* and a subject, *supplies.* "However, Hemingway has written some rather weak novels" is a clause because it contains a subject, *Hemingway,* and a finite verb, *has written.* On the other hand, the group of words "the test being scheduled for Friday" is not a clause, but instead a phrase, because *being scheduled* is a non-finite verb form.

EXERCISES

15. Pick out the clauses in the selections in Exercises 2, 5, 8, and 12.

16. Pick out clauses among the following groups of words: *western dramas were very popular on television; after the news had been given out; who was president in 1903; while the ground crew was working on the plane; until the end of the century; being unable to lift the weight; the motor having been repaired; furthermore, he was not sure of Franklin's plans; after he was graduated from the university; attempting to fix the timer; the books bound in green; or the bus line will discontinue this run.*

Independent and Dependent Clauses

Clauses are divided into two main groups, independent clauses and dependent or subordinate clauses. We must consider various suggestions for telling the difference between the two. It is often said that an independent clause can "stand alone," but that a dependent clause cannot.

This statement means that it is all right to punctuate an independent clause as a sentence, that is, with a capital letter at the beginning and a period at the end:

> However, he was finally elected.

but that it is not all right to punctuate a dependent clause in the same way:

> Although he was finally elected.

Certainly this comment is generally true, but since you want to know the difference between independent clauses and dependent clauses mainly in order to decide on punctuation, it is not very helpful. In effect the comment tells you that a clause that is so punctuated and that is not objected to by instructor or editor is all right.

It is sometimes said that an independent clause expresses a complete thought and that a dependent clause does not. This statement is generally true enough, but it has its weaknesses. The clauses in the paragraph above show very little difference in the meaning expressed: both mean that in spite of some contrary expectation someone was finally elected. A clause may be *grammatically* independent but *logically* dependent on accompanying material for full understanding of its meaning. The clause "later that same year she finished another novel" is *logically* dependent; without some accompanying material you cannot know whether *later* indicates August or November, what year is being spoken of, who *she* is, or what her other novel was. This clause is not *logically* independent in the sense that it could be a detached independent expression, but it is *grammatically* independent. Meaning alone may be an unsafe guide for finding out which kind of clause you are dealing with. Notice in the following sections how this principle works.

The way the clause in question is introduced is likely to be important. Some introductory words signal that the clauses they introduce are dependent. Note the following pair, of which the first is a grammatically independent clause, the second a grammatically dependent one:

> Uncle Ed comes tomorrow
> if Uncle Ed comes tomorrow

The introductory *if* has made the second clause dependent. And note the following:

The two rivers join to form the Ohio
where the two rivers join to form the Ohio

Obviously the difference between these two clauses is that the second starts with the word *where;* as an introductory word *where* has subordinated or made dependent a clause that would otherwise be independent. The following words are likely to make clauses dependent when they serve as introductory elements:

when	where	if	than	although	because	if
why	since	how	after	until	before	though

Clauses introduced by these words are likely to be dependent:

when the new plan was announced
where the extra blankets were kept
if the weather prediction was correct
after the car had been repaired
as the directions indicated

These words (*when, where, if,* etc.) are called *subordinating conjunctions.* They are called *subordinating* because they subordinate or make dependent. They are called *conjunctions* because they join their clauses to the remainder of the sentences in which they appear.[3] (A conjunction is a word that joins.)

Note the following pair of clauses, of which the first is independent, the second dependent:

He was picked to succeed Evans.
. . . who was picked to succeed Evans.

[3] Some of these words are prepositions as well as subordinating conjunctions. A prepositional phrase at the beginning of a clause does not make it dependent. The words given above subordinate only when they refer to whole clauses, not to substantives alone. The clause "since the war was drawing to a close" is dependent; the word *since* applies to the whole group of words. But the clause "since the war the situation has been different" is independent; in this clause, *since* is a preposition, not a conjunction, and refers only to the substantive *war.* Note the following:

dependent clauses: because the process has not been perfected
after the session had adjourned
independent clauses: because of these mistakes the paper was given a failing grade
after the session the legislators returned to their homes

Also, some of the words mentioned (*when, where, why,* and *how*) are used at the beginning of questions: when does the plane come in? where are my chemistry reports? Questions introduced by these words are independent clauses, not dependent.

The independent clause is introduced by the word *he*, the dependent clause by the word *who*. The words *who, which,* and *what* often make subordinate or dependent their clauses as does the word *that* in some of its uses. The following are dependent:

> . . . which was a better gun than the others.
> . . . what had been said at the previous meeting.
> . . . that outsold all rival products by a wide margin.

These words—*who, which, what,* and *that*—are usually called *relative pronouns;*[4] like subordinating conjunctions, they make their clauses dependent.

Some introductory words do not make dependent but instead leave independent the clauses following them. Their clauses are *grammatically* independent, although sometimes *logically* dependent on their context for their full meaning. Words so operating include the following:

however	also	nevertheless
furthermore	still	accordingly
then	thus	consequently

The following clauses are *grammatically* independent:

> however, I finally decided to take the economics course
> then the lights went out
> consequently they went on to Denver on the next flight
> furthermore you should have asked Clark for his consent

These words are called *conjunctive adverbs. Conjunctive* means *joining;* a conjunction is a word that joins. (The meaning of *adverb* and *adverbial* will be given later.)

The clause "and the water pressure was low" is somewhat similar to the clauses in the paragraph above: it is *grammatically* independent although *logically* dependent. It is hard to start any communication with a clause beginning with *and;* logically, something preceding is necessary. But a clause beginning with *and* usually is *grammatically* independent, as is one beginning with *or* or *but*. The following clauses are *grammatically* independent:

---

[4] *Who, which, what,* and *that* are described as *relative* because they "relate" or tie together various sentence parts. In the sentence "he was helped by the man who lived next door," the word *who* serves as the subject for *lived,* makes dependent the clause that it introduces, and shows a relationship between this clause and the rest of the sentence. A pronoun is a substantive with a meaning so wide or varied that its interpretation almost always depends entirely on the context.

and the wheat crop was far over expectations
but the boards were warped out of shape
or you can take the West Side bus

These words are called *coordinating conjunctions—coordinating* because they do not subordinate or make dependent, *conjunctions* because they join.

Finally, a clause is usually independent if it does not begin with a word used especially to introduce or connect. The following clauses are independent:

the water was too cold for us to enjoy our swim
Whitman managed the Sox for three years
a three-day-old calf can run very fast
he and I were selected to represent the fraternity

Clauses lacking introductory elements need less explanation than other clauses, but of the five kinds of clauses dealt with here they are the most common.

These comments on kinds of clauses may be put in tabular form:

Kind of Clause	*Introductory Words Used*	*Grammatical Term for Introductory Words*
dependent	although, though, since, as, if, how, why, when, where, while, because, that	subordinating conjunction
dependent	who, which, what, that	relative pronoun
independent	however, thus, also, then, still, accordingly, moreover, consequently, nevertheless, hence, yet, besides, indeed, likewise, furthermore, nonetheless	conjunctive adverb
independent	and, but, or	coordinating conjunction
independent	(lacking)	

The dependence or independence of a clause does not depend on strict logic about "completeness of thought." Instead, it depends on the feeling, illogically arrived at, of users of the language that one expression of thought is complete, another incomplete. Our introductory words are grouped on the basis of this general feeling. Differences of opinion exist about *for*, *whereas*, and *so*, along with some other words. *So* is often called a conjunctive adverb, but in informal practice clauses beginning with *so* are punctuated in a way different from those beginning with *however* and *also*. Observing how clauses are punctuated in actual use will help you at least as much as the study of textbooks.

EXERCISES

17. Indicate whether each of the following clauses is independent or dependent:

(a) whether the pump will work all right after the repairs
(b) the building was finally razed in 1952
(c) who have not yet satisfied the science requirements
(d) both the Giants and the Dodgers moved to California
(e) furthermore, he gives assignments in unavailable books
(f) we will be unable to reach Camp Everitt before noon
(g) but new men do not receive leave permits for three months
(h) the Oklahoma team went through several seasons undefeated
(i) Maine was originally a part of Massachusetts
(j) or the Republicans will have to find another candidate
(k) thus you will not have to pay a late registration fee
(l) some of the girls wore ski suits to classes
(m) which is confirmed by the Sanders report on cancer
(n) the red dye of the book cover rubbed off on one's clothes
(o) since he was already paying for two insurance policies

18. By adding, changing, or omitting introductory words, change each of the independent clauses in Exercise 17 to a dependent clause, and each dependent clause to an independent clause.

19. Analyze the following into clauses and determine which are independent, which dependent:

The second aspect of the doctrine of usage which frequently troubles people to whom the idea is somewhat new is the fear that the lack of strict and ironclad rules will lead to eventual disintegration. Again history shows such fears to be unfounded. It has been pointed out that the rules for the speaking of correct English date chiefly from the beginning of the eighteenth century. They have existed only two hundred years of the fifteen hundred since the Angles and Saxons first came to the British Isles. Accordingly when English is considered in the light of its millennium of existence as a separate language, one is inclined to feel that the rules have had relatively little effect in either hindering or accelerating the main trends of development. Moreover, we can never be too sure as to just what is meant by disintegration of a language, which innovations are bad and which are good (Albert H. Marckwardt, *What Is Good English?*).

To stress introductory elements as means for choosing between independent and dependent clauses may be somewhat misleading. Dependent clauses sometimes lack subordinating elements. Instead of "a man that I knew at that time," many of us would say and also write "a man I knew at that time." Despite the lack of introductory element, you may be able to feel that "I knew at that time" is a dependent clause—partly because of the sound pattern of this expression when it is spoken. Independent clauses—questions like "who is the Tompkins representative?" and exclamations like "how clear the water seems!"—are sometimes introduced by words here called subordinating conjunctions. Ultimately you must develop your own feeling for the completeness of various clause units. You may look on the study of introductory elements in clauses merely as a necessary first step toward sentence unity.

SU 1   *Do not make period faults*

Do not use incomplete sentences (sentence fragments) in straightforward connected serious writing. An *incomplete sentence* or *sentence fragment* is a phrase or a dependent clause punctuated with a capital letter at the beginning and a period at the end. Sentence fragments are called *period faults*. The average reader will feel that there is something wrong when he meets with them and will doubt the intelligence and knowledge of the writer.

1. Do not confuse phrases with independent clauses. Note the following:

> He decided to vote for Mansfield. A very popular man with a good deal of experience.

The second group of words contains no finite verb and is consequently only a phrase.

> In the last act Leslie, playing the part of the hero, tripped over a light cord. And broke his ankle.

There is no expressed subject for the finite verb in the last group of words. Hence it is only a phrase.

We would not have needed to drive so fast. The takeoff of the plane having been delayed.

The verb form in the last group of words is non-finite, rather than finite, and consequently this unit is only a phrase. As punctuated, these three expressions illustrate period faults.

2. Do not confuse dependent clauses with independent clauses. Note the following:

The substitute quarterback was Fred Baker. Who had not played since the Newton game.

The last group of words is a clause, with a finite verb, *had (not) played,* and a subject, *who,* but the latter word subordinates the clause or makes it dependent.

On graduating from high school I decided to enlist in the army. Since I expected to be drafted anyway.

The last group of words is a clause with *expected* as a finite verb and *I* as subject, but it is dependent because of the introductory word *since.* As punctuated, these two expressions illustrate period faults.

EXERCISE

20. Determine which of the following illustrate period faults:

(a) The Glenside crowd celebrated the victory uproariously. Carrying their quarterback off the field and tearing down the goal posts.

(b) The population of New Hampshire is around 500,000. It stands about forty-fourth in population among the states.

(c) Another sensational paper of the period was the *Graphic.* Which suspended publication in the early '30's.

(d) The listing for Carpenter was finally changed from "missing" to "dead." No trace ever having been found of his plane.

(e) Dade and Duval are the two most populous counties in Florida. Centering around Miami and Jacksonville, respectively.

(f) The task of soliciting for the fund was given to Mrs. Dodge. The only senior member of the club not present.

(g) Keats made a mistake in history in naming the wrong explorer. Picking Cortez instead of Balboa as discoverer of the Pacific.

(h) The court awarded the injured man about 40 per cent of the damages claimed. This award was a blow to the newly formed company.

(i) The vacancy in the history department is to be filled by a man named Emerson. He has a Ph.D. from Pennsylvania.

One simple way to correct a period fault is to change the punctuation and attach the dependent element to the independent clause, either with no punctuation at all or else with a comma:

> PERIOD FAULT: The driverless car picked up speed going down the hill. And crashed into a grocery store on the corner.
>
> CORRECTED: The driverless car picked up speed going down the hill and crashed into a grocery store on the corner.
>
> PERIOD FAULT: Fraley told the whole story to the dean. Who had suspected what had happened.
>
> CORRECTED: Fraley told the whole story to the dean, who had suspected what had happened.

Another simple way to correct a period fault is to change the dependent element (the phrase or clause set off by itself) into an independent clause and to leave the punctuation arrangement unchanged:

> PERIOD FAULT: The appointment should never have been given to Simmons. A thoroughly mediocre officer with a mediocre record.
>
> CORRECTED: The appointment should never have been given to Simmons. He was a thoroughly mediocre officer with a mediocre record.
>
> PERIOD FAULT: The election returns ran pretty much according to predictions. Although there were a few surprises.
>
> CORRECTED: The election returns ran pretty much according to predictions. However, there were a few surprises.

EXERCISE

21. Correct period faults in the following:

(a) The University of Georgia was chartered in 1785. Being the oldest of the state universities.

(b) Jack decided not to pledge Sigma Sigma. Although he had come to like some of the men in it very much.

(c) The poem contains one verse that is hard to explain. The one mentioning the old moon having a new moon in her arm.

(d) Oregon touches four other states. Washington, Idaho, Nevada, and California.

(e) Richardson's death that spring was very costly to the company. It prevented completion of his research project until the following year.

(f) The British decisively defeated Rommel's men at El Alamein. This victory saved Egypt from falling into Nazi hands.

(g) Massachusetts has a number of distinguished universities and colleges. Such as Harvard, M.I.T., Tufts, Amherst, and Smith.

(h) The news was quite unexpected. It took even the president's closest friends by surprise.

(i) Manager Ellis can try Kelly at first base. Furthermore, Clark is also available.

(j) The largest county in continental United States aside from Alaska is Coconino in Arizona. With an area of over eighteen thousand square miles.

It is true that incomplete sentences are often used to communicate thought. One does not usually find full sentences like "This is Davis' grocery" on store windows or like "This novel is called *Seeds of Fury*" on book jackets. It is true that much conversation is conducted in units that are sentence fragments in form. It is true that many experienced writers use incomplete sentences successfully for particular effects in narration and description. In writing narration or description, you may experiment with incomplete sentences, and perhaps what you write will be effective. But until you have some experience in writing, you are likely to find your readers interpreting your incomplete sentences as indications of ignorance or carelessness.

SU 2   *Do not make comma faults*

Do not use a comma to punctuate two independent clauses not joined by and, but *or* or. Use of a comma, rather than a semicolon, between two independent clauses not joined by a coordinating conjunction is called a *comma fault* or *comma splice*. Most teachers and editors regard this as a bad error. Using a comma instead of a semicolon in this situation violates the general feeling for sentence unity—much as a period fault does.

Note the following:

> The coal is taken from the mine to the breaker, there it is cleaned and graded.

The first group of words is an independent clause: it has a finite verb, *is taken,* and a subject, *coal,* and is therefore a clause; it has no subordinating element and is therefore independent. The second group of words is likewise an independent clause; it has a finite verb, *is cleaned,* and a subject, *it,* and is therefore a clause; it does not begin with a subordinating word and is therefore grammatically independent (although it is logically dependent). Between these two clauses there is no *and, but,* or *or.* As punctuated, this sentence illustrates a comma fault, as do the following:

> There isn't enough headroom to take the big tractor under the barn, we have to use the little cub model to clean out.
> Army recovered a fumble on the Navy six-yard line, the ball was still on that line four plays later.
> I had no chance of passing the test, therefore, I simply cut the class and took an incomplete grade.
> Several other staff members disliked this rivalry between the two professors, however, they were in favor of appointing a department head from outside the department.

Sentences like the last two show situations in which conjunctive adverbs come between independent clauses. Conjunctive adverbs like *therefore, however, thus* do not fall into the same group of connectives as *and, but,* or *or.* When one has two independent clauses joined with a conjunctive adverb and uses only a comma between them, the result is a comma fault. The mistake is the same as that illustrated in the first sentence in the group above. Note the last two sentences again carefully. In the first, the conjunctive adverb *therefore* evidently is part of the second clause, but in the second sentence the word *however* evidently is part of the first clause. Use of a comma rather than a semicolon in these sentences makes them at least momentarily unclear. Contrast the comma faults given above with the following:

> The fire was getting worse, and calls were made for help from companies in nearby towns.
> They tried to lighten the ship by dumping part of the cargo, but it remained stuck firmly on the sand bar.

Each of these sentences contains two independent clauses, but the clauses are connected with coordinating conjunctions, and the commas are adequate punctuation.

The simplest ways to correct comma faults are to change commas to semicolons or to make two separate sentences out of the independent clauses. Perhaps because these are the simplest ways, they are often not the best ways rhetorically, but they do make the needed correction.

COMMA FAULT: Reading the copy of the book took longer than had been expected, consequently the publication date was set back.
CORRECTED: Reading the copy of the book took longer than had been expected; consequently the publication date was set back.

COMMA FAULT: Nevada is often called the Silver State, it is also known as the Sagebrush State.

CORRECTED: Nevada is often called the Silver State. It is also known as the Sagebrush State.

Sometimes a comma fault may be corrected readily by adding and, but, or *or between the two independent clauses:*

COMMA FAULT: Kenny and I decided to go to the state university, Bill preferred one of the smaller colleges.

CORRECTED: Kenny and I decided to go to the state university, but Bill preferred one of the smaller colleges.

Often the best correction for a comma fault consists of rethinking what is being said and rewording one clause or the other so that it becomes dependent. Subordinating one clause may make for an effective arrangement:

COMMA FAULT: The traffic was very heavy, we had to hurry to get to the game by two o'clock.

CORRECTED: Since the traffic was very heavy, we had to hurry to get to the game by two o'clock.

The following table summarizes punctuation between independent clauses:

First Clause	Punctu- ation	Introductory Element	Second Clause
independent	,	and, but, or	independent
independent	;	however, thus also, still, then, etc.	independent
independent	;	lacking; no connective	independent

EXERCISE

22. Correct comma faults among the following sentences. The simplest correction is likely to involve a change in punctuation rather than wording. In some cases the best correction will involve subordinating one of the independent clauses:

(a) The forty-seventh state admitted into the Union was New Mexico, the forty-eighth was Arizona.

(b) Very few of the men will vote against the company plan, most of them have come to prefer it to the other.

(c) Nobody liked Professor Jackson very much, as the survey showed, his difficult tests and sarcastic manner alienated students.

(d) Edna was married the week after Commencement, Ruth announced her engagement at the same time.

(e) *Grapes of Wrath* is a rather somber realistic study of a social problem, *Tortilla Flat* is light, racy, and humorous.

(f) My father finally decided to buy the station wagon, it seemed like the best car for the whole family.

(g) Anthracite is usually clean and relatively smokeless, bituminous coal is dirty and smoky in comparison.

(h) Cape Hatteras is not part of coastal North Carolina, it is on an island that stretches east and south of Pamlico Sound.

(i) Once it took as much as twenty-five days for mail to reach the outpost, now it may be brought in in as many hours.

(j) Either the orders were completely misunderstood, or the general staff was guilty of a costly blunder.

(k) Omega Tau was an independent local until 1955, then it became a chapter in a national fraternity.

(l) Delegates from Wyoming seldom cast decisive votes, important issues are usually settled by the time they vote.

As was said earlier, sentence fragments may be defensible in some situations. Placing only a comma between two independent clauses not joined by a coordinating conjunction may also be defended in some situations. If the two clauses are quite short and if they are closely connected in thought or have the same pattern of construction, the comma may be adequate. The following sentence comes from an essay of D. H. Lawrence: "The blackbird cannot stop his song, neither can the pigeon." But the rhetorical effect of such a sentence is quite different from that produced by most of the sentences given in the exercise above and by most of the comma-fault sentences written by students. Teacher and editor usually agree with most of our literate society in regarding comma-fault punctuation as a major error.

SU 3 *Do not write fused sentences*

Sometimes careless students write comma faults without the commas— that is, they sometimes run together without any punctuation at all two independent clauses not joined by a coordinate conjunction. Note the following:

> Thursday night was very cold the water froze solid in the troughs outside.

The first group of words—from *Thursday* to *cold*—is a clause, since *was* is a finite verb and *night* is its subject; it is independent, since it lacks any introductory subordinating element. The second group of words is likewise an independent clause. Either the two should be written as separate sentences, or there should be a semicolon between them. Or another method of revision should be tried. An unpunctuated sentence composed of two independent clauses not joined by a coordinating conjunction is called a *fused sentence:*

> The basketball game attracted a huge crowd the field house doors were closed an hour before game time.
> Builders are using much glass in modern construction often the whole side of a building is composed of glass blocks.

The simplest correction for a fused sentence consists of placing a semicolon between the independent clauses—just as one may correct a comma fault most simply in the same way. But, as with comma faults, the best correction often involves a revision of the wording. There is no defense for, or tolerance of, fused sentences.

EXERCISES

23. Identify and correct fused sentences among the following:

(a) The T. & E. trains are fairly fast and they are much more comfortable than the others.

(b) There was no use at all in trying to repair the car it was a hopeless wreck.

(c) He didn't have enough money to pay the laundry bill he also owed his roommate ten dollars.

(d) Keats' odes are not easy often they employ learned references and difficult figures.

(e) Route 17 circles around the mountain the new parkway will tunnel through it.

(f) Rescue planes searched the area for ten days then hope was given up for the missing ship.

(g) The carpenters raised the old floor with jacks then they replaced the weakened bearing posts.

(h) The half-time score was 21–6 against us no one in the stadium thought that we had a chance to win.

(i) The injured man was taken to the superintendent's office the first-aid supplies were stored there.

(j) Manhattan Island is a borough in the city of New York it is also a county in the state of New York.

24. Indicate which of the following violate sentence unity. Make appropriate corrections where necessary. Do not change sentences which are now correct:

(a) Baker became secretary and treasurer of the Merritt Company in 1958. Having joined the company as assistant treasurer in 1952.

(b) If it rains on commencement day, the ceremonies will be held inside in the main gymnasium.

(c) Much eighteenth-century poetry contains elements of romanticism, however, the movement reaches its peak in the first years of the nineteenth century.

(d) The trouble was that the can hoist was not working there was a hopeless snarl of rope around the pulley block.

(e) Carpenter's career in public office was apparently one hundred per cent honest, but his opponents never let the scandals of the distant past die out.

(f) The population of California continues to grow steadily, the state has passed Pennsylvania as the second most populous in the country.

(g) Anne Devers was a very well-known and quite popular actress, consequently her suicide was front-page news from coast to coast.

(h) We thoroughly enjoyed our vacation in Maine, the lakes, rivers, woods, and hills there are delightful.

(i) To the north of the pass, still small but spreading every minute, was the forest fire that the rancher had reported.

(j) The people at the Tompkins' party did not seem pretentious or aloof, they were very pleasant and made us feel quite at home.

(k) Edwards was discharged from the position. Not to mention the fact that he was roughly aided through the plant gates by two company guards.

(l) The character of the hero changes as the book goes on. Starting as an irresponsible weakling and ending as a dependable strong man.

(m) Frank cherished the delusion that he would become a doctor. Until he realized the years of training that would be necessary.

(n) The man who cast the vote against Ramsay was Sanders. Who was supposed to be an intimate friend of his.

(o) Grant had achieved his lifelong ambition. To spend a year in Paris doing practically nothing.

13

GRAMMAR

This chapter is about grammar. But the word *grammar* means many different things to different people. At present, scholars are widening the meaning of the word so that it includes many new things. To a degree not dreamed of previously, modern grammarians are studying speech sounds, especially the patterns of stress and pitch. They are as much or more concerned with the fact that the final sound in *dogs* is not the same as that in *cats* as they are with the question of whether one should say *radii* or *radiuses*. They find these and similar matters more interesting than many things you were taught in high or grade school. They also find them more important, since they are very significant in teaching English to foreigners and since in the future they may be as significant in teaching English to the native-born.

Even among persons who center their attention on written rather than spoken English, the present period is marked by great changes in thought about grammar. In the past, the subject has often been concerned mainly with such choices of forms as whether *who* or *whom* or *is* or *are* should be used in a certain situation. Most persons now perceive that, as far as meaning is concerned, word order is much more important in English grammar than choice between grammatical forms. Word order is usually the most important determiner of meanings expressed. Through word order we interpret "the policeman shot the bandit" as meaning that the policeman did the shooting and that the bandit was shot. We know, because of word order, that this sentence does not mean

251

the same thing as "the bandit shot the policeman," although the two expressions use the same words—and the same forms of those words. From the order of the words used we know what different actions *sternly* and *fully* refer to in "the judge sternly warned the witness to answer the questions fully." Sometimes you may break textbook rules about choices of grammatical forms. You may say "the baby has drank all the milk." If you do, you will violate the etiquette of the language, but no one will misunderstand you. But if you break away from set principles of word order, you are very likely to drift into nonsense that no one can understand—nonsense like "milk the drank has all the baby."

This book does not have to explain main principles of word order: you already know them. It might be hard for you to explain them to a foreigner or to a first-grader. But you usually follow these principles automatically. On the other hand you may welcome some comments about choices between word forms—between *who* and *whom* and *is* and *are*. Whoever reads your themes will probably look on such matters as fairly important. This is one reason that these comments are given to you. Another reason is that it is useful to know some ready principles about these choices if you are going to write very much. It isn't very practical to have to stop and think doubtfully about what forms to use in every third sentence that you write. A third reason for giving you these rules is that language etiquette is involved in connection with some of them. There is a social difference between "these trucks are for sale" and "these trucks is for sale." You are likely to be downgraded socially if you use the latter.

The following sections, then, try only to teach you some principles for choosing between similar forms. They represent grammar in the old sense of language etiquette, but not in the new sense of detailed analysis of spoken language. Perhaps you can go on to that study. You will find it fascinating and valuable.

To give you grammatical principles this book naturally has to use some grammatical terms. Defining those terms is difficult in this present period. Some grammarians stick to old definitions; some others try to improve on these old definitions by newer procedures. The first group defines a noun, for instance, as "the name of a person, place, or thing." The second group points out flaws in this definition. Some define a noun as a word that will fit the blanks in the following patterns: this_____, these_____s; the_____ was good; he remembered the_____. Some define a noun as a word that shows plural and possessive forms.

Probably the second group will prevail in time. But perhaps you do not know their procedures, and their definitions may not be the same as those that you have had before. In the interests of your understanding both the general subject and the contemporary situation about grammar, this book has tried to compromise and introduce you to ideas used by both groups. Hence, some definitions may not be so cut-and-dried as you might wish.

This book tries to avoid all but the most necessary grammatical terminology. Notice at all times that it is not your aim to be able to give technical terms to words or groups of words. The important thing is to know how certain words and groups of words operate in sentences. Technical terms are used here simply because most teachers and many students are familiar with them, and there is an economy in keeping them. If you can learn the principles for choosing between forms without learning the technical terms, by all means do so. Maybe you can.

The present period has been marked by much research into the different ways used by different people to speak their thoughts. Since people do speak differently and since this fact is being noticed, there is increasing tolerance for different choices between grammatical forms. Some teachers do not care much whether their students say or write "the bell rang" or "the bell rung." On the other hand, all of them do prefer strongly that their students say or write "I would have come" instead of "I would have came." This book tries to call your attention both to those language situations that allow some room for choice and to those that, by general agreement, violate language etiquette. Constructions commonly felt to be violations of language etiquette are called non-standard.

Verb Forms: Principal Parts of Regular and Irregular Verbs

The principal parts of a verb are those few basic forms from which all other forms are made up. You have probably been taught in grade or high school to recite principal parts—like *ride, rode, ridden; go, went, gone; swim, swam, swum; stop, stopped, stopped.* Perhaps, however, you have not been told how each part works.

The Infinitive. The first of these principal parts (*ride, go, swim, stop*) is the simplest infinitive form of the verb, usually given without the *to.* (See p. 229.) This is the form used with *will, shall, may, might, can, could, would, should: will ride, shall go, may swim, might stop,* etc. This is the base form from which the simplest *-ing* forms are made: *riding, going, swimming, stopping.* This form is the present-tense base:

I ride, you go, he swims, and so on. In a sense this infinitive form is *the* verb itself. It is unlikely to cause you much trouble.

The Past-tense Form. The second of the principal parts (*rode, went, swam, stopped*) is the past-tense form. Note two facts about it: (1) in standard written English it is a finite form; (2) it is never joined with another verb form (like *is, was, have, had, being,* or *having*). It is limited to uses like the following: *I rode, you went, he swam.*

The Past Participle. The third of the principal parts of an English verb is the past participle (*ridden, gone, swum, stopped*). This form is used very freely with parts of *to be* and *to have* in compound forms: *is ridden, was gone, being ridden, having gone.* When the past participle is not used with a part of *to be* or *to have,* it is a non-finite form; it is a modifier. The word to which it is most closely connected is not its subject; instead, that word is modified by the past participle. The word modified by a past participle usually shows who or what has received the action shown, not who or what has done it. In the sentence "the horse ridden by Marshall was a chestnut filly," the form *ridden* is closely connected to *horse. Ridden* is here a non-finite past participle modifying *horse,* showing that *horse* is what has received the action. (See p. 234 for more explanation of this use of the past participle.)

Modern English verbs are divided into two groups: (1) Those like *stop,* in which the past tense and the past participle are made up by addition of *-ed, -d,* or *-t* (*stopped*). These verbs are called *regular verbs.* The great majority of the verbs in English are regular. (2) Those like *ride, go,* and *swim* in which the past tense and the past participle are made up by another procedure (*rode, ridden; went, gone; swam, swum*). These verbs are called *irregular verbs.* Their forms may cause some trouble.

Following is a list of principal parts of common irregular verbs:

Present infinitive	Past tense (finite form never used in compounds)	Past participle (often used in compounds; non-finite when used by itself)	Past participle illustrated in compound forms
arise	arose	arisen	have arisen
bear	bore	borne, born	have borne
			was born
begin	began	begun	have begun
			was begun
blow	blew	blown	have blown
			was blown

Present infinitive	Past tense (finite form never used in compounds)	Past participle (often used in compounds; non-finite when used by itself)	Past participle illustrated in compound forms
break	broke	broken	have broken was broken
choose	chose	chosen	have chosen was chosen
come	came	come	have come
do	did	done	have done was done
draw	drew	drawn	have drawn was drawn
drink	drank	drunk	have drunk was drunk
drive	drove	driven	have driven was driven
eat	ate	eaten	have eaten was eaten
fall	fell	fallen	have fallen
fly	flew	flown	have flown was flown
freeze	froze	frozen	have frozen was frozen
give	gave	given	have given was given
go	went	gone	have gone
grow	grew	grown	have grown was grown
know	knew	known	have known was known
lie	lay	lain	have lain
ride	rode	ridden	have ridden was ridden
ring	rang	rung	have rung was rung
rise	rose	risen	have risen
run	ran	run	have run was run
see	saw	seen	have seen was seen
shake	shook	shaken	have shaken was shaken
shrink	shrank	shrunk	have shrunk was shrunk
sing	sang	sung	have sung

Present infinitive	Past tense (finite form never used in compounds)	Past participle (often used in compounds; non-finite when used by itself)	Past participle illustrated in compound forms
sink	sank	sunk	was sung have sunk
speak	spoke	spoken	was sunk have spoken
spring	sprang	sprung	was spoken have sprung
steal	stole	stolen	was sprung have stolen
swear	swore	sworn	was stolen have sworn
swim	swam	swum	was sworn have swum
take	took	taken	have taken
tear	tore	torn	was taken have torn
throw	threw	thrown	was torn have thrown
wear	wore	worn	was thrown have worn
weave	wove	woven	was worn have woven
write	wrote	written	was woven have written
			was written

GR 1 A   Avoid misuse of past-tense and past-participle forms

Should one use *drove* or *driven* in the blank in "Willis had never _____ a truck before"? *Drove* is the past-tense form, the form that is never compounded with other verbs. *Driven* is the past participle, the form that is compounded. *Driven* is the form needed here. "If I had not broke the pencil" is not standard English, since the past-tense form, *broke*, is here used as a part of a compound verb form. The past participle, *broken*, is needed in this sentence. Although many teachers and editors object, others view tolerantly the use of forms containing *-um-* and *-un-* as finite past tenses. Uses like "they sung the opening chorus" and "the bolt sprung back into place" are regarded by many as standard. (Note what your dictionary says about the parts of *drink, ring, shrink, sing, sink, spring, swim*.) Use of the past-tense form in a compounded verb form is not viewed tolerantly; there is common objection to *was began, has rang, will be sank*.

Sometimes problems are caused by the existence of two different past-tense forms or two different past-participle forms. Thus *dive* and *light* each have two past-tense forms, *dived* and *dove* and *lighted* and *lit*. And *hang, bear, prove,* and *forget* each have two past participles, *hung* and *hanged, proved* and *proven, borne* and *born, forgotten* and *forgot*. Aside from telling you to see what your dictionary tells you about such choices, no general suggestion can be given; each situation is pretty much a law unto itself. No general principle will tell you that *dived* is always acceptable but that *dove* is informal, but that *lighted* and *lit* show little difference in use. Sometimes there is a difference in meaning. *Hanged* is restricted to the meaning of putting to death by hanging, and *hung* is the past participle for other meanings of the verb *hang; borne* is the usual past participle of *bear* (as in "burdens to great to be borne"), and *born* is used in reference to the bringing forth of young. Some persons prefer *proved* to *proven* in general uses, holding that *proven* suggests matters legal. But there is no difference in meaning, suggestion, or level between *forgot* and *forgotten*.

Many choices between verb forms, as you see, do not depend on differences of levels, but many others do. *Blowed* and *drug* exist in non-standard English as past tense forms of *blow* and *drag*, but no speaker of Standard English uses them seriously. Use of verb forms not found in conventional educated usage may be informal but is very likely to be non-standard.

EXERCISES

1. Determine which verb form is preferred in each of the following:

(a) These planes have already (flew, flown) several million miles without any serious mishaps.

(b) The surprise attack on the fortress (began, begun) at dawn.

(c) The heavy winds had (blew, blown) the roof off the barn.

(d) If I had (knew, known) about your sister's marriage, I would have (wrote, written) you before.

(e) By midnight the three of them had (drank, drunk) the whole cask of beer.

(f) The cheap shirt was (tore, torn) in three places after I had (wore, worn) it only twice.

(g) The freight train (came, come) down the grade very fast; evidently the engineer had not (saw, seen) the warning signals.

(h) The ride would have been easier if I had not (chose, chosen) a horse that had been (rode, ridden) only a few times before.

(i) This submarine had (sank, sunk) three of the ships in the enemy convoy.

2. Correct the verb forms wherever necessary in the following sentences:

(a) The bell ending the hour had rang before the instructor got around to answering the question.

(b) The fielders' gloves would have lay out in the grass all night if I had not picked them up.

(c) If I had knew about all the reports I would have to write, I would not have took this course.

(d) Anybody who knows anything at all about the game will realize that he should have threw the ball ahead of the runner.

(e) The engine block had cracked when the radiator froze over.

(f) He has never spoken a word to Curry since the night the money was stolen.

(g) Dunn would have given more to the organization if he could have known how valuable it would be to him.

(h) He sprung to his feet at attention when he realized that the lieutenant had spoke to him.

(i) Everett had grew very tired by evening; he had drove the car steadily since six o'clock in the morning.

3. What information does your dictionary give you about the past-tense and past-participle forms of the following verbs: *arise, awake, bear, bite, burst, dig, dive, draw, eat, light, dwell, cast, ring, shine, show, sink, swim, wring, shrink, spring, strive, thrive, weave?*

4. Change the one-word italicized verb forms in the following to two-word forms made up with *have, has,* or *had:*

(a) Valley farmers in these areas *grow* many kinds of tobacco successfully.

(b) The older children *took* the responsibility of caring for the little ones.

(c) The southbound express *comes* into the station on track 4.

(d) The moon *rises* at about nine o'clock the week before Thanksgiving.

(e) On the farm I always *awake* at about six o'clock during the summer.

(f) These lights *shine* on the mountain tops during the summer months.

(g) That week Clark *swam* all the way across the bay three times.

(h) Marcia *saw* the same movie twice during the week.

GR 1 B   *Do not omit the endings of regular forms*

In contrast to irregular verbs, regular verbs cause few problems. You should notice, however, that regular past participles and similar forms end in *-ed, -d,* or *-t.* Sometimes after certain consonants people do not seem to hear these sounds pronounced and consequently leave them out in writing. Sometimes student papers contain sentences like "he thinks that he is a privilege character" and "I hope that I am not prejudice when I make these comments." Participles and similar forms should end in *-ed, -d,* or *-t: privileged, prejudiced.* Although *ice cream* has completely supplanted *iced cream,* one still writes *whipped cream,* not just *whip cream,* with the *-ed* ending of the participle retained.

EXERCISE

5. Add *-ed* or *-d* as needed in the following:

having a collapse lung	had ask for money
the stamps are enclose	an unbalance character
a high-price suit	to play off the postpone game

Nouns and Noun Forms

The word *substantive* was used in the discussion of finite verbs and subjects (see p. 233). A *substantive* is a word or other element that can be used as a subject. The commonest substantives in English are nouns. A noun is traditionally defined as the name of a person, place, or thing, but nouns also name actions (an *explosion,* a *strike,* a *fall*) and qualities (*truth, similarity, hardness*). Definitions of the word *noun* in terms of meanings are likely to be either incomplete or cumbersome.

Hence many grammarians like to use patterns to define *noun.* Some grammarians regard a noun as a simple substantive likely to be used with a preceding *a* or *the.* One contemporary grammarian, C. C. Fries, identifies words like nouns as being capable of use in the blanks of the following: _____is good; _____s are good; the _____ remembered the _____; the _____ went there.[1] Notice how this pattern works: tea or education is good; coupés or salaries are good; the clerk remembered the letter; the dean remembered the incident; the ship or the general went there. *Tea, education, coupé, salary, clerk, letter, dean, incident, ship,* and *general* are nouns since they will fit into the blanks. Notice that there are difficulties in fitting the following words, which are not nouns, into the same blanks: *choose, drown, obey; big, honest, solemn; she, they, which; after, since, till.* Some other grammarians explain nouns simply as words that operate in sentences the way that *soldier, clerk, cat, store, road, star, city, truth, liberty, explosion, decay,* and *construction* do.

---

[1] Charles Carpenter Fries, *The Structure of English,* Harcourt, Brace: N.Y., 1952, pp. 80–81.

EXERCISES

6. By using the patterns given above for identification of words like nouns, find out which of the following words can be regarded as nouns: *adjourn, announce, blame, camera, conspire, diet, experience, germ, impede, late, morale, pardon, promise, rocket, sober, tariff, welcome.*

7. Pick out the nouns in one of the paragraphs used in a preceding exercise.

Nouns have fewer forms than verbs. The most important change in noun form is that between the singular and the plural. In general, the singular is the form used to show only one: *a sailor, the manager, this dog, one church, any town, that chapter.* The plural is the form used to show more than one: *grocers, secretaries, horses, the forests, these tunnels, many equations, three flags, those accomplishments. Number* is the characteristic of a noun or other word that shows whether one or more than one is being spoken of.

GR 2 A *Note irregular plurals of certain nouns*

The great majority of English nouns form their plurals by the addition of *-s* to the singular; some add *-es: faces, factors, factories, falls, famines, fashions, felonies, fiascoes, fillies, fishes, frescoes.* Sometimes the plural form is used to suggest kinds of: *coffees, oils, grasses.* Most variations from the pattern of plurals in *-s* or *-es* cause few problems: *man-men, foot-feet, mouse-mice, child-children, ox-oxen, deer-deer, sheep-sheep, trout-trout.* Sometimes, however, nouns borrowed into English from Latin, Greek, or other languages retain their original plurals. Thus the plural of *larva* is *larvae* rather than *larvas;* the plural of *basis* is *bases* rather than *basises.* Many borrowed nouns like *larva* and *basis* form their plurals according to the following pattern:

Singular Ending	Illustration	Plural Ending	Illustration
-a	nebula, alumna	-ae	nebulae, alumnae
-us	nucleus, alumnus	-i	nuclei, alumni
-um	stratum	-a	strata
-ex, -ix, -is	apex, crisis	-es	apices, crises
-on	criterion	-a	criteria

Often a borrowed word has both a foreign plural and a regular English plural: *nebula-nebulae, nebulas; formula-formulae, formulas;*

radius-radii, radiuses; apex-apices, apexes. Sometimes one of these forms is restricted to a certain meaning or to a certain kind of usage. Scientific accounts of physiology may use the form *vertebrae;* more popular accounts may use *vertebras.* There is a strong modern tendency to regard regular plurals as standard and to prefer them to plurals showing Latin and Greek patterns. *Gymnasiums* and *stadiums,* for instance, are much more common in the college world than *gymnasia* and *stadia.* But *phenomena, alumnae, alumni, data, criteria, bases,* and *strata* are still common.

EXERCISES

8. Look up the following in your dictionary and find the plural forms. If there are two different plurals, note any statement in your dictionary about use or meaning: *formula, nebula, focus, radius, genus, stratum, apex, index, vortex, axis, analysis, cherub, bandit, bureau, ellipsis, genius, opus, species, spectrum.*

9. Correct any errors or questionable choices in the following: *these alumnae, this bacteria, these funguses, the agenda include, according to this data, three memorandums, these phenomenas, many alumni, Christmas bonuses, party caucuses, two stadia, two synopses, many panoramas, several campuses.*

GR 2 B   *Note correct possessive forms of nouns*

1. To form the singular possessive of any noun, you are always safe in adding first an apostrophe (') and second an *-s: man's, soldier's, merchant's, nurse's, horse's, beaver's, newspaper's, organization's.* Sometimes this results in a form that ends in *-s's: James's, Lewis's, Doris's, countess's.* Sometimes these forms are written without the *s* after the apostrophe (*James'*), but you will always be safe in adding it. Notice that the formation of singular possessives never involves such changes as *y* to *i* or use of *-es: Mary's, Larry's, baby's, army's, city's, thief's, Negro's, soprano's, goose's, sheep's, brother-in-law's, secretary and treasurer's, attorney general's.*

2. To form the plural possessive of any noun, first form the ordinary plural and second add an apostrophe at the end: *soldiers', merchants', nurses', horses', babies', armies', thieves', Negroes', sopranos'.* If the form

does not have an *s* at the end, add one after the apostrophe. The plural of *man* is *men,* that of *child* is *children.* To these two forms apostrophes are added: *men', children';* then, since they do not end in *s,* an *s* is added to each one: *men's, children's.* The singular and plural possessive forms are the same for nouns whose singular and plural common forms are the same: *deer's, sheep's.*

EXERCISE

10. Make up the following possessive forms: the possessive plural of *hero, lady;* the possessive singular of *Simmons, navy, family;* the possessive plural of *woman;* the possessive of *Katy;* the possessive of *Burns;* the possessive plural of *salesman;* the possessive of *heiress;* the possessive of *Ellis;* the possessive plural of *grandchild, hostess;* the possessive singular of *jockey, wife.*

GR 2 C   *Don't use possessive forms unless possession is involved*

Aside from common idioms like "a day's work," do not use an *'s* possessive form in a situation in which no possession is involved. Do not use possessive forms—forms with apostrophes—for ordinary uses of nouns. In the sentence "visiting athlete's are housed in Randall Hall," the word *athletes* is an ordinary plural used as subject. There is no defense for use of the possessive form here. In the sentence "veterans' of the Korean action received GI benefits," the word *veterans* is the subject; no possession is showed, and there is no reason for the use of the possessive form.

EXERCISE

11. The following sentences contain possessive forms used incorrectly in place of ordinary plurals. Correct them:

(a) The town's in this area manufacture large quantities of silk's and woolen's.

(b) The university's policy about granting credit's to transfer students' is unusually liberal.

(c) The book's on the upper shelves are reserved for Dr. Anderson's history course's.

(d) Cars over five year's old are parked in the southern part of the lot's.

(e) Sports writers' wording is often somewhat forced, since they must try perpetually for variety in their stories'.

GR 2 D   *Possessive forms may be used before gerunds*

The possessive may often be used effectively before non-finite forms. Notice the following sentence from F. Scott Fitzgerald: "This absorbing information about my neighbor was interrupted by Mrs. McKee's pointing suddenly at Catherine." Use of the possessive here may stress the fact that the pointing interrupted the information and may call attention away from Mrs. McKee as a personality. This construction is often used in contemporary writing:

> Returning, he had heard of Schallenberg's being left behind . . . (George R. Stewart).
> . . . to wander in to do his bloody work without Miss Lizzie's so much as suspecting anyone was in the house (Charles and Louise Samuels).

Often, however, the possessive is not used before -*ing* non-finite forms.

> He recalled what old Amorok had said about Karangak searching for the . . . stone (Theon Wright).
> The brakeman cutting out the burning car saved the train.

Teachers, editors, and others do not entirely agree on this construction; some object to it and mark it wrong or change it, but others accept it. The former group would prefer "Karangak's searching" and "the brakeman's cutting out." Your best procedure is probably to consider using possessive noun forms before -*ing* non-finite verb forms, although sometimes the effect is too formal. Use of either the possessive or the common form may be regarded as standard.

EXERCISE

12. Use possessive forms of nouns before -*ing* non-finite verb forms when feasible in the following sentences:

(a) We were all surprised by the child choosing a book instead of a toy.
(b) Babe Adams winning three games against the Tigers was the highlight of the 1909 series.
(c) The salesman talking too long about his product cost him a possible sale.
(d) Every one was shocked at Wilson being accused of treason.
(e) In view of his record, Richards was extremely irritated by Howells being appointed safety inspector.

(f) But Price fouling a Hillsdale player in the act of shooting cost us the game.

(g) The tone of the conversation was changed by Mary mentioning her father's death.

(h) Dale shaking off the manager's signal cost him his place in the starting line-up.

Pronoun Forms

The noun is one kind of substantive, one kind of word capable of serving as subject. The pronoun is another kind of substantive. The pronoun has been defined as a word used in place of a noun. Thus in the sentence "the men wanted their dinner; they were growing impatient," *they* is substituted for *men*. *They* is a pronoun. However, with several words commonly called pronouns it is difficult to see for what nouns they are substituted, and modern grammarians prefer to think of the pronoun as a substantive that has extremely wide and varied meaning and that usually does not fit the noun patterns for forming plurals and possessives. In any case, common pronouns include *I, you, he, she, it, we, they; who, which, what; these, those; one, some, all, none, everyone, everybody, someone, no one.*

Nominative and Objective Case Forms of Pronouns. The forms of six pronouns indicate case. Case in English is mainly a form characteristic used to stress the way one of these pronouns is used in a particular sentence. The six pronouns in question are:

nominative forms:	I	he	she	we	they	who
objective forms:	me	him	her	us	them	whom

Choices involving case usually do not rest on meaning: *who were you with?* and *whom were you with?* express the same meaning.

USES OF NOMINATIVE FORMS

Subjects of clauses should be in the nominative case. In other words, *I, he, she, we, they,* and *who* are used as subjects. This comment is not very hard to understand. You will see that the case forms used in the following short sentences are those that you would naturally use:

I was taking French.	We work at Erie Heights.
He sent the letter.	They were Swedish.
She wore blue.	Who wrote *Main Street?*

In three situations, however, there is a tendency to use the objective forms (*me, him, her,* etc.) instead of nominatives for subjects:

GR 3 A *Pronouns used as parts of compound subjects should be nominative forms*

In "she and I had leads in the class play," the compound expression *she and I* answers the question "who or what had?" Since this expression is therefore the subject, the two nominative forms *she* and *I* are used. In the sentence "we trainees were ordered to report," *were ordered* is the finite verb; *we* is used rather than *us* because it is part of the subject. Use of objective forms as parts of compound subjects ("me and Harris collected the papers") is non-standard.

GR 3 B *Subjects of elliptical clauses should be in the nominative*

Sometimes we do not say all the words implied in a whole clause if meaning is quite clear without them. Instead of saying "he is stronger than I am strong," we usually say only "he is stronger than I am" or "he is stronger than I." Clauses marked by such omissions are called elliptical clauses; *ellipsis* means "omission." In comparisons we frequently omit parts of clauses: "you are quicker than I," "Mary is prettier than she." *The nominative is preferred if the pronoun is subject of the elliptical clause:*

> I heard the young Emperor discussed in my own family and thought of my brother, eleven years older than I . . . (Pearl S. Buck).
> I greatly admired Miss Idell. Nothing, nothing, I was sure, had ever been as beautiful as she (Robert Penn Warren).
> I knew that with the exception of ourselves everyone in the section had been given his seven days' leave—even two men who had arrived later than we . . . (e. e. cummings).
> The men who govern the instruments are as skilled as they (J. N. Leonard).

Elliptical clauses offer the one common situation in English in which meaning is expressed by choice of case forms rather than by sentence order. "Smith likes Jones better than I" is interpreted as meaning that Smith's liking for Jones is greater than my liking for Jones, but "Smith likes Jones better than me" is interpreted as meaning that Smith's liking for Jones is greater than his (Smith's) liking for me. This point, then, bears on clearness of expression as well as language etiquette. Objective forms as subjects of elliptical clauses are non-standard.

GR 3 C   Who *is used in subject situations*

Various situations involving the word *who* (and the by-forms *whoever* and *whosoever*) cause difficulty partly because the objective form *whom* is seldom used in our spoken language and partly because sentences using *who* often vary from normal order. *Note that each finite verb in a dependent clause should have an expressed subject and that who is, of course, the form preferred for subjects of finite verbs.* In "give the package to whoever calls for it," you may wonder whether the form *whomever* should have been used; you may feel that this form should follow the word *to*. But in the second clause of the sentence, the dependent clause, the finite verb is *calls*. The pronoun is the subject for this. Hence the preferred form is *who*, not *whom*, *whoever*, not *whomever*. The following are correct:

> information addressed to *whoever* may be interested
> I will talk to *whoever* answers the phone.
> Notify *whoever* calls that the shipment is ready.
> regardless of *who* represents the Kenyon Company

Sometimes an unimportant short expression—like *I think, they say, it seemed, you know*—added after the *who* causes uncertainty about the use of the finite verb. In "Roberts is the man who they say will be the candidate," there may be doubt in your mind about the choice between *who* and *whom*. *Who* is used here because the pronoun is the subject for the finite verb *will be*. Again, the determining factor is the fact that the finite verb must have an expressed subject. The following are correct:

> Williams is the man who I think is best qualified.
> The man who they suspected was the murderer committed suicide.
> . . . she called my mother to her bedside and asked her to take care of her small daughter, who she feared would suffer if left alone with the concubines (Pearl S. Buck).
> . . . most of all a Malay pirate, who, he said, was a sort of Saint Francis with beasts, though a perfect Nero with his fellow men (John Buchan).
> He had a far-famed cap or helmet which made whoever wore it invisible (Edith Hamilton).

It all depends on who has the knowledge and what he does with it (Alfred North Whitehead).

Use of *whom* rather than *who* in subject situations is non-standard.

GR 3 D   *Nominative forms are used in predicate nominative situations*

Pronouns meaning the same person or persons as the subject are likely to be in the nominative. In this situation, the forms *I, he, she, we,* and *they* may be used (rather than *me, him, her, us,* and *them*). In "he is president," "I am your friend," "Jenkins is a historian," the words *president, friend,* and *historian* are called *predicate nominatives* (even though, in point of fact, objective forms of pronouns are sometimes used in these situations). Predicate nominatives are substantives that follow verbs—usually parts of *to be*—and mean the same persons or things as the subjects of those verbs. *When a pronoun is used as a predicate nominative, the nominative form may be employed:*

> The stars of the show were she and her brother.
> The only substitutes left on the bench were Jones and I.
> I wanted to tell him not to bother, that it was all right now, that he was he and I was I (Robert Penn Warren).
> I wanted to tell that newsboy it was I—I, the *Daily Globe* reporter (Meyer Levin).

It is I and *it was I*—along with similar constructions like *it was she, it was he, if it had been we, it might have been they*—are standard, although they may sound formal and stilted. *It is me* is used so commonly by all sorts of persons that only an extreme stickler for rules would object very strenuously to its use in ordinary speech. But "it is him" and "it was her" are not regarded so tolerantly and are non-standard. Notice that the nominative form is strongly preferred in both formal and informal English if a dependent clause follows the predicate nominative:

> . . . Coot was an old hand at such things, having been in debtors' prison twice, and it was he who suggested that they bring along a loaf of bread and a bottle of gin (Howard Fast).
> It was she who had chosen the names of her sons for she was very sensible of the dignity of family life (James Joyce).
> The English, incensed at the loss of revenue, had insisted on their right to trade, maintaining that it was not they who had introduced the opium habit to the Chinese (Pearl S. Buck).

Use of objective forms in predicate nominative situations before a following clause is non-standard. Such a sentence, then, as "it was I who made the suggestion" is acceptable, but not, to most people, "it was me that made the suggestion."

GR 3 E *Pronouns in apposition with subjects are in the nominative*

Sometimes a substantive, or a set of substantives, follows directly after another substantive and means the same thing as that preceding one:

The mayor of the town, Samuel Burwell, said . . .
The afternoon newspaper, *The Record,* reported . . .
The Stapleton Company, the town's largest industry, is hiring . . .

In the first of these, the words *mayor* and *Samuel Burwell* mean the same person; in the second the words *newspaper* and *The Record* mean the same thing, and so on. This way of joining substantives together with the same meaning is called *apposition.* The second substantive given in each of these illustrations—*Samuel Burwell, The Record, the town's largest industry*—is said to be in apposition with the first; these expressions are called appositives. *Pronouns in apposition with subjects should have nominative forms.* In "the social committee—Ruth, Eleanor, and I—favored the plan," the nominative form *I* is used since it is part of an expression in apposition with the subject. The following are correct:

The lowest pair—he and Ferris—received a consolation prize.
The buglers in the camp, Tom and I, were awakened first.
. . . we had succeeded, my friend B. and I, in dispensing with almost three of our six months' engagement (e. e. cummings).

Use of an objective form in this situation is non-standard.

EXERCISE

13. Determine which pronoun form is preferred in formal English in each of the following:

(a) Adams and (I, me) were told to clean up the locker room.
(b) My roommate always has more money than (I, me).

(c) Doctors can now give the inoculations to (whoever, whomever) requests them.

(d) The man (who, whom) the paper says will be appointed is Baker.

(e) (She, Her) and Alice were on the probation list at the time.

(f) (We, Us) pledges have to address every full-fledged brother as "sir."

(g) The dean's office has application blanks to be filled in by (whoever, whomever) is interested.

(h) (Who, Whom) did you say was responsible for the account?

(i) Carr knows much more about algebra and trigonometry than (I, me).

USES OF OBJECTIVE FORMS

Objective forms (me, him, her, us, them, whom) *are preferred when the pronouns are objects.* This comment of course will be completely meaningful only if you know what an object is. Most substantives that are not subjects, predicate nominatives, or appositives of subjects are objects. If you can decide that a substantive is not one of these, you can usually be safe in concluding that it is an object of some sort.

The words that have objects include finite verb forms, non-finite verb forms, and prepositions. The direct object of a finite verb form is usually the substantive (noun, pronoun, or other element) that follows the verb form in a sentence arranged in normal order. In "Gannett sent his report to the secretary of the company," *report* is the substantive following the verb; it is the direct object. In "that day Howells sold three new automobiles," *automobiles* is the direct object; it is the substantive following the finite verb *sold*. Italicized substantives in the following are direct objects:

This company manufactures *ink*.   The wreck killed *three men*.
The Yankees beat *the Tigers*.   I ate *the sandwiches*.
Jennings wrote *the letters*.   Keller and Son built *the house*.

Phrases, especially non-finite verb phrases, and dependent clauses may be objects of verbs: we enjoyed *eating the grapes;* he remembered *hating Joe at first;* Kent believed *that the invention would fail;* they asked *if they might borrow the mower*. Sometimes objects of verbs are defined as those words that show who or what has received the action indicated by the verb form. This statement is generally true, although sometimes objects show things that are not affected very much by the actions indicated by the verbs. In "the astronomer saw the comet," the word *comet* is the object, although the comet itself was hardly affected by the experience of being seen. Like subjects, objects are probably best regarded simply as structural units in English sentences.

The objects in the paragraph above are all direct objects. Sometimes finite verbs take two objects; he gave *his friend the money*. When a finite verb has two objects, like *friend* and *money* in this illustration, the first one given is called the *indirect object*, the second, the *direct object*. The indirect object shows that which has been affected less directly, immediately, or forcefully than the direct object; often it indicates that which has been benefited or harmed by an action performed on something else. Note the following:

Subject	Verb	Indirect Object	Direct Object
The Kane Company	offered	me	a job.
Dr. Manning	assigned	him	three extra chapters.
The boss	gave	Nelson and me	a slight raise.
Her father	sent	Betty	a fifty-dollar check.

Non-finite verb forms may likewise take objects. In "having attached the chain," the word *chain* is the direct object for *having attached;* in "to play the music," the word *music* is the direct object for *to play*. The italicized substantives in the following are objects:

keeping *his promise*   calling *Olsen and me*
visiting *them* later   to break *the glass*
having repaired the *set*   to have sent *the note*

Non-finite verb forms may also take indirect objects. In "giving the Red Cross a generous sum" and in "to promise him a promotion," the words *Red Cross* and *him* are indirect objects.

Prepositions likewise take objects. In dealing with prepositions there is no complication about direct and indirect objects. The object of a preposition is the substantive that follows it in a sentence arranged in normal order. In "the new post office will be located in the center of the city at the corner of Elm and Main," the words *in, of, at,* and *of* are prepositions; their objects are the substantives that follow them, *center, city, corner,* and *Elm and Main,* respectively. In the following prepositional phrases the italicized substantives are objects:

at *the gymnasium*   by *the roadside*
beyond *the lines*   over *the fence*
for *him and me*   from *Dick and me*

Nouns and most pronouns show no variation in form between uses as subjects and uses as objects: *the policeman shot the bandit, the bandit shot the policeman.* With *I-me, he-him, she-her, we-us, they-them, who-whom,* there is variation in form, objectives being used in object situations. Most sentences, especially simple ones, cause no problem. You are unlikely to say "he called I" rather than "he called me" or "Parks invited she" rather than "Parks invited her." A few situations, however, require special caution:

GR 3 F   *Pronouns used as parts of compound objects should be objective forms*

In "the real work was done by Quinn and me," the word *by* is a preposition. The compound substantive following it is its object. Since the pronoun is part of the object, the form is *me.* The sentence should *not* be worded as ". . . by Quinn and I" or as ". . . by I and Quinn." In "this will be a secret between you and me," *between* is a preposition and *you and me* is its object. *Me* is here used correctly; the sentence should *not* be worded as ". . . between you and I" or as ". . . between I and you." In "the sergeant ordered us rookies to wait," the form *us* is used rather than *we* because it is part of the object. Note the following:

> She seemed to think that if she didn't speak up, he would most likely leave all his money to his wife, leaving her and Emma without a penny (Charles and Louise Samuels).
>
> Lee made no announcement of the plan, which grew in scope as it evolved between Jackson and him (Clifford Dowdey).
>
> . . . he had made himself, in what was a wilderness, the home he now wishes his mother and me to share (Charles Nordhoff and James Norman Hall).

Use of nominative forms in object situations ("the real work was done by Quinn and I") is non-standard.

GR 3 G   *Objects of elliptical clauses should be in the objective*

In "the inoculations worried Ramsay more than me," the full clause would have been "more than they worried me," and *me* is used rather than *I* because it is an object. *Him* is used rather than *he* since it is the object in "the fall hurt Steve more than him."

GR 3 H   Whom *is used in object situations*

Clauses using either *who* or *whom* often show a word order different from the usual and are occasionally complicated by added elements, such as *they say* or *he thought*. In spoken English many people use *whom* hardly at all, but formal written English may require it. If other words in the sentence are subjects for finite verbs, it is likely that the objective form *whom* will be needed in formal expression. Note the question "whom do you wish to talk to at the company?" In this question the subject is *you*. *Whom* is used because it is an object—specifically the object of the preposition *to*. In "a man whom he had previously known in Cincinnati," *he* is the subject for *had known; whom* is used because it is the object for that verb. In "a lady to whom Turner introduced me," *whom* is used because it is the object of the preposition. In "the candidate whom they say the president himself prefers," *they* is the subject for *say* and *president* the subject for *prefers; whom* is used because it is the object in a clause. Note the following sentences:

> The list of the chief writers through whom the myths have come down to us is not long (Edith Hamilton).
> He was the kind of father whom boys love, who would shut up shop on a fine day and take them fishing (Samuel Eliot Morison).
> Instead of feeling married she was almost wondering who might call her up or whom she might call up (John P. Marquand).

Use of *who* in object situations is generally informal.

GR 3 I   *Pronouns in apposition with objects are in the objective*

In "the coach had some special instructions for the catchers, Underwood and me," *me* is used instead of *I* since it is part of the material in apposition with *catchers*, an object. (See p. 268.)

EXERCISES

14. Determine which pronoun form is preferred in each of the following sentences:

(a) The candy was a present for Mother from my brother and (I, me).
(b) The teacher advised (she, her) and Flora to take the course in algebra.

   (c) The new regulations about student ownership of cars concerned the upperclassmen more than (we, us) freshmen.

   (d) His description fits with that of a man (who, whom) the police want for questioning in connection with several holdups.

   (e) The freshman class passed a motion thanking their upperclass advisers, Wagner, Young, and (I, me), as "enervating influences."

   (f) Northeastern's hopes rest on Abrams, (who, whom) it now seems will start the game at quarter.

   (g) The note from the Alumni Association invited (we, us) recent graduates to join the organization.

   (h) The chapter has invited (she, her) and her sister to the rushing tea.

   (i) It looks as though one would have to choose between (he, him) and Bartlett.

15. In the following, change pronouns that do not accord with formal English grammar:

   (a) Who has the committee picked as the next minister?

   (b) Union leaders who had not supported Faraday knew that it was them that the new orders referred to.

   (c) His sister's decision came as a great surprise to him and his wife.

   (d) Finlay has an important position with the Grant-Hill Company; the editorial committee consists of Jackson, Kellett, and he.

   (e) The new scholarship policy finally gives a break to we athletes.

   (f) Mrs. Lewis asked who they were talking about when she overheard the word "scandal."

   (g) Madden was the accountant who had helped he and his wife make out their income tax return.

   (h) The claim will be investigated by our Mr. Nichols, who you will remember took care of your accident claims a year ago.

   (i) It seemed to we extras in the cast that the director was very fussy about details.

USES OF POSSESSIVE FORMS

Like nouns, pronouns have possessive forms, and, like noun possessives, those forms occasionally cause trouble.

GR 3 J   *Possessive personal pronouns are not punctuated with apostrophes*

Some pronouns use an apostrophe and -s to make up their possessive forms: *someone's, everyone's, no one's, everybody's. But the possessive forms of* I, you, he, she, it, we, *and* they *do not have apostrophes:* my, mine, your, yours, his, her, hers, its, our, ours, their, *and* theirs. These words show possession in themselves.

my car	that car is mine
our dog	that dog is ours
your hat	that hat is yours
its paw	
his pen	that pen is his
her coat	that coat is hers
their house	that house is theirs

(Forms with apostrophes like *you're*, *it's*, and *they're* are contractions of *you are, it is,* and *they are.*) The possessive form for *who* is *whose.* (*Who's* is the contraction of *who is:* "who's ready to go with me?") The personal pronouns and the word *who* are the only English substantives with possessives that are not formed with apostrophes.

EXERCISE

16. Insert apostrophes where they are needed in the following sentences; delete apostrophes that have been incorrectly added:

(a) The bird had broken it's wing when it crashed into the picture window of their living room.

(b) It's no wonder that you lost your glove and have to borrow somebody elses; you should take better care of your things.

(c) It's your' car that is blocking the driveway; our's is parked behind the house.

(d) The house on the corner belongs to the Meyers; they're now away on a trip to Europe.

(e) If you're not sure that the money is yours', you had better let it alone for the time being.

GR 3 K   *Possessive forms may be used before gerunds*

As with noun possessives (see p. 263), the possessive forms of pronouns are often effectively used before non-finite verb forms. Instead of "the victory was insured by him sinking a nine-foot putt," many writers, perhaps a majority, would prefer "the victory was insured by his sinking a nine-foot putt." Note the following: "the accident was caused by his trying to turn to the left from the extreme right lane"; "the sale was delayed by their refusing to sign the quit claim." Study the following expressions:

> . . . he began to recognize that the odds were heavily against his being able to better himself by moving elsewhere (James Hilton).
> This obliviousness of his made it possible for her to get him those shirts and ties and socks without his knowing they were expensive (John P. Marquand).

> It was even said afterward that but for my going out there just then, the murderers might never have been caught (Meyer Levin).

On the other hand the possessive is not always used before non-finite forms:

> The idea of anybody feeling good on a day like this, for instance, made him tired (Katherine Anne Porter).
> . . . to make my father's absence less final and to hold out a hope of him still coming (Conrad Richter).

Perhaps the best advice is to consider using possessive forms of pronouns before -ing non-finite verb forms.

EXERCISE

17. Change objective forms to possessive forms before the -ing non-finite verb forms in the following sentences:

(a) The situation was altered by them deciding not to rent the other cottage.
(b) The mistake in the balance was caused by me forgetting to list the check for cash.
(c) There wasn't enough money that summer to permit us going on a long trip.
(d) The course could be improved a lot by him simplifying the complicated experiments.
(e) This was reason enough to prevent them assenting to the plan.

Adjectives

Adjectives. An adjective fits into one of the blanks in the following patterns and makes sense: the _____ man, the _____ thing, the man was _____, the thing was _____. Notice that each of the following words will make sense in one or all of the blanks: *active, angry, bad, black, capable, careful, clean, dark, dull, easy, exact, fast, feeble, free, great, grotesque, heavy, hot:* "the active (or angry or capable or heavy) man," "the man was bad (or dull or great)," "the black (or clean or dark) thing," "the thing was easy (or free or grotesque or hot)." These words are typical adjectives. Sometimes these patterns do not completely and certainly distinguish nouns from adjectives, but they may be adequate for your present purposes. Similarly, some words commonly called adjectives do not fit these patterns, but they are unlikely to cause you any trouble.

Adjectives are used to modify nouns and other substantives. The word *modify* is here used in its grammatical sense: to *modify* is to describe, characterize, qualify, limit, or restrict. In the phrase "an active man," *active* modifies *man:* in "an angry policeman," *angry* modifies *policeman.* In "a careless, fatal mistake," both *careless* and *fatal* modify *mistake.* In "some one capable of murder," the adjective *capable* modifies the substantive *some one,* a pronoun. In "careful cleaning will protect the fabric from harm" the adjective *careful* modifies the nonfinite verb form *cleaning.*

EXERCISE

18. By using the patterns given above, find out which of the following can be called adjectives: *adroit, arbitrary, becoming, brawny, champion, conserve, demonstrate, empty, fitfully, grisly, immune, jovially, material, noticeable, perhaps, promise, responsible, shabby, soon, thankful, venerable.* Pick out the adjectives from among the words used in any preceding exercise.

In the discussion of pronoun forms you were told *farmer* is a predicate nominative in "he is a farmer" and that *he* is a predicate nominative in "it was he who later turned traitor." These predicate nominatives, or complements, follow *is* and *was,* parts of *to be.* As our patterns show ("the man was _____"), adjectives also follow parts of *to be* and serve as complements. In "he was active," "they were angry," "it was bad," "the car was black," "the secretary was capable," the adjectives serve as complements and modify the subjects of the verbs.

GR 4 A *Use standard comparative and superlative forms of adjectives*

Some adjectives—but not all—have comparative and superlative forms. *Angrier, cleaner, darker,* and *easier* are comparative forms and *angriest, cleanest, darkest,* and *easiest* are superlative forms. As these forms show, short adjectives form their comparatives and superlatives by adding *-er* and *-est,* respectively. Most one-syllable and many two-syllable adjectives follow this pattern. Longer adjectives use the words *more* and *most* to form the comparative and superlative: *beautiful, more beautiful, most beautiful; realistic, more realistic, most realistic.* Some two-syllable adjectives lend themselves freely to either way of forming comparatives and superlatives. If you are uncertain which formation to use, perhaps your dictionary will help you. If it does not, you will probably be safer in using forms made up with *more* and *most* than forms made up with *-er* and *-est*. Note that modern English avoids use of both methods of comparison at once; our language no longer sanctions such forms as *more prettier* and *most difficultest*.

EXERCISE

19. What are the comparative and superlative forms for each of the following: *abject, able, abrupt, acrid, absurd, agreeable, appropriate, beauteous, capable, comic, dismal, eager, fertile, honest, joyful, mellow, proper, petty, scenic, speedy, treacherous, wealthy?*

GR 4 B   *Comparative forms of adjectives are used of two, superlative forms of more than two*

In formal English the comparative form is used in situations in which two—and only two—persons or things are being compared. Note the sentence "Frankie is the stronger of the twins." The comparative form *stronger* is used here rather than the superlative form *strongest* because *twins* indicates that only two persons are being spoken of. In the sentence "Miss Manning is the more competent of the two typists," the comparative *more competent* is used because again only two persons are compared. Note the use of comparatives in the following:

> Citizens of the dual monarchy delighted in comparing the two capitals. Budapest by common consent had much the lovelier women and the livelier parties. Vienna, on the other hand, was more sedate, and its cultural life, in the formal sense of opera, concert and theater, more illustrious. Budapest was held to have a better climate, more tasty cooking, finer dancing, more natural vivacity, a wealthier aristocracy and a more oppressed citizenry. Vienna was more religious, had better music, richer desserts, and more officials (James A. Michener, *The Bridge at Andau*).

Superlatives are used in comparisons involving three or more persons or things: this was the chestnut's fastest time for six furlongs, February was the stormiest month of the year, Ramsey's house was the most expensive one on the block. Because superlatives are used more frequently than comparatives, however, there is a strong tendency to extend their use to comparisons involving only two persons or things: the National is the cheapest of the two trucks, Mt. Bradford is the highest of the two mountains. These uses of superlatives often pass unnoticed in our daily conversation, but they are not sanctioned in formal writing; they may be called informal. On the other hand, it is idle for anyone to object strongly to such idiomatic expressions as "may the best team win" and "to put one's best foot forward."

GR 4 C   *Some adjectives resist comparison*

As said above, although many adjectives can be compared, some cannot be. In *"he* and *they* are nominative case forms," the word *nominative* is called an adjective, yet it resists comparison. In chemistry, some compounds are ferrous; a compound is either completely so or completely not so, and no comparison is possible; comparative and superlative forms of *ferrous* do not exist. There are capital crimes in law; one crime is not more capital than another, and the adjective has no comparative or superlative in this sense. Sometimes, however, in everyday speech and in informal writing, we use the comparative to mean "more nearly" when we have in mind two or more things of which no one is completely *x* but of which one is more nearly *x* than another. We may say, for instance, that Willie's attempt to draw a circle is rounder than Johnny's, ignoring the fact that a figure is either round or not. There can be no comparative or superlative of *perfect* in certain of its religious and philosophic uses, but this fact did not prevent American patriots from speaking of forming "a more perfect union." Sometimes comparatives and superlatives are used for humor: *deader than a doornail, deader than a mackerel.* Comparatives like those of *round, perfect,* and *dead* and similar superlatives often imply a slight change of meaning in the base word and suggest an informal tone.

EXERCISES

20. Which of the following adjectives resist comparison and lack comparative and superlative forms for their primary meanings: *absent, airtight, autocratic, binary, capitalistic, coherent, cubical, distinct, exquisite, fundamental, historical, innate, malignant, neuter, plural, regimental, serial, surgical, tubular, vertical?*

21. Change adjective forms in the following to accord with formal English. Be prepared to explain the reasons for each change you make.

(a) Plane geometry is the easiest kind.
(b) Glencove's winning the championship was the most unlikeliest of these possibilities.
(c) These two weights are more equal than any others in the box.
(d) The two girls were attractive, but Sue was the prettiest.
(e) Naturally Uncle Willie took the comfortablest chair.
(f) As you go farther south the weather naturally becomes more warmer.
(g) Stricken by remorse, he vowed to live a more celibate existence in the future.
(h) The electric outlet on the north wall is more central than the one on the south.
(i) He almost always reads only with his left eye, his strongest one.

Adverbs

A perfect pattern for identifying adverbs is hard to devise, but many adverbs are words other than substantives that will fit one of the following blanks and make sense: he spoke _____, they stopped _____, it operates _____. Notice that the following will fit these blanks: *clearly, easily, regularly, quickly, finally, anxiously, separately, weakly, seriously, frequently,* and many other similar words ending in *-ly; fast, long, straight, slow, late, right, soon, often, always, sometimes, there, then, first, next, seldom, more, less, afterward, alike, also, again, anyhow, outside, well, beyond.* Some grammarians are content to say that adverbs are words that work like *cleanly, rapidly,* and *safely* and let it go at that. With this procedure you are unlikely to make many mistakes, but you should notice that the *-ly* ending does not necessarily show that the word in question is an adverb—since *kindly, friendly,* and *gentlemanly* are adjectives—and you should notice that many words that do not end in *-ly* are called adverbs. As the list may imply, the English adverb, in conventional grammar, includes a miscellaneous class of words with less definiteness of form and pattern than the verb, noun, and adjective.

Adverbs are often defined according to their use as words that modify verbs, adjectives, and other adverbs—in short, adverbs modify words that are not substantives. In "he stopped rapidly" and "it operated smoothly," the words *rapidly* and *smoothly* are adverbs; *rapidly* modifies the verb *stopped* and *smoothly* modifies the verb *operates.* In "a moderately long walk" and "a quite good plan," *moderately* and *quite* are adverbs modifying the adjectives *long* and *good* respectively. In "he did the work very efficiently" and "the tooth hurt almost unbearably," *very* and *almost* are adverbs modifying the other adverbs *efficiently* and *unbearably.*

EXERCISE

22. By using the patterns given above, find out which of the following words may be called adverbs: *behind, queenly, further, beggarly, better, forth, far, blindly, anyhow, otherwise, besides, abroad, boldly, dewy, deep, hence, now, after, both, calmly, once, counter, surely.* Pick out the adverbs used in the sentences in a preceding exercise.

Often it is convenient to think of certain adverbs as modifying not just a single word in a clause but as modifying the whole clause. This is often the situation with conjunctive adverbs, like *however* and *further-more.* In "the evidence was overwhelming; hence there was no surprise about the verdict," the word *hence* may be said to modify the whole clause rather than just one word in it.

GR 4 D   *Comparative forms of adverbs are used of two, superlatives of more than two*

Like adjectives, adverbs are compared; they have comparative and superlative degrees. Several short adverbs show comparison in -*er* and -*est: he waited longer than I, this plane arrived earlier, if the water rises higher in the mine shaft, our work will be finished soonest.* Most adverbs, however, make up their comparative and superlative forms through use of *more* and *most: carefully, more carefully, most carefully; noisily, more noisily, most noisily.* Adverbs like *yet, then, again,* and *anyhow* cannot be compared. As with adjectives, the comparative degree of the adverb is usually used when only two persons or things are concerned in the comparison being made; the superlative is used when three or more are involved. In the sentence "when they took both the car and the truck down the Lenox road they found that the truck went faster," the comparative form *faster* is used rather than the superlative *fastest* because only two things are involved. In "the game was a tie, but certainly Ramsey High had played the more impressively," the comparative form with *more* is used since only two teams were involved.

GR 4 E   *Do not use adjectives in adverb situations, and vice versa*

An adjective modifies a substantive, an adverb something other than a substantive. In "the car is new" and "the noise was constant," the words *new* and *constant* are complements or predicate adjectives; they are joined to the nouns that they modify (*car* and *noise*) by parts of *to be*. The verb *to be* is called a linking verb because its main function is connecting what precedes and what follows. The verb *to be* expresses no action at all; its main function is simply to serve as a formal structural element in the sentence. Other verbs that operate in much the same way and are also called linking verbs include *become, seem, grow, look, feel,* and *taste*. Verbs showing use of the five senses (sight, hearing, etc.) are often linking verbs. In linking uses, these verbs are followed by adjectives rather than adverbs; they may take adverbs after other uses:

> They were becoming weak with hunger (*Become* operates in the same way as *to be;* the adjective *weak* rather than the adverb *weakly* is needed after this linking verb.)
>
> The bolt seems strong enough. (*Seem* is another linking verb; its function in this sentence is to indicate that the bolt gives evidence of being strong. The adjective *strong,* not the adverb *strongly,* is needed here to modify *bolt.*)
>
> He grew impatient when he heard all these objections. (*Grow* in this sentence is a verb to be followed by an adjective modifying the subject *he.* Contrast uses of *grow* as an actional verb in "the corn grew rapidly" and "cancers often grow unpredictably.")
>
> The boss looks happy this morning. (This means that he looks as though he were happy; *looks* is here a linking verb, and the adjective *happy* is used. Contrast "he looked happily across the desk at the new contract.")

A number of other verbs have idiomatic uses in which they express little action and mean little more than *to be, to appear, to come to be,* and consequently take adjectives rather than adverbs after them; contrast the first of each of the following with the second:

The brook ran dry in August.	The brook ran noisily into the pond.
The weather turned cold.	He turned coldly toward the stranger.
You can rest easy about the operation now.	You can rest more easily if you have more pillows.
He stood firm in his determination not to yield.	He stood firmly on the stairs blocking the way.

In some situations it doesn't make much difference whether you use an adjective, with the implication that the verb is a linking verb, or an adverb, with the implication that the verb is at least somewhat actional:

He kept resolute to his vows.	He kept resolutely to his vows.
The children were sitting very quiet in the hall.	The children were sitting very quietly in the hall.

Confusions about linking verbs cause some poor choices in adverb and adjective use. More happen because of carelessness. In "he did the work well," the modifier refers to the verb *did*. Since *did* is a verb, the adverb *well* is used here rather than the adjective *good*. In "he was still worried but was some relieved when he found that his brother had not been badly injured," the adverb form *somewhat* is needed rather than the adjective *some* to modify the participle *relieved*. The word *real* is an adjective; an adverb like *very* or *certainly* is needed in a construction like "it was _____ cold that night." The adverb form *badly* is needed rather than the adjective *bad* in such expressions as "hurt badly."

The paragraph above has stressed using adverbs rather than adjectives in adverb situations. Remember, however, that many adverbs do not end in *-ly*, like *fast, right,* and *late,* and that many other adverbs have both forms, like *slow* and *slowly, loud* and *loudly*. Changing from the normal American "go slow" to "go slowly" is overcorrectness.

EXERCISES

23. In each of the following, indicate which form is preferred in formal English expression. If either form is acceptable, be able to explain in detail:

(a) The custard tasted (bad, badly), and he did not eat any more of it.

(b) Despite these dangers Surrey remained (loyal, loyally) to his king.

(c) Most of Steinbeck's other novels are (considerable, considerably) shorter than *Grapes of Wrath.*

(d) In any case the taxi driver had not made the turn as (careful, carefully) as he should have.

(e) By tradition they sing the second verse of the Alma Mater quite (soft, softly).

(f) I found that if you did not bother to study it college physics (sure, surely) was hard.

(g) With some experience and responsibility he grew more (dependable, dependably) and less (erratic, erratically).

(h) Whatever happened, he could rely on the mate to hold the ship (steady, steadily) on its course.

(i) Nelson felt (uncomfortable, uncomfortably) when he realized his stupid blunder.

(j) He stood (silent, silently) by the rostrum for a long time when he was accused of lying.

24. Some of the following sentences contain adjective and adverb choices that do not accord with formal English. Change them wherever necessary. Make what comments you can about the level of usage illustrated.

(a) You had better go slow about investing in Carpenter stocks.

(b) It was hard to tell which was the worst picture in the double feature.

(c) Captain Powderhorn always talked very brave and then hid somewhere when there was danger.

(d) It will not be long before the pet cub turns wildly again.

(e) More people would elect his courses if he did not always treat his students so sarcastic.

(f) After the old mechanic adjusted the timer the truck started easy enough.

(g) Baker comes very conscientious to every class and then sleeps forty minutes out of the hour.

(h) Jerry was sure happy when he got the news of the appointment.

(i) In kicking Anderson out of the game the referee did not act very fair.

(j) Most of Williams' testimony proved falsely later.

The Concept of Agreement

In "Carson has written several plays," *written* is used instead of *wrote* because the past participle is needed since the verb is a two-word form. The choice between *written* and *wrote* is determined by the verb itself within this sentence. In the sentence "between you and me I believe that he is guilty," *me* is used instead of *I* because the pronoun in question is part of the object of the preposition. In these sentences *written* and *me* are used because of the demands of their own situations.

But in the sentence "the commanding officer of these infantry companies was relieved," we have a different situation: here *was* is used instead of *were* because the choice is governed by the word *officer*. *Was* is used instead of *were* not because of some grammatical characteristic of its own situation, but because it should agree with another part of the sentence, the subject. Since the subject is *officer*, the verb is *was relieved* rather than *were relieved*. In the sentence "the commanding officers of these infantry companies were relieved," *were* is used instead of *was* so that it will agree with *officers*. Nothing about the meaning or the grammatical use of the verbs themselves determines whether one should use *was* or *were* in these sentences. The choice is made entirely because the verb should agree with its subject in number.

English has two argement principles that cause trouble: the principle that subject and verb agree in number, and the principle that pronoun and antecedent agree in number. The latter principle causes us to prefer "everyone has his ticket" to "everyone has their ticket." The next two sections will explain these principles to you in detail.

Subject and Verb Agreement. Subject and verb agree in number. This means that if the subject is singular the verb should be singular and if the subject is plural the verb should be plural. Explanations are needed both about singular and plural subjects and singular and plural verbs. It is simpler here to consider verbs first. On p. 229, you were told that a verb has many different forms. Many of these do not show number by their form; they may be either singular or plural. *Turned* and *will turn,* for instance, may be used with either singular subjects like *he* or plural subjects like *they: he turned, they turned; he will turn, they will turn.* But there is a difference between *turns* and *turn, is turned* and *are turned, has turned* and *have turned, was turned* and *were turned.* You almost certainly say "he turns" but "they turn," "he has turned" but "they have turned." *Turns* and *has turned* are singular forms; *turn* and *have turned* are plural forms.

In situations like this one in which singular and plural forms of verbs differ, an *-s* indicates a singular form, lack of *-s* a plural form:

> SINGULAR FORMS: *turns, saves, earns, writes, builds, opens* (and *is saved, is earned,* etc.)
> *was* (and *was turned, was saved, was earned,* etc.)
> *has* (and *has turned, has saved, has earned,* etc.)
> *does* (and *does turn, does save, does earn,* etc.)

> PLURAL FORMS: *turn, save, earn, write, build, open* (and *are turned, are saved, are earned,* etc.)
> *were* (and *were turned, were saved, were earned,* etc.)
> *have* (and *have turned, have saved, have earned,* etc.)
> *do* (and *do turn, do save, do earn,* etc.)[2]

EXERCISES

25. The following sentences contain both singular and plural verb forms; give the number of each verb form.

(a) The men believe that they are going to receive a bonus.
(b) He is not sure that the bus stops at Hallett's Falls.

---

[2] English nouns and English verbs are generally just the opposite in so far as the meaning of the added *-s* is concerned. The ending *-s* is of course the sign of the plural form of the noun, the form meaning more than one. The ending *-s* is the sign of the singular form of the verb, the form used when the subject means only one; absence of *-s* is the sign of the plural form of the verb.

(c) The caller makes sure that the men who live far from the yards have transportation to work.

(d) Students who have missed the tests are given an opportunity to make them up.

(e) This mountain range extends from Canada to Georgia.

(f) The plane does not leave until 4:10; there is time enough to make the telephone calls.

(g) There was no reason for him to make sarcastic comments about the people who have tried to keep the club going.

(h) The main college was established in 1830; most of the professional schools were founded around 1900.

(i) The Carters are still living in the house where Mr. Carter was born.

(j) Planes coming in from the West are always given priority if there is any congestion at the field.

26. Indicate whether each of the following is singular or plural. If it is singular, give the corresponding plural form, and *vice versa: does operate, are working, have waited, drinks, is hurt, has taken, succeed, is earning, do attend, enjoys, keep, entertain, were talking, has gone, have attempted, tries, finds, care, does stop, arrives, were walking.*

FORM IMPORTANT IN DETERMINING AGREEMENT

For the most part agreement of subject and verb depends on form if there appears to be any conflict between form and meaning—that is, if the form appears to be singular and the meaning plural, or *vice versa.* There are two situations (explained in the sections below) in which form is not more important than meaning, and there are several situations in which the form of the subject may be lost sight of.

GR 5 A   *Unitary subjects may take singular verbs*

Often a subject expressing a measurement, mass, weight, sum, or total takes a singular verb despite the fact that that subject itself is plural in form. Thus one may say "seven years is a long time." In this sentence, the fact that *years* is a plural is lost sight of; both speaker and hearer think of the subject as meaning a period of time rather than a number of separate years; and the singular verb is used correctly. One may say "a hundred dollars is a stiff fine for such an offense." The reasoning in the grammar of this sentence is similar; the subject is thought of as meaning a single sum; and the singular verb *is* is correctly used. The following sentences show satisfactory subject and verb relationships:

Twenty miles is a satisfactory day's march for an army unit.

Two pounds of sugar is needed in this recipe.

Two hundred yards is a reasonably good drive.

Three children is enough, three children in ten years . . . (John O'Hara).

Five years was a long time; he might already be forgotten . . . (Graham Greene).

GR 5 B *Collective nouns as subjects may take either singular or plural verbs*

When a collective noun serves as subject, the verb of the sentence may be either singular or plural, depending on what meaning is attached to the collective noun. A collective noun is a noun that is singular in form—that is, it does not end in *-s* like *miners, students,* or *soldiers,* or otherwise show plural form like *men*. It means a number of persons or, sometimes, animals. *Group, committee, club, class, jury, organization, fraternity, crowd, mob, crew, band, herd,* and *flock* are typical collective nouns. The term *collective noun* is usually not applied to nouns meaning numbers of things, like *fleet, set, collection,* or *galaxy,* and comments about agreement of collective noun subjects and their verbs usually do not apply to such words. A collective noun as subject normally takes a singular verb:

The *group was living* in Livingstone Hall.

The *flock was being kept* in the south fields.

A *crowd* of fifty or sixty people *was charging* up the slope that led to the Palace walls (Robert A. Heinlein).

Though the *jury was* to visit the Borden home later that day . . . (Charles and Louise Samuels).

Her father had been a small military official and the *family was* almost poor (Pearl S. Buck).

Sometimes, however, a plural verb may be used to call attention to the separate individuals composing the group, often to suggest individual action by each of the persons involved:

The *audience are* returning to their seats.

The *gang were* all picked up by the police.

The *staff* of the First Class a la carte restaurant *were having* the hardest time of all (Walter Lord).

While the *jury were* away he walked out of the court before the eyes of the police (Graham Greene).

The Colombo *family were* respectable, but rather happy-go-lucky (Samuel Eliot Morison).

As indicated, this use of a plural verb shows that various individuals are being thought of separately. In "the jury has found him guilty," the thought is that the jury has acted as a formal, organized group, and there is no need to stress the action of the separate persons in it. Use of the plural verb alone in sentences containing collectives is, however, not a very clear way of calling attention to the individuals involved; to do so, you will usually find it better to say so in specific words rather than merely to imply it by use of a plural verb. Rather than saying "the committee were wrangling," you had better say "the members of the committee were wrangling" or "the committeemen were wrangling."

EXERCISE

27. Criticize the subject and verb agreement of the following sentences. Are the sentences effective?

(a) The fraternity eat their meals together in one of the dormitory dining halls.

(b) The congress have returned to their homes without taking any definite action on the question.

(c) The team are being given engraved watches by the alumni association.

(d) The herd were examined by the veterinarian and found free from brucellosis.

(e) The class were confused and irritated by the tricky questions on the test.

GR 5 C *Various pronouns as subjects call for special attention to verbs*

Pronouns like *one, everyone, everybody, anyone, anybody, each one, someone, somebody, no one, nobody* are considered singular in form even though they are general and inclusive in meaning more than one person. The sentence "everyone on the ship escaped" shows that several people escaped, and the sentence "anyone else would have acted the same way" is a general statement applying to all persons. But these words are singular in form and ordinarily take singular verbs when they are subjects:

Everyone is in favor of going.
If anyone calls, give him the message.
Someone who smokes cigars has been here recently.
No one cares much about Tacna-Arica now.

Several, many, and *few* and *a few,* on the other hand, take plurals: *several were finally recovered, many have died of the disease, few of the women were willing to work longer hours, a few of them were waiting by the gate. All* and *none* may take either singular or plural verbs; the choice is usually determined by the number of the noun or pronoun following: *all the sugar was thrown out, none of the cloth was damaged; all the apples were rotten, none of the cows were missing.*

EXERCISE

28. Indicate which form is preferred in each of the following sentences:

(a) Every one of the home owners who signed these petitions (lives, live) on the South Side.

(b) No one who has had experiences like theirs (is, are) likely to blame them very much.

(c) All of the books on the second shelf in the history section (has, have) been moved.

(d) Several of the specific charges that he made in his talk (seems, seem) doubtful.

(e) Someone bringing a message from the cabin (is, are) at the door.

GR 5 D   *Subjects composed of elements joined by* and *usually take plural verbs*

When the subject is composed of two or more parts and those parts are joined with *and,* the subject is compound. Compound subjects take plural verbs:

> Joe and his roommate are going to the city for the weekend. (not *is*)
> The department head and the dean agree that the course should be dropped. (not *agrees*)
> Planes, trains, and buses were all delayed. (not *was*)

> Budapest and Vienna *were* natural rivals (James A. Michener).
> . . . both *he and I have* only just *passed* that strange assessment point—the fiftieth birthday (Meyer Levin).
> Welding, joining and uniting by adhesives *have been perfected* (George Soule).

Use of a singular verb in situations like these would be non-standard.
When a subject composed of a single noun modified by contrasting

adjectives indicates different classes or kinds, it may take a plural verb: *hard and soft coal are both used in these furnaces.*

When the subject is composed of two or more nouns meaning the same person or thing and joined with *and,* a singular verb may be used:

> The secretary and treasurer has not finished the report.
> The direction, planning and master plan was laid down by technicians sent out from Cuzco. . . . (Victor W. von Hagen).
> . . . there was a splendor and nobility about them which no modern hiproofed, standardized monstrosity can approach (Louis Bromfield).

When the parts of a subject joined by *and* indicate a measurement, sum, total, or amount, the verb may be singular:

> The three years and four months has passed quickly.
> Six dollars and seventy-eight cents was what he owed.

GR 5 E *When subjects are composed of elements joined by or or nor, the verbs usually agree with the nearer elements*

When the subject is composed of parts joined with *or* or *nor*, the verb usually agrees in number with the part of the subject closer to it:

> Either the tractor or the truck is all right for the job. (not *are;* the verb takes its number from *truck.*)
> Either the main grid or the tubes are not hooked up right. (not *is;* the verb agrees with *tubes.*)
> Neither the men themselves nor their leader wants any advice from the board. (not *want;* the verb agrees with *leader.*)
> Neither the players nor the coaches were satisfied with the hotel accommodations. (Both *players* and *coaches* are plural, and either would call for *were* rather than *was,* but the fact that *coaches,* the nearer part of the subject, is plural is the determining factor.)

Study the following expressions:

> . . . any poor charcoal-burner or slave was more of a man than he (Robert Graves).
> For most children the writing process is wholly a school activity. No letters or other writing is completed at home where the child can see and imitate the parents (Harry R. Warfel).
> He (Johnny Appleseed) is alive wherever the feathery fennel or the flowering day lilies cover a bank (Louis Bromfield).

GR 5 F *When subjects are followed by such elements as* in addition to, as well as, *and* along with, *the verbs agree with the subjects, not with the nouns following such elements*

Sometimes a subject is followed by a phrase beginning with *in addition to, as well as, along with, together with, with,* or some similar prepositional unit. The verb agrees with the subject in such sentences. The noun or pronoun that follows the prepositional unit is regarded as an object in a phrase. Objects in phrases do not determine choices of verb forms. Verbs agree with subjects, not with objects. In "this man as well as his neighbors is opposed to the zoning laws," the *meaning* is that several persons including this man oppose the zoning laws. According to the *form* of the sentence, however, the subject is *man,* a singular noun; *neighbors* is used in this sentence as the object of a preposition. Since the subject, *man,* is singular, the singular form *is opposed* is used. In the sentence "Frank and Bob as well as their sister are going to State," the word *sister* is singular. In this sentence, however, it is the object in a phrase, and consequently it has no bearing on the number of the verb. The subject is *Frank* and *Bob,* a compound subject, and the verb, *are going,* is plural. Note the following sentences:

> The Carswell Company along with its associates is passing dividends this season. (The singular form *is passing* is used to agree with *Carswell Company,* the subject. *Associates* is a plural, but since it is the object in a phrase it has no influence on the number of the verb.)
> The sons as well as their father were rugged pioneers. (The plural form *were* is used to agree with *sons.* Since *father* can be interpreted as the object in a phrase, the fact that it is a singular does not determine the number of the verb.)

Study the following sentences:

> Human labor, as well as horses and oxen, was used to drag sledges, wagons, and carts (George Soule).
> For he, along with 200 Spaniards in this fateful year of 1533, was engaged in the conquest of an empire (Victor W. von Hagen).
> In 1953 another skull of Rhodesian man, together with associated artifacts [objects made by man], was found about fifteen miles from Saldanha Bay . . . (Ashley Montagu).

It is usually non-standard to let the number of the object in a phrase determine the number of the verb.

The following table may be helpful:

Connective Used in Subject	Verb Number
and	usually plural
or, nor	agrees with nearer item
in addition to, as well as, along with, together with, with	agrees with first item

GR 5 G   *Verbs agree with subjects, not with objects in phrases*

Sometimes a singular subject is followed by a phrase containing a plural: *the list of necessary supplies was drawn up.* Sentences showing this arrangement may confuse you; the plural noun in the phrase may mislead you into using a plural verb form. But the subject is *list*. Since it is singular, the verb is also singular: it is *was drawn*, not *were drawn*. *Supplies* is a plural, but since it is the object in a phrase it has nothing to do with the number of the verb. Note the sentence "the man in charge of scenery, staging, and costumes has an important job." In this sentence the subject is *man*. Hence the singular verb form *has*—not the plural form *have*—is used. The element "scenery, staging, and costumes" is plural in form, but since it is used as the object in a phrase it does not determine the number of the verb.

Sometimes a plural subject is followed by a phrase containing a singular: *the accounts of the Henderson murder vary widely.* In sentences with this arrangement, the singular noun in the phrase may mislead you into using a singular verb form. But in this sentence the subject is *accounts*. Since it is plural, the verb is also plural; it is *vary*, not *varies*. *Murder* is a singular, but since it is the object in a phrase it has nothing to do with the number of the verb. The principle of this section is the same as that of the preceding one about such phrases as *in addition to* and *together with:* objects in phrases do not determine numbers of verb forms. Note the following sentences:

> A complication of diseases then sets in. (*Diseases* is the object in a phrase and does not determine the number of the verb. It is true that the diseases themselves set in, but the form of the sentence rather than its ultimate meaning here determines the number of the verb.)

A series of accidents in atomic laboratories is being investigated. (The subject, *series*, is a singular form here, although it happens to end in *-s*. As object in a phrase the plural form *accidents* does not determine the number of the verb. It is a fact that the accidents are being investigated, but here as in the preceding sentence the form rather than the ultimate meaning determines the grammatical choice.)

The psychological causes of alcoholism are usually traceable to childhood difficulties. (The verb is *are*, a plural, because the subject is *causes*, a plural. *Alcoholism* is the object in a phrase.)

Study the following sentences:

The carrying trade, devoted chiefly to the export of lumber, furs, grains, and other natural products, and the import of manufactures, sugar, and wines, was extensive and profitable (Allan Nevins and Henry Steele Commager).

But the sudden perception of the half-disclosed and half-ridden possibilities relating Crusoe and the sand and the footprint and the lonely island secluded from Europe constitutes romance (Alfred North Whitehead).

GR 5 H   *Verbs agree with subjects, not with predicate nominatives*

The subject rather than the complement or predicate nominative determines the number of the verb. Notice the sentence: *the chief reason for his discontent at home was his wife's relatives.* In this sentence, the subject is *reason,* a singular, and the verb accordingly is singular, *was.* The fact that *relatives* is a plural is immaterial; this word is not a subject but instead a complement, a predicate nominative (see p. 267), and hence does not determine the number of the verb. Note the following:

The result of this policy was dissatisfaction, suspicion, and disloyalty. (There are three things mentioned in the latter part of the sentence, but the subject is a singular form, *result,* and the verb is singular, *is.*)

The next step in the process is the investigations of the subject's previous history. (*Investigations* is a plural, but this fact has no bearing on the number of the verb. The subject, *step,* is singular.)

Study the following sentences:

One of the necessities to improvement of the soil and increase of yields is the application of lime where necessary and the use of more fertilizer (George Soule).

. . . their reply was bewilderment and murmurings that I was only a child . . . (Pearl S. Buck).

Subjects Coming after Verbs

Sometimes a sentence is arranged so that the verb comes before its subject. In the sentence "there is a cabin on the mountain top," the finite verb is *is*. The word *there,* despite its position at the beginning of the sentence, is not the subject. It is the purpose of the sentence to show the existence of a cabin on the mountain top, and the word *cabin* is the subject, although it comes after the verb in the sentence. In the sentence "outside the city are several drive-in theaters" the subject is *theaters.* The main purpose of the sentence is to tell you that the theaters are in existence outside the city. The word *city* is the object in the phrase. The following are typical sentences illustrating this pattern:

Introductory element	Verb	Subject
(Often the word *there;* often a prepositional or non-finite verb phrase)	(Often part of *to be*)	
There	were	several horses in the paddock.
There	is	a gas station on the corner.
On the next page	were	the answers to the problems.
Through these doors	pass	the world's most beautiful girls.
Hanging in the closet	were	three old suits.

Questions usually show arrangements in which subjects come after verbs or after parts of compounded verb forms. In the short question "is the doctor in?" *is* is the finite verb and *doctor* is the subject. In the question "when will the building be finished?" *will be finished* is the finite verb and *building* is the subject. Note the pattern of the following:

	Verb or verb part	Subject	
	Are	you	ready to go?
	Is	he	from Parkersburg?
	Has	the mail	come yet?
	Does	Al	want to buy the tire?
When	did	the murder	take place?
Where	has	the secretary	filed the letters?
Why	didn't	the dentist	pull that tooth?
Which	do	you and Roy	prefer?

EXERCISE

29. Find the subject in each of the following sentences:

(a) Coming from the East every week were trains filled with immigrants.

(b) There were several reasons why the shipments were delayed.

(c) Near the corner of Dwight and Elm is a branch post office.

(d) Have the library hours been changed?

(e) Hidden in the secret drawer was a packet of old letters.

(f) There are three new high schools in the city.

(g) In the southern part of the state are lead and zinc mines.

(h) When does the ferry boat leave for Montauk Point?

(i) Coiled and ready to strike was a copperhead ahead of him in the path.

(j) There is apparently no way to stop the Yankees from taking the pennant.

GR 5 I   *Verbs agree with subjects in sentences showing inverted order*

Sentences in which the subject is placed after the verb are said to be in *inverted order.* (Normal order is subject-verb-object or subject-verb-complement.) *In sentences with inverted order subject and verb agree.* Sometimes inverted order leads to mistakes in subject and verb agreement. Note the sentence "there was still several things to be done before we could leave on the trip." In this sentence the subject is *things* and since *things* is plural, the verb should have been *were*, not *was*. In the sentence "out in the harbor was two tankers just in from Tampico," the subject is *tankers.* Since this is plural, the verb should have been *were* to agree with the subject. Note the following sentences:

Where are the files for the Mackintosh accounts? (Since *files* is the subject, the plural verb *are* is needed.)

There are several complicated sub-assemblies in this machine. (Since *sub-assemblies* is the subject, the plural verb *are* is correct.)

Lying in wait near the islands was a British fleet headed by two battleships. (Since *fleet* is the subject, the singular verb *was* is needed.)

Observe how subject and verb agree in the following:

There is just a chance of a settlement in Ireland, and there are certain events of the first importance impending in Italy and America . . . (John Buchan).

There never were more lovely sailing ships than the wondrous clipper ships (Alan Villiers).

In the center was a great square, larger than the Plaza of Saint Mark's in Venice (Victor W. von Hagen).

Then they . . . were called children's diseases. Among them were measles, scarlet fever, whooping cough and diphtheria (Rudolph Marx).

Principles about agreement between verbs and various kinds of troublesome subjects apply to sentences in inverted order; study the following expressions:

. . . there *were* Moranda and John McHugh at one of the round zinc-topped tables (James Ramsey Ullman).

It was all marsh and forest . . . In it *live* muskrat and mink, raccoon and possum and a wonderful assortment of birds (Louis Bromfield).

. . . there *is* scarcely a house or building—certainly not a settlement—not accessible by road (George Soule).

Without her there *is* no joy nor loveliness anywhere (Edith Hamilton).

There is one exception to this principle that normal procedures for subject and verb agreement are followed in sentences showing inverted order: there may be a certain awkwardness in following a plural verb form like *are* or *were* with a subject whose first part is a singular noun. Faced with such a sentence as "on the shelf were a cup and a saucer," many writers and editors would prefer the singular verb *was:* "on the shelf was a cup and a saucer." In the following sentences, writers have preferred singular verbs:

There *was* an exhilaration and a deep sense of adventure in this thought (Lynn W. Turner).

In the parlour there *was* a piano, eight chairs of all sizes and sorts, innumerable photographs, "ornaments," and absolutely no room for anybody to move about . . . (Liam O'Flaherty).

Along the north wall, near the entrance to the office was a small door inside which *was* a basin, a mirror, a wall-bracket gas lamp, some soap, a towel and a comb (Jim Bishop).

GR 5 J *A single phrase or clause used as subject takes a singular verb*

Sometimes phrases and clauses are used as subjects. (See p. 232.) *A single phrase or single clause so used takes a singular verb, regardless of plural nouns or pronouns within that phrase or clause.* In the sentence "to sit on the bench through eleven straight games was discouraging," the singular verb *was* is used because the subject of the sentence is the phrase "to sit on the bench through eleven straight games." In the sentence "what he should do with the leftover parts was a puzzle to him after he had fixed the clock," the singular verb *was* is used because the subject is the clause "what he should do with the leftover parts." It is worth remembering here that objects in phrases and clauses do not determine the numbers of finite verbs. Note the following:

> How Robinson played on this pride and sense of propriety *was revealed* with his very first questions (Charles and Louise Samuels).
> To be among the dwindling number of people who understood such things *was* to him a kind of secret and valued freemasonry . . . (James Hilton).

EXERCISES

30. Find which form would be generally preferred in each of the following sentences:

(a) Harding and Coolidge (was, were) both opposed to American participation in the League of Nations.

(b) What cities in Pennsylvania (is, are) Jeffers supposed to visit on his trip?

(c) The roughness and rowdiness of these boys from the slums (is, are) alarming.

(d) On the docks about to be shipped out (was, were) twenty cases of submachine guns.

(e) Bourbon and rye whiskey (is, are) about the same in alcoholic content.

(f) Set up on the stage near the speaker's stand (was, were) four or five microphones.

(g) Either the doctor or the nurses (takes, take) care of changing the bandages every day.

(h) There (was, were) several arguments among the fans about the referee's decision.

(i) Neither the general nor his aides (knows, know) about the news as yet.

(j) The part of the story that interested me most (was, were) the naval battles.

31. Accompanying each of the following sentences are directions calling for changes in wording. Making these changes may require making other changes.

(a) The sheep is penned up behind the barn. (Between *the* and *sheep* add the word *three*.)

(b) *David Copperfield* and *Vanity Fair* are acceptable outside reading for the next weeks of the course. (For *and* substitute *or*.)

(c) All of the men have been told to sign the new contracts. (For *all* substitute *each*.)

(d) The bitter criticism of the book on which he built his hopes has left him discouraged. (For *criticism* substitute *criticisms*.)

(e) The department head along with the other professors doubts that many students will take the course. (For *along with* substitute *and*.)

(f) The little maple tree as well as the rose bush in the corner was killed by the spray. (For *as well as* substitute *and*.)

(g) The main cause of the war was bitter economic rivalry between England and France. (For *rivalry* substitute *rivalries*.)

(h) Where does Walters live here in Brookville? (Between *does* and *Walters* add the word *the*.)

(i) Some of the girls were taking courses in geology and geography. (For *some* substitute *a few*.)

32. Correct any errors in subject and verb agreement in the following sentences:

(a) Neither the third baseman nor the left fielder of the Sox were able to field the ball.

(b) There was on the economics reserve shelf several books that had been requested by the History Department.

(c) The shipment of antibiotic drugs being sent to the Emerson Company were delayed.

(d) Along the stream is three or four hunting lodges now closed and boarded up.

(e) Waiting outside the door of the hospital room were her husband along with her two sons.

(f) The resentment that he feels about his cousins seem poorly motivated to the reader.

(g) Willett, along with his co-workers, recommend that the fabrics be tested over again.

(h) The *Chronicle* columnist, who predicted that we would beat A & M, don't feel that we have much chance against Western.

(i) There was several of her elderly neighbors who were glad enough to spread the scandal about her.

(j) The committee were uncertain about how far their powers of investigation extended.

No general comment can be made about the seriousness of disagreement between subject and verb in number. At one extreme a sentence like "he don't care about it" sounds quite crude. At the other extreme are conscious and purposive decisions to break away from agreement requirements in the interests of smoothness: "across the river was an abandoned farm and a summer camp."

Pronoun and Antecedent Agreement

As we saw on p. 264, pronouns include such words as *I, he, they; who, which, what; this, that, these, those; someone, everyone, no one.* The meanings of some pronouns are instantly clear: *I* always means the person speaking; the pronoun *no one* needs no explanation or clarification. On the other hand, many pronouns need some preceding or accompanying word to give them meaning. The word *he,* for instance, can be applied to any one of the billions of masculine creatures that there are and have been on this earth, and such a sentence as "he showed his strength" needs accompanying words to make its reference clear. *They* can refer to any possible combination of persons, things, actions, and qualities; and in being able to indicate anything not a person *which* is almost as broad.

Pronouns like these are usually used in connection with preceding nouns that give them meaning. These preceding nouns are called the antecedents of the pronouns; the word *antecedent* is composed of parts meaning "before" and "going." Note the following:

> The outfielder has more to do than just to catch the balls hit to him. He must often back up other fielders.

In these two sentences the noun *outfielder* gives meaning to the pronoun *he. Outfielder* is therefore its antecedent. Note the following:

> The blue station wagon belongs to a man who works in the accounting department.

Who is another pronoun having very wide possible reference. In this sentence *man* is the word that gives it its meaning, and *man* is the antecedent for *who.*

> Some flies are not killed off even by massive doses of DDT. They appear to be immune to it.

Flies gives meaning to *they* and is its antecedent; *DDT* gives meaning to *it* and is its antecedent.

EXERCISE

33. What nouns in the following sentences are antecedents for pronouns? What pronouns lack antecedents?

(a) I do not like the plan that has been proposed by Simmons; he obviously has not had much experience ushering at commencements.
(b) Jim and Frank found physics very difficult; they had never studied it before.
(c) The car that had passed us on the curve had crashed into a pole. It was a complete wreck, and its driver was dead.
(d) The first book that Sanders wrote was a failure; it sold only a few hundred copies, and he made practically nothing on it.
(e) The man who put the caps on these tanks was very careless; many of them are leaking badly.
(f) The tire that Joe had bought for six dollars wasn't worth it; he got only thirty miles of road use out of it.
(g) These falls are prettier than those at Tanner's Glen, but they are not nearly so high.
(h) The countries that fought the war found that all they gained from it was empty glory.

GR 6 A   *A pronoun and its antecedent agree in number*

If one is singular, the other should be singular; if one is plural, the other should be plural. This principle causes no problem in the great majority of pronoun uses.

In one situation, however, there is a conflict between form and meaning. The words *anyone, everyone, no one,* and *a person* are singular in form. Notice that if you use one of these words as the subject of a sentence you will naturally use the verb *is,* the singular, rather than the verb *are,* the plural. Grammatically these words are singulars. But they are often used in general statements to refer to a number of different people. The sentence "anyone would be irritated by such a trick" is a general statement that you and I and almost every other person would be irritated; the sentence "a person should take good care of his health" does not refer to one specific person; instead it is a general statement in which *a person* means you and me and everybody else. Although they are singular in form, *anyone, everyone, no one, everybody, one,* and *a person* are usually general—or plural—in meaning. Consequently, there is a strong tendency for people to say "does everyone have their money ready?" "one can't be too careful about the kind of friends they make," "no one who really loves their country wants another war."

Use of the plural pronouns in these situations is normal conversational English. Most people from all social groups would normally use plural pronouns in speaking sentences like these. In formal written English, however, many persons prefer agreement between antecedent and pronoun; they prefer "everyone should have his money ready" to "everyone should have their money ready," and "no one who really loves his country wants another war" to "no one who really loves their country wants another war." In the sentence "anyone who wants to take extra credits must get his dean's permission," the antecedent for *his* is *anyone*. Since *anyone* is a singular by grammatical form, the pronoun *his* is preferred in written formal English, although many people would use *their* in speaking this sentence. Note the following sentences:

> Nobody goes about with his knowledge clearly and consciously before him . . . (Alfred North Whitehead).
> . . . the party had been going on forever, and hardly anyone wondered when it would end. Anyone who wanted it to end could go home. He would not be missed (John O'Hara).
> But that is the favorite field of everyone who works on the farm. No one minds working there alone for he returns at night stronger and fresher than when he climbed up to the lonely farm in the morning (Louis Bromfield).

When people make general statements referring to a whole class or group, they often use plural pronouns with singular antecedents in spoken English. Many people would say "a miner must always be careful because they face constant danger." In formal written English the expression "a miner must always be careful because he faces constant danger" would be preferred, with the singular antecedent *miner* taking a singular pronoun *he*. Note the following sentences:

> Here in the jungle a marine killed because he must, or be killed. He stalked the enemy, and the enemy stalked him . . . (John Hersey).
> Rather, each new worker could be trained to do one of these operations, which he could then repeat over and over again (George Soule).

EXERCISE

34. Which form in each of the following sentences would be preferred in formal written English:

    (a) A doctor quickly learns which of (his, their) patients are hypochondriac pests.

    (b) Any member who continues to violate these regulations may find (his, their) membership revoked.

    (c) No woman who really cares about (her, their) reputation would be seen with him.

(d) Each member of the winning team received a watch with (his, their) name engraved on it.

(e) Any driver who has driven a million miles without a mishap has had a fair amount of luck on (his, their) side.

(f) No one who reads Roberts' letters can have any doubt in (his, their) mind about his sincerity.

(g) Not one of the drills was in (its, their) right place in the case.

(h) If any one is surprised by Tom's feelings about his uncle, (he, they) should consider what (his, their) own feelings would be.

Occasionally it is impossible to follow this principle of pronoun and antecedent agreement. In the sentence "I know every one in the room; they are my friends," it would be impossible to use the singular pronoun *he*, along with the singular verb *is*, in the last clause. Note the following:

> . . . everybody looked at Gypo. They saw him sitting on the floor . . . (Liam O'Flaherty).
>
> Everybody rose, panting and full of pride. They swarmed about the gun, examining it with curiosity. They plied Father Prieto with questions about it . . . (C. S. Forester).

In situations like these, in which a series of separate actions by separate individuals is involved, meaning and common sense take precedence over grammatical rule.

GR 6 B *A collective noun as antecedent can take either a singular or a plural form*

Just as a collective noun as subject can take either a singular or a plural verb (see p. 286), so a collective noun as an antecedent can take either a singular or a plural pronoun, depending on the writer's attitude. One can write "the family planned to spend its vacation in Canada" or "the family planned to spend their vacation in Canada." Through the use of the singular form *its*, the first version may stress the notion of the family as a unit; through the use of the plural form *their*, the second may stress the notion of the family as a body of individuals. Either way is all right. Notice the following sentences:

> A defeated army was falling back through the mountains from Espinosa. Such was its condition that an ignorant observer would find it easier to guess that it had been defeated than that it had been an army (C. S. Forester).

. . . a group of university students arrived at the great wooden doors and demanded the right to broadcast to the people of Hungary their demand for certain changes . . . (James A. Michener).

Some grammarians feel that if a collective is regarded as a form singular at one point, it should not be regarded as agreeing with form plurals at another. Note the sentence "the club was holding a meeting to make plans for their annual dance." In this sentence the word *club,* a collective, is the subject; agreeing with it is the singular verb *was.* But *club* is also the antecedent for the possessive pronoun *their* before *annual dance.* It is regarded as inconsistent to treat *club* as a singular in one relationship and as a plural in another. Some grammarians prefer that the sentence should be worded either as "the club were holding a meeting to make plans for their annual dance" or, better, as "the club was holding a meeting to make plans for its annual dance."

GR 6 C   *Relative pronouns agree with their antecedents; when a relative pronoun is the subject of a clause, the verb in that clause takes its number eventually from the antecedent of the relative pronoun*

Most of the sentences above have illustrated agreement in number between antecedents and such pronouns as *he, it, his,* and *its. Relative pronouns* (who, which, *and* that) *also agree with their antecedents in number. This fact becomes important when the relative pronoun is subject for a following verb.* Contrast "the man who was waiting in the hall" and "the men who were waiting in the hall." In the first the relative pronoun *who* is singular because it agrees with its antecedent *man;* in turn *who* is subject for the following verb; since *who* is singular, the verb form used is *was waiting.* In the second, *men* is plural; since pronoun and antecedent agree in number, *who* is plural in this phrase; therefore the verb after *who, were waiting,* is plural. Study the following expressions:

> The colorless Mr. Williams, who exists to us only as a name, appears to have specialized in mathematics (W. E. Woodward).
> He made pleasant remarks and a few jokes, which were applauded lustily . . . (E. M. Forster).
> In the little hall outside the elevator there were the white azaleas which were brought in fresh every week . . . (John P. Marquand).

Confusion about antecedent-pronoun-verb agreement is likely to come up in sentences containing the wording "one of the . . ." In the sentence "this is one of the longest games that have been played in the majors this year," *games* rather than *one* is the antecedent for *that;* consequently *that* is regarded as plural, and, again consequently, the following verb is *have been played* rather than *has been played.* Note the following:

> The colonel looked at Polly in a way which indicated that he was one of those men who know they have a faculty with women (John P. Marquand).

35. Which form is preferred in formal written English in each of the following sentences?

(a) A person who does not bother to register (his, their) gun with the police may be asking for serious trouble.

(b) Any one who would want the country to return to the conditions of the 20's shows that there is something the matter with the way (he thinks, they think).

(c) Everyone who expects to graduate in June must make arrangements now for (her, their) cap and gown.

(d) A student who has once been on probation always has to be careful to keep (his, their) grades up.

(e) The union is holding a meeting now to elect (its, their) officers for the coming year.

(f) This is one of the largest planes that (has, have) ever landed at the local airport.

(g) The letter from Perkins and Sons that (claims, claim) that the goods were damaged in transit has been lost.

(h) Fredericks was one of the men who (was, were) seen entering the blazing warehouse.

(i) The rumor about the assassinations and assassination attempts directed against rightist leaders that (was, were) sweeping through the city demoralized the police.

(j) The party is likely to choose the candidates that (it, they) ran in the last election.

36. In each of the following, indicate which form is correct or preferred:

(a) The Elton is one of the most economical automobiles that (has, have) ever been made.

(b) The sorority was making plans for improving (its, their) rushing procedures.

(c) Any one who thinks that (he, they) might have made a mistake on (his, their) tax returns has a chance to file a corrected return.

(d) Glazing, painting, and hanging all the windows (was, were) a long and difficult job.

(e) Also traveling on the plane (was, were) two representatives of the Standish Company.

(f) The effects of the policy (was, were) widespread unemployment, general depression, and universal discontent.

(g) A series of thefts, burglaries, and similar crimes (is, are) giving the police trouble in the eighth and ninth wards.

(h) Jackson as well as his successors (was, were) resolutely opposed to the idea of a United States bank.

(i) The work went very slowly because the baling machine was not working very (good, well) that morning.

(j) Despite the damage to the landing gear the pilot brought the plane down (safe, safely).

(k) Her father was clearly the (more, most) intelligent of her parents.

(l) Their financial troubles were eased for the time being by (him, his) borrowing five hundred dollars.

(m) The arrangement about extra commissions was approved by (he, him) and Mr. Carver.

(n) These regulations apply to (whoever, whomever) intends to go on all the field trips.

(o) The night taxi drivers, Tony, Steve, and (I, me), were warned about the holdup man.

37. The following sentences show various poor or questionable choices of grammatical forms. Change each one so that it agrees with the demands of formal English. Criticize the grammar of these sentences as they now stand.

(a) The trouble and confusion that has broken out in these sections now show signs of abating.

(b) The detail was simply following their leader's orders in preventing anyone entering the north barracks.

(c) The dean was agitated because some student had parked their car in his private parking area again.

(d) It is only natural for a man to try to protect their family in a situation like that.

(e) Lying in the road was several hundred roofing nails, evidently spilled from the builder's truck.

(f) There don't seem to be much chance of a reduction in tuition rates for out-of-state students.

(g) A careful inventory of the drugs in the warehouse show that none of the narcotics has been stolen.

(h) The camp counselor as well as his campers say that the cow was out in the road.

(i) It usually works out that anybody who bets against the Yankees are in for a disappointment.

(j) The envoys bowed respectful to the baron and then presented him with the king's orders for his arrest.

(k) If he had been gave more information about the horses, he certainly would not have chose the bay gelding.

(l) The shirt had shrank about three sizes, and the laundry had tore several buttons off it.

(m) I could hardly have born all this trouble if you had not wrote me as you did.

(n) Football stadia are now the most modern and expensive buildings on many colleges' campuses.

(o) The hero's action in turning his parents over to the secret police indicate the deterioration of character taking place under totalitarianism.

14

PUNCTUATION

This chapter is about punctuation and similar matters. The word *punctuation*, derived from a Latin form meaning "point," in a narrow sense means use of those points that set off units of expression—points like periods and commas. This book, however, expands the notion of punctuation a bit and includes with treatment of these marks some discussion of italics, capital letters, and similar matters. It is felt in this book that you may be helped most by grouping all these things together.

Why do people punctuate in the first place? Why shouldn't we save time and work and simply omit punctuation? In part, we use punctuation because it is traditional; most people use it and use it more or less conventionally. A page lacking punctuation presents a very odd effect. Some twentieth-century authors—in fact, some of the best—have experimented with leaving punctuation out almost entirely. Although interesting and challenging, their pages are hard to read. This brings us to a second reason for using punctuation: ease in reading. Notice the following:

> Suddenly he appeared to relax his eyes took on their normal expression and he looked at his watch as he did so Gray opened his eyes gosh he said I believe I dropped off to sleep then he started

This is how this passage appeared in Maugham's *The Razor's Edge:*

> Suddenly he appeared to relax; his eyes took on their normal expression, and he looked at his watch. As he did so, Gray opened his eyes.

"Gosh," he said, "I believe I dropped off to sleep." Then he started.

By following the usual punctuation practices, you will make your own writing easier to read.

When we talk, much of our meaning is conveyed by the intonations of our voices—by changes in pitch and stress. Try *saying* the following expressions:

Which is your home town?
Crestline, which is your home town, is a very nice place.

Notice the differences between the *sounds* of these two expressions. Variations in pitch and stress are most important in speaking any language. The punctuation of the written sentence is an attempt to suggest some—but not all—the patterns of speech sounds. Punctuation, especially ordinary punctuation, cannot suggest all intonation details on the printed or written page. Punctuation, however, can suggest some intonations—and the meanings that they express. Notice the difference between the following:

Fish, which live in water, are . . .
Fish which live in salt water are . . .

In the first of these, there is a pause between *fish* and *which* and between *water* and *are,* and the expression between pauses is taken to mean that all fish live in water—an idea added more or less as an afterthought. In the second, there is no pause between *fish* and *which* and between *water* and *are;* the effect of the clause beginning with *which* is to limit the meaning of *fish* only to salt-water kinds. The two expressions are punctuated differently. Punctuation is extremely valuable to us in communicating the feeling for some of the natural intonations of our speech.

Punctuation depends at least somewhat on current style or fashion. In general, the twentieth century uses less punctuation than preceding periods. Since styles change, a textbook cannot give punctuation principles that will always hold good. This book tries to present workable, moderately conservative principles. You will, however, have to watch for future changes in punctuation and be ready to change your practices. Perhaps actually observing styles of punctuation will teach you more than textbook rules. Probably, in doubtful situations, you will fit in with modern trends if you omit punctuation, rather than insert it. It is better to use no punctuation for which you do not have a reason than to sprinkle your writing with punctuation that you cannot justify.

Many good textbooks treat punctuation by listing the various marks used and then giving all the uses for each mark in order. This chapter is organized according to the different situations involving punctuation problems and choices. It discusses first, punctuation after sentences and expressions that serve as sentences; second, punctuation between independent clauses joined together in sentences; third, punctuation of introductory elements in sentences; fourth, punctuation of elements coming within or at the ends of sentences; fifth, punctuation of quotations; and, sixth, punctuation of single words and similar units.

End Punctuation

Sentence punctuation (punctuation at the ends of sentences) is often called *end punctuation:*

PN 1 A   *Use a period at the end of every sentence that is not marked with some other kind of end punctuation*

Use a period at the end of a sentence that expresses a fact or gives a command, and does not ask a question. This principle applies to sentences made up both of single independent clauses and of many independent clauses. You almost certainly know this general rule, but it may be worthwhile for you to note the following sentences carefully:

> The car was a cream-colored convertible.
> And France entered the war a few hours later.
> Consequently, the coach told them to try only line plays.
> Send us the wedding pictures as soon as you can.
> He asked whether the replacement parts had arrived.

Sentences of this kind are often spoken with falling intonation at the end; typically, they are separated from following elements by a slight pause. Punctuation of such sentences is the main use of the period in English.

There is a converse to this principle about placing periods at the ends of sentences: don't use sentence punctuation—capitals at the beginning and periods at the end—with dependent units that are not sentences; don't make period faults (pp. 242–243). Note the following:

Everyone was taking blankets to the game. Since the temperature was
below freezing.

The second group of words is of course not an independent clause, because it is subordinated by the word *since*. Punctuating this group of
words as a sentence is making a period fault.

EXERCISE

1. Which of the following illustrate period faults? Make corrections wherever they are necessary.

(a) The so-called French and Indian wars were not sustained, continuous
actions like other wars. Instead, they were a series of spasmodic, iso-
lated campaigns.

(b) The office girl finally brought him the correspondence files for April,
1957. Which he had requested three days before.

(c) Jenkins always made a larger contribution to the Community Chest
than any one else. Although he was not an especially wealthy man.

(d) In the second inning the rookie pitcher walked two batters. And
threw two wild pitches.

(e) The junior high school section of the building was very pleasant.
The rooms having been newly painted and refurnished.

(f) Among the officials at the game was Ken Leslie. Who had been a
member of the championship State team five years before.

(g) Marysville is located near the Iowa border. About forty miles north
of St. Joseph.

(h) The first two years the sales were rather disappointing. Consequently
the company intensified its publicity efforts.

PN 1 B   *Use a question mark after every direct question*

Use a question mark at the end of each sentence that asks a question:

Are you going home next Friday?
Would he be interested in joining the club?
How far is it from Fort Dodge to Spencer?
Where are the Boston Mountains located?

As far as meaning is concerned, these sentences request an answer from
the person addressed. As far as grammatical form is concerned, they
usually show either inverted order, with verb parts coming before subjects, use of such question words as *who, which, what, how, when,* or
where, or both of these devices. As far as the sound of the spoken
sentence is concerned, they may be said with a rising intonation at the

end. Sometimes single words, phrases, and dependent clauses are used to ask questions and to serve as sentence equivalents; they may be punctuated satisfactorily with question marks:

> You said that the award had been made. To whom?
> Where are you going on your vacation? When?

Do not use a question mark after a sentence that simply reports a question but does not call for an answer from the hearer or reader. Note the sentence "he asked when the train would arrive in Evansville." This sentence tells you that someone asked a question, but it does not ask you for information. Consequently, it is punctuated with a period instead of a question mark, as are the following: "The stranger inquired where the Nanson Company was located," "he wanted to know when Fort Deposit had been made the county seat." Sentences like these are sometimes called *indirect questions.* By contrasting them with the following, notice the difference between indirect questions, which do not take question marks, and direct questions, which do:

> Where is the Nanson Company located?
> When was Fort Deposit made the county seat?

EXERCISE

2. Determine which of the following should be punctuated with periods, which with question marks:

(a) The speaker asked how many in the audience would sign the petition
(b) You don't need a special ticket for stop-over privileges, do you
(c) How long does it take to drive from Durant up to Guthrie
(d) The captain asked the referee what the penalty was for
(e) Do you think that we will have any trouble in getting Owens' orchestra
(f) Why did he decide to buy that Holstein cow
(g) What are some of the better motels near Frankfurt
(h) Who was pitching for the Pirates in the ninth inning

Sometimes questions may be asked without inverted order and without use of question words like *who, how,* or *when.* Such questions are usually spoken with a rising intonation at the end. Question marks are used when such questions are written: "you surely don't think that he is innocent?" "all the reports have already been turned in?" Conversely, sentences having the grammatical form of questions but the intent or effect of orders are sometimes written with periods instead of question marks: "as soon as possible will you please send us items A224 and AX 17."

PN 1 C   *Use exclamation marks after expressions marked by strong feeling*

Exclamation marks may be used after sentences and sentence equivalents to show that strong emotion, force, or urgency is involved:

> What a big ship it is!
> She could think of only one thing: Bob had proposed!
> Oh, stop it! That's just nonsense.
> Get out of this room at once!

The exclamation mark is used less today than it was formerly. Many writers feel that it is a rather obvious device and prefer other means of communicating the fact of strong emotion. Certainly overuse of exclamation marks has a weakening effect:

> Our class was going to New York! to the nation's largest city! We could see the Yankees play at home! We could go to Radio City! We could see the city from the Empire State Building!

Punctuation between Independent Clauses

To review some of Chapter 12, a clause contains a subject and a finite verb. "He had arrived at Newark Airport" is a clause because it has a subject, *he,* and a finite verb, *had arrived;* it is an independent clause because it lacks any subordinating element. "After his arrival at Newark Airport" is a phrase because it contains neither subject or finite verb. You may usually consider a clause independent if it does not start with a subordinating element, like *because, since, although, if, when, who, which.* The problem here is to examine punctuation between independent clauses. Some of this material has been treated in Chapter 12, and you are urged to look back at that chapter.

PN 2 A   *Use a semicolon between two independent clauses that are not joined by a coordinating conjunction*

> The McClintocks remained powerful in the area for three centuries; the Dalloway clan dwindled and died out shortly after these events.

The group of words about the McClintocks is an independent clause, having a subject and finite verb and lacking a subordinating word. The second group, about the Dalloways, is likewise an independent clause, with a subject and finite verb and without a subordinating word. Between the two clauses there is no conjunction like *and*. The semicolon is the usual punctuation for this situation:

> The fire was terribly hot; I could feel it roasting the oil out of my right cheek (William L. White).
> Thinking follows the tracks laid down in one's own language; these tracks will converge on certain phases of "reality," and completely by-pass phases which may be explored in other languages (Stuart Chase).
> Whatever was outside of this tiny territory, before the restless white people came, was as alien to them as the surface of Mars; they did not dream of man's long history on the earth (Ruth Benedict).

Do not use commas rather than semicolons to punctuate sentences of this type. Use of a comma in a situation calling for a semicolon is a comma fault. See Chapter 12 and the following.

PN 2 B *Use a semicolon between two independent clauses joined by a conjunctive adverb*

> Sackett pretended not to hear the order to retreat; instead he commanded his unit to charge.
> South Dakota remained a territory until 1889; then it was admitted to the Union as the fortieth state.

In each of these sentences, the first element is an independent clause without an introductory word. In each the second element is a clause, with subject and finite verb, and in each the connective word (*instead, then*) is a conjunctive adverb. Conjunctive adverbs introduce independent clauses, and these second clauses are likewise independent. (Review Chapter 12; note that the following are conjunctive adverbs: *however, therefore, consequently, hence, indeed, likewise, furthermore, still, then, accordingly, thus, besides, also.*) Sentences illustrating this pattern are punctuated with semicolons. Note the following:

> Pyramus had not come; still she waited for him, her love making her bold (Edith Hamilton).
> Some Spaniards proposed eating the Indians, starting with the Caribs,

who were man-eaters themselves; thus it wouldn't be a sin to pay them in their own coin (Samuel Eliot Morison).

He and his generation had been ahead of me and mine in the stage of historical experience that we had respectively reached; in fact, his present had been my future (Arnold Toynbee).

Do not use a comma between two independent clauses connected with a conjunctive adverb. So doing is making a comma fault. The following are comma faults:

Scientists have long been interested in the firefly, however, no one knows yet how it is able to make light.

Common non-poisonous snakes are usually quite harmless, furthermore, they are valuable in killing rodents.

PN 2 C *A comma may be used between two independent clauses that are joined by a coordinating conjunction*

Sandburg's "Chicago" was famous, and Masters' *Spoon River Anthology* was also widely known.

Betsy Ann had seemed a good long-shot bet, but the odds on her kept going down.

Either there isn't enough water in the well, or there is something seriously wrong with the pump.

And, but, and *or,* along with *for* and *whereas,* are coordinating conjunctions. In each of the sentences given above, both the first and the second clauses are independent. The commas used illustrate satisfactory punctuation. Note also the following:

Al stopped at the corner of Church and Main, for his brother was waiting for him there.

In this sentence the second clause is independent; *for* is usually listed as a coordinating conjunction. To accord with the rule, the comma is used between *Main* and *for.* But there is another reason for it. Note the following:

Al stopped at the corner of Church and Main for his brother.

Here *for* is a preposition. Note the result of punctuating the first sentence without a comma:

Al stopped at the corner of Church and Main for his brother was waiting for him there.

It is now hard to read; it is likely to be momentarily unclear. The reader is likely to suppose at first that *for* is a preposition, but he is surprised to find a verb after *brother*. Then he must reread the sentence with the knowledge that *for* is a coordinating conjunction. The comma prevents the need for rereading. In addition to *and, but, or, for, yet,* and *whereas,* the words *while* and *only* are sometimes regarded as coordinating conjunctions in calling for commas when they start the second clauses of sentences of this type.

EXERCISES

3. This exercise concerns the use of semicolons and commas between independent clauses. By making changes in the punctuation, correct any incorrect sentences in the following. Your instructor may direct you to make corrections involving complete rewriting for rhetorical improvement.

(a) Colorado is sometimes called the Centennial State, it was admitted to the Union in 1876, just a hundred years after the Declaration of Independence.

(b) Dale had spent three-quarters of his money by mid-October, he did not see how he could stay in college throughout the semester.

(c) The word *atom* was composed of Greek elements meaning "not cut or split," and until recently it was believed that the atom could not be split.

(d) The source of the Chippewa River was not far from Lake Superior, therefore they turned to the right and paddled north.

(e) Manager Dwyer called on Edwards to replace Eastman, but the former could not check the Tigers' rally.

(f) The English bicycles were becoming more and more popular, they were much lighter and faster than the American models.

(g) South Carolina was the first state to secede, it was also the scene of the first fighting in the conflict.

(h) Ellis felt that he could not bid hearts again, instead he gave his partner a weak raise and bid three spades.

(i) The yawl was hopelessly aground on the sandbar, we could do nothing but drop our sails and wait for help.

(j) Most of Florida is low and flat, the highest point in the state is only about 325 feet above sea level.

4. Accompanying the following sentences are directions calling for changes in the wording. Make these changes. Making them is likely to require changes in the punctuation also. Make those changes too.

(a) Felton could not say certainly that Maxwell had a liability policy; however, he said that he thought that he did. (Change *however* to *although;* make no other changes in the wording.)

(b) Quiz programs on television may have pleased others, but I did not like them because my own comparative ignorance discouraged me. (Omit *but;* make no other changes in the wording.)

(c) The lifeboats on this tanker will have to be reconditioned, or the inspectors may delay her next sea run. (Change *or* to *otherwise;* make no other change in the wording.)

(d) Because the cows kept straying into the neighbors' fields, Mrs. Fisher installed an expensive new electric fence. (Omit *because;* insert *consequently* before *Mrs. Fisher.*)

(e) The coast guard cutter stayed on the scene until one o'clock, when the abandoned yawl finally sank. (Change *when* to *then;* make no other change in the wording.)

(f) In the sixth race Foley's Caroline Sue did not finish in the money, although she showed good form and ran a good race to finish fifth. (Change *although* to *nevertheless;* make no other change in the wording.)

(g) Boston and New York became exclusive American League territory, St. Louis and Philadelphia had only National League clubs, and Chicago was the only city with clubs in both leagues. (Omit the last clause completely; make no other change in the wording.)

PN 2 D   *A semicolon may be used in formal punctuation between two independent clauses joined by a coordinating conjunction if the clauses are long and complicated*

The ruling passion of the ideal professor is the pursuit of knowledge for its own sake so that he is related to other human beings only indirectly through their common relation to the truth; and those passions, like lust and avarice and envy, are, in his case, ideally excluded (W. H. Auden).

But I see no way of avoiding the moral and intellectual complexities of communication to an audience not all of which is at the same level of sophistication, complacency, or receptivity; and only by listening for this ambiguity and what it signifies can we flexibly protect our cultural role as Socratic questioners and skeptics (Joyce Cary).

The semicolon may imply greater formality, longer pause in speech, and less close connection in thought than the comma; and consequently it may be used satisfactorily in sentences like these.

PN 2 E   *A comma may be omitted between independent clauses joined by a coordinating conjunction if the clauses are short and simple and if they are closely connected in thought*

Griffin scored the touchdown and Brown kicked the point.

I took a plane but Graves came by train.

The dinghy grounded with a sudden jar and Mike jumped out into the backwash of a wave and hauled it up . . . (Hammond Innes).

There was a frantic scuffling behind the first wall of jungle and Roth ground his jaws together to keep from uttering a sound (Norman Mailer).

The writers felt that the clauses in these sentences were all so short that no commas were needed. It is impossible to be very definite about how short clauses should be to allow omission of commas. The punctuation depends mainly on the general formality or informality of the writing in question. In informal, simple, fast-moving narratives commas are often omitted between independent clauses. Perhaps it is correct to say that the comma between independent clauses joined by a coordinating conjunction may be omitted in any kind of composition if the clauses are not over twelve or fifteen words in length. It is, however, often wise to use it before *but* and *for* in any situation in which there might be misreading.

EXERCISES

5. Read the selections quoted in Chapters 7 and 8. To what extent does the practice of the authors quoted accord with principles given just above about the use of semicolon and comma between independent clauses?

6. Each of the following sentences contains two or more independent clauses. Find out what punctuation is needed between the clauses and what alternate punctuation may be possible.

   (a) The small store cannot stock a wide variety of brands   it is wise for the storekeeper to stick to one or two standard ones.

   (b) Mix the sand, gravel, and cement together thoroughly   be sure to keep on mixing until the whole mass is uniform.

   (c) *Right hand* and *left hand* are usually written without hyphens   they do take hyphens, however, when they are used as adjectives.

(d) The Yankees beat the Indians   and the Senators split with the Sox.
(e) Hackett's work suffered when he started to write so much for money cannot be the sole motivation for producing good literature.
(f) Everybody in the line-up hit safely   but George was unhappy at having only a scratch single to show for five times at bat.
(g) Many of the counties have odd shapes   but the ear-like corner containing Kenmore to the northwest makes Ward look positively grotesque.
(h) The organization Democrats were deserted by the left-wingers, who made up a third-party movement and ran Henry Wallace for President, and by the so-called Dixiecrats of the South, who campaigned on racist issues, and were somewhat discouraged   but when the returns were in Truman had beaten Dewey.
(i) The university was located at Ann Arbor, about thirty-five miles west of Detroit   the state college was placed in East Lansing, about fifty miles northwest of Ann Arbor.
(j) Hanson's eyes ached   and he was weary from the detailed work.

Marks for Meaning as Well as Form

So far, this chapter has treated punctuation at the ends of sentences and sentence equivalents and punctuation between independent clauses within sentences. You have seen that the semicolons between independent clauses not connected by coordinating conjunctions are not particularly meaningful, and neither are commas between independent clauses joined by *and, but,* or *or.* Two other marks of punctuation may be used between independent clauses, as well as in a number of other situations: the colon and the dash. Unlike semicolons and commas in these uses, they are more or less meaningful. Unlike semicolons and commas, they are not used mainly because of considerations of sentence form. Unlike semicolons and commas, they are not very common. They are used in exceptional rather than usual situations.

PN 2 F   *A colon may be used before material that explains or completes*

Before explaining how colons are used, it is better to explain how they are *not* used. It is convenient to think of an order of rank among marks of punctuation: periods indicating full stops after sentences, semicolons indicating marked stops between independent clauses without coordinating conjunctions, and commas indicating slight stops between minor elements or between independent clauses joined by coordinating conjunctions. This ranking or ordering is satisfactory. But partly because of the relationship between the words *semicolon* and *colon* and partly because of the form of the mark (:, which looks like something that might suitably fit between . and ;), it is easy to try to fit the colon into the period-semicolon-comma series and to think of it as a light period or a heavy semicolon. This notion is false. A colon is instead a special mark that doesn't fit in the series, one with a significance and a use all its own.

The one main use of the colon is to show that something follows that explains, fulfills, completes, amplifies, illustrates, or restates. In effect, the colon says to the reader, "Pay attention to what follows: it will complete the preceding thought. You need what follows to understand the full meaning of what is being said."

1. Sometimes, like the semicolon, the colon is used between independent clauses not connected by coordinating conjunctions:

> Many freshmen show the same weakness in choosing theme subjects: they fail to see that their own experiences are interesting.
>
> In the back of every mind these days, there is a terrible thought: man has ingeniously devised the means of his own destruction (Brooks Atkinson).
>
> John Cabot's discovery of North America had two important results: it led to English colonization in North America, and it started a great new fishing industry (Willis Lindquist).

These sentences show first an independent clause and second a unit composed of one or two independent clauses. You may ask whether semicolons could have been used in these sentences. They could have been. The sentence by Lindquist, for instance, could have been punctuated as follows:

> John Cabot's . . . results; it . . . industry.

This would have been satisfactory. If the colon is used in this situation, however, the writer is able to say to the reader, "And the following will explain to you more fully that which preceded." Instead of being required by considerations of sentence form, like the semicolon, the colon is often optional.

2. Note the following:

> The assistant night city editor has three important duties: emptying the waste baskets, answering the telephone, and staying awake.

The words following the colon do not make up a clause, but instead a series of phrases. This sentence illustrates another important use of the colon, introducing a list, as does the following:

> What was the nature of the reforms carried out by the states? Many of them had to do with the democratization of political machinery: the initiative and referendum, the secret ballot, the direct primary, and direct election of Senators, corrupt-practices acts, provision for municipal home rule, and woman suffrage . . . Still others had broad social connotations: educational reforms, public-health programs, the conservation of natural resources (Allan Nevins and Henry Steele Commager).

Note that the expression before the colon should have the form of a complete clause. Notice the unsatisfactorily punctuated sentence:

> The supplies that we needed most were: flour, bacon, flashlight batteries, and soap.

These arrangements are preferred:

> The supplies that we needed most were flour, bacon, flashlight batteries, and soap.
> The supplies that we needed most included the following: flour, bacon, flashlight batteries, and soap.

Note the contrast between these two sentences:

> Death rates from other diseases that have almost been conquered have fallen as follows between 1900 and 1950: whooping cough, 12.2 to 0.7; measles, 13.3 to 0.3; typhoid fever, 31.3 to 0.1. Illnesses that have been drastically reduced as a cause of death include chronic diseases of the kidneys, influenza and pneumonia, diarrhea and similar diseases of the digestive system, and syphilis (George Soule).

3. Occasionally the colon is used before a phrase or single word serving as a climax summary of a sentence:

> Dr. Hudson had one terrible weakness: whisky.
> The great social check that acted to keep his activity within limits they phrased as a moral tabu: the tabu on overdoing (Ruth Benedict).

In many situations involving colons, other marks, such as commas or dashes, could also be used. The choice often depends on the writer's preference and on the exact suggestion wanted.

EXERCISES

7. Find five sentences in your general reading or in this book that employ colons. Analyze the effect of this punctuation.

8. Insert colons in the following sentences. If you can, try to analyze the effect that other marks of punctuation might have:

(a) John Ireland summed up Jacobson's character with one sentence he said that he never hit a man when he was up.

(b) There is one rule for merchandising that you should never forget you can fool all of the people long enough to make a profit.

(c) Pennsylvania has three important river systems that of the Delaware, Lehigh, and Schuylkill to the east, the Susquehanna and its tributaries in the center, and the Allegheny, Monongahela, and Ohio to the west.

(d) Jewett's checkbook showed contributions to the following charities the Red Cross, the Cancer Fund, and the Community Chest.

(e) You should take two precautions before visiting those African countries you should be vaccinated again, and you should have some typhus shots.

(f) Keane did not distrust every woman that he met he trusted those under seven and those over seventy.

(g) It is easy to understand what propaganda is it is the sum total of the publicity and public relations of an enemy country.

(h) Delaware has only one sizable area marked by urban and industrial concentration that around Wilmington.

PN 2 G *A dash may be used to signal a change or conclusion or list*

If you are typing you can make a standard dash by typing two hyphens together: --. If you are writing by hand you can make a dash by drawing a straight line about the length of two hyphen lines. Note in the following examples that no space is left between the preceding word, the dash, and the following word.

Before you are told what dashes are used for, you had better be told what they are not used for. Dashes are not general all-purpose marks to be inserted when you do not know what else to use. Instead they are marks that indicate force; as such they should be used sparingly. In most themes there are few situations in which you *must* use dashes, although there may be several in which you *may* use them. You can usually write five hundred or a thousand words effectively and use no more than one dash, or a pair of dashes, in the process.

Like the colon, and unlike the comma and semicolon, the dash is often used to impart an additional meaning or suggestion rather than merely to satisfy considerations of sentence form. Your attention is called to the *often* in the sentence just preceding, for sometimes the dash or an equivalent mark is required by form. Dashes are used as follows:

1. The dash signals a sharp separation between what precedes and what follows; it indicates a decided, often abrupt change or a telling contrast in thought or structure or both. In effect, it says to the reader, "Now stop a moment and get set for a quick change"; it says something like "Hold on; there is an abrupt turn in what follows." It usually shows that there would be in the spoken sentence a noticeable pause, sometimes a pause for suspense. In this function the dash is sometimes used between main clauses:

> I have had a timer apart on a sick Ford many times, but I never knew what I was up to—I was just showing off before God (E. B. White).
> The doctor came promptly—but so, after an hour, did the undertaker.

2. The dash is often effectively used to introduce a terse clarification, an apt summary, or a punch-line conclusion in the form of a clause, phrase, or single word:

> Indeed, he said to a lady that if a man and a dog were drowning in the same pond he would prefer to save the dog—if, that is, there were nobody looking (Virginia Woolf).
> It is a game which also holds the distinction of turning loose annually into the already turbid stream of national life a fresh collection of the world's greatest bores—exfootball-players (Paul Gallico).
> As Mark Twain is supposed to have said, it is very easy to give up smoking—every twenty minutes.

3. Two dashes are often used to set off from other parts of a sentence material inserted more or less abruptly to emphasize, clarify, or explain:

> But remember—though your teachers will work against you here—remember that you are studying primarily for the sake of the intensive specialization and not of the history (Roger W. Holmes).
> Then Mike sat down at the piano and played—or rather tried to play—the "Jersey Bounce."

4. The dash is often useful in situations in which the writer has given a number of details and wishes to pause and summarize with some such expression as *these, all these, all these and other considerations:*

Newspapers, radio, movies, and advertising—these might be called the "big four" of communication (H. A. Overstreet).

5. Like the colon, the dash is used to introduce a list at the end of a sentence, often with an informal effect:

. . . Christianity itself will teach us the noble doctrine of goodness— sweetness, self-sacrifice, generosity, and faith (Hardin Craig).

These rules, for the most part, originated with certain English grammarians of the eighteenth century—notably William Ward, Robert Lowth, and James Buchanan (Albert H. Marckwardt).

EXERCISES

9. Find five illustrations of dashes in the selections in this book or in your other reading. Analyze their use and effect. In which situations could other marks have been substituted?

10. Insert dashes in the following sentences. Analyze the effect of use of other punctuation marks at points where you can insert dashes:

(a) Mr. King had one great ambition in life to break a hundred with honest scoring.

(b) That year the Lions had a most dismal record they lost one hundred and eighteen games.

(c) Some of the romantics Byron and Shelley in particular lived rather unconventional personal lives.

(d) The bug as the homemade farm tractor was called lacked any unnecessary adornments like horn, windshield, lights, and even brakes.

(e) Lambert's initial ignorance, his laziness and carelessness, his utter lack of accomplishment, and his attitude, alternately truculent and offensively blasé any of these might have been reason enough for flunking him.

11. The following sentences illustrate points dealt with in the section on end punctuation and the section on punctuation between independent clauses along with other uses of colons and dashes. If the given punctuation is incorrect, make what corrections are needed. If necessary punctuation has been omitted, insert it. Analyze the effects of various different marks in situations in which you have a choice.

(a) Will you please send as soon as you can two replacement copies of the October 18 issue of your magazine.

(b) Leahy was surprised at being questioned about the load of two-by-fours. Never having had anything whatever to do with the whole matter.

(c) Some of his classmates suspected that Leonard must be a red of some kind. Since he genuinely liked studying politics and economics.

(d) The shy couple asked how far it was from Lancaster down to Elkton, Maryland?

(e) There was a very good reason why buzzers were ringing and people were rushing around   the ship was sinking.

(f) We drove through most of the cities and towns on the Maine coast; Kittery, Portland, Brunswick, Rockland, and Belfast.

(g) It was too late to save the house, the firemen turned their attention to the barns and other buildings.

(h) Lockwood made a mental note that he should bring home some flowers or candy for his wife had seemed rather waspish lately.

Dependent Elements

PN 3   *Use commas to prevent misreading*

Whenever you can prevent possible misreading, insert a comma or commas. Note the following:

> Inside the theater was bright and colorful.
> After milking the cows are turned out into the lane.
> While we were eating the neighbor's child threw his baseball through the dining room window.

Probably you had to read these sentences twice to understand their meaning. In each sentence, an introductory element was probably interpreted as having a noun as object, but on analysis it turned out that that following noun was the subject for what came next. Note how an inserted comma prevents misreading in each of these sentences:

> Inside, the theater was bright and colorful.
> After milking, the cows are turned out into the lane.
> While we were eating, the neighbor's child threw his baseball through the dining room window.

Now note the following:

> Ever since he has been careful about not offending Mr. Marsh.
> A little while after we had our dinner in a restaurant in Phoenix.
> Long before Matthews had learned how to sail a yacht.

In these sentences, one is likely at first to think that *since, after,* and *before* are subordinating conjunctions and to interpret the sentences as dependent clauses; commas after the introductory elements make it clear that they are modifiers and that the units of expression are independent clauses or complete sentences:

> Ever since, he has been careful about not offending Mr. Marsh.
> A little while after, we had our dinner in a restaurant in Phoenix.
> Long before, Matthews had learned how to sail a yacht.

Note the following:

> We had better include Don or Jack may be irritated.
> Every one in the play was invited to the Maynards' midnight dinner
> but Lester was unable to come because his mother was seriously ill.
> The coach had only two days to train a substitute for Jack would obviously be unable to play in Saturday's game.

You can omit punctuation from a sentence made up of two independent clauses with a coordinating conjunction, but you may at least momentarily mislead your reader. Note the clarity of the following:

> . . . include Don, or Jack . . .
> . . . to the Maynards' midnight dinner, but Lester . . .
> . . . to train a substitute, for Jack . . .

The punctuation of series will be treated later in this book, but notice the following at this point:

> The park was filled with elderly people sitting in the sun, clerks and office-workers enjoying a mid-day break, nursemaids taking care of babies and students from the high school four blocks away.

The comma between the next-to-last and last in this series may be helpful:

> . . . nursemaids taking care of babies, and students . . .

Whenever you can help your reader understand your meaning at once and avoid confusion or misunderstanding, by all means insert a comma. This rule, which of course depends on meaning, is more important than all following rules about use of commas for the sake of form alone.

EXERCISE

12. Insert commas in the following sentences in any situations in which they may prevent misreading:
(a) McDonald had picked Meadows for the assignment because of the many men available he had seemed the most reliable.

(b) Ever since the child has refused to come within five feet of the fire-place.

(c) The main floor of the barn was a disorderly confusion of tools and implements, wire and fence posts, tubs and buckets, hay for the cows and puppies and kittens playing around.

(d) As he was eating the custard pie tasted peculiar to him.

(e) We spent the whole morning building the crate for the dog for Mr. Miller was unable to help us.

(f) The western counties in the state are Black Lake Morris Mountain Edward Clinton and Clear Lake.

(g) When Cather started to write about Nebraska people found a new vigor and clarity in her style.

(h) In ironing the frills and ruffles should be left until last.

(i) When Mr. Morgan returns he can take Emily and Dot and Mary can wait here for her father.

(j) After all these troubles and confusions had been entirely unnecesssary.

PN 4   *A comma may be used to set off a long or complicated introductory element*

Sometimes introductory elements in sentences are set off with commas. This matter will be explained shortly, but it is worthwhile to give a negative caution first: in most sentences, the first element is the subject itself. The subject is not set off from the remainder of the sentence with a comma (except for the situations suggested just above). In the sentence "what Newman had predicted many times in his column finally happened," the words from *what* to *column* make up a clause that begins the sentence, but this clause is the subject for *happened,* and there is no comma between *column* and *finally.* In the sentence "skidding on icy roads causes many minor accidents," the words from *skidding* to *roads* make up a phrase beginning with a non-finite verb form, but this phrase is the subject for the verb *causes,* and hence there is no comma between *roads* and *causes.* In the following sentences the first clauses and phrases are subjects for verbs and are *not* set off with commas:

> That I forgot to do this must be put down to the natural agitation of a mathematics teacher caught out in an error (H. F. Ellis).
>
> How the dam was finally built after three years of delays is told in the next chapter.
>
> Standing for several hours or bustling for a place in the galleries would have diminished in appeal as a man grew older (Alfred Harbage).

> To try a scoring shot from three quarters of the way down the floor was merely clowning for the gallery.

Only modifiers—not subjects—are set off with commas. In general, a long or complicated introductory modifier may be set off with a comma, but a short or simple introductory modifier usually is not.

1. A long introductory dependent clause may be set off with a comma:

> If proper controls could be secured and confidence established, the operation of power plants could then be · considered (Harold C. Urey).
> As each new generation saw how the prejudice and vanity of their predecessors proved stumbling blocks to progress, standards of exactness and impartiality were raised (James B. Conant).

A short introductory dependent clause is often not set off with a comma:

> As he ran back the death-rattle was in her throat (Lytton Strachey).
> Years later when we were grown I knew this camp officer again (Thomas Sancton).
> If a person did not work he did not eat.

Usage varies considerably on this matter.

2. An introductory phrase containing a non-finite verb form—a participle, gerund, or infinitive—is likely to be set off with a comma:

> Sitting there, my father read me *The Lays of Ancient Rome* (William Butler Yeats).
> Seen through male eyes, she is big sister who has it easy, who always gets the breaks (Margaret Mead).
> While living first at Harvard and then at Princeton, I found a curious limitation in the attitudes of their undergraduates (Lynn White, Jr.).
> With hair knotted loosely behind, she had something of a warm, maternal look (D. H. Lawrence).

If the phrase is short and simple, the comma is often omitted:

> In swimming one uses many different muscles.

When an introductory participial phrase is immediately followed by a verb with the subject coming last, the comma is not used:

Parked outside was the doctor's Cadillac.
Riding at breakneck speed came messengers bearing the news.
Lying in the mud of Congamond Creek is all that remains of this
heroic ship.

3. Introductory prepositional phrases are usually not set off with
commas: "in the morning the telegram came," "by 1944 it was apparent
that the Allies would win." Longer, more complicated prepositional
phrases may be set off:

> In spite of all their knowledge and interest, most of the students in this
> course had abominable accents . . . (Vincent Sheean)

Such prepositional phrases as *for example, as a matter of fact,* and *on
the other hand* will be considered below. When an introductory prepositional phrase is immediately followed by a verb with the subject coming
last, the comma is not used:

> Only in the nineteenth century was biography fully grown and hugely
> prolific (Virginia Woolf).
> Between the Seattle area and the Columbia River valley to the east
> are the Wenatchee Mountains.

4. *Oh, yes,* and *no, why* and *well* as more or less meaningless introductory elements, and words similarly used are set off with commas:

> No, I don't think I'll go to the dance.
> Why, Perry was here just a second ago.

EXERCISES

13. Find eight illustrations of introductory elements in the selections given
in the first ten chapters of this book and notice how they are punctuated.

14. Insert commas where they are needed after introductory elements in
the following sentences. In some situations the use of the comma is optional. Analyze the effect of using it or omitting it.

(a) To conclude the data should be checked by some one else before
the report is sent in.
(b) Well I don't know of any reason why Pete should not bring the dog.
(c) After drying the fish is ready to be packed and shipped out.
(d) How to fix the coupling link puzzled Andy.
(e) Although Rhode Island is of course the smallest of the states with
a land area of little more than a thousand square miles it at one
time had a winter capital, Providence, and a summer capital,
Newport.

(f) Named "Seward's Folly" when it was purchased from Russia by the United States in 1867 Alaska has turned out to be rich in metal ores and fish.

(g) After scratching both sides of the sedan while driving through the alley Potter was not in a very gay mood when he reached the street.

(h) While watching Proctor noticed that one of the men limped a little.

15. Following are some sentences by professional writers. See how you would punctuate them. The writers' procedures are given below:

(a) If he had heard them he might have been annoyed at some of the names they called him (Katherine Anne Porter).

(b) But as Mrs. Cullen stood facing all this I had an impression of indifference and mere courtesy . . . (Glenway Wescott).

(c) In the surrey with his cousin and Major de Spain and General Compson he saw the wilderness through a slow drizzle of November rain . . . (William Faulkner).

(d) About nine-thirty the guests started really eating and drinking . . . (Octavus Roy Cohen).

(e) As soon as he could do so naturally Arthur asked after Margaret . . . (W. Somerset Maugham).

(f) Returning to London after Margaret's flight Arthur Burdon had thrown himself into the work . . . (W. Somerset Maugham).

(g) As soon as you take the things home you realize that they are revolting (Gilbert Highet).

(h) Looking for the answer in the field itself we arrived at a theory which during the three years since has proven infallible (Louis Bromfield).

Sentences (a), (b), (e), (f), (g), and (h) are punctuated as follows: (a) . . . them, he . . . ; (b) . . . this, I . . . ; (e) . . . naturally, Arthur . . . ; (f) . . . flight, Arthur . . . ; (g) . . . home, you . . . ; (h) . . . itself, we . . . . Sentences (c) and (d) do not have commas.

Middle and Final Elements

A wide variety of sentence elements that must come after others, either within the sentence or at its end, are set off with commas. But before these are explained to you, you should be warned about elements that are not set off. Notice the following sentences:

> Nobody asks whether any of these youths is capable of accepting the education that is to be offered him (William Craig Smyser).
> The consequence is that freedom is no longer the right of any man to hold whatever opinion he pleases (Archibald MacLeish).
> My roommate likes reading detective stories.
> The worst part of the work was sanding the floors.

These sentences show dependent clauses and non-finite verb phrases following other elements, but these dependent clauses and non-finite verb phrases are objects or complements of verbs. Like other objects and complements, they are not separated from preceding verbs by commas: there is no comma between *asks*, a finite verb, and the clause beginning with *whether* in the first illustration because the clause is the object of *asks*. There is no comma between *is* and the clause beginning with *that* in the second sentence because the clause is the complement in the sentence.

You will rarely find a situation in which there is a single comma between verb and object or between verb and complement. You have already been told that there is rarely a situation in which there is a single comma between subject and verb. You may conclude that these important sentence elements—subject, verb, object, or complement—are not set off with commas. Perhaps you can go further and conclude also that commas are used only with other elements, modifiers and appositives for instance. This is correct.

EXERCISE

16. In the following sentences take out the commas that have been incorrectly inserted:

(a) How the thief managed to enter the locked room, remained an unanswered question.

(b) Fairing the lines of a ship, is a job that requires very careful workmanship.

(c) Everybody wondered, why the President did not ask at once for Sanford's resignation.

(d) That the notion of a trinitarian divinity is impossible, is the keynote of unitarian thought.

(e) The theory proposed by Sargent was, that the poem had been written by a single author at Chartres in 1045.

(f) The main point in Scott's system of playing the horses was, refusing to bet on the track favorite.

(g) The slowest part of the process is, picking the pin feathers from the ducks.

(h) For a long time Sears had known, that statehood was assured for Alaska.

An element coming in the middle of a sentence should not be punctuated with only one comma. If an element is to be set off from preceding material with a comma, it should likewise be set off from following material with a comma, and *vice versa*. In other words, *use two commas or none for the punctuation of elements that do not begin or end sentences.* Note the following:

> The ship, which was flying the Greek flag, finally limped into port.
> Shaw did not, at the time, realize the significance of the charges.

These sentences are satisfactorily punctuated. With a slight change in meaning expressed or suggested, they may be satisfactorily punctuated as follows:

> The ship which was flying the Greek flag finally limped into port.
> Shaw did not at the time realize the significance of the charges.

But the following punctuation is completely unsatisfactory:

> The ship, which was flying the Greek flag finally limped into port.
> The ship which was flying the Greek flag, finally limped into port.
> Shaw did not, at the time realize the significance of the charges.
> Shaw did not at the time, realize the significance of the charges.

If you are going to set off a middle element from one part of a sentence, be careful to set it off also from the other part.

EXERCISE

17. Which of the following sentences contain middle elements incorrectly set off with only single commas?

(a) Silverman could not on the other hand, refuse to help an old friend.

(b) Casper, which is located somewhat east of the center of the state is the next largest town.

(c) Sloan who knew the Mohave area well, guided the party back to the road to Kingman.

(d) Under Ivan IV, who lived from 1533 to 1584, the Russians began the conquest of Siberia.

(e) The men in the engine room, having been warned about the danger made for the ladders at once.

(f) Tom's car, which was old and dilapidated broke down completely in Wausau, and we had to take the bus up to Merrill.

(g) You may if you wish, have a shrimp cocktail for a mere dollar and a half more.

(h) Mr. Spalding, whose drug store was the nearest reopened after closing hours to make up the prescription.

PN 5 A   *Non-restrictive clauses and phrases are set off with commas*

Non-restrictive clauses and non-restrictive participial phrases are set off with commas. Restrictive clauses and restrictive phrases are not set off with commas. A modifying dependent clause beginning with *who* or *which* is either restrictive or non-restrictive. A *restrictive clause* is one that is needed in a sentence to identify whatever it modifies or refers to. A *non-restrictive clause* is one that is not needed to identify but which, on the other hand, simply supplies additional, often incidental information. A non-restrictive clause or non-restrictive participial phrase, which is set off with commas, usually may be omitted from the sentence with no great loss of meaning. On the other hand, a restrictive clause or restrictive participial phrase, which is not set off with commas, cannot be omitted from a sentence without considerable change in the meaning or without considerable doubt and uncertainty about identification.

A non-restrictive clause is often used in reference to a person, place, or thing already identified and not needing further identification (George Washington, General Grant's wife, Chicago, Japan, the Empire State Building, my oldest brother, his left foot, the first runner to cross the mark, the combination on our office safe). A restrictive clause is often used in reference to a word needing identification or limitation (a person, the man, a city, a book, a tree, the color, many things, a wreck).

A non-restrictive clause or non-restrictive participial phrase is usually spoken with a brief but perceptible pause before and after: note the sound of the spoken sentence "Mr. Harris, having forgotten his door key, was trying to force open a window in the hall." A restrictive clause or participial phrase is usually uttered without a perceptible pause before or after ("the man trying to force open the window was Mr. Harris himself").

All this may be hard for you to follow at first; notice the following detailed explanation:

> Tom's right forefinger, which had been crushed in the wreck, was amputated.
> The finger that had been crushed was Tom's right forefinger.

In the first sentence the dependent clause *which had been crushed in the wreck* is non-restrictive. Since it is non-restrictive, it is punctuated with two commas, one to set it off from *forefinger,* one to set it off from *was amputated.* The clause is non-restrictive because it may be omitted. If it is, we lose the incidental explanation that it had been crushed in the wreck, but the main thought of the sentence is quite clear: Tom's right forefinger was amputated. It is non-restrictive because the thing to which it refers, *Tom's right forefinger,* is already definitely identified; it is set off from everything else in the world. It is non-restrictive because it would be spoken with a slight pause between *forefinger* and *which* and between *wreck* and *was.*

Now notice the second sentence. In this sentence the clause *that had been crushed* is restrictive. Unless preceding sentences have made the situation quite clear, this clause cannot be omitted. If you read or hear the bare statement "the finger was Tom's right forefinger" you can hardly help wondering about the significance of the comment. Notice that the clause refers to something that needs further identification; *the finger* alone could refer to any of several billion members. Further, the clause is restrictive because the spoken sentence would have no pause between *finger* and *that* and *crushed* and *was.*

Note also that the first sentence, which contains the non-restrictive clause, is punctuated with two commas, and that the second, which contains the restrictive clause, has no commas at all. Punctuating either of these sentences with just one comma would be wrong.

> Franklin D. Roosevelt, who was first elected in 1932, occupied the White House longer than any other President.
> The President who occupied the White House longest was Franklin D. Roosevelt.

In the first of these two sentences the clause *who was first elected in 1932* is non-restrictive and is set off with two commas. It is non-restrictive because it may be omitted from the sentence with the loss of only incidental information but not with the loss of the sense of the main statement: Franklin D. Roosevelt occupied the White House longer than any other President. Once the name *Franklin D. Roosevelt* is given, no further identification is needed. (Situations in which two persons or things happen to bear the same name will be dealt with later.) Further, the clause is non-restrictive because in speaking there would be a slight pause between *Roosevelt* and *who* and between *1932* and *occupied.*

In the second sentence, however, the clause *who occupied the White House longest* is restrictive and is not set off with commas. There have been many Presidents; to omit this clause in this sentence is to provoke the hearer or reader to ask at once "which President?" The expression *the President* needs further identification, and, since it does, the clause modifying it and giving that identification is restrictive. Further, one would say this sentence with no pause between *President* and *who* and between *longest* and *was*.

Punctuating either sentence with only one comma in any position whatever would be wrong.

Often it makes little difference whether you use a full dependent clause or a participial phrase to express your meaning: "cigarettes that are imported from Europe" and "cigarettes imported from Europe" mean the same thing. Principles for punctuating participial phrases are the same as those for punctuating dependent clauses. Note the following:

> Students, coming as they do from almost all levels of our society, have a variety of problems.
> Students coming in to the university from the suburban towns were delayed that morning.

In the first of these sentences the participial phrase represents an additional, more or less incidental thought. Without the phrase enclosed by the commas the sentence keeps its main meaning: students have a variety of problems. *Students* in this sentence means students in general, without limitation. If the sentence is spoken there will be a slight pause between *students* and *coming* and between *society* and *have*. For these reasons the phrase is non-restrictive and is set off with two commas.

In the second sentence there is a different situation. The phrase beginning with *coming* and ending with *morning* is restrictive. It is needed in the sentence: if one says only "students were late" the hearer or reader must ask what students, when, where, and why. In this sentence *students* does not refer to students in general, but instead is limited or restricted to mean a particular group of students at a particular place and time. The spoken sentence would show no pauses between *students* and *coming* and *morning* and *were*. For these reasons the phrase is restrictive and is not separated with a comma from any other part of the sentence. Again, it would be wrong to punctuate either sentence with only one comma.

Sentence order may help you make decisions about the restrictiveness and non-restrictiveness of phrases. Note the following: "the typical automobile, having four wheels, needs four good tires."

For the reasons given above, the phrase *having four wheels* is clearly non-restrictive. Note that the position of the non-restrictive phrase is not necessarily fixed in the sentence; you could vary the order of elements: "having four wheels, the typical automobile needs four good tires."

If a phrase is restrictive, it is less likely to permit a change in its position in the sentence. You can readily say or write the following: "an automobile having defective brakes should not be taken onto the highway." But your feeling for order and meaning will probably tell you that the following is impossible: "having defective brakes, an automobile should not be taken onto the highway."

As the sentences above have showed, use of commas with non-restrictives enables you to show that one statement is general and applies to all persons or things mentioned, another specific and applicable only to a certain limited number. Compare and contrast the following:

> The mountaineers, who believe in these superstitions, avoid . . . (This means that all the mountaineers believe in these superstitions.)
> The mountaineers who believe in these superstitions avoid . . . (This means that only a certain number of the mountaineers—90, 50, or 10 per cent of them, but not all—believe in the superstitions.)
> Women, who cannot be discreet and keep such things secret, cause . . . (This means that *women* is to be understood as referring to all women; by his punctuation the writer has said "and incidentally of course no woman can be discreet.")
> Women who cannot be discreet and keep such things secret cause . . . (This means that there are women who can be discreet and keep secret whatever things are being discussed, and that only indiscreet women, constituting something between one and ninety-nine out of a hundred, are being discussed.)

Whether a dependent clause or participial phrase is restrictive or non-restrictive often depends on the situation. The same clause or phrase may be non-restrictive in one situation and restrictive in another; it may consequently require commas in one situation, no commas in another:

> Dick took a book at random from the economics shelf. This book, which concerned violence in the labor movement, interested him.
> Dick took two books from the economics shelf. The one which concerned violence in the labor movement interested him.

> Anchored in the harbor was a tanker flying the British flag.
> Anchored in the harbor was a battered old tanker. This tanker, flying the British flag, was . . .

If the noun modified by the phrase or clause has been mentioned or identified previously, the clause or phrase will probably be non-restrictive and will take commas.

Sometimes it doesn't make much difference in so far as either correctness or meaning is concerned whether a clause or phrase is punctuated as restrictive or as non-restrictive:

> The heavy snow that had fallen all through the night had blocked the highways.
> The heavy snow, which had fallen all through the night, had blocked the highways.

You may occasionally encounter a situation in which two or more persons or things bear the same name; in such situations the name word (or proper noun) may be followed by a restrictive clause, but if it is, it is usually preceded by the word *the:*

> USUAL SITUATION: John Swanson, who represents the Cardwell Company, is in room 314. (The proper name identifies; the following clause is non-restrictive and is so punctuated.)

> UNUSUAL SITUATION: The John Swanson who represents the Cardwell company is not the John Swanson who has room 314. (There are two John Swansons; the name does not identify either in this situation; both clauses are restrictive because they are needed to identify; neither clause is set off with commas.)

Rules about restrictiveness and non-restrictiveness are applied only rather rarely to prepositional phrases and to other short phrases not containing participles. The great majority of prepositional phrases are not separated by commas from the elements that they modify. Occasionally, however, commas may set off prepositional phrases: "the fire tower, on top of Mt. Marcy, was . . ."

Sometimes prepositional phrases equivalent in meaning to dependent clauses are punctuated as non-restrictive clauses are after proper names: "Mr. Thayer, in charge of the engine room, was summoned . . ."

A final word about restrictive and non-restrictive elements: sometimes your decision that a clause or phrase is restrictive or non-restrictive makes a considerable amount of difference in the meaning expressed:

> Women having such disabilities and weaknesses cannot be employed in this division.
> Women, having such disabilities and weaknesses, cannot be employed in this division.

Sometimes it doesn't make much difference:

> Unemployment that has been hurting the Northeastern states is now lessening.
> Unemployment, which has been hurting the Northeastern states, is now lessening.

But you can never punctuate a dependent clause or participial phrase in the middle of a sentence with just one comma. Use two commas or none.

EXERCISES

18. Determine the difference in the meanings expressed by the following pairs:

the *Saturday Evening Post,* which printed the article, was . . .
the *Saturday Evening Post* that printed the article was . . .

the second hole, which he played very badly, was . . .
the second hole that he played very badly was . . .

the forests, on which our well-being as a town depends, should . . .
the forests on which our well-being as a town depends should . . .

my neighbor, suffering from diabetes, is . . .
my neighbor suffering from diabetes is . . .

his last letter, which told of Howard's unhappiness, was . . .
his last letter that told of Howard's unhappiness was . . .

the baseball fans, who make the neighborhood rather noisy, are . . .
the baseball fans who make the neighborhood rather noisy are . . .

the Sioux, driven from their lands by this arrangement, were . . .
the Sioux driven from their lands by this arrangement were . . .

a baby, needing constant attention, is . . .
a baby needing constant attention is . . .

19. Insert commas where they are clearly needed in the following sentences:

(a) Tom Gant who was playing second base was the next batter.
(b) The officer who issued the ticket was unable to identify in court the man who had been driving the car.
(c) The novel *Compulsion* written by Meyer Levin concerned the famous Loeb-Leopold case which shocked the nation in the 1920's.
(d) The freighter *Clydesider* which was owned by the Norman Company was the nearest ship to the stricken liner.
(e) Students who persist in parking their cars in restricted areas will be given regular police summons.

(f) The Hotel Normandy which stands on the corner of Eighth and Church will be torn down next winter.

(g) The soldiers who crossed the Rhine at Remagen will testify to the truth of this observation.

(h) Carl Smithers whom you mentioned in your last report is doing good work and will fit into the organization all right.

20. Accompanying each of the following sentences are directions calling for a change in the wording. Making the changes called for in these directions may require making changes in the punctuation too. Make such necessary changes.

(a) Workers in the chemical divisions, which are classified as dangerous, should be given special instructions. (Omit the word *chemical*.)

(b) Warned by his record, the authorities sent him to a prison from which escape was impossible. (For *a prison* substitute *Alcatraz*.)

(c) Reemer wore size 12 shoes, which would not have fitted any of the other three men in the group. (Omit *size 12*.)

(d) The procedure required that all outgoing letters should pass over the desk of the president's secretary. (Add after *letters* the words *concerning credits*.)

(e) The Doberman dog, which was imported into the United States from Germany, is a large and powerful animal. (Change *which was* to *that he*.)

(f) These regulations applied to all university students. (Add after *regulations* the words *concerning transfer of credits*.)

(g) After looking around, we finally stopped at the Parkway Motel, which looked clean and comfortable. (For *the Parkway* substitute *a*.)

(h) The book that was required reading for the course was missing from the reserve room. (For *The book*, substitute *L. H. Seever's Essentials of English History*.)

(i) The outfielder who was nearest to the ball slipped and fell in the wet grass. (Change *outfielder* to *left fielder*.)

21. Correct the punctuation of the following sentences:

(a) Astronomy which used to attract only a few students, has become more popular since the sputniks and other artificial satellites.

(b) August, which is usually humid and unpleasant enough was almost unbearable in Cape Prince that year.

(c) The car, that Quillen drove that day, which was a black Buick sedan had been rented from a U-Drive-It establishment.

(d) The case that the law professor spent most of his time on that hour was a breach-of-promise suit.

(e) The Lions' left end who had been hurt on the play, was carried off the field.

(f) The money originally allotted to flood control projects had been turned over to the road commissioner.

(g) The detail ordered to clean up the barracks, had done its work well.
(h) Mrs. Saunderson, who was supposed to preside at the meeting could not come.

PN 5 B *Non-restrictive appositives are set off with commas*

The principle of restrictiveness and non-restrictiveness applies also to words in apposition. Apposition, explained on p. 268, occurs when expressions meaning the same person or thing are placed side by side without an intervening part of *to be*. The second element so treated is said to be in apposition with the first; it is an appositive. Most appositives are punctuated with commas:

> The report was sent to Professor Austen, the person in charge of the division.
> Milton Everest, an able man, was secretary of state at the time.
> The *Lippincott*, the destroyer attached to the convoy, failed to return.
> Layton was glad to land a job with the *Post*, the largest of the morning papers.

Sometimes, however, the element in apposition is necessary to identify the preceding element: *the novel* Grapes of Wrath, *the year 1942, the element cadmium, the word* receive. In these illustrations of apposition the second element is needed to identify or restrict what is meant by the first. They illustrate restrictive apposition. Restrictive appositives, like restrictive clauses and participial phrases, are not set off with commas.

As was the situation with restrictive and non-restrictive clauses, punctuating either kind of appositive with only one comma is utterly wrong unless it comes at the end of a sentence. In so far as spoken sentences are concerned, non-restrictive appositives are usually set off from the rest of sentences by slight pauses, restrictive appositives are not. Contrast the sound patterns of the following pair of sentences: "Lewis' next novel, *Main Street*, analyzed small-town society," "the novel *Main Street* analyzed small-town society."

EXERCISE

22. Insert commas where they are needed in the following:

(a) Our district representative Mr. E. K. Sullivan will call at your office to explain our company policy.

(b) The good ship *Argo* finally weathered all these perils and brought the heroes home.
(c) The color purple was reserved for the gods.
(d) The prep school in my city Burnside Academy was known nationally.
(e) The regular shortstop of the team Marty Ackerman had been hit by a pitched ball and was out of the lineup.
(f) The star Betelgeuse is reported as the largest in the heavens.
(g) The county seat Warner City was a sprawling prairie town with less than a thousand inhabitants.
(h) The women on the jury Miss Dabney and Mrs. Starritt held out for acquittal.

PN 5 C   *Notice uses of commas in addresses and dates*

His address is 572 Fourth Street, Elmwood, Ohio.
The address of the paper—Herald Square, New York City—became known all over the world.
Manhattan Transfer, Newark, New Jersey, was used by John Dos Passos for the title of one of his books.
Portland, Oregon, was named for Portland, Maine.
Trowbridge in Wiltshire, England, was his birthplace.
His sister died on March 13, 1958, during his senior year in high school.

Notice that the last element given—like the state name following a town or the year after the day of the month—has a comma following it if it is not the last word in the sentence.

EXERCISE

23. Insert commas where they are needed in the following:
(a) On April 12 1873 the party left Fort Plank Nebraska and headed west.
(b) The address of the McKinley Building is 425 Fourth Avenue New York New York.
(c) The people of Moscow Pennsylvania and of Moscow Idaho are usually not called Muscovites.
(d) On July 4 1776 the Declaration of Independence was signed.
(e) A card from a friend in Bergen Norway completed the mail.

Elements without Fixed Position

So far this text has dealt with elements like non-restrictive clauses and phrases, appositives, and states in addresses, which necessarily have material preceding them. Other elements set off with commas are often marked by a certain looseness in position in the sentence. Often they may be placed at one of two or three points in a sentence. Any element that can be placed at two or more places in a sentence is likely to be set off with a comma or commas.

PN 6 A   *Absolutes are set off with commas*

Among such elements without fixed position are absolutes. An absolute is a combination of a modifier, often a non-finite verb, and a substantive that is not used as subject, object, or complement of anything in the sentence. Note the following:

> The whistle having blown, the men laid down their tools and started toward the gates.

In this sentence *having blown* is a non-finite verb, which modifies *whistle. Whistle* is a substantive that is not used as subject, object, or complement of anything in the remainder of the sentence. It is not grammatically related to the remainder of the sentence; it is free of any binding connection. Contrast the absolute construction *the whistle having blown* with the following:

> The bell, having been cracked in moving, has a dull and unmusical sound.

In this sentence there is no absolute, since *bell* is the subject of *has* in addition to being modified by *having been cracked.* Notice that an absolute may be called a non-restrictive modifier, and notice also that an absolute can be placed in a sentence at more than one point:

> The whistle having blown, the men laid down their tools and started toward the gates.
> The men laid down their tools and started toward the gates, the whistle having blown.
> Her rage no longer concealed, Marilyn snatched the letter from his hand.
> Marilyn, her rage no longer concealed, snatched the letter from his hand.
> Marilyn snatched the letter from his hand, her rage no longer concealed.

Notice that there is no comma separating substantive and modifier within an absolute:

At seven o'clock, everything being packed and ready, we started on
our trip.

The patrol boats and cutters, all hope having been given up, abandoned the search and prepared to return to port.

Judd walked rapidly across the pasture, his dog at his heels.

EXERCISE

24. Punctuate the following sentences correctly; supply commas where
they are needed; delete those that have been incorrectly inserted.
Which of the following sentences contain absolutes?

(a) The figures having been rechecked several times the reports of the
laboratory were sent out to the client.

(b) Hammonds asked for an afternoon paper containing the closing
stock market quotations.

(c) The first officer of the ship the captain having been injured in the
accident, ordered her to put back to Melbourne.

(d) The coroner filed a routine and cursory report, the cause of the
death being given as coronary thrombosis.

(e) The Zouaves charged forward their brilliant red coats and accoutre-
ments shining in the sun.

(f) All books relating to international law are kept in the stacks near
the top of the steps.

(g) The doctor having been called there was nothing that they could
do but sit and wait.

(h) The brakes seemed to be working perfectly again, the mechanic,
having put in new brake linings and added fluid.

PN 6 B   *Parenthetical elements are set off with commas*

On the other hand, we had no reason to suspect Simmons.

To come to the point, you do not really want this position.

His attitude was, *to say the least,* uncivil.

In some situations virtue is, *they say,* its own reward.

We will not, *at any rate,* have to spend any more money on repairing
the truck.

This is not, *strictly speaking,* the way that the deed is worded.

You should, *in the first place,* never have endorsed the note.

These italicized expressions are called *parenthetical.* Parenthetical expressions supply minor qualifying information or attitudes. Notice that
a parenthetical expression may have the form of a prepositional phrase,
like *on the other hand,* of a non-finite verb phrase, like *to say the least* or
strictly speaking, or of a clause, like *they say.* Notice that these expres-

sions are in effect non-restrictive modifiers and that they may come at more than one place in their sentences:

> On the other hand, we had no reason to suspect Simmons.
> We had, on the other hand, no reason to suspect Simmons.
> We had no reason, on the other hand, to suspect Simmons.

> In the first place, you should never have endorsed the note.
> You should, in the first place, never have endorsed the note.
> You should never, in the first place, have endorsed the note.
> You should never have endorsed the note, in the first place.

Notice the punctuation of these parenthetical items: when they begin or end sentences, they are usually set off with single commas; when they come in the middle of sentences, they are set off with pairs of commas. Notice that punctuating them with only single commas in the latter situation is wrong; the following sentences are mispunctuated: "we had, on the other hand no reason to suspect Simmons," "we had on the other hand, no reason to suspect Simmons." Like phrases and clauses previously discussed, parenthetical elements within sentences should be punctuated with two commas or with none.

Some conjunctive adverbs serve much as parenthetical elements. Notice the following:

> The orders applied to all personnel; however, the sentry at the gate did not challenge the colonel's party.

Notice that *however* in this sentence has the effect of a parenthetical element and that it could be placed elsewhere within the clause:

> The orders applied to all personnel; the sentry at the gate, however, did not challenge the colonel's party.
> The orders applied to all personnel; the sentry at the gate did not, however, challenge the colonel's party.

Conjunctive adverbs that might be placed at one of a number of different places within a clause are set off with commas. *Commas so used have no connection with, or bearing on, semicolons used to separate independent clauses.*

EXERCISE

25. Punctuate the following sentences correctly; supply commas where they are needed; delete commas that have been incorrectly inserted:

(a) George Washington was for example, a rather aristocratic gentleman.
(b) I didn't really like Professor Miller; nevertheless I elected three courses from him.
(c) We did not, to tell the truth really want Jim to come to the dance.
(d) He was to put it bluntly, a pretty green and uncouth specimen.
(e) We could not in truth have made him very welcome.
(f) The reserve planes had to be sent to Christobal, however badly they were needed at other points.
(g) I had thank goodness, enough money with me to pay the bill.
(h) Carlson could not under these circumstances, refuse to help his friend.

As the wording indicates, parenthetical expressions may also be punctuated with parentheses ( ). Parentheses will be discussed below.

PN 6 C *Elements in series are set off from each other with commas*

The cinnamon, nutmeg, and sugar are added later.
He is also taking French 23, History 112, and Geology 11.
The next day we cut the hay in the morning, windrowed it in the afternoon, and baled some of it in the early evening.
He spoke indistinctly, timidly, and apologetically.
The next steps are packing the cans, sealing them, and labeling them.
Worried about his wife and children, tired from the long day's work, and suffering from a heavy cold, Miller started the long drive home.
Ernest was popular in high school, in college, and in his army unit.

Notice the commas in these sentences. The rule about use of commas with elements in series calls for some explanation of the word *series:* the word here means *three or more*—not just two. Unless the situation is peculiar or complicated, mention of only two elements does not call for using a comma to separate; most persons would object to the punctuation of the following:

The cinnamon, and nutmeg are added later.
He is taking French 23, and History 112.

Notice that there is no comma before the first or after the last of a series that serves as subject, verb, object, or complement in a sentence. The following are mispunctuated:

The cinnamon, nutmeg, and sugar, are added later.
He is taking, French 23, History 112, and Economics 14.

Since placing a comma between the next-to-last and the last of the series is rather formal punctuation, you and your instructor may prefer to omit it and punctuate as follows:

> The cinnamon, nutmeg and sugar are added later.
> He is also taking French 23, History 112 and Geology 11.

Today we think it is futile to insist on the comma between the next-to-last and the last of a series, but notice the following:

> Planes, tanks and guns were urgently needed in Russia, France, and the Philippines.
> Planes, tanks, and guns were urgently needed in Russia, France and the Philippines.

Because the use of both procedures is displeasing, you may find it wise at this point in your education to choose one style or the other and to stick to it always. Retaining the comma between the next-to-last and the last item in the series is here recommended because it sometimes aids clarity of expression:

> The standard recipe for waffles calls for some flour, an egg, a cup of milk and salt.
> The standard recipe for waffles calls for some flour, an egg, a cup of milk, and salt.
> Our schedule includes games with Wake Forest, William and Mary and Washington and Lee.
> Our schedule includes games with Wake Forest, William and Mary, and Washington and Lee.

When there is no coordinating conjunction between the next-to-last and the last in a series, the comma is necessary:

> We need bacon, flour, eggs, sugar, soap.
> We got up at five, ate a quick breakfast, arrived at the lake by six.

EXERCISE

26. Punctuate the following sentences correctly, consistently, and clearly; supply commas where they are needed; delete commas that have been incorrectly inserted:

(a) The college has just opened a new humanities building has under construction a laboratory unit for biological sciences and is about to start a new women's gymnasium.

(b) On the lot there were two old highway department trucks with snow plows an old school bus two old pick-ups and a tractor in good shape.

(c) The middle counties include Latah Nez Perce Clearwater Idaho Salmon River and Adams.

(d) He took a bus to Indianapolis a limousine to the airport there a plane to Denver another limousine from the airport and a train to Leadville.

(e) Geology geography and agronomy were combined into a department composed of Professors Shaw and Anderson Assistant Professor Martin and Instructors Lewis and Dubois.

(f) The structuralists say that an adjective may stand in predicate position shows comparative forms and is likely to end in an adjective suffix.

(g) Ripping off the old wooden shingles repairing the wooden roof below and starting the first line of composition shingles took the whole day.

(h) The half-dollar quarter dime and nickel are our common silver coins.

Adjectives in series before the noun they modify are likely to be separated with commas if their order is not fixed by the demands of English idiom: notice the following:

a rare, colorful, parrot-like bird	a threadbare, tattered dress
a huge, modern, powerful earthmover	an expensive, shiny car

In these phrases the order of the adjective modifiers is not fixed; you can say "a colorful, rare, parrot-like bird" or "a tattered, threadbare dress." Since this is the situation the modifiers are separated by commas. Note the punctuation of the following:

the quivering, battered boat	a madcap, lunatic kid
conservative, well-tailored clothes	a thin, tripping tune
a sane, responsible attitude	her warm, dark presence
in sudden, violent swirls	the soft, uneven cooing

Contrast the following: these fresh Georgia peaches, all patriotic young men, Mr. Wilson's old corner grocery.

In these phrases the order of the adjective modifiers is fixed; you will notice that you would be unlikely to say "Georgia fresh these peaches" or "corner old Mr. Wilson's grocery." When the order of the modifiers is thus fixed, those modifiers are not set off from each other by commas. Note the punctuation of the following:

a normal human being
an important political document
the enormous psychical tension
a strong central government

a sedate young ministerial student
four curious state troopers
a brown leather pocketbook
immense social repercussions

EXERCISE

27. Punctuate the following sentences correctly; supply commas where they are needed and delete them where they have been added incorrectly:

(a) The new, athletic council of the university is composed of younger more vigorous and more tolerant men.

(b) The deserted, old, frame house on the corner will probably be included in the city condemnation proceedings this summer.

(c) The smart new sports cars have attracted a good many buyers tired of the heavy uneconomical standard models.

(d) The track favorite, Bluebelle, was a very fast nervous and unpredictable horse.

(e) All new, editorial copy is gone over by the staff stylist, a keen pert attractive young woman.

Many authors today omit commas between adjective modifiers whose order is reversible. The usage varies on this point, and it is up to you to watch how this construction is punctuated in the future.

So far this section has treated main comma uses. The points not covered are quite minor. Main uses are summarized for your convenience on p. 373. In general you will be following modern practice if you put in commas only when you can find reason for doing so; faced with an uncertain situation, you will be following modern practice if you leave out commas.

Other Punctuation Devices

PN 7 A   *Use parentheses as follows:*

Parentheses ( ) are used to enclose quite non-restrictive or parenthetical material regarded as not very important by the writer; often this material does not fit into the grammatical arrangement of the sentence in question:

> Martin Evans (he was a new instructor) offered a plan for the complete reorganization of the department.

Dr. Carter (then past seventy, but still practicing) took care of her.
Colonel Sims (pronounced to rime with *times*) gave the commencement address at the military academy.

Often material enclosed in parentheses could have been punctuated with dashes:

Martin Evans—he was a new instructor—offered . . .

A writer uses dashes when he wants to emphasize material, parentheses when he wants to deemphasize it. Overuse of parentheses, like overuse of dashes, is displeasing.

PN 7 B   *Use brackets as follows:*

Brackets [   ] are rather unusual marks limited to only one specific use: they are used to punctuate explanatory matter inserted by another person in an excerpt taken from some writer's work. Following is a quotation from C. C. Fries as he wrote it, without brackets:

It is true that very often the "meaning" of the "subject" of a sentence is "performer," but one cannot approach a sentence assuming that whatever Class I word represents the "performer" is for that reason the subject.

Note the use of the brackets around the added explanatory material in the following:

It is true that very often the meaning of the "subject" of a sentence is "performer," but one cannot approach a sentence assuming that whatever Class I word [in Fries' system Class I words are roughly equivalent to nouns in conventional grammar] represents the "performer" is for that reason the subject.

Brackets are, naturally, used rather sparingly.

EXERCISES

28. Supply punctuation as needed in the following sentences. Some sentences may be punctuated with different marks or in different ways; analyze the effect of each possible method of punctuation. Aim at a moderately formal procedure, but add no marks unless you have a reason for doing so:

(a) Parimutuel betting is a form of wagering on horses in which those who bet on the winning horse the place horse or the show horse divide most of the total that has been wagered.

(b) Worried observers on the launch wondered whether the canoe could reach the shore safely.

(c) His eyes had a bland kindly look about them, and his mouth was set in a quiet serene half-smile.

(d) The two main kinds of bait used in trout-fishing are live bait which includes worms minnows and grasshoppers and artificial flies.

(e) Primitive man's great accomplishments included discovering the uses of fire making stone tools and weapons and beginning to domesticate animals.

(f) His wallet contained a driver's license a hunting license and a dog license which he had used and a marriage license which he had not.

(g) In October 1957 the launching of Sputnik I the first Russian satellite started a new age of man the age of space travel.

29. Accompanying each of the following sentences are directions calling for changes in wording. These changes are likely to involve punctuation problems. How should the final forms of these sentences be punctuated?

(a) The leader of the prisoners was a tall man. (Add after *tall* the words *gaunt and haggard.*)

(b) Hanging in the closet were three pairs of work pants and an old suit. (Add after *pants* the words *some old shirts.*)

(c) Miller was not guilty of any crime. (Add after *was* the words *strictly speaking.*)

(d) Clark was a good choice for head of the student council; he was to be editor of the campus paper the next year. (Add before *he* the word *furthermore.*)

(e) A police car came racing down the highway; its sirens were screaming. (Omit the word *were.*)

(f) On May 20 they moved from Canton to Fort Wayne. (Add after *May 20* the year *1959;* add after *Canton* the word *Ohio.*)

(g) The element has an atomic weight of 107.88. (Add after *element* the word *silver.*)

30. Some of the following sentences are incorrectly punctuated. Supply marks that are needed and delete those that are incorrectly added.

(a) William F. Cooke and Sir Charles Wheatstone (for whom the Wheatstone Bridge was named, patented the first, practical telegraph in England in 1837.

(b) McDaniels—who never refused any free food) ate the mint jelly and cream cheese sandwiches.

(c) All these five, desperate criminals were captured without a shot being fired.

(d) A few rich intelligent perceptive men could have checked the rebellion at that point.

(e) Electric motors are used in such domestic appliances as fan blowers connected with heating and ventilating systems sewing machines vacuum cleaners and kitchen mixers.

(f) The *Curaçao*, a Dutch paddlewheeler was the first ship, that crossed the Atlantic without using sails.

(g) We had nothing against Williams; on the other hand none of us especially wanted him to come along.

Kinds of Discourse

When you need to show that some one else has said or written something, you can do so in one of two ways. You can simply state that something has been said or written by another person without, however, bothering to give his exact words, and giving only the general meaning of what he said. In *his adviser said that he should take inorganic chemistry first,* the general meaning of what the adviser said is given, but the exact words that the adviser used were certainly not *that he should take inorganic chemistry first.* Instead they were probably something like *you should take inorganic chemistry first.* In *the editor said that he would make a note about the meeting,* the general meaning of what the editor said is given, but his exact words were not *that he would make a note about the meeting;* his exact words may have been *I will make a note about the meeting.* Sentences in which the general meaning, but not the exact wording, of a speaker or writer is given are called indirect discourse. Direct discourse is explained below.

PN 8 A   *Punctuation of indirect discourse:*

Indirect discourse is usually not punctuated; words in indirect discourse are not separated with commas from *he said* and similar tags, they are not enclosed with quotation marks (". . ."), and their first words are not marked with capital letters:

> Sumner said that he would not support Crosby under any circumstances.
> The mechanic retorted that most machines would work better if they were lubricated occasionally.
> Her cousin wrote that she would be unable to visit her after all.

PN 8 B   *Punctuation of direct discourse:*

In contrast to indirect discourse, direct discourse gives the exact words said by a speaker or written by a writer. In the illustration immediately preceding, the cousin's words were probably something like *I will be unable to visit you after all*. In the one above that, the mechanic's words were probably something like *most machines will work better if they are lubricated occasionally,* and Sumner's exact words were probably *I will not support Crosby under any circumstances,* or perhaps *I would not.* . . . Direct discourse showing the exact words would be punctuated as follows:

> Sumner said, "I will not support Crosby under any circumstances."
> Sumner said, "I would not support Crosby under any circumstances."
> The mechanic retorted, "Most machines will work better if they are lubricated occasionally."
> Her cousin wrote, "I will be unable to visit you after all."

The *he said* (or *asked, answered, replied, wrote*) tag may of course come in the middle of the quotation or at the end, as well as at the beginning:

> "I will not," Sumner said, "support Crosby under any circumstances."
> "Most machines will work better if they are lubricated occasionally," the mechanic retorted.
> "I will not be able to visit you after all," her cousin wrote.

In connection with these illustrations of direct discourse, note the following points:

1. Every word said by the speaker or written by the writer is enclosed in double quotation marks, regardless of where the *he said* tag is placed. Note the incoherent effect of the following:

> "I cannot give you a final report," the assayer said, until I finish all the tests.

Nothing but what the speaker has said or the writer has written should be enclosed in quotation marks; the following is extremely misleading:

> "I think that Mr. Everitt should be on the new pulpit committee, said Mrs. Ferguson."

2. *He said* and similar tags are commonly separated from the exact words of the speaker or writer, enclosed in quotation marks, by a comma or commas:

> The librarian asked, "How long should these books be kept on reserve?"

"I want," my grandfather said, "to see the boy graduate from my own college."

"And may God have mercy on your soul," the judge said solemnly.

Note that whatever the situation is, the order is always first comma, then quotation marks when these punctuation marks are used together.

3. The first words of sentences and similar units in direct discourse are capitalized:

"Paper-bound books and cheap long-playing records are very valuable methods of disseminating culture to the masses," the lecturer said. Simmons said in reply, "Of course! He would do it that way."

EXERCISES

31. Identify each of the following as either indirect or direct discourse. Note the punctuation, which is correct. Then translate each illustration of indirect discourse to correctly punctuated direct discourse, and vice versa.

(a) Ferris asked the air-lines representative what flights he could take to give him a five-hour stop at Atlanta.

(b) Reynolds replied, "Mr. Ewell has always been most considerate to both of us. I do not understand why you dislike him so much."

(c) The referee told captains of both teams that the game was being played too roughly and that he would call personal fouls for the slightest infractions of rules in the future.

(d) The motorcycle cop told Davis that his license had expired and wrote him an additional ticket.

(e) "You should have an X-ray taken of that aching right shoulder," said the doctor to Mrs. Madison.

(f) The personnel manager said that we would have to fill out each of the papers before our application could be considered.

(g) "I like deep-sea fishing," said Kenny, "much more than any one else in my family does."

(h) The department head said that he knew of course that the classroom was inadequate but that there was nothing at all else available at that hour.

(i) "The early polls suggest," said the commentator, "that the western part of the state is safely in the Republican column."

(j) The grocer said that he did not have a case of the fruit in stock but that he could order one for us very quickly.

32. Supply quotation marks, commas, and capital letters needed in the following to punctuate direct discourse; delete those incorrectly or unnecessarily used to punctuate indirect discourse:

(a) The freight agent said "that he could not release the shipment without having a receipted consignment slip.

(b) "Many big leaguers now, said the old manager, couldn't possibly have made the grade twenty years ago."

(c) After looking at the plans, Hildreth said, "Let's employ Andrews at any price; after looking at the finished building he said "that Andrews would have cost too much at a dollar a year."

(d) "We will be very sorry to see Richmond leave our office," the manager wrote, and we hope that he will be very successful in his new position.

(e) The editorial says as follows, Few men have done as much as Dr. Thomas in winning national recognition for the college. He will be sadly missed when he retires in June.

(f) The contract is worded as follows: when the manuscript is ready for publication, it will be published at the Publisher's own expense.

(g) "No," said the income tax adviser, "you cannot charge off veterinarian's bills unless you are in the business of breeding and selling dogs.

(h) Years ago, they say, she was a beautiful, famous, and rather wealthy actress.

(i) The prosecuting attorney asked the druggist, "did the accused ever try to buy strychnine at your store?"

(j) Carter asked whether "he could bring a guest with him to the club."

Punctuation Devices Used with Single Words

Our last group of punctuation marks and similar devices is composed of those commonly used with single words rather than with independent clauses, dependent clauses and phrases, and similar arrangements of words. This group of marks includes apostrophes, hyphens, italics, capital letters, etc.

PN 9 A *Apostrophes are used to show the omission of letters*

An apostrophe is used to show the omission of letters, especially in the blending together of two words to form a contraction. Often in speech we say *isn't* rather than saying the two words *is not*. We omit the *o* of the *not* in this form. When we write this form, we show the omission of the *o* by writing in its place an apostrophe: *isn't*. Similarly with a number of other contractions of *not*: *wasn't, hasn't, hadn't, wouldn't, shouldn't, mayn't, mightn't*, etc. When a verb form, such as a part of *to be*, ends in *e*, like *are, were, have*, the *e* is retained in the written form of the contraction even though the letter is not sounded in speech; note the spelling of *aren't, weren't, haven't*. *Does not* contracts to *doesn't*, and *do not* to *don't*, a plural form acceptable in "they don't" but non-standard with a singular subject in usages like "he don't." *Am not* is one of the origins for the contraction *ain't*, a useful form but one much objected to. With negative contractions in today's English we use only one apostrophe; the contraction of *shall not* is usually written as *shan't*, not *sha'n't*. *Won't* is the contraction of *woll not*, a by-form of *will not*.

Contractions also occur when combinations of pronouns (and nouns) and parts of *to be* and other auxiliaries are spoken quickly. Instead of *you are* and *I will*, we are likely to say *you're* and *I'll*. The apostrophe is used to indicate the omission of the letters in the written form:

I am	I'm	I have	I've	I will	I'll
you are	you're	you have	you've	you will	you'll
he is	he's	he has	he's	he will	he'll
she is	she's	she has	she's	she will	she'll
it is	it's	it has	it's		
we are	we're	we have	we've	we will	we'll
they are	they're	they have	they've	they will	they'll

The contraction of *it will* sometimes occurs in speech but is rarely written. Notice that three of these contractions sound about the same as possessive personal pronouns: *it's, you're, they're*. Notice that these contractions are written with apostrophes and notice also that the possessive forms that sound about the same are *not* written with apostrophes: *its, your, their*. Notice the difference in the forms used in the following:

> It's too late to change things now.
> The puppy was licking its paw.
>
> You're supposed to be at the meeting in Old Main now.
> Will you let me use your car tonight?
>
> They're not at home now.
> Their house will be for rent during the next year.

Contractions involving nouns and parts of *to be* and other auxiliaries follow the same principles; note the following:

> Mary's not ready. Raymond's been expelled from school.
> Ruth's a sophomore. Dorothy's received the letter by now.

Contractions are informal. Sometimes even the most common ones, like *I'm, she's, we'll,* are objected to in formal writing. Less common forms—even though many of them occur in almost everyone's speech—are even more likely to be objected to, and you had better not write "the dean'll excuse the absence" or "the players'll take special buses," even though, along with most other people, you *say* forms like these.

PN 9 B   *Apostrophes are used to punctuate possessives of nouns but not of personal pronouns*

Possessive forms are dealt with above (see pp. 261, 273) but are briefly summarized here for your convenience:

1. To form an ordinary possessive singular of a noun add an apostrophe and then -*s: this student's grade, this mechanic's work, this cow's horns, Paul's decision, England's navy.* Do not alter a final *y* on a noun to form a possessive singular: *this lady's hat, the baby's formula, the country's resources.* If the singular form ends in *s,* you may form the possessive either with or without adding another *s: Charles'* or *Charles's, Tompkins'* or *Tompkins's.* Many pronouns follow nouns in forming regular singular possessives: *somebody's, anyone's, everyone's.* But, on the other hand, possessives of personal pronouns do not take apostrophes: *my, mine, your, yours, his, her, hers, its, our, ours, their, theirs. Whose,* the possessive of *who,* likewise has no apostrophe. The forms *it's, you're, they're,* and *who's* are contractions.

2. To form the possessive plural, first find the usual plural form and then add an apostrophe: *the farmers' trucks, the soldiers' uniforms, the drivers' union.* Note the possessive plurals of words ending in -*y: ladies' hats, babies' clothes, the puppies' food, these countries' peoples.* Some plurals in English do not end in -*s.* For them, you find the usual plural form, add an apostrophe, and then add an -*s.* Note the following possessive plurals: *the men's demands, children's shoes, women's affairs, the salesmen's cars.* Forms like *deer's* (as in "the deer's tracks") or *sheep's* (as in "the sheep's wool") may be either singular or plural possessives.

The apostrophe is usually used in the writing of the plurals of letters, numbers, symbols, and words mentioned as words:

> The word *accommodate* has two *m's.*
> The proper name *Merritt* is usually spelled with two *r's* and two *t's.*
> The broken faces of the *8's* permitted the police to identify the typewriter promptly.

B-29's were used in bombing Japanese cities.
Commercial writing is likely to overuse *&'s*.
There are seven *that's* in this short sentence.

EXERCISES

33. Form contractions for the following. Insert apostrophes at the right places: *does not, we had, dare not, they will, can not, you are, do not, who is, John is, we have, should not, ought not, Ruth is, have not, could not, they are.*

34. Scan the pages in a contemporary novel that often attempts to represent conversation. Note the number of contractions used. Do the same for a more formally written book, a history text, for instance. Compare the results. Notice the actual speech of persons around you. To what extent do they say clearly the word *not* and the auxiliary verbs like parts of *to be* and *to have?*

35. Form possessive singulars of the following words: *navy, clerk, man, teacher, city, county, jockey, assistant, tailor, child, lady, horse, fish.* Form possessive plurals of the same words. Form possessives of the following proper names: *Jenny, Roberts, Samuels, Evans, Tommy, Wesley, Jones, Farley, Peters, Lucy.*

36. Supply apostrophes where they have been omitted in the following; delete those unnecessarily added; and change the position of those inserted in the wrong places:

   (a) The city's central schools are not serving childrens' lunches this year.
   (b) Perhaps Dickens novel's shouldn't be judged by the standards of modern fiction.
   (c) The different lawyer's comments left Jenning's more confused than before.
   (d) Lord and Kellys store is having a sale of lady's hats.
   (e) Illinois Governor Stevenson was President Trumans choice as Democratic candidate.
   (f) The Tiger's pitching staff wasn't very good that year.
   (g) Professors' don't seem to be able to write more than three pages' without using several *howevers*.
   (h) Winters has two of the Ivor-Johnson Companys old .32s.

PN 9 C *Hyphens are used as follows:*

The following mark is a hyphen: -. Notice that the hyphen is only half the length of the dash: —. By far the most common use of the hyphen is to show the division of a word broken at the end of a line because there is not enough space left to accommodate it. Divide words only when you must, not when you might. In general, American practice, as recommended in dictionaries, is to divide words so that a preceding syllable is likely to end in a vowel, a following one to begin with a consonant: *fa-vor, rea-son, no-ti-fy,* but there are many exceptions to this. Do not attempt to divide words so that a single letter stands on one line. Do *not* divide words as the following are divided:

a-	o-	i-	e-	u-	are-	radi-	rode-	read-
bout	ver	dea	ver	pon	a	i	o	y

Do not divide words so that a consonant or group of consonants appears without a vowel on one line, like the following:

leng-	twi-	nex-	hur-	pea-	wi-	spu-
th	st	t	l	ch	sh	rn

Do not attempt to divide monosyllables like *ask, rest, strength, damn, light, tack, church, wrest.* Forms like *called, turned, stopped, missed, walked, reached* are regarded as monosyllabic forms, despite their spelling, and are usually not divided. Try to divide words in accordance with their component parts, like prefixes and suffixes.

EXERCISES

37. Check the syllabic divisions used at the ends of lines in this book.

38. See pp. 382–383. With the aid of your dictionary find how the following words are divided into syllables:

abandon	dissipation	lexical	revolution
angular	enthusiastic	matriculate	seminary
barricade	figurative	multiply	solidarity
bravery	generation	omission	testament
certainty	harmonious	persecute	structural
concentrate	imitation	precipitate	tuberculous
cynical	investigation	radicalism	verbalize

Hyphens are sometimes used in writing various compound words. (As here used, the term *compound word* means a word made up by combining two or more other words: *self-satisfied, fireproof, dry-clean, football, handwrought, warm-blooded, heat-treat, whereas.*) Unfortunately it is impossible to give you definite, clear-cut principles about when to use hyphens and when not to use them with compound words. Usage varies widely. The best advice that can be given you is to consult a recognized, reputable dictionary.

EXERCISE

39. According to your dictionary, are the following combinations printed with hyphens or not?

air base	bird seed	call boy	country dance
air borne	birth control	canvas back	day coach
all clear	block signal	cat boat	dill pickle
atom bomb	blue blooded	check off	down hill
back bone	blue green	city state	dust bowl
bank account	book review	color guard	even minded
beech nut	brown bread	comic section	fancy dress

In general today there is less tendency to hyphenate noun compounds than there once was; there is apparently a tendency to prefer to write compounds solidly as one word (*football, footwear*) or as two words (*foot brake, foot rot*) rather than with hyphens. Compounds definitely stressed on the first element are likely to be written solid: *cloudburst, cookbook, corncrib, cowboy, crossbar, earthquake, battleship.* Combinations that show more even stress, without reducing the second element, are likely to be written as separate words.

Hyphens are used in noun compounds to suggest recent formation (*mock-up*), in compound numerals (*thirty-one, seventy-eight*), in compounds of nouns to mean a person or thing that is both items mentioned (*owner-manager, secretary-treasurer*), in compounds in which the first elements ends in *-er* (*runner-up, higher-ups*), and in compounds beginning with *self* (*self-esteem, self-reliance*). Other parts of speech—except adjective units—are likely to accord with nouns in so far as hyphening is concerned.

Use of the hyphen in compound adjective phrases is common:

a first-rate man	a stone-paved patio
a twelve-inch rule	a jet-propelled car
a single-action gun	an ever-present danger
warm-blooded animals	an ill-timed suggestion
a blonde-haired girl	a spliced-together rope
a broad-shouldered man	warmed-over dinners
a yard-wide margin	a low-lying area
a rust-resistant alloy	a high-pitched voice
a fever-ridden area	blue-black ink

Note that many of these compound adjective forms would *not* be written with hyphens if they were used as predicate adjectives, not as attributive adjectives (that is, as adjectives coming before the nouns that they modify):

people who are well educated	well-educated people
people who were grown up	grown-up people
a figure that was half shabby	a half-shabby figure
a tribute that was well deserved	a well-deserved tribute
the teams were well matched	well-matched teams

The hyphen is often used to prevent misreading or make reading easier and quicker: *re-enlist, re-creation* (contrast *recreation*), *anti-imperial, re-address, pre-election, semi-independent, co-worker, un-American, anti-British, pre-Silurian, pro-Churchill.*

EXERCISE

40. Insert and delete hyphens in the following sentences:

(a) After a six-week period, the newly-arrived men are given reinoculation shots.

(b) His seventeen year old high school friends were never tired of his stories of his older brother, now an all American halfback.

(c) For the rookies, playing a responsible part in fighting a five alarm fire was a never to be forgotten experience.

(d) Never-the-less some of these queries are taken care of in a series of well-planned foot-notes.

(e) The Indian delegation, along with other proRussian groups, voted against the seven point program.

(f) A fast-flying snowball thrown by one of the grade school urchins ruined both his new pearl gray hat and his sense of selfpossession.

(g) The publicity minded store-keeper decided on a sales-program involving loss-leader items, throw-aways, and full-page news-paper ads.

(h) Even if you live in a onehorse, out-of-the-way town, it is hard not to be agitated about the ever present possibility of air-raids with atom-bombs.

PN 9 D *Capital letters are used as follows:*

Like other punctuation practices, use of capital letters varies from period to period. During the twentieth century there has been a tendency to decrease rather than increase the use of capitals, and some expressions are now written or printed in small or lower-case letters that once would have been printed or written with capitals. In doubtful situations it is better to use small letters than capitals.

A proper noun is traditionally defined as a noun meaning only one particular person, place, or thing (Woodrow Wilson, Cincinnati, *the Lusitania*). Most proper nouns are not preceded by articles. Proper nouns and adjectives derived from them begin with capital letters:

William F. Gilman	Hoover Dam
Mary Dexter	the Empire State Building
George Washington	Long Island Sound
Henry VIII	Lake Superior
Black Beauty	the Colorado River
Frenchman	Williams County
Chinese	Philadelphia
Methodist	Smithport
Catholic	Chesapeake Bay
The American Medical Association	Mount Rainier
Aetna Insurance Company	Sunday
Western Union	January
Tulane University	Christmas
Memorial Hospital	the Franco-Prussian War
Hotel McAlpin	S. S. *Windsor Castle*
The New York Times	*Othello*
the Chicago Cubs	*Il Trovatore*

The first word of every sentence, the pronoun *I* and the important words in titles (*Three Keys to Language, Language in Thought and Action*) are capitalized. It would be possible to give rule after rule and classification after classification about the use of capitals, but the following negative cautions and explanations of doubtful situations may solve most of the problems that you face in writing that you are now doing.

1. Nouns indicating family relationships are not capitalized when they are used with possessive adjectives or with articles:

My father works in a bank.
The mother was given psychiatric care.

Nouns indicating family relationships may be capitalized when they are used without articles or pronouns or when they are used with names.

Just after the war Father got another position.
My Aunt Julia lives in Kansas.

2. Although words indicating days, holidays, and months are capitalized (*Thursday, Labor Day, March*), names for the seasons (*spring, summer, fall, autumn, winter*) are usually not capitalized:

> That summer I visited in Wyoming.
> The winter was unusually severe.

3. Do not capitalize the direction words *north, east, south,* and *west,* and their derivatives, unless these words refer to definite sections of the United States or the world.

> We drove south to Mt. Jackson.
> The east wind was piling up drifts along the roads.
> The captain ordered a north-north-west course.
> The West was opened up and settled rapidly after 1840.
> There is considerable Republican strength in the Southwest.
> Japan and China are the dominant powers in the Far East.

4. Do not capitalize the words *freshman, sophomore, junior,* and *senior* in ordinary uses:

> He is a junior at Notre Dame.
> During my freshman year I was often homesick.

Expressions like *Freshman Week* and *the Junior Prom* are capitalized.

5. In general, do not capitalize the names for academic subjects:

> He is majoring in history.
> He took a course in abnormal psychology.
> Geography and geology will be combined into one department.

When proper nouns or proper adjectives designate academic subjects, they are capitalized: *studying French and German, English history courses, Greek literature, a course in European governments.* Official catalogue course designations are likely to be capitalized:

> Although I was pretty good in chemistry, I almost flunked Chemistry 37.
> You ought really to have a course in English history and one in Victorian poetry. I'd recommend History 122 and English 58.
> Dr. Colter's course, the History of the Industrial Revolution, will not be given next semester.

Official names of departments, schools, branches, and bureaus should be capitalized: the Department of Economics, the Graduate School of Arts and Sciences, the Bureau of Entomology.

6. In general, do not capitalize names for titles, ranks and positions unless there is a proper name accompanying. Do not capitalize *doctor, professor, secretary, president, captain, commander, chief, superintendent, judge,* etc., as used thus:

> The doctor arrived in about a half an hour.
> In 1959 he retired as professor of sociology.
> The class elected Jim secretary.
> The building superintendent said that the office was locked.

Capitalize these words when there is a proper name accompanying:

Doctor Clements	Corporal Franks
Chief of Police Emery	Director Graham
Professor Daniels	Judge Harland
Treasurer Ingraham	Marshal Jackson

A limited few title words expressing great dignity may be freely capitalized: *President* (of the United States), *Vice President, Chief Justice* (of the Supreme Court), *Secretary of State.* But *judge, senator, representative, chairman, commissioner,* etc., are usually not capitalized.

7. Do not capitalize the words *school, high school, college, university, institute,* etc., unless the specific name of the institution accompanies:

attended school in Portland	the Portland Public Schools
my high-school days	at the Westmont High School
going to college	going to Ursinus College
university athletics	the University of Iowa team

8. In doubtful situations consult your dictionary. Many words start out as proper nouns and adjectives and become common nouns and adjectives later. Italic type was once closely associated with Italian printing, and the adjective was first written with a capital (*Italic*). Now, however, it has become commonized and is written with lower-case letters. A number of other words have undergone similar commonizing: *china, jersey, guillotine, derringer, derby.* But this process of commonizing takes a very appreciable period of time, and during that period there may be uncertainty about capitalization of lack of it. In today's world should you write *diesel* or *Diesel? victrola* or *Victrola?* In such situations use your dictionary. (See p. 381.)

EXERCISE

41. Which of the following are capitalized? Which are printed lower-case? Which are written either way? What preferences does your dictionary show?

graham crackers	a caesarean section	the reaumur scale
crepe de chine	duncan phyfe furniture	bodoni type
the caucasian race	roentgen rays	cayenne pepper
drinking benedictine	a bowie knife	a stuka
an irish setter	a doberman dog	cape cod cottage
a homeric style	french dressing	zero fahrenheit

42. Change lower-case letters to capitals where necessary in the following:

(a) On tuesday, march 16, professor everitt of the department of history here and the visiting professor from the university of winnemac will both talk to the international affairs club.

(b) That winter my father and my uncle edwin took me with them on their hunting trip in northern michigan.

(c) During my senior year in high school i took courses in english, french, political science, and history.

(d) The sheriff was driving west on route 36 at the time; he was following a new gray ford station wagon with kansas plates.

(e) Some of the eighteenth-century democratic notions of european thinkers considerably influenced the framing of the united states constitution.

(f) Senator marshall of alaska joined the bloc of republicans in opposing the president's views on general foreign policy and on the singapore commitments.

(g) During the fall of that year—in mid-october, to be more exact—i went to a u.s. navy boot camp in maryland.

(h) The section on minor parties in ferguson's book, *american political parties*, gives a good account of the dissolution of the american socialist party.

43. Following are a number of sentences. Each is accompanied by directions calling for the addition of certain words. Making these additions is likely to call for changes in capitalization or lower-casing. Make these changes.

(a) Just as Father had done thirty years before, I took a general preparatory course in high school. (Before *Father* add the word *my;* before *high school* add the word *Oakmont.*)

(b) The orderlies at the hospital had especial reason to be timid in the presence of doctors. (Before *hospital* add the words *West Side;* after *doctors* add the words *Smith and Jenkins.*)

(c) During the winter he quit the job with the railroad and started to work for the construction company building the bridge. (Before *railroad* add the word *Pennsylvania;* before *construction company* add the word *Weston;* before *bridge* add the words *Fourth Street.*)

(d) After graduating from Colver College, he started graduate work at Ohio State University. (Omit the word *Colver;* change *Ohio* to *the.*)

(e) The Democrats elected Governors Maddox and Miller in Indiana and Illinois and senators in Illinois and Iowa. (Omit the names *Maddox and Miller;* add after *senators* the names *Green and May-berry.*)

(f) That semester I was taking biology, organic chemistry, vector analysis, and history. (After *biology* insert the number *14;* indicate that *vector analysis* is the catalogue designation of a mathematics course; add *English* before *history.*)

(g) My Uncle Joe, who had just retired as president of the Mason Lumber Company in St. Louis, was to visit us over the weekend. (Omit *Joe;* change *the* to *a* and omit *Mason;* add *Labor Day* before *week-end.*)

(h) The office of the doctor is located in an old house at the foot of the main street. (Omit the second *the* and add *Thomas* after *doctor;* omit the last *the.*)

PN 9 E   *Italics have three main uses*

The most common printed letters are those in roman type. This sentence is printed in roman type. In addition to roman, another type, italic, is used possibly 3 per cent of the time. Italic type shows more slanting and less full-bodiedness than roman type. *This sentence is printed in italic type.* To show italics in writing on a typewriter or in writing by hand, underline once.

Italics have had various uses in the past, and in special situations they have various uses today. What follows here is by no means a complete resumé of all these uses; instead, this book presents only a negative caution about italics and gives three main uses for them. A style book or a section on punctuation at the beginning of your dictionary may give you other uses for italics.

In general, do not attempt to use italics for emphasis. True, today's professional writers occasionally do use italics to emphasize. You can find sentences like the following: "he *was* hardheaded, practical, clear-cut, and he *did* possess an infinite genius for details" (Nathan Schachner). The author is here stressing the truth of the over-all comment. But use of italics in the following sentences is immature and unsatisfactory: "Mr. Williams was guilty of *murder*," "we had the most *thrilling* time," "we were *champions* of the Big Valley Conference," "the suit was *simply* charming."

Although there are other acceptable ways of writing titles, titles of full-length works, those that may be printed as books themselves (rather than titles of shorter poems, short stories, and single essays) are likely to be put into italics, as also are titles of newspapers, magazines, longer musical compositions, and works of art, and often names of ships and airplanes: *The Return of the Native, For Whom the Bell Tolls, The New York Times, The Saturday Evening Post,* Verdi's *Il Trovatore,* the sinking of the *Titanic.*

Sometimes the distinction between italic for titles and ordinary roman is quite meaningful:

> Shakespeare's *Hamlet* often seems melodramatic.
> Shakespeare's Hamlet often seems confused and indecisive.

(Punctuation of titles of shorter works, with quotation marks, will be dealt with below.)

English has borrowed a number of words and phrases from foreign languages. When these words and phrases are felt to be completely part of the English language, they are printed in ordinary roman type. When, however, they are still thought of as being foreign, they are often printed in italics. Notice here that the wording "are still thought of" is quite subjective; it is often difficult to tell when a word is "still thought of" as foreign rather than English. The only thing to do is to consult your dictionary (noticing, as p. 384 indicates, that different dictionaries treat this matter differently). You will probably find that your dictionary regards *bona fide, dilettante,* and *resumé* as fully naturalized into English, but *comme il faut, fait accompli,* and *ante meridien* as foreign words.

EXERCISE

44. With the aid of your dictionary, discover whether each of the following is written in italic or roman type:

> sang-froid, status quo, enfant terrible, beau geste, ad valorum, viva voce, nisi, bourgeoisie, prima facie, attaché, quasi, sauté, faux pas, élan, de facto, hors de combat, coup d'état, ensemble, in medias res, ante bellum.

Notice the sentence "the word *receive* is spelled with the *e* before the *i.*" In this sentence the combination of letters r-e-c-e-i-v-e designates the word itself, with no regard for its meaning, and *e* and *i* designate the letters. In cases like this italics are used:

> *Rage* and *fury* were borrowed from French and Latin respectively.
> In the preceding sentence the word *respectively* is satisfactorily used.
> Academic writing often has too many *however*'s.
> His *7*'s look remarkably like *9*'s.

PN 9 F *Quotation marks have various secondary uses*

As we saw earlier, the main use of quotation marks is to punctuate direct discourse, to show that the words enclosed are the exact words of speaker or writer. In addition to this main use, quotation marks may be used to enclose titles of shorter works, often of works unlikely to be printed by themselves in full book form:

> He read Sandburg's "Fog" and "Chicago" in Evans' *Twentieth Century American Poetry.*
> "Smoke Gets in your Eyes" was the hit number in the review called *Roberta.*
> Brown and Spencer's collection entitled *Exposition and Persuasion* contains a selection called "Change in Science Means Social Change" from Waldemar Kaempffert's book *Explorations in Science.*

Quotation marks may enclose meanings of words under consideration:

> The accent is on the first syllable of *gallant* when it means "brave," but it is often on the second when it means "given to showy courtesies to ladies."
> Many people still object to the use of the verb *aggravate* with the meaning of "vex, irritate, annoy."

Once in a while a writer finds it necessary or effective to use a word in a new or unusual sense, or to indicate that others use a word in an odd, new way. In these circumstances the word in question may be enclosed in quotation marks:

> Childbirth, whether it is "natural"; i.e., follows the rules invented by Dr. Read for participating in the delivery, as millions of women had done before the development of obstetrics, or whether it is more completely managed by the doctor with the aid of anesthetics . . .
> Tea is what Dichter calls a "prejudiced" product, as are prunes, and cigarette holders for men. There is something about these products that gives many consumers the creeps. Tea, for example, carries the stigma of effeminacy and feebleness.

Sometimes slang and other informal expressions are enclosed in quotation marks when the general style of the writing is more-or-less formal; note the following sentence from Thornton Wilder:

> They do not fling themselves into causes; they are not easily moved to enthusiasms; the expression on their faces is impassive, is "dead pan."

EXERCISE

45. Underline for italics and insert quotation marks where necessary or desirable in the following sentences:

(a) When the lion cubs reach the age of ten or twelve months, they become noisy, active, and mischievous. Often these teen-agers disrupt the peace of the whole pride of lions.

(b) The report dealt with ramifications of the meaning of the phrase academic freedom. It took exception to the trustees' interpretation of the words detrimental to the university.

(c) The phrase honi soit qui mal y pense may be translated as meaning let evil come or accrue to him who thinks it.

(d) As used among today's grammarians the word structure seems difficult to define precisely.

(e) Chapter 7, entitled The Aftermath of the War, had been assigned for Thursday.

(f) The character Tom Jones in Fielding's novel of the same name is one of the most likable young men in English fiction.

(g) To the chagrin of the Navy the mighty battleship Missouri was stuck for nearly a week on a sandbar in Chesapeake Bay.

(h) After one trip to the laundry, the unshrinkable shirts that he bought for a dollar apiece were three sizes smaller.

PN 9 G   *Abbreviations are customarily punctuated with periods*

Mr. Bennett	Jan. 15, 1960	Fannin & Co.
Dr. Evans	the Dennett Bldg.	Ralph Gannett, Jr.
St. Louis, Mo.	Iowa Ave.	Mt. Everest

Many writers and some publishers like to dispense with periods after abbreviations; periods are not used in some situations in which they might be (abbreviations of governmental agencies and military organizations, for instance: *FCC, ICC, FBI, SAC;* and names of radio and television stations: *WJZ, KDKA*); and it may well be that after a while most abbreviations will be written without periods. At this time, however, you had better continue to use them.

In ordinary writing you can usually use abbreviations with proper names, as in *Mr. Walker; Dr. Eldridge; Col. Stephens; Frank Dailey, Sr.; Norman Woods, Ph.D.* But there is likely to be objection to the use in ordinary writing of other abbreviations, especially to those for given names (*Chas.* for *Charles*), names of countries and states (*Gr. Brit., Nebr.*), names of months and days of the week (*Nov., Wed.*), and common words easily written (*co.* for *company, chap.* for *chapter, oz.* for *ounces, ft.* for *feet, ave.* for *avenue, dep.* for *department, frt.* for *freight, govt.* for *government*). University speech contains many shortened forms like *lab, prof, ag, chem, econ, gym, soph,* etc. These shortened forms are usually felt to be too informal in most writing. Treating them as abbreviations and putting periods after them does not change this feeling.

EXERCISE

46. The following sentences show a number of abbreviated forms. Which are inappropriate in ordinary writing, formal or informal?

(a) The ad men's convention will be held in Chi. during the first week of Feb.

(b) A young hist. instr. may expect his students to read a doz. vols. throughout the sem.

(c) Mr. and Mrs. Marshall have moved out of Wisc. to Ill., and consequently their sons at the col. should be charged out-of-state tuition rates.

(d) The firing of the econ. prof. at the local univ. was being investigated by the Amer. Assoc. of Univ. Profs.

(e) Dr. Norman, the dr. in charge of the cardiac div., pronounced Thos. Smiley dead after he failed to recover from the 2nd shock.

(f) Fed. banking laws prohibit nat. banks from considering 5-yr. mortgage arrangements.

(g) The grocery bill for twenty-three dollars and fifty-eight cts. itemized six lbs. of coffee and nine qts. of milk among other things.

(h) The understanding between Col. Nelson and the construction co. doing the work was that the barracks would be finished by Oct.

PN 9 H   *Numbers are treated as follows:*

In ordinary writing do not use numbers for sums, amounts, or quantities that can be expressed in a few words:

> NOT: He is 17 years old. I have 12 dollars with me. I bought 10 pounds of sugar. The college is over 100 years old. I saw him 9 weeks later. I am carrying 21 credits.
>
> INSTEAD: He is seventeen years old. I have twelve dollars with me. I bought ten pounds of sugar. The college is over a hundred years old. I saw him nine weeks later. I am carrying twenty-one credits.

Use numbers for sums, amounts, or quantities that cannot be expressed easily in a few words:

The ratio is 3.1416
The population figure is 517,683.
My telephone number is El Dorado 8–5546.
The literacy rate for this area is 96.16.
The oil bill was $137.68.
The hole is 2.78 inches from the center.

Use arabic numbers for addresses, room numbers, page and chapter references: 375 Broadway; the paragraphs on pages 47, 48, and 53. Use Arabic numbers for dates: March 21, 1915; January 3, 1960.

Whenever you can, avoid beginning a sentence with an Arabic number:

NOT: 1603 is the date for Queen Elizabeth's death.
$57.22 was left in the checking account.
3.92 is the record for the mile.

Any revision is preferred:

Queen Elizabeth died in 1603.
The sum of $57.22 was left in the checking account.
The record for the mile is 3.92.

EXERCISES

47. Wherever necessary, revise the procedure of expressing numbers in the following sentences:

(a) After three hours the patient's temperature had gone down to one hundred and one and three fifths.
(b) After we had waited 2 hours and 30 minutes, flight 182 finally came in.
(c) There are one hundred and twenty eight students in the lecture session of Economics one hundred and fifty eight.
(d) The 500 unsold copies of the novel were remaindered at 35 cts. apiece.
(e) Wood's hand was a flat bust: the 2 and 8 of spades, the 10 of hearts, and 3 and 6 of diamonds.
(f) She died at the age of 78 on May fifteenth, nineteen fifty two.
(g) A. & M. kept its 6-point lead until the end of the 3rd quarter.
(h) 500,000 dollars was lost by the insurance company on account of the storm.

48. The following sentences show a variety of poor choices of punctuation involving apostrophes, hyphens, capitals, and italics, quotation marks, and in use of abbreviations and numbers. Suggest whatever changes are preferable.

(a) Dr. Evans' was enjoying a well earned 6-weeks vacation in Fla. during Jan. and Feb.

(b) Keat's sonnet called *On First Looking into Chapmans' Homer* has always been a highly regarded product; it's literary position seems assured.

(c) My mother went to College at Wellesley; she graduated in the class of nineteen twenty one.

(d) Several of Roberts' novels, like "Northwest Passage" and "Arundel," use archaic sounding and old fashioned words like "astonied" and "fair" as an adverb.

(e) Tom's half grown Kerry Blue terrier was taken to the vet's; the sore on it's left front leg wasn't healing properly.

(f) Washington's and Lincoln's Birth-days were Holidays in some of the states.

(g) 1956 was a difficult year for the Ferris company, since it underwent a 12-percent decrease in total sales' that year.

(h) Nelly's attempts to sell mens' neck-ties at the Grant brothers store were'nt very successful.

(i) James Joyces' novel "Ulysses" was attacked by many self appointed custodians of public "morality."

(j) The more sane and level headed members of King Charles staff were'nt optimistic about his chance's of winning the battle of Zemstov.

PN 10   *Punctuation marks together; minor uses*

Sometimes there are confusions and uncertainties when two punctuation marks or devices come together. Many students—and also many other people—are baffled about which mark comes first. The following section tries to explain some of the more common problems.

Quotation Marks

Probably quotation marks cause the greatest uncertainty. Before anything else, notice that quotation marks *never* go directly above any other mark of punctuation, whatever it is. Do not write quotation marks above other marks. Do *not* punctuate as the following are punctuated:

> The stuttering umpire was trying to say "out", but he found that he could say "safe" more readily.
>
> Miller answered at once, "Not on your life".

It is a fair statement of general American practice to say that, whatever the situation, the order is always comma-quotation mark and always period-quotation mark:

The mayor simply said, "No comment," and then he asked the reporters to leave.

The prisoner said very solemnly, "Again I swear before God that I am innocent," but the jury refused to believe him.

"The trouble," the mechanic said, "is evidently in the transmission."

The meaning expressed by a sentence determines whether quotation marks come before or after question mark or exclamation point. If the whole sentence is a question or an exclamation and happens to end with an element in quotation marks, then the question mark or exclamation mark comes last, outside the quotation marks:

The bride's answer to the question about obeying her husband was "no"!

Wasn't this letter to me marked "strictly personal and private"?

If on the other hand the whole sentence simply states a fact and ends with a quoted question or exclamation—if the quotation itself is a question or exclamation—then the question mark or exclamation point comes first, with the quotation marks outside and following:

The tabloid headline was composed of just one word, "War!"

The instructor stopped and asked, "Have you any questions on diminutive alliteration?"

Parentheses

Sometimes there is uncertainty about which comes first, the closing parenthesis—that is,)—or comma, period, question mark, and so on. In general, if the element within parentheses or brackets is a complete sentence, the period or question mark accompanying that sentence comes inside—not outside—the closing parenthesis or bracket:

The next three pages of the diary were illegible. (They were later deciphered but contained no information of value.)

If on the other hand the element within the parentheses is not a complete sentence, the period or question mark comes outside the closing parenthesis:

The matter of the claim was referred to Samuel Ewarts (then in charge of Indian affairs in the territory).

The reserves were stationed at St. Angelina (about twelve miles away).

Question Marks

Very occasionally you will find a question mark enclosed in parentheses to indicate doubt about the comment made:

> The party left Fort Slocum in February (?) and traveled up the Little Bear River.

Colons

The colon may be used to formally introduce a quotation of some length. The quotation after the colon may be enclosed in quotation marks if it is not printed with special indentation.

> Sledd criticized the old definitions as follows: "Hard as the statement may seem, the traditional definitions do not enable us to classify our words as belonging to one part of speech rather than another. For one thing, definitions like that of the noun are in terms of meaning, while others, like that of the pronoun, are in terms of function or use."

Naturally, in a situation like this the quotation marks follow the colon. Many people would prefer to treat this situation by omission of quotation marks and use of special indentation for the quoted passage:

> Sledd criticized the old definitions as follows:
>
> > Hard as the statement may seem, the traditional definitions do not enable us to classify our words as belonging to one part of speech rather than another. For one thing, definitions like that of the noun are in terms of meaning, while others, like that of the pronoun are in terms of function or use.

The usual procedure is not to capitalize the first word after a colon preceding an explanatory series, unless of course that word is a proper noun:

> They were worried about three uncertainties: whether the radio message had been picked up, whether the rescue party could reach them, and whether the captain could live another twenty-four hours.

Periods

Use of periods with other marks has been discussed above. Sometimes three periods are used as "ellipsis points," marks of punctuation to indicate ellipsis or omission. Suppose you wish to quote part but not all of the following sentence from Ruth Benedict:

> The "great man" theory of history had a spectacular development in the hands of Carlyle and is now generally held to be either inadequate or naïve.

You might quote it with three periods indicating the omission of some words:

> The "great man" theory of history . . . is now generally held to be either inadequate or naïve.

EXERCISE

49. The following sentences show a variety of situations in which marks of punctuation come together. Correct those that need correction:

(a) All the blame for the accident was finally placed on the shoulders of Mr. King (who had conveniently died before the investigation.)
(b) Was tomorrow's weather prediction the usual "fair and warmer?"
(c) The letter of recommendation effectively ruined his chances by saying that he was "usually cooperative".
(d) "Most of the new buildings", said the president; "will be ready for occupancy in the fall".
(e) He talked for an hour about his various problems (most of them more imaginary than real.)
(f) The woman kept crying, "Help, help, I'm poisoned"!
(g) "Can we really make this attempt", the lecturer asked, "to feed and clothe the whole world"?
(h) The Braves and Dodgers played the longest game ever, a twenty-six inning tie finally halted by darkness. (Major-league parks were not lighted in those days).

SUMMARY OF MAIN PUNCTUATION USES

Period .		
	1. Use a period at the end of a sentence expressing a fact or giving a command.	Pn 1 A
	2. In general, use a period to punctuate an abbreviation.	Pn 9 G
	3. Three periods may be used for ellipsis marks.	Pn 10

Do not use periods to set off dependent elements.

Question mark ?	Use a question mark at the end of each sentence that asks a question.	Pn 1 B
	Do not use a question mark after a sentence that indicates that a question has been asked.	
Exclamation mark !	An exclamation mark may be used after a sentence or sentence equivalent to show strong emotion.	Pn 1 C
	Do not overuse exclamation points.	
Semicolon ;	1. Use a semicolon between two independent clauses that are not joined by a coordinating conjunction.	Pn 2 A
	2. Use a semicolon between two independent clauses joined by a conjunctive adverb.	Pn 2 B
	3. A semicolon may be used between long and complicated independent clauses joined by a coordinating conjunction.	Pn 2 D
Comma ,	1. Use a comma between two independent clauses joined by a coordinating conjunction.	Pn 2 C
	2. Use a comma to prevent misreading.	Pn 3
	3. Use a comma to set off a long and complicated introductory element, or an introductory element containing a non-finite verb form.	Pn 4
	4. Use a comma or commas to punctuate a non-restrictive clause or phrase.	Pn 5 A
	5. Use a comma or commas to punctuate a non-restrictive appositive.	Pn 5 B
	6. Use commas to punctuate names and addresses.	Pn 5 C
	7. Use a comma or commas to punctuate an absolute.	Pn 6 A
	8. Use commas to punctuate parenthetical expressions.	Pn 6 B
	9. Use commas to punctuate elements in series and to punctuate coordinate descriptive adjectives before substantives.	Pn 6 C

Do not use a comma instead of a semicolon between independent clauses not joined by a coordinating conjunction.

Do not use commas to separate substantives used as subjects from the remainder of the sentences.

Do not use commas to set off objects and complements from the remainder of the sentence.

Do not use a single comma to punctuate a middle element.

Do not use commas to punctuate restrictive elements.

Do not use commas before the first or after the last of a series.

Colon :	Use a colon to introduce material that explains, completes, or fulfills.	Pn 2 F

Do not use a colon as a loose equivalent of a comma, period, or semicolon.

Dash —	Use a dash to signalize an abrupt change, a forceful conclusion, an explanatory comment, a summation.	Pn 2 G

Do not use a dash as a loose equivalent for other marks of puncuation.

Parentheses ( )	Use parentheses to enclose unimportant non-restrictive explanatory material.	Pn 7 A
Brackets [ ]	Use brackets to punctuate explanatory material inserted in material quoted from some one else.	Pn 7 B
Quotation marks " "	1. Use quotation marks to enclose the speaker's or writer's exact words.	Pn 8 B
	2. Use quotation marks to enclose titles of shorter works and to enclose words being used in special senses.	Pn 9 F
Hyphen -	Use hyphens to indicate division of words broken at the end of the line and between	

	the parts of certain compound elements, especially adjective units.	Pn 9 C
Apostrophe '	1. Use apostrophes in contracted forms and to indicate other omissions of letters.	Pn 9 A
	2. Use apostrophes in the possessive forms of nouns and pronouns other than personal pronouns and *who* and to form plurals of letters, numbers, symbols, and words mentioned as words.	Pn 9 B

Do not use apostrophes with possessive forms of personal pronouns.

Capitals	Use capitals for proper nouns and adjectives.	Pn 9 D

In general, do not use capitals for relation words, names of seasons, direction words, academic classes, academic subjects, rank words without names accompanying, etc.

Italics	Use italics for titles of full-length works, for foreign words, for words and symbols being used in themselves.	
		Pn 9 E

EXERCISES

50. Insert whatever punctuation is needed in the following sentences. Be prepared to discuss the effects of different marks.

(a) The salesman asked whether the hotel would cash a check for him.

(b) No one realized the significance of the missing key it demonstrated that the death could not have been suicide.

(c) He had over ten thousand dollars in his checking account consequently he could hardly have been worried very much about financial matters.

(d) The emperor ordered the killing of all the settlers and visitors from Italian Rome and before nightfall over thirty thousand had been killed.

(e) I left at ten but Al stayed on.

(f) President Wilson had the same experience he had less influence since he could not be a candidate for another term

(g) He needed a number of office supplies and materials stationery, envelopes, ink, stamps, carbon paper.

(h) The father announced that they must all stop what they were doing and look for the missing child some one of those days.

(i) Sound symbolism, alliteration, assonance, rime, meter, rhythm all these contribute to the appeal of poetry.

(j) The left fielder who was playing far back had to race in to catch the fly.

(k) The only grounds for divorce is very difficult to obtain in that state are adultery and desertion

(l) When we started the car seemed to be in perfect operating order.

(m) If the plan is unsuccessful and our enemies do maintain their control of this island chain lying across our path then perhaps we will try to bypass them and let them wither on the vine.

(n) In attempting to bolster up his argument the attorney quoted several similar decisions from Indiana and Illinois.

(o) Her wedding ring which had disappeared at about the time of the theft was finally found behind one of the kitchen cabinets.

(p) The Secret Service which has the duty of guarding the president and vice president is part of the Treasury Department.

(q) World War II lasting from 1939 to 1946 cost much more than all previous wars put together.

(r) The box that contained all the family silver had evidently been put in another ship at St. Joseph Missouri

(s) Mike Connelly the leader of the prisoners revolt was serving a life sentence plus ninety nine years

(t) The battleship Maine was blown up in Havana harbor on February 15 1898 this event triggered American entry into the war

(u) Beers used the color mauve to describe the period in his book called the Mauve Decade

(v) Everything having been arranged to every ones satisfaction the people bound for Twin Falls Idaho joined major Roberts wagon train aiming for the oregon trail

(w) On thursday noon the ship burning fiercely and shaken by explosions plunged beneath the water the captain still on the bridge

(x) It is not necessary on the other hand to replace all of the bridges at once

(y) Warner could not under the circumstances account for Jeffers actions

51. Correct the punctuation of the following sentences:

(a) Clyde thought that he might as well enlist and ask to go to the Radar School at camp Schofield. Since he would soon be drafted other-wise.

(b) Mr. Bennett asked, "will the old barn floor be strong enough to support the new tractor, the bailer and the spreader"?

(c) The ill tempered motor-cycle cop asked dr. Jenkins' where the fire was?

(d) When they asked him for his opinion on the matter prof. Cartwright was embarrassed (since he had never made any pretence at knowing any-thing about Comparative Religion.)

(e) The beauty of various word's is a subjective matter inter-mixed with considerations of meaning, for instance, mother and smother have about the same sound but call-forth different responses.

(f) "Do you think, the Senator asked, that the people will take a do nothing attitude and sit back idly while their liberties' are being destroyed"?

(g) But it turned out that Judge Brennan ignored the jury's suggestion about "leniency," instead he sentenced Morris to a ten year term at the Allbright penitentiary.

(h) One of the university of Michigan teams had scored two hundred and eighty seven points in 5 games, it was known as the "point a minute team".

(i) "Black Swan" had always done his' best on a wet, or muddy track, for that reason Johnnie did'nt want to bet on him.

(j) The official tests showed that the scales registered 1 lb. at what was actually fifteen and five eights oz., an official warning was sent to the Benedict and brother Company from the city Department of Weight's and Measures.

(k) To the North was Sachem county, to the South lay the Narrakiota indian Reservation.

(l) In Chandless' poetry, especially in such short products as *The Reign of Night* and *Altamaha,* the word "mother" is used with a play on the now forgotten meaning of "constricting hysterical seizure".

(m) The Three valley League was obviously in bad shape, the only active team's remaining were: Centreville, Duryea, Eastchester and Plainville junction.

(n) I was shocked to hear of mr. Adam's death, he had been director of our Junior Class play and had helped in many other High-School activities.

(o) The childrens' drawing—if it could be so-called, of a horse was not very successful, however, Willy saved the day by labeling it "Daddy".

(p) One of my great-aunt's Aunt Julia, was killed in the crash of a Chicago-San Francisco plane in the Wasatch Mountain range in Northern Utah, none of my other relatives would ever travel by plane after-wards.

(q) You should define all new words like leading edge and blip and phrases that "rookies" may not know, should be explained.

(r) The red-faced old woman who kept the candy store, unable to catch up with the stone-throwing brat shook her fist's at him, and turned back to her dingy store.

(s) What caused the mens' deaths, was obviously *asphyxiation* according to the report sent to the Coroner by police-chief Ackerman.

(t) Danvers claimed, that his old truck was all-right, he thought that the garageman was just trying to discriminate against him, when he said "that it's brakes needed tightening."

(u) Having witnessed such a never to be forgotten event as the Presidents assassination, Kessler, who was a first class "bore" made sure that his friends' would'nt ever forget it, either.

(v) Louis's duties were: calling each driver ½ hour before departure time, giving him way bills and consignment slips, and noting exact times of departure, he wasn't very good at the last of these.

(w) The patients' own physician, having received the clinicians' reports ordered an immediate emergency appendectomy.

(x) While the fireman was racing up the stairway collapsed and came crashing down, then we knew that the childrens' lives could be saved only by a miracle.

(y) Books relating to history, sociology, and economics, are kept on the 4th level of the stacks, these volumes, which are about geography should be on the 6th.

52. Make up your own sentences—mature sentences of mature length and content—to illustrate each of the following items:

indirect questions
use of exclamation marks
two independent clauses joined by a coordinating conjunction
two independent clauses joined by a conjunctive adverb
two independent clauses lacking a connective word
two independent clauses separated by a colon
two independent clauses separated by a dash
a colon before a series
a comma needed to prevent misreading
a long dependent clause serving as an introductory modifier
an introductory phrase containing non-finite verb forms
a restrictive adjective clause
a non-restrictive adjective clause
a restrictive non-finite verb phrase
a non-restrictive non-finite verb phrase
non-restrictive apposition
an absolute phrase
a parenthetical phrase
elements in series
two or more descriptive adjectives placed before the substantives modified
direct discourse
indirect discourse
five contractions
hyphenated adjective units
a title of a short work; a title of a longer, book-length work
sequence of quotation marks and commas or periods

53. Analyze the punctuation of the paragraphs and other selections in any preceding chapter of this book. Explain reasons for each mark of punctuation used.

15

DICTIONARY
USE

As a college student you need a modern dictionary of acceptable size and coverage. For practical purposes a modern dictionary is one that has been copyrighted within the last five years. Many older dictionaries were excellent works in their own times, but a dictionary fifteen or twenty years old may give you no better practical service than an automobile fifteen or twenty years old. A dictionary of acceptable size and scope for the college student today is one having over a hundred thousand entries, one of the so-called desk dictionaries.[1]

Elementary, high-school, and secretarial dictionaries are not good enough for you. Even a desk dictionary may not give you all the information that you may need on a particular problem of writing or interpreting. You may occasionally need to use the *Oxford English Dictionary* (sometimes still called the *New English Dictionary*), which gives copious information about the historical development of words, or the Merriam Company *Webster's New International Dictionary*, the best-known of the larger dictionaries.

A modern desk dictionary must be compact in presenting its great store of information; space limitations prevent long essays at each entry. Under the circumstances dictionary makers must use conventional short

[1] *Webster's New Collegiate Dictionary.* Springfield, Mass.: G. & C. Merriam Company, 1961; *The American College Dictionary,* N.Y.: Random House, 1961; *Webster's New World Dictionary,* Cleveland and N.Y.: World Publishing Company, 1961.

cuts. Sometimes persons unfamiliar with dictionaries do not find information given, or they misinterpret it. The following comments and exercises are designed to prevent your doing so and to make you familiar with your dictionary.

How to Find the Information in Your Dictionary

The main problems that you face in using your dictionary are, first, finding the entry that you want, and, second, interpreting that entry. You usually have little difficulty about the first of these: all dictionaries arrange their entries in alphabetical order. A few problems, however, may arise:

1. Modern technical and scientific words sometimes employ odd combinations of letters. *Rh factor,* for instance, is a rather unusual term. Such words are entered in the expected alphabetical order; *rh factor* is to be found between *rheumatism* and *rhinestone.*

2. Hyphens, apostrophes, capital letters, and other marks of punctuation called for in various entries do not change the alphabetical position of words concerned, and two-word forms appear at their regular places: *dog-legged* comes between *dog Latin* and *dogma; Bright's disease* comes between *brighten* and *brill; Empire Day* comes between *empire* and *empiric.*

3. Some dictionaries use a printing device known as the *run-on.* After a base word has been explained in full, they print, at the end of the entry, its derived forms, often without explanation of pronunciation or meaning. Thus you may find in your dictionary at the end of the entry for *large* the run-on derived form *largeness.* The word *large* may be followed by *large-hearted* and *large-minded,* so that, strictly speaking, *largeness* is not given in alphabetical order. Usually, forms that are run on would have come very close on the dictionary page to the base entry if they had been given their own separate entries. Derived forms coming far from their base forms on the dictionary page are often given their own separate entries. Some dictionaries omit less common derivations and avoid the use of run-ons altogether. They give every word its own separate independent entry, however obvious its method of formation, pronunciation, and meaning.

4. Some dictionaries list names of persons and places in separate sections, usually in supplements after the last words in *z-.* When you are using such a dictionary, look at the last pages to find who Dostoevski was or where Corregidor is. Names of mythological, legendary, and

fictional characters, like *Bellerophon, King Lear,* and *Pecksniff,* are, however, found in the main body of words, as are names of characters important in religion, like *Moses* or *Judas.* Other dictionaries give names of persons and places in the main body of words. In such a dictionary you will find *Dostoevski* given between *dossier* and *dot* and *Corregidor* between *corrective* and *correlate.*

5. Dictionaries likewise differ in their treatment of abbreviations. Some give abbreviations in special supplements. In using a dictionary that follows this procedure, you will find near the end of the book the information that *civ.* means "civil" or "civilian" and that *lv.* means "leave" or "livre." A dictionary with a "single-alphabet" listing puts all abbreviations in the main body of the work, so that one finds *civ.* between *city-state* and *civet* and *lv.* between *luxury* and *lycanthrope.*

6. The most difficult problem that some students have in finding information in a dictionary comes about through their inability to spell the first parts of words in question. Neither a dictionary nor a textbook like this can help you much if this is your problem. All that can be suggested is that you search for spellings other than those that you had in mind. If you can't find *ommission,* try *omission,* the correct form; if you can't find *perscription,* try *prescription.*

EXERCISE

1. Find enough of the following words and expressions in your dictionary to familiarize you with its procedure: *ars poetica, boogie-woogie, Brabant, candidness, cannel coal, Daedalean, ddt, Falkland Island, Fl layer, Grimm's Law, guildsman, Guinevere, Helvetius, horse latitudes, L beam, liveliness, monk's cloth, officially, Q fever, Romanist, roller skate, Sa., sadistic, S. Afr., Saint Elmo's fire, Schubert, Sisyphus, x-ray.* Does your dictionary use run-ons? Where do you find abbreviations?

How to Interpret Information

Unfortunately, many users of dictionaries do not perceive or understand all the information offered them. Since makers of dictionaries must present information compactly, they use simplifications and short cuts, which in turn must be explained to you. The typical dictionary treatment gives you the following information:

1. *The form of the word under consideration.* Most information about the form of the word is given in the word entry itself, which is almost

always printed in boldface (heavy type). The word entry, of course, gives the spelling. (Variant spellings will be discussed shortly.) The word entry *separate* tells you that this word is spelled with an *a* between the *p* and the *r;* the word entry *accommodate* tells you that there are two *m*'s in this word. The printing of the word entry usually shows whether the word begins with a lower-case (small) letter, as most words do, or with a capital letter. Your dictionary is likely to include *garrote, garter, gas,* and then *Gascon.* The printing of the word entry for the latter word shows you that it is usually capitalized. Note entries in your dictionary for *Platonic, Pliocene, Plutonian, Polish, Pomona,* and *Populist.* If your dictionary maker finds that the word in question is written sometimes with a lower-case letter and sometimes with a capital, he may give both forms. If the word in question is capitalized in some senses and not capitalized in others, the dictionary maker will tell you this by italicized notes, usually in brackets, before certain of the definitions. Some dictionaries, for instance, print *Pygmy* with a capital letter, but before the definition of the sense "very short person, dwarf," they add a note showing that the word is not capitalized in this sense. To be sure about capitalization, you should scan the whole treatment of the word in question in your dictionary.

EXERCISES

2. Look up enough of the following to be sure how your dictionary treats problems of capitalization: *saint bernard dog, salmon pink, salvation army, samaritan, sam browne belt, samoyed, sandalwood, sanhedrin, sargasso, saturn, saturnine, saxon, scabiosa, scandium, schick test, schnauzer, scotch.* Which of these words have meanings that are not capitalized?

3. How does your dictionary treat the problem of capitalizing or lower-casing the following words: *calliope, calvary, cancer, capitol, capuchin, illuminati, italic, lion, locofoco, logos, lombard, long tom, lord, love, lucifer, moll, sapphic, satan, savior, scaramouch?*

The printing of the entry word shows whether or not that word can be divided into syllables with hyphens for end-of-line division. If the entry word is printed without any marks separating any of the letters, that word is not divided and must always be printed or written as a unit. Note the entries for *spring, springe, sprint, spruce, spur, spurt,* and *squall* in your dictionary. Dictionaries show division into syllables by printing raised periods or dots between letters. Your dictionary may print the entry word *talisman* as *tal·is·man*, the entry word *tamarisk* as *tam·a·risk*. These printings show that these two words may be divided correctly at the ends of lines as follows: *tal-isman* or *talis-man*, *tam-arisk* or *tama-risk*.

Some dictionaries give two different kinds of information at once by their printing of entry words: they use raised periods to show part of the syllable division but also use accent marks to show which syllables are strongly stressed when the words are spoken. Thus for *millennium* your dictionary may print the entry word as mil·len'ni·um. This printing tells you two facts at once: that the word divides into four syllables (*mil-len-ni-um*, with *mil-lennium,* *millen-nium*, and *millenni-um* as acceptable end-of-line divisions), and that the syllable *-len-* receives the greatest stress when the word is pronounced, that it is sounded as MilLENium rather than MILlennium or millenNIum. Most of today's dictionaries print the accent mark after the syllable to be stressed rather than before it, although many of today's linguists prefer to reverse this procedure. Sometimes secondary accents are shown. Your dictionary may show for the word *millenary* the following entry: *mil'le·nar'y*. The printing of this entry shows two facts: that the syllabic division of the word is *mil-le-nar-y* and that the syllables *-mil-* and *-nar-* receive primary and secondary stresses respectively.

EXERCISE

4. How does your dictionary show syllabification of words? Does the form of the entry word tell you only the syllabification, or does it also tell you which syllables are stressed? Find the syllabification of the following words: *effective, effeminate, efflorescence, effusive, egocentric, idiosyncrasy, ignominious, ignorant, illegible, illumination*. Determine the position of primary and secondary stresses in these words *if your dictionary gives you this information in the printing of the entry word.*

The printing of a compounded unit also shows whether it is written as a single word (like *football*), written as two separate words (like *foot brake*), or hyphenated as a compound (like *foot-loose*). A dictionary maker is often likely to include only the form that seems to him most common in well-printed publications. Following your dictionary is safe procedure for you, although you may find alternate printings in your reading. When you use your dictionary, be careful to distinguish between the raised periods used to show syllable division and the hyphens used to separate parts of compounds; notice, for instance, the difference between *fol′ low·er* or *fol·low·er* and *fol′ low-up* or *fol·low-up.*

EXERCISE

5. For each of the following—all of which are here printed solid—discover whether your dictionary calls for writing as two words, as a hyphenated compound, or as one word: *antislavery, blackguard, catchall, cottonseed, dieselengine, eggplant, fieldday, grasswidow, illbred, lazytongs, many sided, newsstand, pepperandsalt, PreRaphaelite, restcure, shamefaced, sportshirt, Texasleaguer, trustworthy, warmblooded.*

The printing of the entry will likewise show whether or not the word in question is customarily written with an apostrophe (like *cat′s-eye*) or without.

2. *The usual printing of the word.* Some words and phrases borrowed from foreign languages are still looked on as not entirely part of the English language. These words are usually put in italics when they are printed, and are usually underlined when they are handwritten or typed. *Ad hoc* (as in "a committee *ad hoc,*" one appointed to take care of one particular situation) illustrates this point. Dictionaries usually give information about such words, but their procedures differ widely. Before words still regarded as foreign, some dictionaries print a double bar (‖) or a double dagger (‡). You may find in your dictionary such entries as ‖ *con do·lo′re* or ‡ *de no·vo.* Other dictionaries handle this situation in a totally different way: entry words are printed without special marks, but before the definition or definitions the name of a foreign language is given in italics. In the treatment of *raison d′être* you may find in your dictionary the word *French* just before the definition to show that the phrase is still regarded as French and that it should be italicized or underlined.

EXERCISE

6. Find out whether, according to your dictionary, each of the following is regarded as an English word to be printed and written without especial treatment or whether it is regarded as a foreign word to be italicized or underlined: *a priori, capriccio, conge, dolce, fille de chambre, in perpetuum, motif, intelligentsia, parfait, pis aller, quasi, strabismus, Weltanschauung, zinfandel.* Find out how your dictionary treats words still regarded as foreign.

3. *The variants of a word.* A variant is a form that shows a spelling variation without, however, an accompanying difference in meaning. *Grey* is a variant of *gray*. Sometimes variants arise because of different spelling preferences in different areas: *honor* is the form preferred in the United States, *honour* in Great Britain. Sometimes different spellings develop without regional preferences being involved: a frenzied Malay may run *amok* or run *amuck* anywhere. Desk dictionaries include as many contemporary variant spellings as possible, although they usually do not enter many variants from earlier periods. Variants are entered in a number of ways: a variant form is often given in boldface immediately or very nearly after the entry word; your dictionary may contain the entry: *mi'ter, mi'tre.* This kind of entry indicates that both forms are common and acceptable, although the first may be slightly more frequent than the second. The dictionary maker often uses this procedure when he has found no strong preference between the two. The device of joining variants with *or* is sometimes used with the same meaning. Your dictionary may have an entry for *snow line* or *limit.* This means that the dictionary maker has found no particularly strong preference between the two. Sometimes the second form given may be prefaced by the word *also*, printed in ordinary roman type. Your dictionary may have the entry: *e·col'o·gy* . . . Also *oe·col'o·gy.* This means that although the form *oecology* exists the dictionary makers have found *ecology* more common and want to show that it is preferred. Some dictionaries do not give variants just after the entry word, but instead put them at the end of the whole entry, after the definition or definitions. Sometimes dictionary makers omit mention of variant forms at main entries. Note the treatment in your dictionary for *defense* and *defence* and for *labor* and *labour.* Some dictionaries indicate very specifically that variants entered are variants; your dictionary may have something like the following: *pe'an* . . . Var. of PAEAN. Other dictionaries are less specific; they treat this matter simply as follows: *pe·an* . . . n. paean.

EXERCISES

7. How does your dictionary treat variants? How does it treat the following forms: *abridgement, accoutre, eon, esthete, grey, kidnapper, quinin, glamour, entrust, caulk?* What are the preferred forms for the following? what comment, if any, does your dictionary make about these variants: *absinth, labour, saviour, calibre, cigaret, mould, cheque, jiujitsu, waggon?*

4. *The pronunciation of the word.* After the bold-face entry comes an indication of pronunciation. Almost all dictionaries give the pronunciation in special symbols printed in roman type and enclosed in parentheses. This material enclosed in parentheses between the entry word and the part of speech indication has nothing to do with the written form of the word. After the bold-face entry word *coal* you will probably find something like the following: (kōl). This is the dictionary maker's way of showing the pronunciation. The indication of pronunciation shows nothing about the spelling of the word. All dictionaries show in the pronunciation the position of stresses in words of more than one syllable; they do so by placing stress marks *after* syllables to be stressed. For *dubiety* your dictionary may have in the pronunciation parenthesis something like the following: dû·bī′ e·tĭ or dōō-bĭ′-ə-ti. The accent mark (′) indicates that the second syllable is stressed, that the word is pronounced duBIety. For *dubious* your dictionary may have something like: dū′bĭ·ŭs or dōō′bĭ-əs, the position of the accent mark showing that the word is pronounced DUbious.

The various sounds in words are indicated by various symbols; in determining existent pronunciations, deciding which ones should be included, and choosing symbols to represent sounds, dictionary makers face grave problems. No other branch of dictionary making is so difficult and so likely to cause controversy as the recording of pronunciation. Except for calling your attention to the keys explaining pronunciation symbols on inside cover pages of dictionaries, this book can tell you little more about pronunciation. Before trying to use your dictionary to learn about pronunciation, be sure that you understand the symbols used. Note that most dictionaries have prefaces that explain pronunciation principles in detail.

When there are two reasonably well-established pronunciations for the same word your dictionary is likely to list both; thus for *drama* your dictionary may have something like one of the following: (drä′må; drăm′å) or (drä′mə, dram′ə). The preferred pronunciation is given first, although often the dictionary maker's preference is not very strong. To save space, some dictionary makers "cut back" certain pronunciations of the word in question. It may be that in your dictionary *condense,* for which (kŏn·děns′) is given, is immediately followed by *condensed;* in that case your dictionary maker may give only (-děnst) to show the pronunciation of the latter word. This means that the pronunciation of the first syllable is the same as that given for the first syllable in the entry just above. Dictionary makers often try to save space by omitting unnecessary indications of pronunciation, especially in their treatments of compounds and of homonyms. *Homonyms* are words the same or similar in form and sound but different in etymology and meaning. Some dictionaries do not give a separate pronunciation for a homonym that comes after another homonym; perhaps your dictionary does not include pronunciation indications for the second entries for *jag* and *jam*.

EXERCISES

8. Determine which syllable receives the main stress in the preferred pronunciation of the following: *secretive, rotogravure, industrial, photographer, acclimate, acrimony, barbarian, communist, cajole, beneficent, catholicism, definitive, enigmatic, interpellate, libertine, momentous, pontifical, reclamation, subsidiary, spiritous, theatrical.*

9. According to your dictionary, what pronunciation is preferred for each of the following words: *culinary, aquatic, route, tomato, duke, mayonnaise, tune, medicine, menagerie, caffeine, literature, respiratory, miniature, victuals, mongrel, senile, nougat, pageant, patent, grimace, garage, rouge, coupé, coupon, coyote, sacrilege, schedule, rodeo, sumac, greasy?*

5. *The part of speech indication.* Most dictionaries give the part of speech for the word being treated by printing an abbreviation in italics after the pronunciation parenthesis. The abbreviations used are usually simple and easy to understand, like *n., adj.,* and *prep.* Many dictionaries use *v.i.* and *v.t.* for "intransitive verb" and "transitive verb" respectively. The dictionary maker usually does not reprint the word entry if the word in question is used in different parts of speech; your dictionary is likely to give adjective, adverb, and verb definitions under the single entry for *free;* verb and noun definitions under the single entry for *freeze;* and adjective, noun, verb, and adverb definitions under the entry for *fresh.* The fact that your dictionary does not show that a certain word has a certain grammatical use does not mean that the word in question is never so used, but often it indicates that the use in question is rare. Dictionaries often omit treatments of the adjective uses of nouns, not because they are regarded as incorrect but merely because they are too obvious to need dictionary entry. Thus your dictionary may have no entry for *apple* as an adjective to cover its use in "apple pie" and "apple tree."

EXERCISE

10. How many part-of-speech indications do you find in your dictionary for each of the following words: *call, calm, carry, choice, common, foul, frame, free, front, full?*

6. *The inflections of the word.* An inflection is a variation in form to show number, case, tense, degree of comparison, or some similar grammatical feature. Dictionaries usually give necessary information about inflectional forms just after the part of speech indication. Many use semicolons or commas to set off information about inflections from the part-of-speech indication given just before, but some dictionaries give inflectional forms within brackets.

Most dictionaries do not give entirely regular inflectional forms of nouns, verbs, and adjectives; instead they include inflectional forms only when there is some problem about their formation. Such a word as *crisis* presents a problem; hence your dictionary will have a note like the following: *pl. crises.* When the noun in question has two different plurals your dictionary will list both; at *radius* your dictionary is likely to have the note: *pl. radii, radiuses.* Preferred forms are given first, but often the dictionary maker is unable to find a very strong preference between forms. Sometimes one plural form is common in certain senses, another in other senses. Note, for instance, how your dictionary treats the plurals of the word *genius.*

EXERCISE

11. What does your dictionary tell you about the plural forms of the following: *automaton, axis, bacillus, bacterium, banjo, barrack, basilica, beau, beef, bellows, Bolshevik, bourgeois, brother, buffalo, cactus, caesura, calico, calyx, camera, catalysis, cerebrum, chassis, chateau?*

Giving forms for entirely regular verbs, like *turned* or *turning* for *turn* or *killed* or *killing* for *kill,* is not felt necessary in a desk dictionary, but usually forms of verbs are given when they present any problem. Your dictionary is likely to give for *ring* the forms *rang* and *rung* and perhaps *ringing* and for *rise* the forms *rose* and *risen* and perhaps *rising.* The forms of verbs like *omit* and *regret* are regular enough in so far as grammar goes, but in treating these two verbs your dictionary is likely to give the forms *omitted* and *omitting* and *regretted* and *regretting* because in each one the doubling of the final *t* of the base form is a spelling problem. Dictionaries often give forms for verbs ending in *y* (like *parry* and *harry*). If there are two acceptable forms for the past tense or two for the past participle, your dictionary will tell you so.

EXERCISE

12. What does your dictionary tell you about the forms for the following verbs: *awake, babble, bar, bear, burst, catch, cavil, chagrin, dive, double, drag, entice, grow, harry, heave, impel, level, lie, mimic, ply, prove, refer, reply, ride, scrub, shine, steal, submit?*

Comparative and superlative forms for adjectives and adverbs are likewise given only if the forms are irregular or if their formation creates a spelling problem. Notice how your dictionary treats the comparative and superlative forms of *far* and *fat* and *haughty*.

In giving inflectional forms many dictionaries use the cutback device as a space saver. In giving the plurals of *dictum,* for instance, your dictionary may have something like the following: *pl.* -TA, -TUMS. This means, of course, that the two plural forms are *dicta* and *dictums*. For the verb *defy* your dictionary may give the following: -FIED, -FYING, meaning that the past tense and past participle are *defied* and the present participle is *defying*.

7. *The etymology of the word.* To give the etymology of a word is to explain its manner of formation or to show the form, in earlier English or in a foreign language or in both, that gave rise to the modern English form. It is standard dictionary practice to give etymological information in square brackets, but in some dictionaries the bracketed etymological treatment is given immediately after the part of speech indication (and the treatment of inflectional forms), and in others it is given at the end of the whole entry, that is, after the last definition and note on the word being discussed. All dictionaries present etymologies quite compactly, and you must study the procedures used in your own to understand the etymologies fully. You will find that many etymologies begin with the abbreviation for a foreign language and continue with a foreign word printed in italics. Thus in the etymology for *froth* in the Merriam Company *Webster's New Collegiate Dictionary,* you will find "ON. *frotha*" and in that for *frown* "OF. *froignier*." These treatments indicate that *froth* is borrowed into English from the Old Norse form *frotha,* and *frown,* from the Old French form *froignier*. Like other dictionaries, the

Webster's New Collegiate explains in a preface the language abbreviations used; this is given just before the treatment of the first words in *a*.

Sometimes the etymologist seems to give much less information. At the entry *terminus*, for instance, the *Webster's New Collegiate* gives only the following: [L.]. This very brief etymology tells you that the word *terminus* came into English from Latin with no change in form (the etymologist did not feel it necessary to reprint the form *terminus* in his treatment) and similarly with no change in meaning (since the first definition of the English word gives the meaning that *terminus* had in Latin, the etymologist felt that he was excused from indicating it).

If you are using the *American College Dictionary*, the etymologies that you encounter will be somewhat different from those just discussed. For *froth* your dictionary will have something like the following: [ME *frothe?* t. Scand . . .]. This means that the modern word *froth* evidently comes from a Middle English form *frothe*, which in turn was taken or borrowed from the Scandinavian. The etymology for *terminus* will be something like the following: [t. L.: boundary, limit, end]. This means that the English word *terminus* is borrowed from Latin without change of form and that in Latin the word meant "boundary, limit, end."

If you are using the World Publishing Company *Webster's New World Dictionary* you will probably meet with longer etymologies. This dictionary has attempted to cover etymology in more detail than other desk dictionaries. For *froth* you will probably find an entry that begins as follows: [ME. *frothe;* ON. *frotha, frauth;* basically akin to AS. (*a*)-*freothan* . . .], meaning that our modern word derives from the Middle English form *frothe*, that that form was borrowed from Old Norse *frotha* or *frauth*, which forms are related to the Anglo-Saxon verb *afreothan* or *freothan*. For *terminus* you are likely to find: [L.; see term]. This means that the word has entered English from Latin without change in form or meaning and that more etymological information is available at the entry *term*. The etymologies of the *Webster's New World Dictionary* often attempt to trace forms back to those in Indo-European, the parent language of most of the important European languages, and an explanation of these etymologies lies outside the sphere of this book.

To the dictionary maker, etymologies are important for many reasons, one of which is that etymology tells him whether he is dealing with one word or several. In your dictionary you will probably find only one entry word *jay*, although this entry may be followed by four or five definitions. All of these represent one series of meaning developments tracing back to a single source. On the other hand you are likely to find two or three entries for *jack, jag,* and *jam;* the reason for this is that there are different original base forms—or *etymons*—for these.

One thing you must notice about etymologies: the words given in ordinary roman type within the etymology brackets do not attempt to tell you what the modern English entry word means. In the etymology for *ocarina,* for instance, you will find in every dictionary the English word *goose;* in the etymology for *occur* you are likely to find the English word *run.* The dictionary maker is emphatically not trying to tell you by these treatments that the modern word *ocarina* ever means "goose" in English or that the modern word *occur* ever means "run" in English. Instead he is telling you that these words or their parts expressed these meanings in foreign languages at the time when the words themselves were evolving.

Occasional attention to the dictionary etymologies can help you a good deal toward mastering English. You may find that a little knowledge of etymology helps you to understand the connotations of words. In the etymology for *recalcitrant,* for instance, you are likely to find some mention of kicking, and the phrase "the recalcitrant minority" may be the richer for you if you can picture its members as always kicking, perhaps like unruly animals kicking in their stalls. *Meticulous* may mean to you not so much "very careful" as "careful through fear of making errors" if you see that the Latin form *-met-* meaning "fear" is the base of the word. *Gregarious* may have an additional value for you if you know that at its base is the form *-greg-* meaning "herd, flock."

Many people are fascinated by the exotic suggestions of some dictionary etymologies. Notice for instance that the etymologies of the everyday words *sugar* and *coffee* suggest the far-away and romantic because of their references to Turkish, Arabic, Persian, and Sanskrit. And many people are fascinated by etymologies that derive today's common words from names of persons and places. The etymology for *guillotine* in your dictionary will tell you that the device in question was named for the French physician who supported its use as a humane measure; the etymology for *damask* will tell you that the fabric was named from the city of Damascus, in which it was evidently first made. People likewise find interesting the odd changes in meaning that have taken place in the development of some of our English words; they are pleased, for instance, to discover from the etymology of *delirium* that the original Latin form of this meant deviating from a straight furrow in plowing.

EXERCISES

13. What abbreviation does your dictionary use in its etymologies for each of the following names for languages: *French, German, Greek, Latin, Arabic, Persian, Sanskrit, Chinese, Old French, Low Latin, Low German?* What other abbreviations does it use in its etymologies?

14. Although the following are all borrowed words, they are all more or less common in English today. From what foreign language does each one come, according to the etymologies given in your dictionary: *alarm, antique, brace, canal, continent, crown, educate, escape, gap, grand, inflate, kettle, mountain, odd, prison, rapid, sense, social, touch, unit?* The etymologies of the following words show that they came from more distant and exotic languages. Find out from what language each came: *albatross, benzoin, borax, check, cobra, esker, Fenian, goulash, hegira, kangaroo, khaki, mulligatawny, mummy, raccoon, rhinoceros, sequoia, seraph, taboo, totem, yacht.*

15. Find out which of the following words are "native" in the English language: *ale, belt, bottom, cold, contract, edge, end, food, game, horse, inn, mark, move, pin, prince, run, send, take, town, wrong.* (Notice that native words have not been borrowed from foreign languages; their etymologies are written entirely in terms of AS. or OE. and ME. forms.)

16. What names for persons and places do you find in the etymologies for the following: *Airedale, bourbon whisky, bowie knife, canary, canter, derby, delftware, Fourierism, Frankenstein, graham flour, hector, limerick, macabre, maffick, magenta, maudlin, mausoleum, oersted, pander, peavey, pierrot, ruthenium, Seidlitz powder, tabby, uranium?* The etymologies of the following words have been regarded as especially interesting, since they show unusual meaning developments. Look up each one: *atom, belladonna, checkmate, codeine, cynical, dainty, easel, eliminate, fascism, falk, graft, hecatomb, knight, limeu, paregoric, pioneer, radar, rhesus, seminary, slave, supercilious, syphilis, tory, urchin.*

17. The discussion of etymology given above has indicated that dictionary etymologies may aid in understanding the connotations of words. See how this principle works with the following words: *immure, expedite, inflated, imply, congregate, ardent, autonomy, duress, precursor, embrace, aberration, magnify, eulogy, extravagant.*

8. *The spheres and levels of usage of a word.* Two kinds of notes are printed in dictionaries right before the definitions of words: subject labels and diction or usage labels. A subject label shows the specific subject or field in which the word in question has the meaning given in

the definition following. General words and meanings of course lack subject labels. Many dictionaries print subject labels (and abbreviations for them) in italics; you may find in your dictionary such labels as *Law, Civil Engineering, Forestry, Football*. Some dictionaries prefer to show the subject field by such a phrase as "in law," "in civil engineering," or "in forestry," with the word *in* printed in ordinary roman and the word giving the specific subject field printed in italics. You will find that one of the definitions of the noun *check* in your dictionary is something like "a position of danger of being captured requiring some defensive play on the next move." Your dictionary is likely to preface this definition with the word *chess* in italics, or with the phrase "in chess," to show that this meaning is found in connection with chess. Dictionary use of subject labels is not entirely consistent; the dictionary maker is likely to use a label when he thinks that it will be helpful.

EXERCISES

18. In your dictionary look up twelve words pertaining to a subject that you are interested in—baseball, dancing, radio, or automobiles, for instance. Be sure that you find the definitions that pertain to your special field of interest. How many of these definitions have subject labels? What appears to be the policy of your dictionary on the use of subject labels? In what particular fields of activity are the following words used: *aliquot, bevatron, deuterium, erg, hash mark, kedge, pig boat, quantic, skivvies, snooker, thallus?*

Usage labels are printed like subject labels in many dictionaries—that is, in italics before the definition or definitions in question. Some dictionaries, however, print usage labels in roman type in square brackets. The usage label is the dictionary maker's way of calling attention to some peculiarity, often an added suggestion or connotation in the usage of the word in question.

One such label is *Obs.*, meaning "obsolete." An *obsolete* word or meaning is one no longer part of the current language, although it was previously current, perhaps, for instance, in Shakespeare's days. For *manor* in the sense of "main mansion on an estate; main house of its lord," your dictionary probably has the label *Obs.* or [Obsolete], meaning that the word is no longer in use. Somewhat similar to obsolete words are archaic words and senses. Archaic words are still used, but they are likely to be found mainly in poetry, historical novels, and other writing that suggests the past. The adjective *olden,* the adverb *mayhap* for "perhaps," and the noun *miscreant* for "unbeliever, heretic, infidel" illustrate archaic words. Notice that the label *Archaic* calls to your attention a suggestive or connotative value of the word over and above the meaning indicated by the definition, the statement of its denotation or meaning.

Some words and meanings are marked *Poetic* to show that they are more likely to be found in poetry than in prose; your dictionary may so label *mead* (a synonym for *meadow*), *orb* in the sense of "eye, eyeball," or *pennon* in the sense of "wing." Occasionally words and meanings are labeled *Humorous* or *Jocose* to show that their use is an attempt to be funny; your dictionary may use one of these labels with *murphy* for "potato" or with *pate* for "top of the head." The label *Slang* is frequently used; your dictionary is likely to use it in its treatment of some of the following: *Mickey Finn, mike, old man* (meaning "father,") *once-over, onto* (in "I was onto his tricks"), *oscar, panic* (in "this act will panic the audience").

Perhaps the most common usage label is *Colloq.* or *Colloquial.* This label should be interpreted as meaning something like "more fit for ordinary informal conversation than for formal writing." Your dictionary may label as colloquial usages like the following: *make* in "to make the team," *manage* in "don't worry; he'll manage all right," *old timer, pal,* and *pan* in "the critics panned the play."

Of these various labels, *archaic, poetic, humorous, slang,* and *colloquial* are similar in indicating connotations. *Orb* may mean "eye" and *pal* may mean "friend," but in addition to denoting meanings these words suggest situations—*orb* in this sense poetic usage and *pal* informal conversational usage. Since these labels do express connotative values, they are often rather subjective; that is, they may rest as much on the dictionary maker's impression and judgment as on the objective evidence that he has before him. Consequently dictionaries often vary in the labels used for a particular word or construction.

Another usage label is *Dial.,* meaning "dialect." A dialect is a form of a language in use in a particular area but not in use everywhere the language in question is spoken; it is a regional division of a language. As a label, *Dial.* indicates that the word or meaning being treated is used only in a certain area. *Redd* or *redd up* for "arrange, make tidy" is a dialect word found mainly in Pennsylvania; *poke* for "paper bag" is a dialect word from the South. Your dictionary may use the label *Dial.* for these two. If the word in question exists only in English but not in American dialects, it is likely to be labeled *Dial. Eng.;* your dictionary may so treat *nesh* for "delicate or sickly" or *mew* in the sense of "cage for young birds." If the dictionary maker can be specific in giving you information about regional use he will be, often omitting the label *Dial.* and using instead only an indication of the area concerned. A word used all through England but not in the United States is likely to be marked *Eng.*, one used throughout British but not American areas to be marked *Brit.* Notice how your dictionary treats *navvy* (meaning "laborer") and *chemist* in the sense of "druggist." Dictionary makers use a variety of specific labels, usually easily understood, like *Obs. exc. Dial., Now Chiefly Dial., Scot. & Dial. Eng., Now Chiefly U.S., Southern U.S., U.S. Colloq.,* and so on.

EXERCISE

19. Scan the columns of your dictionary for usage notes. Find three words or meanings that are marked *colloquial,* three marked *archaic,* and three marked *dialect.*

20. How does your dictionary label each of the following: *fere* ("companion"), *harken, emprize, olden, busk* ("prepare"), *misdoubt, familiar* (n.), *wight* ("person, creature"), *ken* (n.), *romaunt, eldritch, rill* ("brook"), *bruit* (n.), *reck* (v.), *quaff, feat* (adj.), *fain* (adj. and adv.), *fealty, leal, puissant, perpend, meet* (adj.), *perchance, passing* (adv., "to a reasonable degree"), *minion, pard* ("leopard"), *main* ("ocean"), *missay, maker* ("poet"), *minish, marl* ("earth"), *mickle?*

21. How does your dictionary label each of the following: *hock* ("pawn"), *hoosegow, cool* ("excellent"), *galoot, fiddle* ("violin"), *hooch, spunk, shinny, knock* ("criticize adversely"), *ballyhoo, codger, misses* ("wife"), *argufy, mooch, fib* ("childish lie"), *spiel, ornery, fluke* ("lucky chance")?

22. Look up each of the following in two or three desk dictionaries. What differences do you find in the usage labels assigned: *wacky, soap opera, hooey, kilter, palaver, dumb* ("stupid"), *spiv, complected, nitwit, moonshiner, ruction, splurge, pep, rambunctious, one-horse* (adj.), *snide, pet* (v. "kiss and caress"), *riled up, pesky, spook, black Maria, pundit, high* ("drunk"), *deadpan?*

9. *The definition or definitions of the word.* Dictionaries differ in their arrangements of definitions of words with several senses. Some dictionaries, notably the Merriam Company *Webster's New Collegiate Dictionary,* follow what is called *historical order.* In this dictionary, meanings are given in the order, in so far as it can be determined, in

which they developed in the history of the English language. The earliest meaning is given first, the next second, and so on. Other dictionaries, notably the *American College Dictionary*, enter definitions according to the frequencies of the meanings involved, in so far as they can be determined. In this dictionary, the first definition of a word gives the most common meaning, the second the next most common, and so on. Other dictionaries use modifications of these two main procedures, notably arrangements involving logical semantic developments.

EXERCISE

23. In what order does your dictionary give the definitions for the following words: *dial* (n.), *dot* (n.), *entry, feather, grace, holy, judge* (n.), *log, mortal* (adj.), *picket, ridge, shell, stretch* (v.)? Compare the treatments given in the *New Collegiate Dictionary*, the *American College Dictionary*, and the *Webster's New World Dictionary*.

The unit of meaning that defines a word is what is given between semicolons if the definition is at all complicated. Your dictionary may have something like the following for *logic:* "The study dealing with the rules and criteria of value in thought; the science of formal reasoning." This indicates that the word *logic* may express either the first or the second of these two closely related meanings. Notice that the meaning unit in a dictionary definition is *not* composed of material set off by commas. For *lordly* your dictionary may have something like the following: "of, pertaining to, or befitting a lord"; in this definition the dictionary maker is emphatically not trying to tell you that the word *lordly* means "pertaining to."

Definitions consisting only of synonyms are not typical formal definitions. The dictionary maker sometimes defines by synonyms when they are quite accurate; he has no interest in running up the cost of his product in situations in which he can economize, and many users of dictionaries seem to welcome definitions that include synonyms.

The typical definition, however, is usually composed of two parts, the genus and the differentiae. To place something in its *genus* is to show the general class of things or actions to which it belongs. Your dictionary may begin its first definition of *ink* with the words "a fluid" or "a liquid"; it may begin its first definition of *saddle* with the words "a leather seat." *Fluid* or *liquid* and *seat* are genus words in these definitions. Your dictionary may continue its definition of *ink* by differentiating ink from other fluids or liquids: "employed in writing or painting." These and other similar refining comments make up the *differentiae,* the parts of the definition that set the thing being defined off from other things in the same class. The differentiae for *saddle* will consist of comments like "for a person riding on a horse or on a bicycle." These definitions of *ink* and *saddle* show the form often aimed at by the dictionary maker. After a definition written in this form he may add synonyms. He tries to limit the genus term as narrowly as he can; he tries to call *coffee* a beverage rather than a liquid and a *chisel* a tool rather than a thing. Often, however, he is compelled to use wide genus terms. He may define *horse* first as "a large herbivorous animal," but to take care of secondary uses of the word he may find himself forced to add a following definition like "something on which one rides, sits, or exercises as though on a horse." Formal definition of nouns in terms of genus and differentiae is usually possible for first meanings but sometimes not for following meanings.

EXERCISE

24. Look up definitions in your dictionary for the following words: *deteriorate, elastic* (adj.), *fantastic, genteel, grant* (v.), *grave* (adj.), *house* (n.), *loot* (n.), *multiply, pain* (n.), *plant* (n.), *querulous, risk* (n.). To what extent does the dictionary maker define by synonyms? To what extent does he utilize formal definitions involving genus and differentiae?

Some critics of dictionaries make much of counting numbers of meanings given in different works. They like to tell you that one dictionary has fifteen "meanings" listed for *force* in its various uses, another has twenty-eight, a third twenty-two. It is interesting to notice how many different definitions are necessary in a desk dictionary for such words as *bid, bill, bind, bite,* and *black.* But often counting numbers of dictionary definitions does not mean much in itself; it actually shows rather little about the coverage given by different dictionaries. Some dictionaries prefer to shorten and simplify individual definitions wherever possible; this preference involves subdividing meanings. A dictionary so written may have for the noun *start* two definitions like the following: "1. a sudden startled reaction; a sudden brief moment of shock or uncertainty. 2. a sudden startled motion." Another dictionary may prefer to combine these two notions as parts of a single definition and define somewhat as follows: "a sudden startled reaction, as of shock or uncertainty; a sudden involuntary motion." Sub-divisions of meanings often depend on editorial policy or preference at the moment rather than on objective logic; so long as the whole treat-ment of the definitions includes somewhere and somehow the meaning being sought for, the division of meanings does not matter much. You should remember in this connection that the dictionary definition is often expressed rather broadly so that it will fit with hundreds or thousands or even millions of uses of a word in the sense in question.

EXERCISE

25. How many definitions are given in your dictionary for each of the fol-lowing words: *city, deal, face, guard, hand, king, mill, pace, read, spark?* How many are given in another similar dictionary? Does either dic-tionary contain any meanings omitted from the other?

Usually one may presume that if the maker of a desk dictionary gives a definition for a certain meaning of a word he has evidence that the word has been used with that meaning at least five, eight, or a dozen times in different well-written books or articles. The statement by the dictionary maker that the word has meant the meaning that he defines is usually a safe one. On the other hand, makers of a desk dictionary often do not try to list all the existent meanings of a word.

10. *The idiomatic use of the word.* English shows many situations in which certain prepositions or adverbs are required after certain other words, especially verbs. Thus we must use *to* after *defer;* one defers *to* another's opinion, not *at* it or *of* it. These compulsory choices are idiomatic uses (see p. 201 in Chapter 10); as often as he can, the diction-ary maker gives information about such uses. Sometimes he does this by adding after his definition a short example of the use in question, often prefaced with the word *as.* At the appropriate definition of *report* v. your dictionary may have an illustration like "he reported for duty" to indicate that the preposition *for* is idiomatic here. Sometimes the dic-tionary maker may add an explanatory note set off with a dash from the definition in question.

EXERCISE

26. Look up the verbs at the beginning of the following phrases. Find out what prepositions should be used in the blanks. To what extent is your dictionary helpful in giving you this information?

a poem admitting ___ two interpretations
aiming ___ success
accounting ___ his friend's absence
allowing ___ possible delays
amounting ___ a hundred dollars
answering ___ that description
blame him ___ the accident
bidding ___ our support
applying ___ him for help
attended ___ serious consequences

11. *The synonyms of the word.* A synonym of a word is another word of closely similar meaning. *Difficult* and *hard, climb* and *ascend,* and *wound* and *injury* are synonyms. Few synonyms are entirely interchangeable; between synonyms there are usually differences in connotation or in areas of use. Every desk dictionary includes a number of synonymies, paragraphs that differentiate among sets of synonyms. The following synonymy is from the *American College Dictionary* at the end of the treatment for *brave:*

> —Syn. 1. BRAVE, COURAGEOUS, FEARLESS, GALLANT refer to confident bearing in the face of difficulties and dangers. BRAVE is the most comprehensive; it is especially used of that confident fortitude or daring that actively faces and endures anything threatening. COURAGEOUS implies a higher or nobler kind of bravery, esp. as resulting from an inborn quality of mind or spirit which faces or endures perils or difficulties without fear or even with enthusiasm. FEARLESS implies unflinching spirit and coolness in the face of danger. GALLANT implies chivalrous, impetuous, dashing, or showy bravery.

At the conclusion of the treatments for *courageous, fearless,* and *gallant* are synonymy cross references like the following:—Syn, *See* brave. The synonymy paragraph is the clearest treatment by the dictionary of differences among synonyms. Other indications of differences are given in the etymologies, the usage labels, and the definitions.

EXERCISE

27. Find all the differences that you can among the words in the following sets of synonyms. Make full use of all that your dictionary tells you:

defraud, cheat, gyp, swindle
drunk, souse, sot, soak, alcoholic, boozer, drunkard, inebriate
fool, dope, simpleton, gull, dupe, patsy, moron, oaf, lout

scram, depart, go away, leave
sophisticated, suave, smooth, hep, urbane, cosmopolitan
hut, shack, hovel, lodge
stout, fat, chunky, plump, thickset, corpulent, tubby, stocky
walk, stroll, amble, march, plod, saunter, hike, trudge
fluster, upset, startle, agitate, ruffle, disturb, unsettle

It is not the primary purpose of a dictionary to serve as a word finder; it is not the intent of the dictionary maker to produce a book intended to help you find synonyms. This is done by various books on synonyms. One of these is *Roget's Thesaurus* (in various editions), which simply lists synonyms. In it you will find under *wonder,* for instance, such synonyms as *astonishment, amazement, wonderment, admiration, awe, fascination,* and *surprise.* Although this book includes a great number of words and their synonyms, it does not call to your attention how these various synonyms differ from each other. A number of other collections contain discriminated synonymies, notably the Merriam Company *Webster's Dictionary of Synonyms.*[2] This book discusses *wonder, wonderment, amaze, amazement,* and *admiration* together, pointing out differences in their suggestion and use and illustrating with quotations from prominent authors.

EXERCISE

28. By using your dictionary, find as many synonyms as you can for the following: *agile, awkward, caress, confuse, dark, eager, fashion, hate, include, kill, meager, offer, profane, recoil, scold, small, talkative.* What additional synonyms are given in *Roget's Thesaurus?* What additional information do you find in *Webster's Dictionary of Synonyms* or a similar book?

This chapter is actually just an introduction to the mass of information contained in your dictionary. To understand how much information it offers you, by all means read the introductory matter in which the dictionary maker explains his purposes and procedures further. To learn some of this information and to apply it, use your dictionary and keep using it. No matter how good your dictionary is, it will not help you in any way if you do not use it. Look up any word about which you are uncertain or curious—and keep on doing so every day.

[2] *Webster's Dictionary of Synonyms,* Springfield, Mass., 1942.

EXERCISE

29. Review this chapter on dictionary use. Then be prepared to explain in full any information conveyed by any part of each of the following three entries:

Webster's New Collegiate treatment for *manage*

man'age (măn'ĭj), *n.* [It. *maneggio*, fr. *maneggiare* to manage, fr. *mano* hand, fr. L. *manus.* In Eng. influenced by F. *ménage* housekeeping.] **1.** *Archaic.* Management. **2.** *Archaic.* The action and paces of a trained riding horse. **3.** A riding school; manège. — *v. t.;* MAN'AGED (-ĭjd); MAN'AG·ING (-ĭj·ĭng). **1.** To train (a horse) in the manège; to put through his paces. **2.** To control and direct; to conduct; guide; administer. **3.** To render and keep (one) submissive; to wield with address. **4.** To treat with care; to husband. **5.** To bring about by contriving; to contrive. — *Syn.* See CONDUCT. — *v. i.* **1.** To direct affairs; to carry on business or affairs. **2.** *Colloq.* To achieve one's purpose.

American College treatment for *metal*

met·al (mĕt'əl), *n., v.,* **-aled, -aling** or (*esp. Brit.*) **-alled, -alling. 1.** any of a class of elementary substances, as gold, silver, copper, etc., all of which are crystalline when solid and many of which are characterized by opacity, ductility, conductivity, and a peculiar luster when freshly fractured. **2.** an alloy or mixture composed wholly or partly of such substances. **3.** *Chem.* **a.** a metal (def. 1) in its pure state, as distinguished from alloys. **b.** an element yielding positively charged ions in aqueous solutions of its salts. **4.** formative material; mettle. **5.** *Printing, etc.* **a.** type metal. **b.** the state of being set up in type. **6.** *Brit.* broken stone used for roads or railroad track ballast. **7.** molten glass in the pot or melting tank. **8.** *Her.* either of the tinctures gold (*or*) and silver (*argent*). —*v.t.* **9.** to furnish or cover with metal. [ME, t. OF, t. L: m.s. *metallum* mine, mineral, metal, t. Gk.: m. *mĕtallon* mine]

Webster's New World treatment for *child*

child (chīld), *n.* [*pl.* CHILDREN (chil'drən)], [ME. *childe,* pl. *childre* (now dial. *childer; children* is double pl.); AS. *cild,* pl. *cild, cildru;* akin to Goth. *kilthei,* womb; IE. **gel-t,* a swelling up < base **gel-,* rounded; sense development: rounded—swelling—womb—fetus—offspring; cf. CALF (animal)], **1.** an infant; baby. **2.** an unborn offspring. **3.** a boy or girl in the period before puberty. **4.** a son or daughter. **5.** a descendant. **6.** a person like a child in interests, judgment, etc., or regarded as a child; immature or childish adult. **7.** a person regarded as the product of a specified place, time, etc.: as, a *child* of the Renaissance. **8.** a thing that springs from a specified source; product: as, a *child* of one's imagination. Abbreviated **ch., c., Ch.** (in senses 3, 4, 5).
with child, pregnant.

16

SPELLING

English spelling is neither entirely consistent and logical nor entirely inconsistent and illogical. It does, however, have a great number of inconsistencies. We are inconsistent in spelling *proceed* with two *e*'s between the *c* and the *d*, but *procedure* with only one. If *comparative* is spelled with an *a* between the *r* and the *t*, we might expect *comparison* to have an *a* between the *r* and the *s* but instead it has an *i*. The words *rough, thought, though* and *through* suggest the rather bewildering number of values attached to the spelling *-ough*. The spelling of many of our words does show unreasonable quirks. The result of lack of complete consistency is that although one may be reasonably sure about, say, six or seven letters in an eight-letter word, he must often learn the others by heart.

Our Society Values Correct Spelling

The second fact that you should know about English spelling is more important: for good or ill, whether it is logical or not, whether we like it or not, English spelling is a part of our culture. Our society values it—in fact, values it rather highly. Our society attaches a value to your correctly writing *allotted* (with two *t*'s instead of one), *repetition* (with an *e* between the *p* and the *t*), and *changeable* (with an *e* between the *g* and the *a*). Whether our society should feel as it does in attaching a value to such matters is beside the point here: the important thing is that it does. If your letter of application has the misspellings *acheivement, equiped, excellant,* and *concideration* (instead of the correct forms *achievement, equipped, excellent,* and *consideration*), you probably won't get the job regardless of what good qualifications you have. This attitude may be unfortunate in so far as criticism of writing is concerned. The sentence "saftey is the first principal of driveing," with *safety* and *driving* misspelled and with *principal* used instead of *principle,* is probably a better sentence than the sentence: "a procedure calculated to insure maximal safety may be regarded as the primary principle in the operation of a motor vehicle." But the social attitude about the value of spelling is an existent fact. "Accurate spelling is expected of all educated people. Incorrect spelling is penalized heavily in our society. Indeed, misspelling is the commonly accepted sign of illiteracy."[1]

If You "Never Could Spell. . . ."

Although very, very few persons can correctly spell every word in the language without considerable hesitation, it cannot be a very difficult mental feat for you to learn the spelling of those words that you use frequently. It is well to concentrate on them and to let *zymurgy, phthisic,* and *hegemony* go for a while. You may resent spelling, feel that you "never could spell," that you have always been "a poor speller." But you cannot become a good speller any younger in your life. Now is the time to change from the habit of misspelling, which has never done you any good and which will hurt you more and more in the future unless you correct it now. And you can change now.

A book like this can give you some rules and principles for spelling. It will do so shortly. But the rules and principles that can be given do not apply to all words. Because, as has been said, English spelling is often inconsistent and illogical, there are many words that you simply have to learn individually and know by heart. There are two steps in this process.

Look at Word Parts Closely

First, and more important, look closely at these words; examine them in detail; look at each letter. Contrary to what may have been taught you in the grades in reading, do not try to absorb the whole word as a meaningful unit all at once. It is not your problem merely to recognize the word but to know in detail the parts of it. Concentrate on the letters

[1] Thomas Clark Pollock and William D. Baker, *The University Spelling Book* (Englewood Cliffs, N.J.: Prentice-Hall, Inc., 1955), p. 1.

used at the one or two places at which you are likely to go wrong in spelling. Note, for instance, the following:

environment	business	consistent
occasion	similar	athletic
embarrass	dependent	ridiculous

If you are "not a very good speller," the chances are that you have simply glanced at these nine combinations of letters, come to realize what words are being given, and gone on to read this sentence. This is *not* what you are to do here—unless you *want* to continue to be a bad speller. Look at the words again in detail, letter by letter, syllable by syllable. Try it again. Have you noticed that *environment* has an *n* between the *o* and the *m?* Have you seen that *business* is spelled with an *i* after the *s?* Have you noticed that the last syllable of *consistent* has an *e* in it? that *occasion* has two *c*'s and one *s?* that *similar* ends in *l a r,* with nothing between the *l* and the *a?* that there is nothing between the *th* and the *l* in *athletic?* that *embarrass* has two *r*'s and two *s*'s? that *dependent* contains no vowel other than *e?* that the first vowel in *ridiculous* is *i?*

Let us try another list. Do not treat this too rapidly; do not be satisfied merely with recognizing what words are given; instead, look carefully at the details of their spelling:

prevalent	loneliness	existence
curiosity	explanation	hypocrite
adequate	boundary	concede
favorite	changeable	sergeant

Look at them again and, after so doing, see if you can answer the following questions quickly: what is the vowel in the last part of the noun meaning person who shows hypocrisy? what vowels come in the middle of the noun meaning quality of being curious? what is the vowel in the last syllable of the noun formed from *to exist?* what is the vowel in the middle of the noun meaning process of explaining? what is the vowel in the last syllable of the noun meaning favored one?

Then Learn the Words

After looking carefully at the spelling of a word, learn it. How best to do this is your own problem, since it depends on how you have trained your own mind. You may try spelling it over and over again to yourself. You may try writing it a number of times, especially after waiting an hour or so after looking at it. You may want to keep a list of words that you have learned recently, adding to it words that you have misspelled and then learned. You may wish to think of memory aids; you may want to recall that it is curious that *curiosity* is not spelled like *curious + ity*. These matters depend on you.

Learn the Rules—and Their Opposites

Some rules and principles for certain spelling situations follow, but before studying them, you should notice two things. First, most rules have exceptions. Second, when you learn a rule, notice that often you can learn and apply its opposite or converse. When you are told, for instance, that a final consonant is likely to double before a suffix beginning with a vowel if the base word is accented on the last syllable (*regret, regretted, regretting*), notice also that the final consonant is *not* likely to double under the same circumstances if the accent of the base word is *not* on the last syllable (*barter, bartered, bartering; blacken, blackened, blackening*).

SP 1 *Notice the numbers of syllables in words*

Be sure that your spelling shows the right number of syllables for the word in question. A syllable is a word division that contains a vowel sound. (The definition is adequate here, although of course words like *cat* and *man* and *set* are single syllables themselves.) If you are a little uncertain about the number of syllables in words, perhaps it will help you to note that the following words contain three syllables: *absolute, adequate, consider, definite, extremely, imagine, occurrence, operate, professor, quantity, together, tragedy.* Similarly, notice that the following are four-syllable words: *accidental, accommodate, arithmetic, comparative, dissatisfy, exaggerate, psychology, ridiculous, significance, undoubtedly.* Sometimes the following words are misspelled because the italicized syllable vowels in them are omitted:

Three-syllable words:

bound*a*ry	bus*i*ness	court*e*ous	crit*i*cism	crit*i*cize
cru*e*lty	cur*i*ous	hyg*i*ene	l*i*able	marr*i*age
now*a*days	soph*o*more			

Four-syllable words:

anxiety	appropriate	colloquial	continuous	enthusiasm
experience	hurriedly	ingenious	laborious	luxurious
mathematics	medieval	original	parliament	temperament
temperature				

Five-syllable words:

accidentally	accompaniment	contemporary	curiosity
enthusiastic	liability	notoriety	sociology

Some other words are frequently misspelled because of a tendency of poor spellers to add syllables. The following are two-syllable words:

athlete	Britain	lightning	nervous
usage	village	villain	

The following are three-syllable words:

athletic	barbarous	devastate	mischievous
poisonous	similar	tremendous	

The following are four-syllable words:

available	unanimous

SP 2 *Do not omit consonants*

Rather than leaving out vowels with resulting loss of whole syllables, you may make spelling mistakes by leaving out consonants. This often happens in the spelling of consonant clusters, as in the following words. Do not omit:

c in *arctic, practical*
d in *candidate, handkerchief, sandwich*
g in *recognize, recognition*
h in *exhausted, exhilarate*
n in *environment, government*
p in *impromptu*
r in *February, library, reservoir, surprise, persevere, quarter*
t in *quantity, mortgage, representative, attempt, contempt, evidently, excerpt*

SP 3 *Notice i after a consonant and before a vowel*

The letter *i* sometimes functions more as part of a consonant group than as a single vowel by itself. Notice the word *Grecian*, for example.

Although it would be possible to pronounce this word with three syllables with *i* having a vowel value, most of us pronounce this word with only two syllables. But we do not pronounce the *c* as we pronounce it in *city* or *civil*—that is, with an *s* sound—instead we pronounce the *ci* combination as *sh*. It is the function of the *i* in this word to lead us to sound the *ci* combination as we do. Notice that *ci* is similarly pronounced in *commercial, efficient, physician,* and *sufficient.* Do not omit the *i* after the *c* in these words. Notice, too, that after *t* the *i* is also important in pronunciation. The combination of *ti* in *Christian* is usually pronounced as *ch.* The same combination (*ti*) is pronounced as *sh* in *nation,* as also in the last part of *fictitious.* The letter *i* between a consonant and a vowel may have the consonant sound of *y.* Contrast both the sound and the spelling of *familiar* and *similar.* Be careful not to omit the *i* in situations in which it affects the sound of the preceding consonant. Such misspellings as *efficent, familar, and convenent* are especially irritating to many people. Notice the following words carefully:

auxiliary	behavior	beneficial	brilliance
brilliant	Christian	commercial	conscience
conscientious	conscious	convenience	convenient
deficiency	deficient	efficiency	efficient
especial	especially	familiar	financial
influential	initiate	peculiar	politician
substantial	sufficiency	sufficient	

SP 4   *Try to notice word relationships*

Sometimes an allied or related form may give you a hint as to how a word is spelled. If you hesitate, for instance, about a vowel in the last syllable of the word *grammar,* you may rightly guess that it is *a* if you think of the word *grammatical,* in which the *a* is clearly pronounced. The following sets may help you:

advantage advantageous	ecstasy ecstatic
analysis analytic	explanation explanatory
apology apologetic	fantasy fantastic
arithmetic arithmetical	importance importation
column columnist	medicine medicinal
continuous continuity	narrative narration
courage courageous	origin original
difference differential	vegetable vegetate

Some words frequently misspelled are associated with other words by common root elements. Thus *refer, defer, transfer, offer,* and *differ* are all linked by a common root meaning "bear, carry," which is also found in *fertile*. Your spelling problems may be made somewhat easier by knowing root elements. Knowing that *aggravate* contains the same root element as *grave* or *gravity* may help you; the spelling of *accommodate* (with two *m*'s) is easier if you know that its root element is also found in *commodity* and *commodious*. You may find it useful to remember the following pairs:

absolute solution	conscience science
accumulate cumulative	consequently sequence
achieve chief	definite finish
acquaint quaint	destruction destroy
across cross	familiar family
adequate equate	immediate mediate
appetite petition	impromptu prompt
apparent parent	laboratory labor
attempt tempt	prejudice judicial
benefit benevolent	recommend commend
buoyant buoy	surround round
candidate candid	villain villa

Only one common root element creates much of a problem in so far as variation in its form is concerned—the verb element pronounced "seed" in *precede*, *proceed*, and *supersede*. This element is usually spelled *-cede*: *accede*, *concede*, *intercede*, *precede*, *recede*, and *secede*. Three verbs—*proceed*, *succeed*, and *exceed*—use the *ceed* spelling. *Supersede*, originally from a different Latin base, is spelled with an *s* instead of a *c*; it is the only common verb so spelled.

The preceding part of this section has stressed similarities among related words. Unfortunately, related words occasionally show confusing differences in spelling. Note each of the following pairs carefully:

curious curiosity	hinder hindrance
comparative comparison	maintain maintenance
despair desperate	pertain pertinent
disaster disastrous	pronounce pronunciation
enter entrance	remember remembrance
explain explanation	

SP 5 *Learn the* ie-ei *rule*

Many writers have to stop for a moment to think about the sequence of *i* and *e* before they write *believe* and *receive* and similar words. The well-known jingle (page 409) may help you spell such words.

> *i* before *e*
> except after *c*
> and when sounded as *a*
> as in *neighbor* and *weigh*

But the jingle needs some explanation and reservation:

1. *i* before *e*. This is the sequence in most common words: *friend, thief, grief, brief, shield, wield, believe, achieve, relief.*
2. except after *c*. A *c* immediately preceding reverses this order: *ceiling, deceive, receive, receipt.* (*Ch* does not operate as *c* alone does: *chief, mischief, achieve.*)
3. when sounded as *a*. Words in which the combination has an *a* sound are spelled *ei*: *neighbor, weigh, weight, freight, vein, veil, rein.*
4. There are a number of miscellaneous exceptions to the *ie-ei* rule: *either, neither, weird, leisure, foreign, seize, sovereign, counterfeit, forfeit, financier, species.*
5. When the combination has the sound of *i* as in *bite* or *ride* it is usually written *ei*: *height, Fahrenheit.*
6. The rule does not apply to plurals of nouns: *mercies, captaincies, democracies.*
7. This rule does not apply at all when the two letters *i* and *e* come together but are sounded individually, that is, when each vowel is part of its own syllable: *quiet, medieval, society, deity, deicer.* It does not apply when the *i* follows a *c* to indicate the *sh* sound: *efficient, proficient.* (See Section 3.)

SP 6   *Notice spelling of prefixes*

A prefix is a short form used before a word or word form to modify its meaning. In *untie*, the syllable *un-* is a prefix; in *commit*, *com-* is a prefix. *Un-* is a living prefix, in the sense that it is still used to form words; *com-* is no longer living, although of course it appears in a number of words.

Prefixes cause two problems in English spelling: (1) choice between similar prefixes, (2) choice of letters used in the joining together of prefix and following element. These two problems are often interrelated and will be treated together in the following discussion. One over-all comment can be made here about the second of these problems: usually all letters involved in both prefix and following elements are retained. Thus *misspell* is made up of the prefix *mis-* and the word *spell*; it has two *s*'s. *Unnecessary* has two *n*'s because it is composed of the prefix *un-* and the word *necessary*.

A number of prefixes, most of them no longer living and no longer used to form new words, show a tendency to adjust in form to the following element. One common prefix used with elements of Latin origin was *com-*. If this were joined to the word elements *-lapse* and *-rupt* it would produce the rather awkward forms *comlapse* and *comrupt*. Consequently these two words have emerged as *collapse* and *corrupt*. *Ad-* was another common prefix. *Adpear* and *adfect* would not have been as easy to say as the words we actually have: *appear* and *affect*. In *collapse, corrupt, appear,* and *affect* the first one of the double consonants comes from the original prefix, the second from the word form to which the prefix has been added. Retention of the prefix consonant in such situations is one reason for the rather large number of doubled consonants in English.

The following list of prefixes is limited to those that seem to cause trouble in English spelling. In many cases comments about what these prefixes mean are to be interpreted very widely and loosely:

> *a-* (in, on, but meaning varies). *across, arise, arouse, among.* Causes no doubling.
>
> *ad-* (to, toward, very, but meaning varies). Results in doubled consonants in *address, addition, adduce,* and, with change of form, in *accommodate, accept, accompany, accustom, affect, affirmative, aggravate, aggression, allot, apparent, appear, appreciate, appropriate, associate, attempt, attitude, attend, attract.* Spelled *ac-* before *qu: acquaint, acquit.*
>
> *ante-* (before). *antedate, antecedent.* But note *anticipate.*
>
> *anti-* (against). *antidote, anticlimax.* Often used with hyphen, as in *anti-labor.*
>
> *be-* (around, about, away, but meaning varies). *begin, belief, become, before, behavior.*
>
> *com-* (with, together, very, but meaning varies). Results in doubled consonants in *command, communicate, commercial, committee, communist,* and, with change of form, in *collaborate, collapse, connect, correct, correspond, corrupt.*
>
> *de-* (away, from, down, but meaning varies). *deceive, defer, definite, describe, desperate, destruction, descend, despair.*
>
> *dis-* (away, off, opposing, not). Results in doubled consonants in *dissimilar, dissent, dissatisfy, dissolve,* and, with change of form, in *different, difficult, diffident.* Spelled *di-* in *digress* and *diverge.*
>
> *ex-* (away, from, out). Results, with change of form, in doubled consonants in *eccentric, effect, efficient.*
>
> *for-* (away, from, off, but meaning varies). *forbid, forgo, forget.*
>
> *fore-* (before, previous). *forecast, foreclose, forerunner, foresight, foresee, foretell, forewarn.*

in- (in, into). Results in doubled consonants in *innate* and, with change of form, in *illuminate, immigrate, irrigate.*

in- (not, opposing). Results in doubled consonants in *innocent* and, with change of form, in *illegal, illiterate, illogical, immaterial, immature, immense, immovable, irregular, irrelevant, irresistible, irreverent.*

inter- (within). *intercede, intercept, interfere, interpose, interpret, interrupt, intervene.*

intro- (between). *introduce.*

mis- (not, wrongly). Results in doubled consonants in *misshape, misspell, misstate, misstep.* No doubling in *misapply, miscarry, misdeal, misjudge, misplace.*

ob- (against, toward, over). Results, with change of form, in doubled consonants in *occasion, occupy, offense, oppose, opportunity, oppress.*

per- (through, thoroughly, but meaning varies). *permit, perceive, perfect, perform, permission, persevere, persist, persuade, perhaps, pertain.*

pre- (before in time or place). *precede, prefer, prejudice, prepare, prevalent, predominant.*

pro- (before, but meaning varies). *proceed, profess, professor, pronounce, proportion.*

re- (again, back). Results in doubled vowels in *re-echo, re-enter, re-enlist.*

sub- (under, beneath, but meaning varies). Results, with change of form, in doubled consonants in *succeed, success, sufficient, suffocate, suggest, suppose, suppress, supplement, support, surround, surrender.*

sym- (with, but meaning varies). Results in doubled consonants in *symmetry* and, with change of form, in *syllable.*

trans- (over, across). Results in doubled consonants in *transship.* Note spelling of *transcribe* and *transpire.*

un- (not). Results in doubled consonants in *unnatural, unnecessary, unnerve, unnumbered.*

SP 7   *Notice spelling of suffixes*

A suffix is a short form used after a word or word form to modify its meaning. In *improvement* the syllable *-ment* is a suffix; in *conclusive* the syllable *-ive* is also a suffix, although we have no independent word *conclus* or *concluse.*

Suffixing may cause doubling of consonants

Sometimes the final consonants of words are doubled when suffixes are added: *set-setting, refer-referring,* but *bite-biting, beat-beating.* Doubling occurs only when *all three of the following conditions exist:* (1) the consonant is final, that is, when the word does not end in *e:*

plan planning	occur occurring	cure curing	describe describing
bat batting	omit omitting	make making	confide confiding

(2) the consonant is single, that is, when the word does not end in two or more consonants:

bet betting	drag dragging	excel excelling	rest resting
win winning	bar barring	defer deferring	reject rejecting

(3) the consonant is preceded by a single vowel:

sin sinning	allot allotting	moan moaning	detain detaining
pad padding	begin beginning	read reading	exceed exceeding

(The *u* of the *qu* combination is not here considered as a vowel: *acquit acquitting, equip equipping.*)

Notice how these principles work; let us try making up some *-ing* forms:

hope	*Hope* ends in *e.* There is no doubling.	hoping
ebb	These words do not end in single consonants.	ebbing
cast	There is no doubling.	casting
cheer	In these words the vowels are not single.	cheering
beat	There is no doubling.	beating
get	These words end in consonants. In each the con-	getting
drip	sonant is single. In each case it is preceded by	dripping
swim	a single vowel. Therefore there is doubling.	swimming

So far, our illustrations have concerned *-ing* forms alone but the same principles apply with other suffixes beginning with vowels: *-ed, -er, -able,* and so on. Often these principles mean that after a short vowel there is doubling, after a long vowel no doubling. Notice the following:

to scrap the old ships
scrapping the old ships
the old ships were scrapped

to can the fruit   *Scrap, can,* and *wag* have single final
canning the fruit   consonants preceded by single vowels.
she canned the fruit   These vowels are short.

to wag its tail
wagging its tail
the dog wagged its tail

to scrape the hull
scraping the hull
they scraped the hull

to cane the chair seat
caning the chair seat
he caned the chair seat

In *scrape, cane,* and *wage* the consonants are not final; instead the words end in *e.* Vowels in these words are long.

to wage war
waging war
they waged war

So far this section has been concerned with one-syllable words. With words of two syllables there is an additional complication: final consonants are doubled only if the second syllable of the word in question is accented. Let us consider the word *begin.* The *n* is final; it is single; it is preceded by a single vowel (*i*). In this word the accent falls on the second syllable, one says beGIN, not BEgin. Hence there are two *n*'s in *beginner* and a total of three in *beginning.* In *omit* the single final consonant *t* is preceded by the single vowel *i;* the accent is on the last syllable. Hence there are two *t*'s in *omitted* and *omitting.* Compare with this word the word *vomit:* since the accent in *vomit* falls on the first syllable, the *t* is not doubled in *vomited* and *vomiting.* Sometimes the forms derived from a single base differ. *Referred* and *referring* show doubled *r*'s, since in these words the accent is on the second syllable, but *reference* does not show a doubling, since in it the accent is not on the second syllable. The position of the accent is so nearly even in *kidnap* that we have both *kidnaped* and *kidnapped.* Sometimes *l* is doubled in unaccented syllables (*traveller, totalled, quarrelling*), but this procedure is more British than American. Most Americans prefer *traveler, totaled, quarreling.* Some words borrowed from French, like *chagrin* and *ricochet,* resist doubling: *chagrined, ricocheted.*

The letter *c* has two sounds: the "hard" sound of *k,* as in *cat* and *cot,* and the "soft" sound of *s,* as in *cent* or *city.* When a word ends in "hard" *c,* like *picnic* or *panic,* its *-ing* and *-ed* forms are likely to show a *k* added after the *c: picnicking, picnicked, panicking, panicked.*

Words ending in consonant plus suffix beginning with consonant

Although a number of suffixes begin with consonants, the suffixes *-ly, -ness,* and *-ment* seem to cause more trouble than the others when they are added to words ending in consonants. The principle is to add the suffix to the word without changing the form of either:

| barbarously | continuously | ruggedness | embarrassment |
| conveniently | curiously | wastefulness | equipment |

Often this results in doubled consonants; note that the following are correct:

really	evenness	drunkenness
cruelly	openness	stubbornness
coolly	thinness	keenness

Be sure to retain the final consonant of the original word form in the following:

| carelessly | differently | environment |
| evidently | strictly | government |

Many adverbs end in -ally, some being formed from adjectives ending in -al with -ly added, some from adjectives ending in -ic with -ally added. Note the -ally endings on the following:

really	formally	accidentally	influentially
finally	originally	incidentally	mathematically
generally	basically	athletically	characteristically
actually	practically	optimistically	

Adverbs made from adjectives ending in two l's are not spelled with three: *fully, illy, dully.*

Words ending in vowel plus suffix beginning with consonant

1. Words ending in e. The usual procedure is simply to add the suffix: *abatement, lamely, tameness, meddlesome, largely, hopeless, lifelike.* Be sure to retain the e in each of the following:

likely	scarcely	absolutely	immediately
surely	extremely	severely	decisively
lively	adequately	sincerely	comparatively
lonely	separately	desperately	approximately
merely	divinely	negatively	definitely

Note also the words *safety* and *ninety.*

The following are exceptional in omitting the e although the suffixes used do begin with consonants: *wholly, duly, truly, argument, judgment, acknowledgment, ninth.*

2. Words ending in y. Words ending in y fall into two groups: those

in which the final *y* is preceded by a consonant, like *angry* and *envy*, and those in which it is preceded by a vowel, like *bay* and *enjoy*. In adding a suffix beginning with a consonant to words of the first group, change the *y* to *i* and add the suffix:

accompany + ment	accompaniment	noisy + ly	noisily
merry + ment	merriment	lively + hood	livelihood
icy + ness	iciness	likely + hood	likelihood
lonely + ness	loneliness	beauty + ful	beautiful
hungry + ly	hungrily	duty + ful	dutiful

If another vowel comes before *y* at the end of a word, one usually adds the suffix without change: *joyful, coyness, employment. Daily* and *gaily* are exceptions.

Words ending in consonant plus suffix beginning with vowel

The usual procedure in dealing with the combination of a word ending in a consonant and a suffix beginning with a vowel is simply to add the suffix without addition or subtraction of letters: *acquaintance, characterize, consideration, consistent, difference, foreigner, interesting, occasional, performance, similarity.*

The chief problem that comes up here is whether or not to double the consonant. Since in each of the following the accent falls on the second syllable and in each one the second syllable contains a single vowel, the final consonant of the base word is doubled: *acquittal, remittance, controllable, admittance, abhorrence, rebellion, demurrer. Deference, preference,* and *reference* do not show consonant doubling because their accents fall on the first syllables.

Words ending in vowel plus suffix beginning with vowel

1. Words ending in *e*. The usual procedure is to omit the *e* and add the suffix: *declare-declaration, defense-defensible, arrive-arrival, compose-composure, hate-hated, come-coming, dine-diner.* The following are sometimes misspelled:

lose + ing	losing	use + ing	using
dine + ing	dining	hide + ing	hiding
prove + ing	proving	argue + ing	arguing
write + ing	writing	believe + ing	believing
argue + able	arguable	desire + able	desirable
guide + ance	guidance	continue + ous	continuous

Sometimes the final *e* is retained to indicate the soft sound of *c* (*s*) or *g* (*j*). According to the rule the combination of the word *peace* and the suffix *-able* would be spelled *peacable*, but this could be mispronounced as *peakable;* hence the correct spelling is *peaceable*, with the *e* retained, which is not likely to be mispronounced. Note the following: *advantageous, changeable, chargeable, forceable, outrageous, manageable,* and *vengeance. Mileage* is a common exception to the rule. A few *-ing* forms are spelled like *singeing* and *dyeing* to prevent confusions.

2. Words ending in *y*. If a consonant comes before the *y* at the end of a word, the *y* is changed to *i* before a suffix beginning with a vowel except for suffixes like *-ing, -ish,* and *-ism,* which begin with *i.* The word *studious* is made up of *study* and the suffix *-ous;* note that *y* has been changed to *i.* When *bury* and *-al* are joined, the result is *burial,* with the same change. Note also *pitiable, marriage, loveliest,* and *fortieth.* A suffix beginning with *i* is simply added to a word ending in *y* without change in or addition to either. To form the present participles of *study* and *hurry,* one simply adds *-ing* to them: *studying, hurrying.* Note *babyish, Toryism.* Note also the unusual formations *beauteous, piteous,* and *bounteous. Flyer* is an acceptable alternate spelling for *flier.*

If a vowel comes before the *y* at the end of a word, a suffix beginning with a vowel is added without addition or change: *betrayal, conveyance, boyish, buoyant, employer.* The verb forms *paid* and *said* are exceptions to the general rule, as is *gaiety.*

SP 8   *Notice formation of noun plurals*

Formation of the plurals of nouns involves problems of suffixing. The great majority of English nouns simply add *-s* to form the plural, regardless of the last letter of the singular form. After sibilants (*s, sh, ch, x, z*), *-es* is added: *gases, masses, dishes, ditches, boxes, topazes.* An *f* as the last consonant in the singular is often changed to *v* in the plural: *calf-calves, wolf-wolves, wife-wives, thief-thieves,* but *roof-roofs, safe-safes, chef-chefs.* A number of words ending in *o* add *-es* to form the plural: *buffaloes, cargoes, echoes, mosquitoes, Negroes, potatoes, tomatoes, vetoes.* Many others, especially those in which another vowel comes just before the final *o,* simply add *-s: bamboos, cameos, folios, banjos, casinos, lassos, pianos, sopranos, torsos, zeros.* A noun ending in *y* preceded by a consonant forms its plural by changing *y* to *i* and adding *-es: army-armies, lady-ladies, fly-flies, ferry-ferries, penny-pennies,* but *toy-toys, essay-essays.* The plural of *child* is of course *children,* and our language has a few sets like *foot-feet, tooth-teeth, louse-lice, mouse-mice.* The formation of foreign plurals—the process whereby the plural of *basis* is *bases,* that of *radius* is *radii,* and that of *phenomenon* is *phenomena*—is dealt with on pp. 260–261. Most compounds form their plurals by adding *s* to the last part or by otherwise inflecting it: *atom bomb-atom bombs, dog fight-dog fights, toothpick-toothpicks, horseman-horsemen.* (To form possessive singulars one does *not* change *f* to *v* or *y* to *i* or add *-es* after *o;* note the following possessive singular forms: *wife's, lady's, Negro's;* nominative and objective plural forms *wives, ladies, Negroes;* possessive plural forms *wives', ladies', Negroes'.*)

SP 9 *Notice variant forms*

Some words have more than one acceptable spelling: *ax-axe, center-centre, dispatch-despatch, enclose-inclose, humor-humour.* Your dictionary is your best source of information about preferences between variant forms (see p. 385). It is better, in situations in which you have a choice, to use forms that accord with the rules and principles given in the foregoing sections, that is, to prefer *leveled* to *levelled* and *riveted* to *rivetted.* It is better to use American rather than British forms and to prefer *color, favor,* and *labor* to *colour, favour,* and *labour, center* and *miter* to *centre* and *mitre,* and *apologize* to *apologise.*

Spelling List

Following is a list of the words most commonly misspelled in student writing. Since the words in this list occur in about three-quarters of the misspellings in college themes, they are singularly important. That is why they are presented to you in detail. The first column presents the word in question in its ordinary form, with no unusual printing device. The second column gives its division into syllables; this will often be helpful to you in learning its spelling. The third column prints in bold-face parts of words causing spelling mistakes and confusions. The fourth column attempts wherever possible to explain spelling difficulties. Numbers given in parentheses in this column refer to parts of the foregoing section. The fifth column gives grammatical forms and more common derivatives of the base words being treated. Go over these words carefully. Do not be content with merely reading them, with merely perceiving what words are given here. Notice every letter of them. Notice the first *u* in *continuous,* the first *e* in *noticeable,* the two *r*'s and the two *e*'s in *occurrence*. And learn the spelling of these words thoroughly—so that you remember them not merely until the end of this day, or this week, or this semester, but until well into the twenty-first century.

absence	ab sence	absence	like *presence* (4)	absences
absent	ab sent	absent	like *present* (4)	absently
absolute	ab so lute	absolute	last part related to *solution* (4)	
absolutely	ab so lute ly	absolutely	*e* retained before -*ly* (7)	
accident	ac ci dent	accident	-*ad* prefix (6)	accidents
accidental	ac ci den tal	accidental	note *t* (2)	
accidentally	ac ci den tal ly	accidentally	*accidental* and -*ly;* two *l*'s (7)	
accommodate	ac com mo date	accommodate	*ad*- prefix (6)	accommodated accommodating
achieve	a chieve	achieve	*a*- prefix (6); *ie-ei* rule (5)	achieved achieving achieves
achievement	a chieve ment	achievement	*ie-ei* rule (5); *e* retained (7)	achievements
acquaint	ac quaint	acquaint	*ad*- prefix (6); last part *quaint*	acquainted acquainting acquaints
acquaintance	ac quaint ance	acquaintance	*a* in first and third syl.	acquaintances
acquire	ac quire	acquire	*ad*- prefix (6)	acquired acquiring acquires
acquit	ac quit	acquit	*ad*- prefix (6)	acquits
acquitted	ac quit ted	acquitted	second syl. accented (7)	
acquitting	ac quit ting	acquitting	second syl. accented (7)	
across	a cross	across	*a*- prefix (6); *a*- and *cross*	
adequate	ad e quate	adequate	*ad*- prefix (6); last part *equate* (4)	inadequate
adequately	ad e quate ly	adequately	*e* retained before -*ly* (7)	
aggravate	ag gra vate	aggravate	*ad*- prefix (6); middle syl. related to *grave* (4)	aggravated aggravating aggravates

allot	al lot	allot	*ad-* prefix (6); last part *lot*	allots allotting
allotted	al lot ted	allotted	second syl. accented (7)	
almost	al most	almost	one *l*	
among	a mong	among	*a-* prefix (6)	
analysis	a nal y sis	analysis	*ana-* prefix; last part as in *paralysis*	analyses
analyze	an a lyze	analyze	*ana-* prefix (6)	analyzed analyzing analyzes
apology	a pol o gy	apology	*apo-* prefix (6)	apologies
apologize	a pol o gize	apologize		apologized apologizing apologizes
apparent	ap par ent	apparent	*ad-* prefix (6)	apparently
appear	ap pear	appear	*ad-* prefix (6)	appeared appearing appears
appearance	ap pear ance	appearance	*a* in each syl.	appearances
appreciate	ap pre ci ate	appreciate	*ad-* prefix (6); related to *precious;* for *-ci* see (3)	appreciated appreciating appreciates
argue	ar gue	argue		argued arguing argues
argument	ar gu ment	argument	*e* drops before *-ment,* an exception (7)	arguments
arise	a rise	arise	*a-* prefix (6)	arising arises
arithmetic	a rith me tic	arithmetic		arithmetical
athlete	ath lete	athlete	two syl. (1)	athletes
athletic	ath let ic	athletic	three syl. (1)	athletics athletically
barbarian	bar bar i an	barbarian	four syl. (1)	barbarians
barbarous	bar ba rous	barbarous	three syl. (1)	barbarously
begin	be gin	begin		begins
beginner	be gin ner	beginner	second syl. accented (7)	beginners
beginning	be gin ning	beginning	second syl. accented (7)	beginnings

belief	be lief	belief	*ie-ei* rule (5)	beliefs
believe	be lieve	believe	*ie-ei* rule (5)	believed believing believes
beneficial	ben e fi cial	beneficial	related to *benevo-lent* (4); for *-ci-* see (3)	beneficially
benefit	ben e fit	benefit	related to *benevolent* (4)	benefited benefiting benefits
boundary	bound a ry	boundary	three syl. (1)	boundaries
business	bus i ness	business	*y* to *i* (7)	businesses
candidate	can di date	candidate	related to *candid* (4)	candidates
career	ca reer	career	no doubled *r*	careers
careless	care less	careless	*e* retained before *-less* (7)	carelessly
carry	car ry	carry	two *r*'s	carried carrying carries
category	cat e go ry	category	first part related to prefix of *catechism* (4)	categories
certain	cer tain	certain		certainly
challenge	chal lenge	challenge		challenged challenging challenges
changeable	change a ble	changeable	*e* retained before *-able* for soft sound of *g* (7)	changeably
character	char ac ter	character	associate with *act*	characteristic
choose	choose	choose	two *o*'s in present form	choosing chooses
chose	chose	chose	one *o* in past tense	
chosen	cho sen	chosen	one *o* in past part	
coming	com ing	coming	*e* drops; no doubling (7)	becoming unbecoming
comparative	com par a tive	comparative	*a* in this word	comparatively
comparison	com par i son	comparison	*i* in this word	comparisons
competitive	com pet i tive	competitive	related to *compete* and to *petition* (4)	competitively

competitor	com pet i tor	competitor	related to *compete* and to *petition* (4)	competitors
completely	com plete ly	completely	*e* retained before *-ly* (7)	
conceive	con ceive	conceive	*ie-ei* rule (5)	conceived conceiving conceives
conscience	con science	conscience	*con-* and *science;* for *-ci-* see (3)	consciences
conscious	con scious	conscious		consciously
consider	con sid er	consider		considered considering considers
consistency	con sist en cy	consistency		consistencies
consistent	con sist ent	consistent		consistently
continuous	con tin u ous	continuous	four syl. (1); *e* dropped before *-ous* (7)	continuously
controlled	con trolled	controlled	second syl. accented (7)	
controlling	con trol ling	controlling	second syl. accented (7)	
controversy	con tro ver sy	controversy		controversies
convenience	con ven ience	convenience	for *-ni-* see (3)	conveniences
convenient	con ven ient	convenient	for *-ni-* see (3)	conveniently
courteous	cour te ous	courteous	three syl. (1)	courteously
courtesy	cour te sy	courtesy	*e* as in *courteous*	courtesies
criticism	crit i cism	criticism	*critic* and *-ism* (7); three syl. (1)	criticisms
criticize	crit i cize	criticize	*critic* and *-ize* (7); three syl. (1)	criticized criticizing criticizes
curiosity	cu ri os i ty	curiosity	five syl. (1)	curiosities
curious	cu ri ous	curious	three syl. (1)	curiously
deceive	de ceive	deceive	*ie-ei* rule (5)	deceived deceiving deceives
decide	de cide	decide		decided deciding decides
decision	de ci sion	decision	for *-si-* see (3)	decisions
defer	de fer	defer	last part related to *fertile* (4)	defers

deference	def er ence	deference	first syl. accented (7)	deferences
deferred	de ferred	deferred	second syl. accented (7)	
deferring	de fer ring	deferring	second syl. accented (7)	
definite	def i nite	definite	de- and finite (4), (6), related to finish	definitely
describe	de scribe	describe	de- ("down") and scribe (4), (6)	described describing describes
description	de scrip tion	description	related to describe (4)	descriptions
desirable	de sir a ble	desirable	e drops before -able (7)	desirably
desperate	des per ate	desperate		desperately
destruction	de struc tion	destruction	related to destroy (4)	destructions
difference	dif fer ence	difference	dis- prefix (6); related to fertile	differences
different	dif fer ent	different	dis- prefix (6); related to fertile	differently
disappoint	dis ap point	disappoint	dis- and appoint (6)	disappointed disappointing disappoints
disastrous	dis as trous	disastrous	e dropped from disaster (1), (4)	disastrously
dissatisfy	dis sat is fy	dissatisfy	dis- and satisfy (6)	dissatisfied dissatisfying
effect	ef fect	effect	ex- and -fect- (6); related to last part of perfect (4)	effected effecting effects
effective	ef fec tive	effective	effect and -ive (7)	effectively
efficiency	ef fi cien cy	efficiency	for -ci- see (3)	efficiencies
efficient	ef fi cient	efficient	for -ci- see (3)	efficiently
eighth	eighth	eighth	one t dropped in adding -th to eight	
eliminate	e lim i nate	eliminate		eliminated eliminating eliminates

embarrass	em bar rass	embarrass	two r's, two s's	embarrassed embarrassing embarrasses
entertain	en ter tain	entertain		entertained entertaining entertains
enthusiasm	en thu si asm	enthusiasm	four syl. (1)	enthusiasms
enthusiastic	en thu si as tic	enthusiastic	five syl. (1)	enthusiastically
equip	e quip	equip		equips
equipped	e quipped	equipped	second syl. accented (7)	unequipped
equipping	e quip ping	equipping	second syl. accented (7)	
exaggerate	ex ag ger ate	exaggerate	two g's; related to gerund (4)	exaggerated exaggerating exaggerates
exaggeration	ex ag ger a tion	exaggeration	exaggerate and -ion	exaggerations
excel	ex cel	excel		excels
excelled	ex celled	excelled	second syl. accented (7)	
excellence	ex cel lence	excellence	first syl. accented— exception to rule (7)	excellences
excellent	ex cel lent	excellent	first syl. accented— exception to rule (7)	excellently
excelling	ex cel ling	excelling	second syl. accented (7)	
exercise	ex er cise	exercise		exercised exercising exercises
existence	ex ist ence	existence		existences
experience	ex pe ri ence	experience	four syl. (1)	experiences experienced experiencing
explanation	ex pla na tion	explanation	the i in explain is dropped (4)	explanations
extremely	ex treme ly	extremely	e retained before -ly	
familiar	fa mil iar	familiar	for -li- see (3); related to family (4)	familiarly
fascinate	fas ci nate	fascinate		fascinated fascinating fascinates

favorite	fa vor ite	favorite		favorites
February	Feb ru ar y	February		
finally	fi nal ly	finally	*final* and *-ly* (7)	
foreign	for eign	foreign	exception to *ie-ei* rule (5)	foreigner
forty	for ty	forty	*u* from *four* dropped	fortieth
fourth	fourth	fourth	*u* from *four* retained	
further	fur ther	further		furthermore
government	gov ern ment	government	note the first *n* (2), (7)	governments
grammar	gram mar	grammar	note *grammatical* (4)	grammars
guarantee	guar an tee	guarantee	begins like *guard*	guaranteed guaranteeing guarantees
harass	har ass	harass	one *r;* contrast *embarrass*	harassed harrassing harasses
height	height	height	*ie-ei* rule (5); final *t*, not *th*	heights
hindrance	hin drance	hindrance	*e* of *hinder* drops (1), (4)	hindrances
hypocrisy	hy poc ri sy	hypocrisy		hypocrisies
hypocrite	hyp o crite	hypocrite		hypocrites
imaginary	im ag i nar y	imaginary	*e* drops before *-ary* (7)	
imagine	im ag ine	imagine	one *m;* related to *image* (4)	imagined imagining imagines
imitate	im i tate	imitate	one *m*	imitated imitating imitates
immediate	im me di ate	immediate	*in-* prefix (6); related to *mediate* (4)	immediately
incidental	in ci den tal	incidental		incidentally
independence	in de pend ence	independence		
independent	in de pend ent	independent		independently
indispensable	in dis pen sa ble	indispensable	from *dispense*	

influential	in flu en tial	influential	mid-part *fluent;* for *-ti-* see (3)	influentially
interest	in ter est	interest	three syl. (1)	interested interesting interests
interpret	in ter pret	interpret	note second *r*	interpreted interpreting interprets
involve	in volve	involve	*in-* prefix (4)	involved involving involves
irresistible	ir re sist i ble	irresistible	*in* ("not") pre-fix (6)	irresistibly
knowledge	knowl edge	knowledge		knowledgeable
laboratory	lab o ra to ry	laboratory	five syl. (1); from *labor* (4)	laboratories
led	led	led	*a* drops from *lead* in past tense	
leisure	lei sure	leisure	exception to *ie-ei* rule (5)	leisured
license	li cense	license		licenses
likelihood	like li hood	likelihood	*y* to *i* before *-hood* (7)	
likeliness	like li ness	likeliness	*y* to *i* before *-ness* (7)	
likely	like ly	likely	*e* retained before *-ly* (7)	likelier likeliest
livelihood	live li hood	livelihood	*y* to *i* before *-hood*(7)	
liveliness	live li ness	liveliness	*y* to *i* before *-ness* (7)	
lively	live ly	lively	*e* retained before *-ly* (7)	livelier liveliest
loneliness	lone li ness	loneliness	*y* to *i* before *-ness* (7)	
lonely	lone ly	lonely	*e* retained before *-ly* (7)	lonelier loneliest
losing	los ing	losing	contrast *loose*	
maintain	main tain	maintain	*ai* in both syl.	maintained maintaining maintains
maintenance	main te nance	maintenance	*e* in the second syl., not *ai*	

maneuver	ma neu ver	maneuver		maneuvered maneuvering maneuvers
marriage	mar riage	marriage	*y* to *i* before *-age* (7)	marriages
marry	mar ry	marry		married marrying marries
mathematics	math e mat ics	mathematics	four syl. (1)	
merely	mere ly	merely	*e* retained before *-ly* (7)	
necessary	nec es sar y	necessary	one *c*, two *s*'s	necessaries necessarily
necessity	nec es si ty	necessity	one *c*, two *s*'s	necessities
nineteen	nine teen	nineteen	*e* retained before *-teen* (7)	nineteenth
ninety	nine ty	ninety	*e* retained before *-ty* (7)	nineties
ninth	ninth	ninth	*e* dropped	
noticeable	no tice a ble	noticeable	*e* retained before *-able* for soft sound of *c* (7)	noticeably
occasion	oc ca sion	occasion	*ob-* prefix (6); two *c*'s, one *s*	occasions occasioned occasioning
occur	oc cur	occur	*ob-* prefix (6)	occurs
occurred	oc curred	occurred	accent on second syl. (7)	
occurrence	oc cur rence	occurrence	accent on second syl. (7)	occurrences
occurring	oc cur ring	occurring	accent on second syl. (7)	
omission	o mis sion	omission	one *m*	omissions
omit	o mit	omit	one *m*	omits
omitted	o mit ted	omitted	accent on second syl. (7)	
omitting	o mit ting	omitting	accent on second syl. (7)	
operate	op er ate	operate	one *p*; related to *opera*	operated operating operates
opinion	o pin ion	opinion	one *p*; for *-ni-* see (3)	opinions

opportunity	op por tu ni ty	opportunity	*ob-* prefix (6)	opportunities
optimism	op ti mism	optimism		optimisms
optimist	opti mist	optimist		optimists
origin	or i gin	origin		origins
parallel	par al lel	parallel		parallels
				paralleled
				paralleling
perceive	per ceive	perceive	*per-* prefix (6); *ie-ei* rule (5)	perceived
				perceiving
				perceives
perform	per form	perform	*per-* prefix (6)	performed
				performing
				performs
performance	per form ance	performance	*perform* and *-ance*	performances
persistence	per sist ence	persistence	*persist* and *-ence*	
persistent	per sist ent	persistent	*persist* and *-ent*	persistently
possess	pos sess	possess	two doubled *s*'s	possessed
				possessing
				possesses
possession	pos ses sion	possession	two doubled *s*'s	possessions
practical	prac ti cal	practical	contains word *act*	practically
precede	pre cede	precede	*-cede* (4)	preceded
				preceding
				precedes
precedent	pre ced ent	precedent	*precede* and *-ent* (7)	precedents
prefer	pre fer	prefer	*pre-* prefix (6); related to *fertile* (4)	prefers
preference	pre fer ence	preference	first syl. accented (7)	preferences
preferred	pre ferred	preferred	second syl. accented (7)	
preferring	pre fer ring	preferring	second syl. accented (7)	
prejudice	prej u dice	prejudice	*pre-* prefix (6); related to *judicial* (4)	prejudices
preparation	prep a ra tion	preparation	*prepare* and *-ation* (7)	preparations
prepare	pre pare	prepare	*pre-* prefix	prepared
				preparing
				prepares
prevalent	prev a lent	prevalent	related to *prevail*	prevalence

privilege	priv i lege	privilege		privileges privileged
probable	prob a ble	pro**bable**		probably
procedure	pro ce dure	procedure	one *e* in *-ced-*	procedures
proceed	pro ceed	proc**eed**	contrast *precede* (4)	proceeded proceeding proceeds
professor	pro fes sor	pro**fes**sor	*pro-* prefix (6); related to *confessor* (4)	professors
prominent	prom i nent	prominent		prominently
psychology	psy chol o gy	**psycho**logy	first syl. used in many other words (4)	psychological psychologist
pursuit	pur suit	pur**suit**	*e* drops (7)	pursuits
quantity	quan ti ty	quantity	note first *t* (2)	quantities
quiet	qui et	quiet		quiets quieted quieting quietly
really	re al ly	really	*real* and *-ly* (7)	
receive	re ceive	rec**eive**	*ie-ei* rule (5)	received receiving receives
recognition	rec og ni tion	recognition	note *g* (2)	recognitions
recognize	rec og nize	recognize	note *g* (2)	recognized recognizing recognizes
recommend	rec om mend	recommend	*re-* prefix (6); compare *commend* (4)	recommended recommending recommends
refer	re fer	re**fer**	related to *fertile*	refers
reference	re fer ence	reference	first syl. accented (7)	references
referred	re ferred	referred	second syl. accented (7)	
referring	re fer ring	referring	second syl. accented (7)	
relief	re lief	relief	*ie-ei* rule (5)	reliefs
relieve	re lieve	reli**eve**	*ie-ei* rule (5)	relieved relieving relieves

religion	re li gion	relig**ion**		religions
remembrance	re mem brance	remem**brance**	*e* in *remember* drops (1), (4)	remembrances
repetition	rep e ti tion	repetition	related to *repeat*	repetitions
responsible	re spon si ble	responsible		responsibly
rhythm	rhythm	**rhythm**		rhythms
ridiculous	ri dic u lous	ridiculous	related to *deride* (4)	ridiculously
safety	safe ty	safety	*safe* and *-ty* (7)	safeties
seize	seize	seize	*ie-ei* rule exception (5)	seized seizing seizes
sense	sense	sense		senses sensed sensing
separate	sep a rate	separate		separated separating separates
sergeant	ser geant	ser**geant**		sergeants
shining	shin ing	shining	*e* drops before *-ing* (7)	
significance	sig nif i cance	significance		significant
similar	sim i lar	similar	three syl. (1)	similarly
sophomore	soph o more	sophomore	three syl. (1)	sophomores
speech	speech	speech	contrast *speak* (4)	speeches
studying	stud y ing	studying	*study* and *ing* (7)	
succeed	suc ceed	suc**ceed**	*sub-* prefix (6); *ceed* (4)	succeeded succeeding succeeds
succession	suc ces sion	suc**cession**	*sub-* prefix (6); related to *cession* (4)	successions
suppose	sup pose	su**pp**ose	*sub-* prefix (6)	supposed supposing supposes
suppress	sup press	su**pp**ress	*sub-* prefix (6)	suppressed suppressing suppresses
surprise	sur prise	surprise		surprises surprised surprising

surround	sur round	surround	*sur-* and *round*	surrounded
				surrounding
				surrounds
technique	tech nique	technique		technique
temperament	tem per a ment	temperament	four syl. (1)	temperaments
tendency	tend en cy	tendency		tendencies
themselves	them selves	themselves	*them* and *selves*	
therefore	there fore	therefore	*there* and *fore*	
thorough	thor ough	thorough		thoroughly
together	to geth er	together		
tragedy	trag e dy	tragedy		tragedies
transfer	trans fer	transfer	*trans-* and *fer:* related to *fertile* (7)	
transferred	trans ferred	transferred	second syl. accented (7)	
transferring	trans fer ring	transferring	second syl. accented (7)	
undoubtedly	un doubt ed ly	undoubtedly		
unusual	un u su al	unusual	four syl. (1)	unusually
usage	us age	usage	two syl. (1); *e* drops before *-age* (7)	
useful	use ful	useful	*e* retained before *-ful* (7)	
various	var i ous	various	*y* to *i* (7)	variously
vary	var y	vary		varied
				varying
				varies
villain	vil lain	villain	two syl. (1)	villains
weird	weird	weird	*ie-ei* rule exception (5)	weirdly
written	writ ten	written		

17

GLOSSARY
OF USAGE

Language, whatever else it is, is something of a folk custom, a folkway. Just as folk customs change, so language changes. Language usages that would have been impossible in polite society at one time may be accepted now. Folkways, however, are not very logical or consistent, particularly where change is involved. Customs A and B may change easily and readily, but changes in custom C may be resisted. So with language. The fact that usages A and B are accepted does not mean that usage C is accepted.

Our code of etiquette on language consequently includes usage matters that do not lend themselves to general treatments like those on sentence unity, grammar, and punctuation. You were told in the chapter on grammar that the past-tense form of a verb is not used in compounded forms. This principle will guide you away from *have broke* and *has stole* and many similar forms. But no general principle will guide you away from using *ain't*. *Ain't* is a natural contraction for *am not,* just as *aren't* is a natural contraction for *are not*. According to logic, the one should be as acceptable as the other. But, as you know, many people object strongly to *ain't*. In this situation, our society has not been consistent about language etiquette.

Most freshman English texts call attention to details—like the objection to *ain't*—that do not lend themselves to statements of general principles. This book also presents details for you to notice. But first you may be interested in knowing about some of the situations in which a changing language causes problems—the situations in which our society has not been consistent and logical in its language judgments:

1. Functional change occurs when a word belonging to one part of speech comes to be used as another part; it happens when a word that was originally only a noun comes to be used as a verb too, and *vice versa*. English shows thousands of illustrations of functional change. We have, for instance, the following verbs evolved from nouns through functional change: *worship, blaze, gleam, cripple, pride, wheel, file, hook, saw, stitch, dust, bloom, blast, flock, snow, edge, fork, hammer, pin, mind*. But thousands of other words have not undergone functional change. If we try to say "she cannot command obey from her pupils, and her teach is poor," we will not be talking acceptable English, no matter how many verbs other than *obey* and *teach* have yielded new nouns through functional change. When a word starts to undergo functional change, that is, when it is used as a part of speech different from its original one, some people accept and employ the new use, but others object to it. Modern English has seen widespread use of the word *like* as a subordinating conjunction, but many people object to uses such as "he dresses like his brother does." Many other connective words have changed function in English, and perhaps the objection is not logical. But it exists in our society.

2. The word *semantic* means "pertaining to meaning," and semantic change is change in the meaning of a word. English has thousands of illustrations of semantic change. The word used in Old English to describe the awesome dragon that brought about Beowulf's death was *worm*. The meaning of this word has changed through the intervening centuries so that the word now applies mostly to harmless earthworms. The word *nausea* is related to the word *nautical;* it once referred only to seasickness but has changed so that it now applies to any marked queasiness. *Steward* once meant something like "guard over the pig sties," but has changed so that it can apply to dignified court positions. If you look at an unabridged dictionary, you will find that the great majority of common words show semantic change. On the other hand, the scope of semantic change is, after all, limited. If it were not, every word could mean everything. *Mother* has not come to mean "battleship," "detour," "cinnamon," "elevation," or "trout."

When a word is in the process of changing meaning, some people use it freely in its new meaning, but others avoid that new meaning and object to it. The word *unique,* for example, is now commonly used in the sense of "unusual, strange, noteworthy as startlingly different." Some people prefer, however, to use it only in its earlier sense—that of "single, sole, only one extant," as in "the manuscript of the play is unique," meaning that it is the only one in existence. Semantic changes cause problems in usage.

3. New words are being made up every day. Some become common and are accepted as parts of the language. Some fade out almost unnoticed and are soon forgotten. Generally, words formed by standard processes of adding prefixes and suffixes are likely to be accepted if there is a real need for them. But new words and forms are evolved by other methods. Sometimes the ending of an established word is dropped or clipped off to make a new form. Some people object to words so formed. *Reminisce* was formed by dropping the last syllable of *reminiscence*, and *enthuse* by dropping that of *enthusiasm;* both of these new words have been objected to. The fact that there is rarely objection to *edit* and *donate,* which were both formed by dropping the last syllables of longer words, does not lessen the objection to *reminisce* and *enthuse.* Logic and meaning are sometimes used in judgments of word forms. Thus *irregardless* is objected to, since it means the same thing as *regardless* but should according to its form mean the opposite. But no one objects to *unloosen,* which means about the same thing as *loosen.*

There are likewise changes in grammatical forms. Such changes are natural and normal in English; there have been a great many changes in grammatical forms in the history of the English language. Many verbs that were formerly irregular have become regular—verbs like *sigh, creep, help, yield, milk, starve, mourn, shave,* and *bake,* which form their past tenses with *-ed* or a variant of it. But in most cases there is no apparent logical principle that determines which forms will change, which forms will not. If we can say "he mowed the field" and "he rowed the boat," we really ought to be able to say "he knowed the fact" and "he growed the plants." But these latter two uses are objected to strongly.

To turn from verbs to nouns, many plural forms from Latin and Greek have emerged as singulars in today's English; there is no objection to *insignia* and *stamina* as singulars, although they were originally plurals. But there is some objection to *data, phenomena,* and *bacteria* as singulars. Neither the acceptance of *stamina* as a singular nor the objection to *phenomena* as one is entirely logical.

4. The grammar of one age may be rejected in part and objected to in a following age. At one time it was general practice in English to stress a negative idea by doubling or tripling negatives. Chaucer and Shakespeare often used this device. Later, however, it became fashion-

able to use only one negative word and to gain stress only by other devices, like use of such words as *certainly* or *positively*. But not everyone is fashionable. Many persons retained old ways and continued to use double negatives. The man who says "I never want to eat no squash nohow" is not breaking away from an old established pattern; he is being stubbornly conservative in keeping a way of speaking that went out of fashion more than two centuries ago. Sometimes, as with functional and semantic change, formal English may be more conservative than other varieties; sometimes non-standard English may be more conservative in retaining the usages of the past.

People often lack consistency in grammatical preferences. In early English many verbs were limited to either transitive or intransitive uses. (A *transitive* verb is one that takes an object; in "he built the house," "they bought the house," "she rented the house," "we repaired the house," the verbs *built, bought, rented,* and *repaired* are transitive because each has an object, *house*. An *intransitive* verb is one that does not take an object; in "we looked at the house," "they thought about the house," "we moved into the house," and "this was the house," the verbs *looked, thought, moved,* and *was* are intransitive because they do not take objects.) Many formerly intransitive verbs came to be used with objects and many transitive verbs without them. These usages were, by and large, accepted and became part of English; no one now objects to "they swam their horses across the river"; "the nurse walked the invalid down the hall"; "this slaughterhouse kills on Fridays"; "he tries to buy low and sell high." But acceptance of these usages has not brought with it acceptance of all similar usages. There is still determined opposition to use of *set* and *lay* as intransitives, aside from certain established idioms.

5. As used here, *idiom* means a commonly used set or fixed sequence of words for which literal word-for-word interpretation is difficult. "To make up one's mind" is an idiom. One doesn't, strictly speaking, do any making, nor is there any idea of up-ness, of rising or ascent, connected with the process. But the phrase is fixed; it is a standard part of the language. Other similar expressions include "to be at odds," "to be off," "to make friends with," "to bear down," "to beat a retreat." Once an idiom is fixed, there is resistance to changing it. Many people use *in regard to* but object to the slight variation *in regards to*. Often there is little reason for preferences in idioms; there is no logical reason, for instance, why everyone has accepted "commenced speaking" but some persons have objected to "commenced to speak."

Sometimes logic is used in criticizing idiomatic expressions. A logical analysis may find certain words unnecessary. In "to fill up," for instance, the *up* is unnecessary; the expression means little more than "to fill." Usages like this are called *redundant*. Many teachers object to redundancy or tautology in formal English. Their objections are often well taken; it is hard to defend expressions like "at 9 A.M. in the morning." On the other hand, natural speech and writing are often not so sparing of words as they might be, and some redundant constructions seem to show a pleasing rhythm. Most service station men say "Fill it up?" (or "Fill her up?") rather than "Fill it?" and the redundancy does not appear to bother their customers.

6. If an expression becomes associated with one particular activity, it is sometimes disconcerting to hear or see it used in connection with another, especially one considerably different. The term *rhubarb*, meaning "squabble," has been fairly well established in accounts of baseball games, but it would be disconcerting to hear or see it used in connection with a more serious activity, as in "the Russian delegation caused a big rhubarb at the United Nations." *Party* in the sense of "person entering into a contract" is well established in legal usage, but it has been objected to as a synonym for *person* in writing concerning other activities.

7. *Homonyms* are words that are either the same or quite similar in pronunciation but different in meaning and etymology. The verb *bear* meaning "carry, support, sustain" and the noun *bear* meaning "large shaggy animal" are homonyms. Occasionally it happens that distinctions between two homonyms are lost. If there is a difference in pronunciation or spelling, one form may drop out of the language. English at one time had the homonymous verbs *think* and *thenk;* the latter has of course dropped out. But once people have taken the trouble to learn the differences between homonyms they are often not very tolerant of confusions between them. In the list of words following, there are several homonymous sets. Notice the differences among them—the differences among "the core of the apple," "the cadet corps," and "the undertaker took away the corpse," and between "the letter was censored" and "the letter was censured."

The following comments sometimes try to discern between *standard* and *non-standard English*. These terms mean in this list what they meant in Chapter 2; review that chapter if you are in doubt. There are numbers in parentheses after most of the following paragraphs; these numbers refer to sections in the preceding introductory discussion.

a, an: *a* is used before a word beginning with a consonant sound (*a* college, *a* city, *a* desk), *an* before a word beginning with a vowel sound (*an* apple, *an* evening, *an* inning). Notice the importance of the first sound of the following word, rather than the first letter in its spelling: *a* ewe, *a* European, *a* unit, *a* university, *an* hour, *an* honest man. Wording like "a apple" or "a error" is non-standard. (5)

above: informal when used as an adjective, as in "subject to the *above* qualification," or as a noun or pronoun, as in "note the above." These usages suggest business and legal affairs and may be objected to elsewhere. (1, 6)

accept, except: *accept* is a verb meaning "to receive, often willingly," as in "Evans *accepted* the nomination." *Except* is usually a preposition; in its occasional verb uses it means "leave out, exclude," as in "older men are *excepted* from freshman regulations." (7)

ad: this abbreviated form for *advertisement* or *advertising* is usually regarded as informal. Some old abbreviated forms like *mob, cad, bus,* and *piano* have won their way to use in most formal English, but others like *phone, photo, lab, bike,* and *gym* remain informal. If you can see without much thought that a form is a clipped or abbreviated form, you can usually regard it as informal. Clipped forms for academic subjects, like *econ, phys ed, poly sci, trig,* and *chem,* are informal, but *gent* for *gentleman* is non-standard. (3)

advice, advise: *advice* is a noun, as in "to give him some *advice*"; *advise* is a verb, as in "to *advise* him." (7)

affect, effect: as a verb, *affect* is likely to mean "to influence, condition, make a change in," as in "soil conditions *affect* the growth of plants." As a noun, *affect* is used mostly in psychology. *Effect* as a verb means "to produce, make, accomplish," as in "this change in the rules was *effected* in May." *Effect* is often a noun, as in "the *effect* of these rules." (7)

after: following *after* with a non-finite verb form suggesting past time has been regarded as redundant; "after finishing the report, he took a vacation" has been preferred to "after having finished the report. . . ." (5)

aggravate: informal in the sense of "annoy, irritate," as in "the noise that the children made *aggravated* their mother." In formal uses *aggravate* means "intensify, make worse, make more serious," as in "the tense situation was *aggravated* by several border clashes." (2)

ain't: always non-standard, although widely used as a contraction for "am not," as a general negative contraction for other forms of *to be,* as a contraction for *have not* and *has not.* (3, 5)

alibi: legal in the sense of plea that a person accused was at another place than the scene of a crime, as in "his *alibi* for the Los Angeles murders was that he was in Boston at the time." Informal in the sense of "excuse, mitigating reason," as in "oversleeping as an *alibi* for cutting the class." (2, 6)

all ready, already: *all ready* is an adjective phrase meaning "entirely in readiness," as in "the truck was *all ready* to leave." *Already* means "previously, by the time in question," as in "he had *already* bought his ticket." (7)

all the farther, all the longer, all the faster, etc.: these constructions, as in "this is all the farther I go," "that was all the longer the rope would reach," are informal or non-standard. Wording like "this is as far as I go" is acceptable in any style.

all together, altogether: *all together* is an adjective or adverb phrase meaning "assembled together, united in a group," as in "the men were all together in the hall." *Altogether* means "entirely, completely." He was *altogether* too hasty in making that decision. (7)

allusion, illusion: an *allusion* is a passing reference or suggestion, as in "making *allusions* to old scandals," "*allusions* to Plato in Cicero's works." An *illusion* is a deceptive appearance or false perception, as in "the red glass in the window produced the *illusion* that the building was on fire." (7)

almost, most: *almost* is an adverb meaning "nearly, practically," as in "the cake is *almost* done," "*almost* all the books are here." *Most* is not used as an equivalent for *almost* in formal English. (7)

already. *See* all ready, already.

altogether. *See* all together, altogether.

alumnus, alumni, alumna, alumnae: *alumnus* and *alumni* are masculine singular and plural forms, respectively: an *alumnus* of Notre Dame or Colgate, *alumni* of Notre Dame or Colgate. *Alumna* and *alumnae* are feminine forms: an *alumna* of Smith, the *alumnae* of Wellesley. *Alumni* is the plural form usually used in reference to coeducational institutions: the *alumni* of Michigan. (3)

A.M., P.M.: A.M. and P.M. mean "in the morning" and "in the afternoon or evening," respectively. Expressions like "at 8 A.M. in the morning" or "by 3 P.M. in the afternoon" are redundant. Use of A.M. and P.M. is usually restricted to situations in which a specific time is given, and expressions like "I'll do it this P.M." are non-standard. (2)

among, between: it is often said that *among* should be used in reference to situations concerning three or more, as in "divided equally *among* the three of us," and that *between* should be used only in situations concerning two and no more. But use of *between* in the former situation, especially when a common relationship is involved, is usual even in formal English, as in "a pact between the three countries." (2)

amount, number: *amount* is likely to be used of things measured or weighed rather than counted, *number* of things readily counted, as in "the *amount* of money," "*amount* of manpower," "*amount* of hair," but "the *number* of dollar bills," "*number* of men," "*number* of hairs." Usages like "the *amount* of books he has read" are informal. (2)

an. *See* a, an.

analysis: the plural form is *analyses,* as in "these analyses have been made." (3)

and, but: starting sentences with *and* and *but* is quite correct procedure even in most formal English. Sometimes starting a sentence with *and* or *but* may give additional emphasis, as in "He boasted that he would become president of the company. And he did just that." Like any other special writing device, use of *and* or *but* at the beginning of a sentence should be employed only with moderation. (4)

and etc.: *etc.* is the abbreviation of *et cetera,* which means "and others." The expression *and etc.* is redundant and non-standard. (5)

angry, mad: *mad* is now so commonly used to mean "angry" that it seems useless for anyone to object to this wording. It must be called standard, although it may be regarded as informal. (2)

any one, anyone: *any one* may stress the idea of individuality, of any one single individual person or thing, as in "if *any one* here in this group wants further proof." *Anyone* is the common indefinite pronoun serving as a synonym for *anybody,* as in "if *anyone* calls, say that I am out." (7)

anywheres: non-standard, as in "we couldn't find the ball *anywheres*"; *anywhere* is standard. (3, 5)

apex: the plural forms are *apexes* and *apices.* The former is now more common. (3)

appendix: the plural forms are *appendixes* and *appendices.* The former is now more common. (3)

arise, arouse: *arise* is an intransitive verb and does not take an object. He will *arise* at six. *Arouse* is transitive and does take an object. To *arouse* still more trouble. (4)

as: (a) *as* is likely to be unclear as a subordinating conjunction, since it means both "at the time that, while" and "since, because." A sentence like "*as* the bus was approaching the corner, I started for the door" is ambiguous, since *as* may express either meaning—or both. Whenever possible, replace *as* as a subordinating conjunction with a more clear word like *because* or *when.* (b) *As* is non-standard as an equivalent for *that* or *whether,* especially in sentences showing uncertainty or doubt. "I am not sure *that* I want to buy the saw" is preferred to "I am not sure *as* I want to buy the saw." (5) (c) As a subordinating conjunction, *as* is preferred in formal English to *like.* "We wrapped the goods *as* the foreman ordered" is preferred to "we wrapped the goods *like* the foreman ordered." See like.

aspect: informal in the general sense of "characteristic," as in "his bad temper is his worst *aspect*." (2)

at: non-standard and redundant in sentences in which other words express the idea of place, location, or situation, like "where is it *at?*" instead of "where is it?" (5)

awful, awfully: *awful* is informal as a synonym for *poor* or *very poor,* as in "the grade-B movie was awful, and we walked out before it was over." *Awfully* is informal as a synonym for *very,* as in "I was *awfully* tired after the game." (2)

axis: the plural form is *axes.* (3)

back of, in back of: informal as equivalents for *behind,* as in "the car was parked *in back of* the house." (5)

bacteria: a plural form, as in "these *bacteria* have been identified." The singular form, used much less commonly, is *bacterium.* (3)

bad: non-standard when used as an adverb in constructions like "he was hurt *bad.*"

basis: the plural form is *bases.*

because. *See* reason is because.

being as, being that: these constructions are non-standard as equivalents for *since* and *because* in sentences like "*being that* the car wouldn't start, we drove to the city in the truck" and "*being as* I am a freshman, I don't know about fraternity organization." (5)

beside, besides: *beside* is usually a preposition meaning "by the side of," as in "the tree *beside* the house." *Besides* is usually an adverb meaning "additionally, other, else," as in "*besides,* I did not like the way he acted"; "we have to pay the interest *besides.*" (3, 7)

bet: principal parts are *bet, bet, bet.* (3)

between. *See* among, between.

biased: *biased*—not just *bias*—is the adjective form meaning "showing prejudice or partiality," as in "maybe I am *biased* about him."

bid: for the majority of the meanings and uses of *bid,* many of them archaic, acceptable principal parts are *bid, bade* or *bid, bidden* or *bid.* For the sense of making a bid or offer, as at an auction, principal parts are *bid, bid, bid.* (3)

bike. *See* ad.

blame: the construction *blame it on,* as in "they *blamed the wreck on* the engineer," is non-standard. Standard English freely uses constructions like "they *blamed* the engineer for the wreck." (5)

born, borne: *born* is the past participle of *bear* in the sense of bringing forth young, as in "he was *born* in 1940." *Borne* is the past participle of *bear* in other senses. This single beam has *borne* the whole weight of the floor. (7)

borned: non-standard. *See* born, borne.

borrow: usually followed by *from* in Standard English. Use of *off* rather than *from,* as in "I borrowed five dollars *off* my roommate," is non-standard. (5)

both: using *the* to modify *both,* as in "*the both* of them," "*the both* brothers," is non-standard. (5)

breath, breathe: *breath* is a noun, as in "out of *breath* after the run." *Breathe* is a verb, as in "we could hardly *breathe* in the stifling room." (7)

broadcast: although the form *broadcasted* is sometimes used, the forms *broadcast,* (as in "the station *broadcast* the news"), and *broadcast* (as in "the news *broadcast* by the station") are always acceptable standard English. (3)

burst: the principal parts in standard English are *burst, burst, burst.* The form *bursted* is non-standard. (3)

bust: non-standard as a verb form, although no one can object very strongly to its use in such set phrases as "boom or *bust.*" (3)

but: (a) *see* and, but. (b) In constructions like "there aren't *but* two games left on the schedule," *but* acts as a negative, and the effect is that of an unintended double negative. *See* double negatives. The construction is non-standard. (5)

but that, but what: "There is no doubt *but that* the bill will pass" is formal but heavy. "There is no doubt *but what* the bill will pass" is not formal; at best it is informal. Neither construction adds much to the simpler expression of meaning: "There is no doubt *that* the bill will pass." (5)

can, may: in strictly formal English *can* is limited to situations involving ability, as in "he *can* swim across the lake." *May* is used in situations involving permission, as in "you *may* swim with the other group"; "*may* I hand the paper in later?" (2, 3, 5)

can't hardly. *See* double negatives. *Can't hardly* may be called an unintended double negative. As such, it is non-standard, as in "he *can't hardly* lift the weight." Either "he can't lift the weight" or "he *can hardly* lift the weight" would fit with the English of any level. (5)

can't help but: sometimes objected to as an unintended double negative. *See* double negatives. Following *can't help* with a non-finite verb form ("you can't help admitting that he is right"; "you can't help liking him") is always satisfactory. (5)

capital, capitol: the word *capitol* means only the building in which legislature meets, as in "funds were needed to redecorate the *Capitol.*" The word *capital* is used for all other meanings. (7)

cast: acceptable principal parts are *cast, cast, cast.* (3)

cause: redundant in a sentence in which another word or phrase also expresses the idea of reason or cause, as in "the *cause* of the fire was on account of defective wiring." The following expressions are preferred: "the *cause* of the fire was defective wiring"; "defective wiring caused the fire"; "the fire happened because of defective wiring." (5)

caused by: incoherent, when used without clear reference to a specific noun, as in "the train was late, *caused by* the heavy snow." The following are preferred: "the train was late because of the heavy snow," "the lateness of the train, *caused by* the heavy snow . . ."

chem. *See* ad.

cite, sight, site: *cite* is a verb meaning "call up, summon, notice," as in "*cited* for contempt of court," "*cited* for distinguished service." *Sight* is a noun meaning "thing seen" or a verb meaning "to see." *Site* is a noun meaning "place, locale, location," as in "this field is the new school *site.*" (7)

complected: non-standard and objected to as a shortened form of *complexioned.* A single adjective—like *fair, blond, dark,* or *swarthy*—will usually free you from need to use either *complected* or *complexioned.* (3)

complement, compliment: *complement* means "that which fulfils or completes," as in "a regiment without its full *complement* of men." A *compliment* is an expression of praise or pleasure, as in "many *compliments* on her appearance." (7)

considerable: non-standard in noun and adverb uses, as in "he lost *considerable* on the sale" and "her health has improved *considerable.*" (1, 3)

contact: informal as a verb meaning "communicate with," as in "the salesmen were *contacting* various prospects," "he *contacted* the main office." (1)

continue on: *on* is redundant in this phrase. (5)

corps, corpse: *corps* means an organized group, especially a military unit, as in "the U.S. Army signal *corps.*" *Corpse* means a dead body. (7)

crisis: the plural form is *crises.* (3)

curriculum: plural forms are *curriculums* and *curricula.* (3)

daren't: the standard contraction for *dare not.* The contraction *daresn't* is non-standard. (3)

data: a plural form, with *datum* as a rather rarely used singular. Use of *data* with a plural verb, as in "these data are now being processed," is standard. There is an increasing tendency, however, to use *data* as a singular, as in "this *data* is. . . ." (3)

dessert, desert: the word for sweet food, like ice cream or pie, eaten after a meal is *dessert.* (7)

device, devise: *device* is a noun, *devise* a verb. (7)

did not ought, didn't ought: *see* ought.

differ: *differ from* is the usual idiom in situations involving dissimilarity, as in "this year's model *differs from* last year's." *Differ with* is the usual idiom in situations involving disagreement, as in "I *differ with* you in your interpretation." (5)

different: in situations in which the wording can be used, *different from* is always acceptable. *Different than* seems informal to some. *Different than* is inevitable when a full clause follows. (5)

directly: now occasionally used, with informal effect, as a subordinating conjunction, as in *"directly* I receive the news, I will call you."

disremember: non-standard. (3)

do, done: the principal parts of *do* are *do, did, done.* Use of *done* as a past tense, as in "he *done* it very well," is non-standard, as is use of *did* as a past participle, as in "I could have *did* the work faster with a little help." (3)

don't, doesn't: *don't* is the contraction for *do not, doesn't* the contraction for *does not.* Use of *don't* with a singular subject like *he, she,* or *it* ("he *don't* care much about it") is non-standard. (7)

dorm. *See* ad.

double negatives: earlier English freely used double and even triple negative for emphasis, as works of Chaucer and Shakespeare illustrate. Eighteenth-century writers on language, however, sometimes attempted to use logic in their judgments; they concluded that two negatives really should have an affirmative effect. This is true only in such sentences as "he is not uncooperative," which means that he is cooperative to a degree. Except in sentences like this, the double negative dropped out of standard English. Non-standard retained the older usage. In non-standard "he didn't have no gun" is a strong way of saying that he had no gun, and "he don't do no work around here" a strong way of saying that he doesn't do any work. The words *hardly, barely, scarcely,* and *only* have negative effect, and using them with negatives like *no, not, none,* and *never* produces an unintended double negative. Hence there is objection to "he couldn't hardly reach the rope" instead of "he couldn't reach the rope" or "he could hardly reach the rope," and objection to "I hadn't scarcely enough money" instead of "I had scarcely enough money" or "I hadn't enough money." The double negatives objected to are non-standard. (4)

doubt if: "I *doubt if* I will go" is informal; "I *doubt that* I will go" is formal. (5)

drownded: a non-standard form of *drowned.* The standard principal parts of *drown* are *drown, drowned, drowned.* (3)

drug: a non-standard form for *dragged.* The standard principal parts of *drag* are *drag, dragged, dragged.* (3)

due to: there has been objection to use of *due to* in adverbial units, as in "I was late due to a flat tire." No one has objected to use of *because of* or *owing to* in such situations, and no one objects to "my lateness was due to a flat tire." (1)

ec, econ. *See* ad.

-ed: adjectives are often formed by adding *-ed* to nouns: *moneyed, winged, talented, bearded.* There is sometimes a tendency to drop the *-ed* of such forms and of past participles. Many people now say *butter toast* and *whip cream* instead of *buttered toast* and *whipped* *cream.* At this time, however, standard English calls for retention of the *-ed,* as in *biased, prejudiced, privileged, armored, old-fashioned,* and *good-* (or *fair-*) sized. (3)

effect. *See* affect, effect.

else: the possessive form is *else's,* as in "that car is somebody *else's,*" "everyone *else's* answers were different from mine." (3)

eminent, imminent: *eminent* means "prominent, outstanding, distinguished by rank or accomplishment," as in "doctors, lawyers, clergymen, and other *eminent* men in the community." *Imminent* means "likely to happen in the near future," as in "his death is *imminent.*" (7)

enthuse: formed by dropping the last syllable of *enthusiasm, enthuse* is informal rather than formal. (3)

equally as good, equally as well: objected to since the *as* is unnecessary. There is no objection to "equally good," "as good as," "as well as."

etc. *See* and etc.

everyone, every one: *everyone* means "everybody, any or all capable of being included." *Every one* means "each separate individual." (7)

every place. *See* place.

everywheres: non-standard for *everywhere.* (3)

exam. *See* ad.

except. *See* accept, except.

expect: informal in the general meaning of "think, guess, suppose," as in "I expect that he is in New York by now." (2)

explicit, implicit: *explicit* means "clearly and definitely stated," as in "an *explicit* prohibition of this procedure in the regulations." *Implicit* means "implied, to be understood, although not stated fully and clearly," as in "an *implicit* suggestion to let the prisoners escape." (7)

factor: in formal English, means only "cause or condition contributing to an effect," as in "harsh treatment of the natives was one *factor* leading to the revolt." Used informally as a vague synonym for "aspect, character, thing." (2)

farther, further: *farther* may suggest actual physical distance, as in "Detroit is *farther* away from New York than Cleveland is." *Further* may suggest "additionally, in addition" or "to a greater extent or degree," as in "he did not speak *further*" and "I want no *further* interruptions." But many authors do not observe this distinction, and use of either form for either meaning is standard. (2, 7)

faze: an informal synonym for *agitate, disconcert, discourage.*

fewer, less: *fewer* is commonly used in reference to things that can be counted: *fewer* men, *fewer* sales, *fewer* coins. *Less* is commonly used in reference to things that cannot be counted: *less* manpower, *less* business, *less* money. Use of *less* in reference to things counted, as "*less* men," "*less* coins," is informal. (2)

flunk: both noun and verb are informal.

focus: plural forms are *focuses* and *foci,* the latter being more formal and more likely to be used in science and mathematics. (3)

folks: suggests informality. *Relations* and *relatives* are more formal.

formally, formerly: *formally* means "in a formal manner," as in "the hostess greeted her guests *formally.*" *Formerly* means "previously," as in "he was *formerly* the president of the company." (7)

former, latter: in formal English these two words are used only in situations in which two persons or things are involved, but not more than two. Use of either word in a situation involving more than two seems informal, as in "Brown, Jones, and Williams were all concerned; the *former* had the largest interest." (2)

forth, fourth: *forth* means "forward, onward," as in "going *forth* to battle." *Fourth* means "between third and fifth." (7)

funny: standard but informal in the sense of "strange, provoking interest and calling for explanation," as in "it's *funny* that he had so much money just after the robbery." (2)

further. See farther, further.

gent: non-standard for *gentleman*. See ad. (3)

get, got: (a) *Got to* is a somewhat informal equivalent for *must, have to.* After *have* it is unnecessary: "I have to go to St. Louis" means about the same thing as "I have got to go to St. Louis." (2, 5) (b) *Get* and *got* are used in a number of other idioms, many of them informal or non-standard. In writing formal English, you may find it advisable to try to find other wording. (c) In formal English *get* is likely to mean only "acquire, come into possession, usually by one's own efforts." *Get* and *got* are often used unnecessarily: it is adequate to say "the dog has fleas" rather than "the dog has *got* fleas." (2)

good and: an informal intensive as in "it is *good and* cold tonight." (2)

gotten: the principal parts of *get* are *get, got, got* or *gotten.* Choice between *got* and *gotten* often depends on which sounds smoother in the sentence in question, although *gotten* is sometimes regarded as old-fashioned. *Got* is the only past participle form used when the notion of ownership or possession is involved.

growed: non-standard for *grew* or *grown.* (3)

guess: some regard this as informal in the sense of "believe, suppose, think," as in "I *guess* I have enough money with me." (2)

gym. See ad.

had better: in "you *had better* leave now," *had better* is good idiom at any level. Omitting the *had* and saying just "you better go now" may seem informal. (5)

had ought, had not ought, hadn't ought: non-standard. *See* ought.

hardly: has negative effect. "Dinner isn't *hardly* ready yet" and "he can't *hardly* walk" are unintended double negatives. (4)

hardly ever: an acceptable idiom, as in "he *hardly ever* goes to church these days." But *hardly if ever* is not an acceptable idiom.

healthful, healthy: *healthful* is used to describe places, situations, climates, as in "this area is supposed to be especially *healthful*." *Healthy* describes persons. Attempts have been made to limit *healthy* to this use alone, but it is used so widely to describe places, situations, and climates too that it must be called standard in this sense. But *healthful* is not used to describe persons. (2, 7)

herself. *See* self words.

himself. *See* self words.

hisself: non-standard for *himself; see* self words.

hope: the established idiom is *in the hope of; in hopes of* has been objected to. (5)

hypothesis: the plural form is *hypotheses.* (3)

if: in formal English *whether* is preferred to *if* after verbs like *say, ask, doubt, wonder,* etc. "He asked *whether* the meeting would be held" is preferred to "he asked *if* . . ." The latter usage is so common and so natural to many that it must be regarded as standard. (5)

illusion. *See* allusion, illusion.

imminent. *See* eminent, imminent.

implicit. *See* explicit, implicit.

imply. *See* infer, imply.

in back of. *See* back of, in back of.

infer, imply: *infer* means to gather from what is implied or suggested, to conclude from facts or indications, as in "the detective *inferred* from these bits of evidence that Smith was the murderer"; "I *inferred* from his tone that he disliked me." *Imply* means "suggest, indicate indirectly," as in "to *imply* that he was lying without saying so outright." (7)

infinitives. *See* split infinitives.

inside of: the *of* is redundant. (5)

into. *See* in, into.

irregardless, irregardlessly: non-standard for *regardless, regardlessly.* (3)

is when, is where: definitions and explanations that begin with *is when* and *is where* are usually objected to. "A cut is an unexcused absence from class" is preferred to "a cut *is when* you miss a class without an excuse."

kind, sort: *kind* and *sort* are singular forms, and there is consequently a feeling that they should be modified by the singular forms *this* and *that* rather than the plural forms *these* and *those*. *These kind* is not without some defense, but it is hardly formal American English. (3, 5)

kind of, sort of: these expressions are often used as qualifying adverbs, as in "it was *kind of* hot in the theater." Formal English would require other wording, like *somewhat, rather*. (5)

knowed: non-standard.

last, latest: *last* is used to indicate the final item in a series, *latest* to indicate the most recent in time, as in "the *last* propeller planes that the squadron had were replaced by the *latest* jets." (7)

latter. *See* former, latter.

lay, lie: the principal parts of *lay* are *lay, laid, laid*. In its main meaning, *lay* is a transitive verb. As such, it is followed by an object or used in the passive: "*laying* the dishes on the table"; "they *laid* their packs on the ground"; "the papers were *laid* on the shelf." In some meanings, *lay* is intransitive; note how your dictionary treats it. The principal parts of *lie* are *lie, lay, lain*. *Lie* is usually an intransitive verb; as such it is not followed by objects: "he *is lying* on the couch in the living room"; "the dead men *lay* where they had fallen"; "the patient *has lain* still for the past hour." There is objection to using *lay* intransitively in its main meaning. Usages like "Rover, *lay* down" and "he *laid* still watching the fire" are non-standard. (4)

learn: using *learn* with a personal object—that is, an object indicating a person—is non-standard, as in "the teacher learned him arithmetic." *Teach* is standard.

lead, led: *lead* (rhyming with *bed*) is the noun indicating a heavy metal, as in "*lead* mines." *Lead* (rhyming with *bead*) is the present tense of the verb meaning to go before and direct or conduct, as in "the guide will *lead* us to the lake." *Led* is the past tense of this verb, as in "the guide *led* us to the lake." (3, 7)

leave, let: the principal parts of *leave* are *leave, left, left*. The most common meanings of *leave* are "to allow to remain," as in "*leaving* the glasses on the table," and "to withdraw from," as in "she is *leaving* college" and "we *left* him behind." The principal parts of *let* are *let, let, let*. The main meaning of *let* in most speech and writing is "to permit," as in "*letting* him have the money," "her father *lets* her drive the car." *Let* is often followed by a verb form, an infinitive without the *to. Leave* is not. *Let go of* is standard; *leave go of* is non-standard. *Let* sometimes has the meaning of "leave," but only in the idioms *let alone* and *let be*, as in "that dog is bad-tempered; *let* her alone" and "I'm tired; *let* me be." Use of *leave* in these idioms is non-standard. Confusion of *let* and *leave* is common, but use of a form of *leave* for *let* in its main meaning is non-standard, as in "they *left* the rabbits go." (3, 7)

less. *See* fewer, less.

let's: (a) *let's* is the contraction of *let us*. The expression *let's us* is redundant and non-standard. (5) (b) *Let's don't* is usually regarded as quite informal; *let's not* is better for any writing. (5)

lie. *See* lay, lie.

like: many persons heartily dislike the use of *like* as a subordinating conjunction, that is, as a word introducing a dependent clause, and strongly prefer *as* instead. Many regard use of *like* in "do it *like* he ordered" as non-standard and approve instead "do it *as* he ordered." There is no objection to "do it the way he said." *See* as. (1)

loose, lose: *loose* is usually an adjective with the meaning of "not firm, tight, taut, or compact," as in "a *loose* bolt," "a *loose* knot," "*loose* sand." *Lose* is a verb meaning "to fail to have kept" or "to suffer defeat": "to *lose* one's keys," "to *lose* the big game." (7)

mad. *See* angry, mad.

math. *See* ad.

may. *See* can, may.

medium: the usual plural is *mediums; media* is used for some scientific and artistic meanings. (3)

memorandum: plural forms are *memoranda* and *memorandums.* (3)

moral, morale: *moral* is an adjective meaning "excellent or blameless in conduct," as in "a very *moral* man," and a noun, meaning "principal teaching," as in "the *moral* of the story." *Morale* is a noun meaning "spirit and attitude, especially as concerns courage and determination," as in "the *morale* of the troops was high." (7)

most. *See* almost, most.

myself. *See* self words.

nebula: plural forms are *nebulas* and *nebulae;* the former is more common. (3)

no account: non-standard as an adjective unit.

no doubt but that: the *but* is redundant; "there is no doubt that he will win" is preferred to "there is no doubt but that he will win." (5)

nohow: non-standard.

no place. *See* place.

not hardly, not scarcely. *See* double negatives.

nowheres: non-standard for *nowhere.* (3)

nucleus: the usual plural form is *nuclei.* (3)

number. *See* amount, number.

oasis: the plural form is *oases.* (3)

of: often confused with the unstressed *have* of such spoken verb forms as *could have driven, would have done, might have found,* and with the *-'ve* of the written contractions of these forms. The word *have* is often used to make up verb forms; the word *of* is not. Forms like *might of come* and *would of called* are non-standard attempts to write *might have come* and *would have called*. (7)

off of: the *of* is redundant. "He got off the bus at Elm Street" is preferred to "he got *off of* . . ." (5)

OK, Okay, okay: informal. (3)

old-fashioned: the correct form in all uses. Note the *-ed* ending.

on account of: informal or non-standard as a subordinating conjunction, as in "*on account of* I was sick, I didn't go on the trip." *On account of* may be used as a preposition at any level, as in "*on account of* sickness I didn't go on the trip." (5)

oneself. *See* self words.

only: (a) as an equivalent for *but* as a coordinating conjunction between clauses, *only* is informal, as in "I wanted to buy the shirt, *only* I didn't have enough money." (1, 2) (b) Sentences like "he hadn't *only* two dollars with him" and "there weren't *only* three minutes left in the game" show unintended double negatives. (4)

ought: not used in Standard English, either formal or informal, with another verb form coming before it; *had ought, did ought,* and similar forms are non-standard. (5)

our'n, ourn: non-standard for *our* or *ours.* (3)

out of, outside of: the *of* is redundant. "He went out the door" is preferred to "he went *out of* the door." (5)

owing to. *See* due to.

parenthesis: the plural form is *parentheses.* (3)

passed, past: *passed* is the past tense and past participle of *to pass,* as in "the time *passed* slowly," "the bus has *passed* the corner." *Past* is a noun meaning "previous time," as in "the great men of the *past,*" or an adjective meaning "occurring in the past," as in "*past* periods." (7)

pay: for most of the meanings of the word *pay* acceptable principal parts are *pay, paid, paid.* (3)

per: strongly suggests business and commercial usage, and is not very appropriate elsewhere. (6)

personal, personnel: *personal* is an adjective meaning "of or pertaining to an individual person," as in "putting aside *personal* interests to serve the public." *Personnel* is a noun meaning, among other things, "group of people engaged in a common activity," as in "the *personnel* of the bureau." (7)

phase: in formal English likely to mean "aspect, appearance," as in "the various *phases* of the moon"; and informal in more extended, less definite meanings, as in "took part in various *phases* of athletics." (2)

phenomena: a plural form; the singular form is *phenomenon.* (3)

phone. *See* ad.

photo. *See* ad.

place: free adverbial use of this word, as in "I couldn't find my hat any *place*," is informal; more formal wording would require *anywhere*. (1)

plenty: non-standard or informal as an adverb meaning "very, quite, to a marked degree, as in "he was *plenty* surprised when I came." (1)

P.M. *See* A.M., P.M.

possessive pronouns: the possessive personal pronouns are *my, mine, our, ours, your, yours, his, her, hers, its, their, theirs*. No possessive personal pronoun takes an apostrophe; the forms *you're, it's*, and *they're* are the contractions of *you are, it is* (or *it has*), and *they are* respectively. *Mine, ours, yours, hers,* and *theirs* are the forms used in constructions like "that book is mine," "that house is theirs." The forms *ourn, yourn, hisn, hern,* and *theirn* are non-standard. (3)

precede, proceed: *precede* is a verb, usually transitive, meaning "to go, come, or be before," as in "the color guard *precedes* the regiment." *Proceed* is an intransitive verb meaning "to go or move onward or forward," as in "the column *proceeded* slowly down the valley." (7)

prefer: idiomatically followed by *to* rather than *more than*. "I *prefer* Smith to Jones" is acceptable; "I *prefer* Smith more than Jones" is not. (5)

prejudice: the adjective form is *prejudiced,* as in "perhaps I am *prejudiced*." (3)

prepositions at ends of sentences: use of a preposition at the end of a sentence or clause is entirely correct practice. "This is the man I was talking about," "I liked the program I was listening to," "replacing the post the car crashed into"—these and countless other similar expressions are entirely acceptable in any kind of English. Few critics and teachers pay much attention now to the old rule that a preposition should not be used to end a sentence. (4)

pretty: informal as an adverb with the meaning of "considerably, moderately, rather," as in "it's *pretty* cold out tonight." (1, 2)

principal, principle: *principal* is an adjective meaning "chief or main," as in "the *principal* reason for his decision," and a noun meaning "main officer," as in "the *principal* of the school," or "main sum, in contrast to interest." *Principle* is a noun meaning "law, rule, or truth," as in "the *principles* of aerial navigation." (7)

proceed. *See* precede, proceed.

prophecy, prophesy: *prophecy* is a noun; *prophesy*, a verb. (7)

proved: the usual past participle is *proved. Proven* may suggest matters legal. (6)

quiet, quite: *quiet* is adjective, noun, and verb meaning "calm, still." *Quite* is an adverb meaning "completely, very, really," as in "the hall became *quite* quiet when he started to speak." (7)

quit: acceptable principal parts are *quit, quit, quit*. (3)

quite a number, quite a few, quite a bit: these idioms are informal, along with others beginning with *"quite a."* (5)

radius: plural forms are *radii* and *radiuses*. (3)

raise, rise: the principal parts of *raise* are *raise, raised, raised*. *Raise* is usually a transitive verb and as such is followed by an object: "to *raise* the sunken ship," "he *raised* his hat when the flag went by." Acceptable principal parts of *rise* are *rise, rose, risen*. *Rise* is usually an intransitive verb and as such is not followed by objects: "*rising* at dawn," "prices *rose* to alarming new levels." Although use of *raise* as an intransitive verb is not entirely uncommon, it is non-standard. (4)

raise: objection to use of *raise* as in sentences like "they *raised* three children" is disappearing. (2)

re: a preposition meaning "about, concerning," as in *"re* your request for sick leave," this word usually suggests business or commerce. (6)

read where, see where: "I read in last night's paper that new missiles were being tested" is preferred to "I read in last night's paper where . . ." (5)

real: informal as an adverb with the meaning of "quite, very" or of "really," as in "it was a real exciting game." (1)

reason is because, reason is due to: since both *reason* and *because* express notions of cause or reason, the expression *the reason is because* is redundant. The same thought applies to *the reason is due to* and *the reason is on account of*. Rather than these constructions, formal English prefers wording like "the reason is that . . ."; "it happened because . . ."; "it occurred on account of . . ." (5)

refer back: the work *back* is redundant. (5)

regard, regards. *See* in regard to.

regardless, regardlessly. *See* irregardless, irregardlessly.

remember of: the *of* is redundant, and the phrase is regarded as non-standard. (3)

reminisce: formed by clipping the last syllable from *reminiscence*, this word is informal. (3)

repeat again: the *again* is redundant and misleading unless a third rather than a second performance is meant. (5)

respectfully, respectively: *respectfully* means "with respect," as in "he spoke *respectfully* of his father." *Respectively* means "each for each in the order given," as in the sentence "Smith and Clark make ninety and seventy dollars a week *respectively*." This means that Smith makes ninety dollars and Clark makes seventy. The word is meaningless in such a sentence as "he owns a sedan and a station wagon respectively." (2, 7)

rid: acceptable principal parts are *rid, rid, rid*. (3)

rise. *See* raise, rise.

said to: non-standard or perhaps informal in the reporting of orders, as in "the sergeant *said to* stay here," "he *said to* fold the paper lengthwise." (5)

scarcely. *See* double negatives.

seldom ever: not a standard English idiom. Use *seldom* or *never* or *hardly ever*. (5)

self words: (a) the acceptable forms for pronouns ending in *-self* and *-selves* are as follows:

myself	ourselves
yourself	yourselves
himself	
herself	themselves
itself	

The first four of these forms are made up with possessives (*my, our,* and *your*). The language, however, has been inconsistent in this matter, and other forms are made up with objectives (*him, them*). *Hisself* and *theirselves* are non-standard. (b) It is not formal English to use a *-self* word as part of a subject when there is nothing accompanying it to identify it. Uses like "the doctor and myself took the taxi together" are objected to, and "the doctor and I took the taxi together" is preferred. (3, 5)

set, sit: the principal parts of *set* are *set, set, set*. Most of the time *set* is a transitive verb and is consequently followed by an object: "*setting* the silver on the table," "this workman *sets* the springs into place," "they *set* their guns in the rack." *Set* has a number of acceptable intransitive uses: "the hens are *setting*"; "the glue will *set*"; "the sun has *set*"; "we are *setting* out." See your dictionary for these and similar expressions. The principal parts of *sit* are *sit, sat, sat*. Aside from a few idiomatic uses, like "he *sits* on his horse well," *sit* is intransitive and is not followed by objects: "Zimmer *sits* in the last row," "we *sat* for hours waiting in the station." *Set* as an intransitive verb used in the main meaning of *sit* is non-standard, as in "*set* down on the couch there," "the old lady was *setting* in the rocking chair."

shall, will: (a) Old grammars have complex rules governing the use of *shall* and *will*. They usually say that for expression of simple futurity *shall* is preferred with first-person subjects, as in "I *shall* call," "we *shall* go," and *will* with second- and third-person subjects, as in "you *will* find out," "he *will* come," "it *will* be finished soon." On the other hand, for expression of promise, determination, command, and so on, *will* is preferred with first-person subjects and *shall* with second- and third-person subjects. Expressions like "thou *shalt* not kill" and "they *shall* not pass" illustrate this latter usage, but very few twentieth-century Americans interpret the comment "I *will* write" as an expression of promise or determination. Statements given in the old grammars about *shall* and *will* did not show the actual usage of the language, and attempts to teach them were unsuccessful. *Will* is the usual future auxiliary for most situations at all levels in American English, and very few persons object to its use with first-person subjects. (4, 7) (b) Acceptable contractions of pronouns and *shall* and *will* are *I'll, we'll, you'll, he'll, she'll,* and *they'll.* All of them are informal. Negative contractions are *shan't* and *won't.* (3)

should, would: (a) Old grammars give rules for *should* and *would* that parallel those for *shall* and *will.* According to these rules, *should* is preferred with first-person subjects, *would* with second- and third-person subjects, in the majority of their uses. Most Americans are likely to use *would* in most situations, and almost no one objects to usages like "I *would* go if I were you" and "we *would* like to hear from you." *Should* is always used rather than *would* to express ideas of obligation, as in "you *should* send a thank-you note," or of likelihood or probability, as in "the letter *should* arrive by tomorrow." (b) In formal English *would* is usually not used after *if.* (c) Acceptable contractions of pronouns and *should* and *would* are *I'd, we'd, you'd, he'd, she'd, they'd,* all of which are informal. Negative contractions are *shouldn't* and *wouldn't.* (3)

sick, ill: *ill* may suggest greater formality than *sick.*

sight, site. *See* cite, sight, site.

slow, slowly, "go *slow*" and "he went very *slow*" are correct standard English idiomatic expressions. They may be used quite correctly in the most formal English. If one wishes to, he may substitute *slowly* for *slow,* but it is never necessary to do so. But *slowly* is usually the better choice as an adverb to modify other verbs. In a sentence like "she arose *slowly* and with much pain from her hospital bed," there would be little defense for *slow.* (3)

so: (a) *So* as an intensive adverb, as an equivalent of *very* or *quite,* as in "the bride looked *so* pretty," is informal. In the most formal English there is no objection to *so* in this usage if a *that* clause follows, as in "the atomic bomb is *so* powerful *that* no city can be safe." (1, 2, 5) (b) *So* as a conjunctive adverb equivalent to *therefore,* as in "I was never very good at languages, *so* I did not take German" offers two problems in today's English composition. Because a succession of *so* sentences of this type is displeasing, it is often useful to revise to a form like "since I was never very good at languages, I did not take German." In informal English, sentences employing *so* as a conjunctive adverb may be punctuated with a comma between the clauses, although some persons prefer a semicolon. (1) (c) In formal English, *so that* is preferred to *so* in expressions giving cause or reason; "we pushed our way through the crowd *so that* we could see the candidate" rather than "we pushed our way through the crowd *so* we could see . . ." (5)

some: non-standard as an adverb equivalent of *somewhat,* as in "the experience left him *some* poorer but wiser." (1)

sort. *See* kind, sort.

sort of. *See* kind of, sort of.

split infinitives: at one time many English textbooks warned against split infinitives. A split infinitive occurs when an adverb or adverbial unit is placed between the *to* and the verb word in an infinitive: "to poorly sing," "to carelessly drive," "to with all his strength try" illustrate split infinitives. In general, the split infinitive is simply part of the natural idiom of the English language, and few people object to it these days. The split infinitive raises two problems: (a) Some split infinitives are awkward: "I refused to under the circumstances work for him," "he did not expect her to thus rudely answer." Rewording would improve these sentences. The objection to them is not that they contain split infinitives, but that they contain awkward split infinitives. (b) But fear of splitting an infinitive may make a sentence ambiguous. In "he should be told carefully to adjust the switches in the cellar," it would be better to show clearly that *carefully* modifies *to adjust* rather than *should be told;* the best way to do this would be to split the infinitive and to write *to carefully adjust.* (4)

stationary, stationery: *stationary* is an adjective meaning "fixed in place," as in "a *stationary* obstacle," "a *stationary* press." *Stationery* is a noun meaning "paper and writing materials," as in "buying a box of *stationery.*" (7)

statue, stature, statute: *statue* means "sculptured or molded figure," as "a *statue* of the general in the park." *Stature* means "height; height; height and girth," as in "a man of large *stature* well over six feet tall." *Statute* means "ordnance or law," as in "punishable by fine according to these *statutes.*" (7)

strata: a plural form. *Stratum* is the singular. (3)

sure: (a) non-standard or informal as an adverb; *certainly* or *surely* is formal. In most writing "it certainly is a fast car" is preferred to "it sure is a fast car." (1) (b) *Sure and* is an informal equivalent for *sure to* in sentences like "be *sure and* write to us." (5)

suspicion: non-standard as a verb, as in "he never *suspicioned* what was going on in his own house." (1)

synopsis: the plural form is *synopses.* (3)

than: (a) *See* different. (b) *Than whom,* as in "Chase, *than whom* no first baseman was more graceful," is an acceptable idiom, although it may sound both formal and awkward. (5)

than, then: *than* is the conjunction used in comparisons, as in "New York is larger *than* Chicago." *Then* is the adverb meaning "by that time," as in "*then* he turned around and went out." (7)

that: (a) *that* is non-standard as an adverbial intensive, that is, as an equivalent for *very* or *so,* regardless of whether or not a dependent clause follows. Both the following are non-standard: "I was *that* tired," "I was *that* tired I fell asleep with my clothes on." (5) (b)

Sometimes the subordinating conjunction *that* is unnecessarily repeated; there is no need for two *that's* in a sentence like "I knew *that* if I went *that* my little brother would want to come too." (5) (c) *That* is sometimes preferred to *which* in restrictive clauses; some persons feel that "the building *that* we saw" is smoother than "the building *which* we saw." (5) (d) *That* may be used freely as an equivalent for both *who* and *whom* in reference to persons and *which* in reference to things. (5, 7)

that there. *See* this here.

their, there, they're: *their* is the possessive form of *they*, as in *"their* house." *There* is the common adverb meaning "to or at that place," as in "we moved *there* later," and the common introductory element in sentences like "*there* are three cars parked across the street." *They're* is the contraction for *they are*, as in *"they're* in Canada on a vacation trip." (7)

them: non-standard as a substitute for *those*, as in "them papers." (1, 2)

then. *See* than, then.

thesis: the plural form is *theses*. (3)

this here, that there: non-standard, as in "use *this here* hammer" or "I want *that there* blade." But "I want that blade there" would be satisfactory at any level. (5)

they: use of indefinite *they*, as in "in England *they* have to pay still higher taxes" and *"they* did not have good roads in colonial America," is uncommon in formal English. (2)

thorough, through: *thorough* is an adjective meaning "complete, not cursory," as in "a *thorough* examination of the evidence." *Through* is the common preposition and adverb, as in *"through* the woods," "to go *through*." (7)

thusly: non-standard for *thus*. (3)

to, too, two: *to* is the common preposition, as in *"to* the town," *"to* him," and the "sign" of the infinitive, as in *"to* go." *Too* is the adverb meaning "also, in addition, more than enough, excessively," as in "Robert works there *too*," "it is *too* cold for swimming." *Two* is the number between one and three. (7)

used to: (a) notice that the common idiom is *used to*, not *use to*. In formal English there is no entirely satisfactory negative for this phrase, although *used not to* will usually serve. *Didn't use to* is not uncommon, but it is not formal English. Notice the spelling of the phrase. *Didn't used to* seems to express the past time twice. (b) *Used to could* is non-standard; *used to be able to* is standard but cumbersome. In many sentences, the word *could* alone, with a time modifier, will express the idea. (5)

unique: in the sense of "rare, strange, unusual," as in "this was the most unique play of the game," *unique* is now standard, although it is not used much in formal English. (2)

up: often redundant in phrases like *end up, connect up, divide up, settle up, split up, polish up, open up, finish up,* etc., which suggest informality. If you are trying to write formal English and you find situations in which *up* can be omitted, you had better do it. (5)

vertebra: plural forms are *vertebras* and *vertebrae.* (3)

want: (a) *want* in the sense of "ought, had better," as in "you *want* to keep the moving parts lubricated at all times," is informal. (2) (b) It is non-standard to follow *want* with a complete dependent clause, as in "he *wants* that you should work in the mailing room now." The wording "he *wants* you to work in the mailing room now" fits in with English at any level. (5)

weather, whether: *weather* is a noun meaning general atmospheric conditions, as in "the *weather* has been fine lately." *Whether* is the conjunction used to indicate alternates, as in "I don't know *whether* to buy the car or not." (7)

what. *See* but what, but that.

when. *See* is when.

where: (a) *see* at; (b) *see* is when; (c) *see* read where.

whether: (a) *see* if; (b) *see* weather, whether.

which: used in reference to people, as in "the men *which* were in the hall," *which* is non-standard. Use of *who* (or *whom*) or *that* is standard. On the other hand, use of *which* in reference to a collective noun used as a singular is standard, as in "the club *which* was meeting in the room." (5) (b) Possible possessives for *which* are *of which* and *whose.* The best procedure is to revise away from the need for a possessive for *which.* (3, 5) (c) *See* and which. (d) *See* that.

while: (a) *while* means both "when" and "although," the latter as in "*while* I was afraid to drive across the ford, I had no other choice." *While* is consequently ambiguous in some situations. In "*while* the flood waters were still low, the family decided to leave the farm," which does it mean? Check situations in your own writing in which *while* may be ambiguous and substitute other connectives. (2) (b) Use of *while* as a synonym for *and* or *but,* as in "Tom and Dick went to college *while* Harry stayed home" is informal. (2)

will. *See* shall, will.

without: non-standard or very informal as a subordinating conjunction meaning "unless," as in "*without* you have a ticket, they will not let you into the armory." (1)

would: (a) *see* should, would. (b) It is usually informal to use *would* in verb forms (like *would write, would be hurt, would have gone*) in clauses beginning with *if:* "if I *would* take Spanish"; "if the president *would* die in office." After the word *if* the one-word past tense is preferred in formal English: "if I took Spanish," "if the president died in office." (5)

would rather. *See* had rather.

yet: when *yet* introduces the second of two independent clauses in a sentence, as in "he seemed nervous, *yet* he was calm inside," the usual punctuation between the clauses is a comma—unless of course both clauses are quite long. In this situation *yet* functions as a co-ordinating conjunction. (1)

you: it is informal standard English to use *you* in indefinite situations to mean "anyone," "people in general," as in "*you* drive on the left instead of the right in England" or "if *you* were drafted into the army in the Civil War *you* could buy a substitute." In formal English *one* may be preferred in this situation. (2)

you was: non-standard—and illiterate. (3)

yourself. *See* self words.

EXERCISE

Find out which of the indicated choices is preferred in formal English in the following:

1. He felt that (a, an) advanced (math, mathematics) course would be a (real, quite) bad mistake for him.
2. (There, Their, They're) (sure, surely) too busy now to take as much interest in the club as they (used, use) to.
3. She was still (mad, angry) and would not (except, accept) the invitation to (sit, set) down and discuss the matter.
4. Tom and (I, myself) had (laid, lain) the tools on the kitchen floor (so, so that) we could reach them easily.
5. It seems (like, as though) the (effect, affect) of the taxes will be to discourage new industries.
6. She (set, sat) still on the porch (irregardless, regardless) of the (eminent, imminent) danger.
7. (Most, Almost) anybody would (of, have) been (aggravated, irritated) at such crude attempts at humor.
8. It was (real, quite) cold outside when the sergeant (told us, said for us) to (raise, rise) and fall in.
9. Being in a hurry was not a good (alibi, excuse) for (letting, leaving) the new boards (lay, lie) out in the wet grass over night.
10. I read in the paper (where, that) the salvage company was planning to (raise, rise) the old ship (lying, laying) in the mud of the inlet.
11. Just (among, between) us three here, she is (altogether, all together) too free in the (allusions, illusions) she makes to Mabel's divorce.
12. James (let, left) go of the dynamite cap (plenty, very) fast when we told him of (its, it's) explosive force.

13. The (amount, number) of people at the game this (P.M., afternoon) will be very large.

14. (Like, As) I said before, this is a purely (personnel, personal) matter involving (myself, me) only, and I (can't hardly, can hardly) see why (its, it's) any one else's business.

15. If you (leave, let) your tools (laying, lying) around (anywhere, anywheres), (its, it's) no wonder that you cannot find them later.

16. (On account of, Due to) her (old-fashion, old-fashioned) ways, Grandmother (didn't never, didn't ever) tip a Pullman porter more than five cents when she got (off of, off) the train.

17. The (assent, ascent) straight up the mountain seems (awfully, very) steep, and I don't know (as, that) I want to try it.

18. (Let's us, Let's) have no (doubt but that, doubt that) our team (can hardly, can't hardly) (loose, lose) this game.

19. (Since, Being that) there was another car parked (real, very) close (beside, besides) ours, I (couldn't hardly, could hardly) open the door.

20. Don't leave this brace unfastened; (like, as) the directions tell you, bolt it (so, so that) it isn't (lose, loose) at all.

21. (As, Since) there (won't be but, will be only) two other councilors in the camp at that time, he (can not, may not) have the day off.

22. You (had ought, ought) to know better (then, than) to (let, leave) your catcher's mitt (lay, lie) out on the field over night.

23. The radio station (broadcast, broadcasted) a report that the candidate had not been (born, borned) in the United States.

24. The old man got tired of seeing his grown sons (laying, lying) around loafing all day and decided to (learn, teach) them a lesson.

25. The cause of the wreck at the (sight, site) of the new post office was (on account of the snow and ice, the snow and ice) on the street.

26. (Regardless, Irregardless) of what he thought, I did not mean to (infer, imply) in what I said that I thought he was (kind of, somewhat) dishonest.

27. This Signal (Corps, Corpse) unit did not have its full (complement, compliment) of men.

28. This candidate (ought, had ought) to know by now that he (can hardly, can't hardly) hope to win.

29. (This data differs, These data differ) very noticeably (from, with) the figures in the rough estimates.

30. This (genus, genius) of weeds has (got, gotten) out of control in some areas.

31. He (don't, doesn't) really help very much (unless, except) he comes here (directly, as soon as) I call him.

32. It seems somewhat (funny, strange) that Sam's new wife (seldom if ever, seldom) mentions her (relatives, folks).

33. Even the strongest team of horses (could not hardly, could hardly) (of, have) (dragged, drug) that big stone out of the field.

34. There will be (less, fewer) people dressed (formally, formerly) for this affair than there would (of, have) been in (past, passed) years.

35. Many of the town's more (imminent, eminent) men were (enthused, enthusiastic) about the project.

INDEX

459